A GUIDE TO
STAINED GLASS
IN BRITAIN

A GUIDE TO
STAINED GLASS
IN BRITAIN

PAINTON COWEN

MICHAEL JOSEPH

First published in Great Britain by Michael Joseph Ltd.
44 Bedford Square, London WC1
1985

ISBN 0 7181 2567 3

Designed and produced by
BELLEW PUBLISHING COMPANY LTD.
7 Southampton Place, London WC1A 2DR

Design: Prue Bucknall

Printed in Great Britain

Title page: Temptation of Christ, *c.*1223, from Troyes Cathedral,
now in the Victoria & Albert Museum, London.

iv

CONTENTS

LIST OF COLOUR PLATES

DEDICATION
For Annick and Geraldine.

FOREWORD

The production of this guide would have been quite impossible without the help of numerous people. To visit all the churches and places where stained glass might be found, from Land's End to John O'Groats, would take an individual a lifetime — and by the time the results were published, much of it might be out of date! I have therefore drawn heavily upon the published and unpublished work of many people, and I am deeply grateful for their efforts.

I would particularly like to express my thanks to David O'Connor, Jim Bracken, Birkin Haward, Barry Comberton, David Evans, Nigel Morgan, David George and The Revd O.S. Bennett for their help with English glass; to The Revd Canon T.H. Hill, Keith London, Mostyn Lewis and Rodney Bender for information on Welsh glass, Rona Moody for help with Scottish windows and to the Dean and Chapter of York Minster for permission to reproduce photographs of the cathedral's glass. Also to members of the Society of Master Glass Painters who furnished me with lists of their own works that they would most like to see publicised (I asked each to select twelve windows) and for their help in pointing out other windows.

I must also thank the many friends and relations who have helped out by putting me up and looking after me during my travels around Britain, and for others such as my stepfather Charles Gordon and Jane Reeves who have given a hand with some of the paperwork and checking; Jill Kerr and Dennis King for giving me their time and some valuable leads; also Frederick Warne Ltd for their assistance in the early days. So, too, must I thank all those who have contributed via their publications — they are listed in the bibliography. Thanks are particularly due to the Council for the Care of Churches whose library and records on churches have been of great assistance. Most of all, I would like to mention the help given by many incumbents and members of their congregations who, despite no doubt already over-filled work days, responded so warmly to my circular letter asking them questions about the glass in their churches and allowed me to photograph their windows.

Inevitably this guide has to be a selection — and a selection is to a great extent personal. It is by no means definitive, particularly with regard to the glass of the last 50 years or so. Because of the great mass of glass belonging to this period and the near impossibility of seeing it all, let alone passing judgement on it, I have attempted to give as good a cross-section of what can be seen as is possible, and have refrained in many instances from offering opinions. I would rather people went to visit the places – and support those churches that need help – in order to see the glass for themselves, unencumbered by my particular prejudices. In the case of the nineteenth-century glaziers, I have concentrated on their early works, before the period when most of them slipped into more overtly production-line

1

practices that resulted in so much monotonous stained glass. As I mention in the text, much work needs still to be done here, although Martin Harrison's book on Victorian glass has been an invaluable help and is essential reading for anyone interested in stained glass of this period.

I must ask readers to forgive me for utilising poetic licence in listing Herefordshire and Worcestershire as two separate counties despite their recent fusion into one. I have kept the old names in these two cases to facilitate use of the gazetteer, i.e. by not listing Worcestershire under 'H', as I am, doubtless, not alone in having difficulty in adjusting to the new politically-created counties. Moreover, I apologist to those in other counties to whom such things are important for not listing their counties by the older and more familiar names!

Finally, I would like to thank those people in churches and cathedrals around the country who allowed me to photograph their windows for this book.

Opposite: Angel Musician, C15, Orchardleigh Church, Somerset.

PART ONE
AN INTRODUCTION TO STAINED GLASS IN BRITAIN

THE MAGIC OF STAINED GLASS

*The glass in the windows, through which pass the
rays of light, is the mind of the doctors, seeing
heavenly things as in a glass darkly.*

HONORIUS OF AUTUN

Standing in the Trinity Chapel of Canterbury Cathedral and looking at the 'Miracle Windows', a visiting stained glass enthusiast might well be forgiven for thinking that for a moment he had been miraculously translated to France (*see illustration on* p.5). Indeed, the magical atmosphere of this chapel is very largely created by the glowing, deeply-coloured early thirteenth century glass, work of the same school – possibly even of the same glaziers – that created the equally stunning windows at Chartres and Saint Denis – birthplaces of the Gothic. In the year 1144, Abbot Suger stood in the new choir of his church at St Denis outside Paris surrounded by such glass and reflected on what he and many others had achieved in the completion of this important new building. St Denis brought to focus under one roof the most advanced techniques and trends in church architecture, and the results were astounding. In particular, new visions appeared in walls relieved of much of the roof's weight by the innovatory flying buttresses. Stained glass, which until then had been seen only in single and often isolated windows of wealthy establishments, became an instrument of mass-communication for the Church. For reasons not yet fully explained, the use of stained glass began to spread widely as the twelfth century progressed. So mesmerised was Suger by its effect in one building that he was moved to put into words what the experience meant to him. He described the church as being 'pervaded by the wonderful and uninterrupted light of the most radiant windows', and wrote that he himself had become transformed by the light that had passed through its jewel-like glass:

> Then it seems to me that I see myself dwelling, as it were, in some strange region of the universe which neither exists entirely in the slime of the earth nor entirely in the purity of Heaven; and that by the grace of God, I can be transported from this inferior to that higher world.

The abbey church of St Denis showed what could be achieved with the new medium of stained glass and caught the imagination of some of the age's most ingenious and skilled craftsmen, so that within a few years – if not a few months – demand for new windows came from all quarters. For example, at least three very large windows were produced at Chartres just after the consecration of St Denis in 1144 – they are now under the great rose window in the west front.

One of the 'Miracle Windows', Trinity Chapel, Canterbury Cathedral, *c*.1220. It was believed the murdered St Thomas à Becket performed healing miracles for pilgrims to his tomb at Canterbury. This window tells a story in nine scenes running from left to right along the bottom, then top and finally middle row as follows: Sir Jordan Fitzeisulf's household is struck by plague. The family nurse dies and his son falls ill. Sir Jordan vows to make an offering to St Thomas' tomb, but forgets. The son recovers but St Thomas warns the leper, Gimp, in a dream of the consequences of Sir Jordan's neglect. Gimp tells the dream and, after more people fall ill, Sir Jordan makes the offering.

Stained glass was one of the chief glories of the newly emergent style in architecture that only centuries later was given the adjective 'Gothic'. Many of the common people believed that the secrets of the glass's manufacture resided with alchemists. To the more speculative of the scholar-monks at the Abbey of St Denis – already well versed in the writings of the Irish mystic John the Scot – the glass evoked the transcendent properties believed to exist in light and jewels, which could heal and transform. To the Church it was an invaluable teaching aid permanently communicating the essential elements of the Faith and its founders. Stories and personalities of the Bible could be shown to all in a form comprehensible to the majority who could not read or understand Latin. That which had

5

previously been illustrated in painting, mosaic and sculpture now blazed stronger than ever in light transmitted through the magical glass.

Above all, the building of many of the churches and cathedrals in the twelfth and thirteenth centuries was seen by many people as a kind of preparation for the Holy City of the New Jerusalem, which was to appear 1000 years after the writing of St John's Revelation. According to the saint, the foundations of the walls of the Holy City were:

> garnished with all manner of precious stones. The first foundation was jasper; the second, sapphire; the third, a chalcedony; the fourth, an emerald;
>
> The fifth, sardonyx; the sixth, sardius; the seventh, chrysolyte; the eighth, beryl; the ninth, a topaz; the tenth, a chrysoprasus; the eleventh, a jacynth; the twelfth, an amethyst.
>
> And the twelve gates were twelve pearls: every several gate was one of the pearls: and the street of the city was pure gold, as it were transparent glass.
>
> REVELATION 21:19

However, to the great Bernard of Clairvaux, head of the more strict order of the Cistercians, this was no New Jerusalem. He regarded the luxury of St Denis with disapproval, not so much from an aesthetic point of view but because of the power that such beautiful things had over the unsuspecting mind, particularly to 'distract the brothers' away from their contemplation and studies of the Divine. (The Cistercians subsequently sanctioned *grisaille* – a more sober form of stained glass that has an overall grey-green colour, often painted with natural or geometrical designs, and only occasionally incorporates small pieces of colour, *see* p.22.) In fact, Suger talked about *leading* the mind upwards, which implies that some needed leading as opposed to those who, like the brothers, were already well on their way. In retrospect, the views of Suger and St Bernard can be seen as being necessary and complementary to each other, the former representing the path to awareness through the experience of beauty and exciting the senses, the latter catering for the more contemplative and cerebral approach encouraged by austerity. In terms of architecture, the two approaches are reflected in the refreshingly simple and calm Cistercian abbeys that contrast with buildings containing rich and exuberant stained glass.

At its highest, stained glass can instruct and inform, at both the conscious and unconscious levels, or, to quote Suger again, it can 'illumine men's minds so that they may travel through it to an apprehension of God's light'. However, whether we are capable of undergoing or even understanding this kind of experience in our present age would seem to be highly unlikely – if all people could come to 'an apprehension of God's light', then surely the world would be a better place! Nowadays most of us visit Chartres along with a host of other sites, possibly as part of a package deal that takes in Versailles and the Louvre in the same day. It may be easier to peruse the brochure, trust in what a learned guide recites parrot-fashion, read what some worthy art historian has to say about the windows, or

Opposite: St Dunstan, C14 under both C14 and C15 canopies; Cockayne Hatley, Bedfordshire.

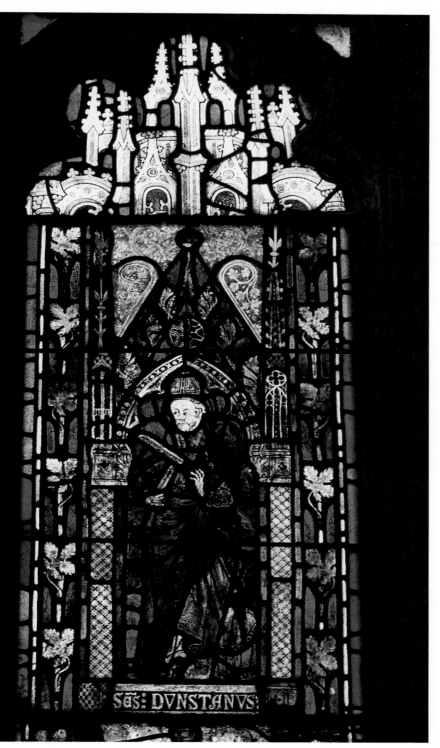

just take a photograph and pass on our way, rather than delve into any mystery that may reside there, hidden from a passing glance. It would seem that the only mysteries left to our rational minds are scientific ones: that the true sense of mystery, of opening the mind to the unknown – whether it be represented by natural or artificial beauty – is no longer part of our intellectual tradition. Such areas are invariably labelled 'mystical' or dismissed as 'religious', irrelevant to our modern and highly informed age, implying that the need for such enquiry is the result of immaturity or some psychological inadequacy compensating for internal unhappiness.

We have virtually lost the knowledge of how to become at one with what we are looking at, an experience similar to the one T. S. Eliot described on hearing music 'so deeply that it is not heard at all, but you are the music while the music lasts'. So often art – and religious art in particular – is consumed rather than experienced, whether we walk through art galleries and look at it, or make notes about it, classifying and comparing it for a thesis, lecture or book, or whether we collect it for investment or private pleasure. The emphasis is on seeing as much as possible in the time available rather than in making time available for seeing as much as possible in one place — or in a single object.

Whether George Herbert had stained glass in mind when he wrote 'Elixir':

> A man that looks on glass,
> On it may stay his eye;
> And if he pleaseth, through it pass,
> And then the heaven espy.

matters not. What we see, or what we allow ourselves to see, is very much up to us, just as a deeper meaning can be found in just about anything we turn our attention to, or as William Blake put it in 'Auguries of Innocence':

> To see a World in a Grain of Sand,
> And a Heaven in a Wild Flower,
> Hold Infinity in the palm of your hand,
> And Eternity in an hour.

In terms of looking at stained glass, our experience is, in one sense, the opposite of that of God, of whom the psalmist wrote, 'a thousand years in Thy sight are but as yesterday.' In the almost 1000 years that stained glass windows have been with us, the world has moved, it believes, from what is often called the 'Dark Ages' to Civilisation, and in the West, Christianity has played a key part in that evolution. During all those years, stained glass – filled with religious images that reflect the contemporary Christian view of history and the universe – have moved through a cycle of growth that began in the eleventh and twelfth centuries, flowered in the thirteenth and fourteenth, began to wither in the fifteenth, faded in the second half of the sixteenth century (when such images came to be deemed superstitious), declined and almost died in the seventeenth and eighteenth, and moved on to a kind of renaissance in the nineteenth and twentieth centuries.

We can, then, travel round our churches and museums, looking at this legacy to see and judge for ourselves. If we so choose and it pleases, then we can learn and perhaps 'travel through it to an apprehension of God's light', 'travel' being the keyword here. One window may change our lives — yet that window will probably be different for each of us – but first we have to find it or, as the mystic might put it, the window has to find us. Whatever 'secrets' a window (ancient or modern) may hold in store, they cannot be discovered if we are over hasty in our opinions as we are encouraged to be today; nevertheless we must praise that which does immediately resonate with something inside us, all the while bearing in mind that what seems to be a 'bad' or ugly window may, on reflection, have something to say. Much that is good has been lost because of the prevailing opinions of a so-called enlightened age.

To the medieval mind, light was a magical substance – that is, one that had supernatural properties. In the magnificent opening words of St John's Gospel, Christ is described as the Light of the world, words with which Abbot Suger would undoubtedly have been familiar. One cannot help but wonder, therefore, whether he was also acquainted with the medieval lyric that so aptly described the overall purpose of the stained glass windows, newly arrived in the many churches and cathedrals called 'Notre Dame': 'As the sun that shines through glass, so Jesus in his mother was.'

The Crucifixion between the sun and moon; a C15 fragment from Durham Cathedral.

9

THE LEGACY OF
STAINED GLASS IN BRITAIN

Britain is a unique place in which to observe and study the art, craft and iconography of stained glass. Although it tends to lack the concentration and quantity of the early (i.e. twelfth- and thirteenth-century) windows that are to be seen in such places as Chartres, Paris (Sainte Chapelle) and Bourges in France, Britain compensates for this by having an instructive and, at times, beautiful corpus of stained glass spread widely over a large part of the country. Despite immense losses over the centuries, numerous panels and fragments of glass survive and are still being unearthed: at least 2500 locations have one or more fragments. Among them are to be found parts of an iconographic programme that was, in essence, the same all over Europe, embellished at times by the personal insight of a glazier of genius who transformed products of the craft into great works of art. In certain schools, such as those at Norwich and York, can be seen an almost universally high standard of glazing in the design and drawing – an experienced eye can detect these 'schools' and even the hand of an individual artist at work in different locations, even if his name has long since been lost.

From the middle of the sixteenth century until the mid-nineteenth, the rudiments of this medieval art and craft were all but lost; the techniques of glass manufacture certainly were (even though coloured glass was rarely made in Britain), while all that survived were the painting of enamels on to glass and the process of silver staining, both of which produce quite different effects to that of glass coloured throughout its whole mass. With the revival of interest in Gothic art and architecture early in the last century, much research and experiment was carried out into the manufacture of medieval glass. The results led to a kind of rebirth in the art of stained glass, and some fine windows appeared from the mid-1850s onwards, despite the mass production that soon set in. In the 1860s, William Morris and his associates played a vital role in resisting the impersonal approach to the design and manufacture of stained glass windows that had been gradually creeping into the business after the International Exhibition of 1851, but by the 1880s and the 1890s even they were accused of resorting to production-line techniques when demand for their windows had become so great.

The loss of glass over the centuries has been enormous. Puritan iconoclasts of the seventeenth century certainly took their toll, but far more has probably been lost through the combination of ignorance, neglect and the removal of glass by less than scrupulous glaziers in the name of 'restoration' (as at Winchester College where the heavily darkened late fourteenth-century glass was deemed to be beyond repair in the early 1800s and replaced by imitation panels, the originals being sold). Unless church windows are looked after, the lead that holds them together may 'rot' after a hundred years or so and they can easily fall to pieces.

Interesting reset C15 fragments at North Tuddenham, Norfolk, that display the high quality of the Norwich School of glass painters.

Old windows were threatened in the eighteenth century, when prevailing taste considered much of the work of the Middle Ages to be 'barbaric' and thus it was called 'Gothic', after the barbarian Goths. Many that survived were then at risk of removal for the benefit of collectors, although it could be argued that some of the glass now in private homes and museums might well not have survived if it had remained in the church whence it was taken. This is certainly true of many French windows, which were mercifully removed and sold before they could be smashed by ideological zealots of the Revolution. Many English churches, museums and collectors willingly acquired this glass (*see* p.56).

This makes the comprehension of the stained glass now in our churches a complicated business. Anything can be expected, from fragments of the church's own original stained glass, to some good medieval panels that could be indigenous (possibly moved to a different position within the church), or might have come from another English church, or they might be foreign, bought in the nineteenth century by a wealthy vicar or donated by a generous parishioner. Sorting out what the church might have had before the Reformation from some *in situ* remains or by analysing a few reset broken pieces can provide many hours of fun. (A pair of binoculars is a vital piece of equipment to carry when looking at glass in tracery lights.) However, the first thing that invariably comes to one's attention upon opening the door is the Victorian glass; either beloved or hated by generations of local worshippers, it all too often displays the worst characteristics of nineteenth-century 'art' with its sentimentality or empty factory-line mannerisms. On the other hand, opening that door can lead to something undreamed of – a window that shatters all one's prejudices about Victorian or modern stained glass. That moment of entering and those that follow can indeed be magical.

THE STONE THAT HOLDS

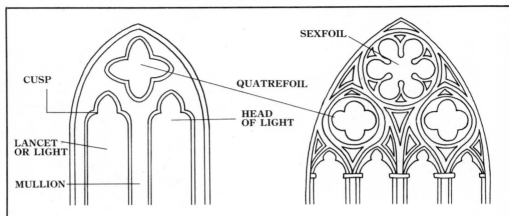

CUSP

SEXFOIL

QUATREFOIL

HEAD
OF LIGHT

LANCET
OR LIGHT

MULLION

1 In the twelfth and early thirteenth centuries, **plate tracery** comprised the framework surrounding the stained glass. In this, openings, or **lights,** were made in the thick flat areas of stone that make up the inner parts of the window. This type often gives the appearance of the openings having been cut out of the stone wall. The long thin main lights are called **lancets**.

2 **Geometrical tracery** arrived in the early to mid thirteenth century. The quatrefoil and sexfoil openings (resembling four- and six-lobed flowers) were generated out of more carefully shaped and thinner stone **mullions** of 'bar tracery', built up within the opening.

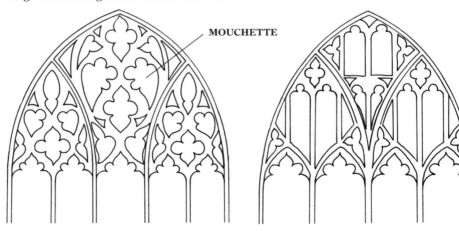

MOUCHETTE

Curvilinear or flowing

Perpendicular

5 With the Transition period between the Decorated and Perpendicular during the second half of the century, reticulated form gave way to flowing **curvilinear tracery**, of which the east window at Carlisle is a fine example. In addition, the

more symmetrical openings of reticulated tracery lights often evolved into more flowing and often asymmetrical shapes such as the **mouchette**.

THE GLASS – THE TRACERY

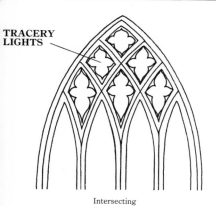

TRACERY LIGHTS

Intersecting

Reticulated

3 Y-tracery and **intersecting tracery** date from the late thirteenth and early fourteenth centuries. The first was formed by continuing the simple curves generated by a single mullion within a simple Gothic arch, and the latter by the intersection of the curves springing from two or more mullions.

4 By the fourteenth century, bar traceries began to take on a more flowing and waving form creating more irregular openings with the 'ogee' S-shape predominating; this is **reticulated tracery** which is typical of the Decorated period of architecture in the first half of the fourteenth century.

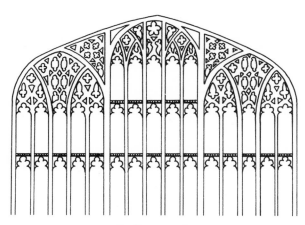

Rectilinear or panel

6 With the advent of the **Perpendicular** era, tracery lights became more ordered and straight-sided – as the name 'Perpendicular' implies. (*See illustration on opposite page.*)

7 In its last form at the end of the Gothic era (*c.* 1540), we find the often elaborate and multiple form of **rectilinear tracery** – or **panel tracery** – with its straight-sided openings beneath the barely recognisable flattened Gothic arches.

SOME MAKERS' MARKS

The practice of signing a stained glass window – either in writing or by placing a symbol in the bottom left or right hand corner – was not common in the Middle Ages. Over the past 150 years or so it has become much more common, but even during the nineteenth century many windows remains unsigned: the O'Connor Brothers seem to have nearly always signed their work, as did the Continental firms, but most of the larger British firms generally did not. Thus Clayton & Bell's windows nearly always have to be identified by recognition of style and the same is true with Heaton, Butler & Bayne, Lavers, Barraud & Westlake, and Burlison & Grylls. Kempe & Co signed their windows after 1900 with the wheatsheaf emblem, and Powell of Whitefriars used their little friar figure in the twentieth century. More recently signatures and emblems have become more common. Here are some of them:

1 M. Farrar Bell, 2 Goddard & Gibbs, 3 Alfred Bell, 4 J.E. Nuttgens, 5 Reginald Bell, 6 Sir Ninian Comper, 7 C.E. Kempe (after 1900), 8 Geoffrey Webb, 9 William Wailes 10 William Warrington, 11 John Thornton of Coventry, 12 Walter Tower, 13 Thomas Willement, 14 Caroline Townshend and Joan Howson, 15 Christopher Webb, 16 Hugh Easton, 17 Francis Skeat, 18 Thomas of Oxford, 19 James Powell & Sons, Whitefriars, 20 Celtic Studios, 21 & 23 Martin Travers, 22 M.E. Aldrich Rope, 24 Holland of Warwick

THE MAKING OF STAINED AND COLOURED GLASS WINDOWS

Recent research into medieval glass production has substantially changed the traditional picture of how coloured glass was made during the twelfth and thirteenth centuries. It was formerly believed that the basic ingredients consisted of a large quantity of sand fused by high heat with beechwood ash roughly in the proportion of three to one, to which was added a small amount of metallic oxide to obtain the desired colour. To a certain extent this was true in that certain colours were produced this way. However, it seems now that for most colours only sand and ash were used, the latter providing the required lime and metal oxides. Hereby lies the curse and blessing of medieval glass, the curse being that beechwood is rich in potash and, over the centuries, this has caused the glass to corrode badly. The blessing, however, was that the natural content of iron and manganese oxides in the ash (up to 2 per cent) gave rise to a whole range of colours that depended upon the state of oxidation in the furnace and how long the glass was kept molten.

In 1977, the researcher Christine Sellner, using electron spin resonance to analyse numerous samples of medieval glass as well as performing actual experiments, proved that virtually any colour was obtainable by this process. Dr Roy Newton has gone on to suggest that, since the operation was somewhat hit and miss, different colours became associated with different 'houses' in the glass-making areas, each craftsman knowing his own recipe and sticking to it rather than trying to produce many different colours. By collecting the products of these different houses, travelling pedlars – the middlemen of their time – would have known where to obtain all the colours. In the light of this research, one could well ask: Was this, then, the 'secret' that surrounded much of medieval stained glass production?

However, whether controlled oxidation or the addition of metallic oxides were used, the basic process of making pieces of medieval glass is fairly well known. The dome-shaped furnaces were lined with clay and fired by wood, creating a high enough temperature – about 2,700°F (1,500°C) – to melt the ingredients. This 'melt' of molten glass produced in clay pots placed in the furnaces was transformed into sheets of 'pot-metal' glass by one of two methods. The first involved extracting a lump of molten glass from the clay pot with a metal blow pipe. After being blown into a bubble, the glass was coerced by swinging and further blowing into a cylindrical shape as it gradually solidified. At a crucial moment this cylinder was cut along its length and the sides opened out to create a sheet of flat glass. This glass was called muff. 'Crown glass' was produced by extracting a quantity of the melt and spinning it around on a heated rod so that the centrifugal force spread it out into a disc shape of anything up to two feet (0.60m) in diameter. (Elongated trails of bubbles trapped into the melt often formed concentric circles in the glass and betray that it was made by this method.) After the rod had been broken off, the disc

15

was reduced to whatever sizes of sheets were desirable (or possible). At the centre was left the knob — the 'bull's eye' — which was often used in domestic glazing as it still is today in 'olde worlde tea shoppes'. In rare cases, bulls' eyes were worked into a window in a church; there is a good example of this in the figure of St John the Baptist in Beverley Minster's east window (Humberside), where the bull's eye is used for St John's hand, creating an almost sculptured effect; another example is in the Tiffany window in St Cuthbert's, Edinburgh (*see illustration on* p.234).

Ruby – that is, red – glass when produced either by controlled oxidation or by the addition of copper oxide was too deep in colour, almost opaque. For this reason, it was produced by a process known as 'flashing'. In this, clear glass was extracted from the 'melt', blown so that it formed a small bubble and then was dipped into a crucible of molten red so that a thin layer of the red glass stuck to it. Repeated dipping (sometimes as many as a dozen applications) built up the thickness until the desired density of ruby was obtained. Such glass often has an uneven colour, which, in the hands of a good glazier, could be used to great artistic effect.

Much of our knowledge of how the medieval glazier then transformed this coloured glass into a window is described by the contemporary writer Theophilus whose book, *On the Various Arts*, dates from either the eleventh or twelfth century. He, too, noted the variation of the colours in the melt but does not describe this aspect of the art in too much detail, either because this section of the treatise is missing, it was regarded as a trade secret or he simply did not know. He goes on, however, to describe how the 'cartoon' (or life-sized drawing) for the envisaged window was drawn either on to paper or on to a whitewashed table top that defined the positions of the lead and glass within the composition, each glass position then being labelled with a colour. Glass was cut from the main sheets in the first instance by placing a red hot iron on its surface and judiciously applying a lump of saliva to the right spot, the glass fracturing – with any luck – exactly where desired. The selected piece was then trimmed into shape using a grozing iron, a flat piece of metal with a notch at each end for chipping off bits of the glass.

When all the coloured and clear pieces had been selected and cut to shape, they were then ready to be painted with a pigment made from a mixture of iron filings, resin and wine (or urine) to create features such as hands, feet, face, drapery folds, lettering, etc. The shading of these details was brought about by applying light washes of pigment – a technique called smear-shading – dabbing little dots of paint on to the various areas according to the required density. The shadings or washes of colour could subsequently be picked or scratched out, either with the hard end of a brush or with a special pointed instrument that, like an etching pen, could give further fine detail to such features as costume decorations or jewellery. Lettering was also often picked out in reverse from a wash of a dark shade or of black. Occasionally back painting can be seen on the outside surface – it creates a kind of three-dimensional effect that was used in a brilliant manner, for example, on the fish in the water beneath the feet of St Christopher in a window at Beckley (Oxon). Firing in the kiln at about 1110°F (600°C) then fixed the painting and shading, an operation that had to be done carefully so that the fine details could be preserved (i.e. it

Opposite: The Tree of Jesse, *c.*1533, Ḷlanrhaeadr, Clwyd in north Wales.

17

could not be fired too much) and made to last (i.e. it could not be fired too little).

In the early fourteenth century, it was discovered that, when silver nitrate was applied to the surface of the glass, it subsequently turned yellow on firing in the furnace. This 'silver staining' was applied to what would become the outer surface, the pigment being on the inner face. Its potential was soon realised, namely that yellow/gold could be applied to selective areas of a piece of clear glass for such features as crowns, hair, borders, etc. When flashed red glass had been abraded away (scraped off), yellow stain could be applied to the clear undersurface, but this treatment was hardly used until the fifteenth century, and then only rarely – examples can be seen at Fairford in Gloucestershire (*see illustration on* p.108) and Llanrhaeadr in Clwyd (*see illustration on* p.16). Likewise, the yellow staining of blue glass in order to give green in selected areas is also comparatively rare.

The pieces were then ready for leading together, an operation carried out either on the cartoon or on the whitewashed table. Pieces of lead with I-shaped cross-sections, invariably made by the glazier himself, were measured and cut so that every piece of glass was entirely surrounded and the lead junctions soldered together to form a panel. (Today this leaded panel is then cemented with a compound of plaster of Paris, linseed oil, lamp-black and red lead that seals the glass to the lead, prevents rattling and helps keep out the rain.) A large window would have been made up from a number of these panels fitted into the window by an iron armature (in the case of large thirteenth-century windows) or, later, by saddle-bars (horizontal and occasionally vertical iron bars) on the inside of the opening on to which the window is fixed by ties that help take the weight and prevent wind blowing it in.

This process remained substantially the same all through the Middle Ages and is still – with certain refinements such as the use of diamond cutters and steel pliers instead of grozing irons – the way that a good many windows are made today.

From *c.* 1530 onwards, however, painting in enamels became increasingly more common. This was partly because the technique was easier and cheaper than using pot-metal glass, partly because the trend was towards more realism, which painting made more easily possible, and, finally, coloured glass was unobtainable after 1630 and virtually all colouring during the seventeenth and early eighteenth centuries was achieved by enamels. Crude attempts at producing pot-metals over the next hundred years were unsatisfactory, and it was not until the late 1850s, when so-called 'antique glass' became available, that the craft found new life.

Much of the colour range seen in medieval glass reappeared, together with some new colours never produced before, but the method of glass manufacture was different from the medieval process, which is possibly why it does not look quite the same, even allowing for corrosion and deterioration over the ages and, of course, artistic differences. Later in the nineteenth century, new types of glass were developed. An example was Norman slab, an attempt to imitate the glass made in medieval times, which was generally rather thick and uneven, produced by blowing the molten glass into a rectangular mould that created sides with glass thicker at the centre. Popular with the Arts & Crafts fraternity, it can still be obtained (at a price and to order) today.

Present-day coloured glass is made as it was in the nineteenth century, using a range of metallic salts for colouring – cobalt blue, manganese for purple, chromium for green, selenium for red, copper for green or red depending on the conditions, iron or uranium oxide for yellow, nickel oxide for brown. Flashed glass is also available now, in red, blue and green. This century saw the development of the 'streaky' glasses that mix two colours when the glass is in the liquid state, and 'reamy', in which the colour density varies. New techniques have been evolved, such as aciding to replace the laborious business of abrading flashed colours from their bases. This involves covering the areas that are to remain with beeswax or bitumen and immersing the glass in hydrofluoric acid for minutes or hours, depending upon its colour and the degree of removal required; part-removal of flashed layers can, by subsequent treatment with staining or paint, create some remarkable effects – Karl Parsons and Harry Clarke use a lot of aciding in order to create the very rich and varied colour schemes of their windows (*see illustration on* p.69).

Other new techniques include appliqué, the process of sticking pieces of coloured glass directly on to the surface of another sheet; the fixing substance has until recently been epoxy resin, although recent research is beginning to throw doubt on its long-term properties (it is no longer used for sticking together pieces of old glass for this reason). Similarly, fused glass, as the name implies, involves fusing plates of coloured glass by heating them to just below the melting point of glass.

Finally, apart from making windows in fibre-glass, which has not proved particularly popular, there is the process of making them out of *dalle de verre*, that is, out of 'pavingstones' of glass – or large thick plates of cast glass, set into a frame of either reinforced concrete or lighter (both artistically and physically) epoxy resin. This has been particularly popular over the past thirty years or so and enables great walls of glass to be created.

October – sowing; Norwich School, 1480-1500; originally at Coslany, now at the Victoria & Albert Museum, London.

WINDOW DESIGN, CONTENT AND ICONOGRAPHY

Since most stained glass was originally to be found in churches, it is only natural that the majority of the themes of windows we see today are religious. During the Middle Ages, subjects were selected from a conventional iconographic programme, into which elaborations were sometimes woven in connection with such things as local or popular saints and their legends. Apart from these main themes, we find some fascinating details in the ancillary material that makes up a large proportion of each of these compositions – such as the canopies, border settings, donor figures, heraldry and backgrounds – and which often illustrates, in passing, details of agricultural and domestic life of the time.

CANOPIES

From an early design stage in the evolution of medieval stained glass, most saintly figures were depicted in a setting appropriate to their dignity, that is, placed within some kind of frame and beneath a canopy that established their presence as the main item in a particular light or opening in a window. In the very earliest examples of figures in stained glass, the prophets in the Cathedral at Augsburg in West Germany are portrayed in their lancets without any embellishment apart from texts over their heads that serve as both canopies and borders. In the case of the twelfth-century figures at Canterbury, these sit beneath simple architectural curves that spring from styled capitals at the side. At Chartres, these simple surrounds have been slightly elaborated to form niches, similar in most respects to those of Early English architecture. Indeed, as time went by, the canopies began to mirror the architecture of their eras more and more, sometimes in great detail. As windows grew in height, so too did the canopies until, in the fourteenth century, they sometimes towered many times higher than the panel beneath them, as at Tewkesbury Abbey. During the Perpendicular period, the process of elaboration continued, though the heights rarely exceeded those of the eccentric examples of preceding years. Some of the most fantastic canopies of all can be seen at New College, Oxford, executed by Thomas Glazier towards the end of the fourteenth century, where it is hard to find two the same. However, in John Thornton's east window at York Minster, so many scenes are employed to convey the events from Genesis to Revelation that the canopies are merely perfunctory and pushed to the upper limit of the lights. At Gloucester Cathedral, on the other hand, they play a more prominent role; they are found in the middle as well as at the top of the huge east window, so that they link the successive rows of figures together.

Opposite: C14 canopy top, border and tracery lights at Gedney, Lincs.

In the early sixteenth century, the practice of copying the prevailing architecture in the windows continued, so that Renaissance elements in design gradually displaced those of the Gothic era, and we find that, whenever canopies were used, they are depicted as little alcoves set between pillars beneath Roman arches, while the scenes themselves have burst out of their confines, often spreading across many lights with no border or canopies at all. Heavy Renaissance alcove canopies and plinths continued to be employed in the painted windows of the next two centuries up to the end of the Georgian era, until the Gothic revival brought back into fashion the elaborate fifteenth-century models, which, in the hands of Heaton, Butler & Bayne, Clayton & Bell, Kempe & Co. and a host of lesser firms, persisted right up until the outbreak of the First World War. With the Pre-Raphaelite-inspired glaziers in particular, we find some interesting transformations of conventional forms into beautifully patterned canopies of foliage and interweaving natural forms – there is a fine example at Mere (Wilts) by Henry Holiday, and a host around the country by Morris & Co. and the later Arts & Crafts glaziers.

GRISAILLE

The use of *grisaille* – clear glass embellished by painting on natural motifs and set in a geometric design – originated in the twelfth century, partly under the influence of Cistercian society and partly by virtue of its cheapness compared with coloured glass. It had the advantage of moderating the amount of light that came into the building, imparting more than panels of deeply coloured stained glass, yet subduing the glare of full sunlight unrestricted by clear glass. A forerunner of *grisaille* can be seen at Brabourne in Kent where a mid-twelfth century window with a high percentage of coloured glass can be seen. It has a strong geometric and flower-like pattern, but lacks any painting on the surface of either the coloured or clear glass. By the thirteenth century, *grisaille* proper had arrived. Essentially it consists of a repeating framework of a geometric pattern with lozenges, circles or squares, within which flower and leaf motifs are painted on to the clear glass creating a pattern that acts as a counterpoint to the main geometric pattern reinforced by the leading. Colour is only sparingly used. The finest example of the species in Britain is unquestionably the glass in the Five Sisters Window at York Minster of *c.* 1250. Here each Sister – five foot wide and over fifty feet high – has a different repeating pattern, whilst the leaf pattern on the glass can often be seen to be breaking out of its geometric confinement and growing – as it were – into the pattern next door. Other examples of early *grisaille* can be seen at Stockbury in Kent, at Lincoln and Salisbury Cathedrals.

By 1270 we begin to find figure subjects or heraldic shields being placed against a *grisaille* background. The style became particularly popular during the Decorated period – good early examples can be seen at Chetwode in Buckinghamshire and at Stanford on Avon in Northamptonshire. At Merton College, Oxford, the numerous figure panels of *c.* 1292 are sandwiched between layers of *grisaille* that has itself become much more 'naturalised' in that the patterns are generated from an ivy tree trunk that grows up the centre of each window. So, too, the leaf designs in this nature-obsessed Decorated era were based on a greater variety of species – we find

C13 geometric *grisaille* at Stanton St John, Oxfordshire.   Grotesque at Stanford-on-Avon, Northants, C14.

ivy, bramble, hawthorne and maple in addition to the more common trailing leaves of oak and vine: good examples can be seen at Eaton Bishop and Brinsop in Herefordshire, Mamble in Worcestershire and at Bere Ferrers in Devon. Soon, however, the elaborate underlying structure of *grisaille* as determined by the leading gave way to a more simplified repeating pattern of diamond-shaped quarries across which the trailing leaves and branches are painted; this can be seen in an early stage at Merton College, Oxford. By the fifteenth century *grisaille* was largely replaced by quarries each having a single design that was often repeated.

BORDERS

One of the many charming aspects of medieval windows was the care lavished upon borders, a tradition that no doubt stemmed from the creation of illuminated manuscripts. They are at their most beautiful, intricate and interesting in the naturalistic/geometric forms that are to be found in early thirteenth-century glass – alas, something of a rarity in this country outside Canterbury Cathedral. Geometric design was something of an obsession at this time – it permeates the background settings against which the main scenes are placed, while the scenes themselves are invariably placed inside a strong geometric medallion (*see illustration on* p.5). This can be seen in Canterbury and, in a different form, is present in the north rose window there, but by the end of the century it had disappeared.

Some of the archers at Middleton, Greater Manchester, c.1503; note their arrows and names alongside their bows.

At Merton College, Oxford, we can see in the window of *c.* 1295 the form that was to prevail, although later slightly modified, for at least the next 200 years: the border, much reduced in thickness and acting as an outer skin between the perimeter of the light and the surround of the canopy that houses the central figure, comprises alternating pieces of red, green and gold bearing little images of castles and fleur-de-lis that often flow all round the lights. In other fourteenth-century windows, we find combinations of heraldic charges (emblems that would appear on a shield) such as lions, leopards' heads and covered cups, as well as naturalistic foliage of vines and maple or oak leaves, that weave a continuous strip all round the outside of the panel. This style sometimes continues up into the tracery lights, framing the little figures and scenes inside their mouchettes or other shapes characteristic of the Decorated era (*see illustration on* p.21). Many of these heraldic motifs act as a kind of paean to the monarch: the castles of Castile having come to England through Eleanor of Castile, wife of Edward I; the fleur-de-lis symbolising France, the leopards and lions being emblems of the monarch, and the covered cups signifying Galicia over which Castile ruled.

The magnificent 'Monkey's Funeral' border in York Minster is a unique and charmingly executed example of a more elaborate border from this time. So, too, are the intriguing borders of the Lenton school of glaziers of Nottinghamshire, with their bizarre faces, animals and grotesques (*see illustration on* p.23).

As the Decorated period gave way to the Perpendicular, the same kind of treatment continued, although the individual pieces that made up the borders tended to be much more perfunctory, often comprising only a single emblem painted on clear glass with yellow staining. Borders with the radiant sun, or sun *ensoleille,* emblem of Edward IV, became popular during the period 1461-83. After this time, borders were gradually dispensed with as pictorial windows became more popular and the scenes reached to the extremities of the window openings.

DONOR FIGURES

The precedent of portraying the donor at the bottom of a window seems to have been set in 1144 by Abbot Suger at St Denis, where he can still be seen today in one of the apse windows. Strangely, examples are absent from thirteenth-century windows until *c.*1298, when Henricus de Mamesfeld gave to Merton College the fourteen three-light windows in which he himself appears no fewer than twenty-four times, twice with each of the twelve Apostles. Thereafter, donor figures crept into fourteenth-century windows, sometimes up in the tracery lights (as with the quarryman William Campion at Helmdon) or, more commonly, at the bottom where, kneeling, they request that we pray for them – they are often accompanied by their coats-of-arms to make sure that they are easily recognised. Occasionally they can be seen in the act of handing over a model of the church or a window to the saint to whom the church is dedicated. York Minster has many fine examples of this, notably the 'Bell Founders' window in the north aisle where the whole composition is liberally sprinkled with bells – the donor, Richard Tunnock, seen giving a window to St William of York, has one on his satchel, and on each side of him are scenes illustrating details of the bell-making trade. At Tewkesbury, some fine windows were given in the fourteenth century to the Abbey by Lady Eleanor de Clare, and she appears naked, kneeling at the base of the Last Judgement scene below the rose window; also here are the fine large figures of the knights Robert Earl of Gloucester, Lady Eleanor's husband Gilbert de Clare and others. These windows are rare instances of benefactors being portrayed the same size as the holy figures next to them.

There are, all over the country, some fine donor figures in the Perpendicular windows of the fifteenth century, particularly at Long Melford (Suffolk) and East Harling (Norfolk), both of the Norwich school, and a splendid knight in armour among the high-quality fragments at Birtsmorton church (Worcs). Figures of wives and children often appeared with that of a donor during the fifteenth century, generally lined up with the sons behind the father and daughters behind the mother. Everyone is depicted in their Sunday best, or in their best suit of armour, with ermine and the latest fashions abounding – everyone, that is, except the aforementioned Lady Eleanor at Tewksbury in her birthday suit and the member of the Heydon family at West Wickham (Bromley, London) who is even further reduced – to a skeleton!

Royal donors, as at Little Malvern (Worcs), were generally given grander settings to befit their stately offices, either set beneath fine surrounds or kneeling at desks. By the sixteenth century, both they and donors of lesser importance had grown larger in proportion to the rest of the window (e.g. at St Margaret's, Westminster), although nowhere do they become as domineering as some examples from the Continent, where they not only rival the main holy figures but sometimes even displace them from the central panels!

HERALDRY IN STAINED GLASS

A basic knowledge of heraldry is helpful to the serious student of stained glass: if the main terms are understood, then it is possible to recognise a coat-of-arms from a description given in heraldic language, and this in turn can help identify donors/benefactors and hence, with some antiquarian research, can date the windows with which they are associated. Moreover, in the testing business of sorting out what's what in a sea of fragments of medieval glass leaded together either into an undifferentiated mass or into a pretty pattern, the identification of heraldic pieces can be useful not only for the above reasons but also in helping to avoid the mistake that some of the heraldic charges (*see glossary on* p.28) might have something to do with the iconography. The use of heraldic devices (or emblems) in border design has been mentioned – such pieces are common among fragments and naturally assist in identification. Students of heraldry, on the other hand, can also derive many hours of pleasure deciphering heraldic glass. The coats-of-arms of many of England's old families appear in windows, sometimes found again and again across the country, families such as Warenne, de Clare, Mortimer, Berkeley, Bohun, Valence, Fitzalan, Beauchamp, Despenser, Percy, Neville and Roos.

Heraldry first appeared in an organised form in France in the early thirteenth century, prompted by the recently introduced closed visor to a suit of armour that made identification of knights on the battlefield virtually impossible. It was soon represented in stained glass, and examples from this time exist in a number of windows at Chartres – the transept rose windows utilise heraldic charges as the background 'mosaic', of France in the north rose and the House of Dreux in the south. England, however, was slow to adopt the practice, the first surviving example being the shields now in the west window of Salisbury Cathedral. In early examples, the heraldry is placed against *grisaille* in the lowest layer of the window – for instance, in the east window of Gloucester Cathedral and at Tewkesbury Abbey. Shields were divided into two parts or halves (*per pale, per fess* and *per bend*) after 1340 when, with the assumption of the title of King of France by Edward III, the royal coat-of-arms with its three lions became united with the fleur-de-lis of France. At about this time, shields of arms also started to appear in tracery lights above the figure panels, and in the following century, they can sometimes be found in canopies while those in the traceries are often held by angels.

Towards the end of this century, there is evidence of flashed red glass that was abraded and the exposed clear glass stained yellow, a very useful technique to help simplify the making of heraldic panels. The subdivision of heraldic fields beyond the quarter (i.e. with more than four coats-of-arms on the shield) gradually became more complicated at this time, making the glaziers' task more difficult; by the mid-sixteenth century, many of them chose to portray such elaborate alliances by

Arms of the Grocers' Company and Lady Margaret Slaney, painted by John Oliver, 1664; Northill, Beds.

enamel painting and yellow staining rather than involving themselves in much fiddly leading, only occasionally adding pieces of pot-metal. These techniques were also encouraged by the heraldic designs themselves that were becoming even further embellished with the addition of supporters, scrolls, helms and crests. By the seventeenth and eighteenth centuries, when foreign pot-metal glass was unobtainable and heraldic achievements had become immensely elaborate, it was all paint and stain. Nevertheless, some of these heraldic devices are splendid, notably the works of Henry Gyles and William Peckitt; and fine windows by Gyles of 1663 can be seen at Acomb (N Yorks) where Charles II's elaborate coat-of-arms is painted complete with supporters, mottos and Garter wreath. A fine pair of windows from about the same time can also be seen at Northill, Beds (*see illustration above*).

In general, heraldic glass has survived purges against windows better than figure and scenic panels, possibly because the coats-of-arms were often placed out of reach of the Puritans in tracery lights; some Parliamentarians might also have had problems in reading them and therefore ignored them, content with having destroyed the images of sacred figures.

HERALDIC GLOSSARY

Metals, Colours and Furs

Metals: gold (*or*)
silver (*argent*)

Colours: blue (*azure*)
red (*gules*)
black (*sable*)
green (*vert*)
purple (*purpure*)

Furs: ermine
vair (a squirrel-like fur)

Field Divisions

Field divided into halves horizontally (*per pale*)
Field divided into halves vertically (*per fess*)
Field divided into halves diagonally (*per bend*)
Field divided into quarters (*quarterly*)
Field divided into quarters diagonally (*per saltire*)
Field divided into thirds (*per pall*)

Ordinaries

Horizontal strip divided into two (*a chief*)
Horizontal strip divided into three (*a fess*)
Vertical strip divided into three (*a pale*)
Diagonal strip divided into three (*a bend*)
Inverted V-shaped strip (*a chevron*)
Y-shaped strip (*a pall*)
Horizontal-vertical cross strip (*a cross*)
Diagonal cross strip (*a saltire*)
Inverted triangle on shield (*a pile*)

Some heraldic terms are self-explanatory. Here are some of the less obvious ones:

achievement the shield or shield-shaped surface on which a coat-of-arms is depicted, also the shield with the bearings.

bezant a gold disc.

cadence a charge (*qv*) that indicates a family relationship.

canton a square in the top left-hand corner of a field.

cartouche a shield with an elaborate shape, common in the seventeenth century.

charge an emblem placed on the field (*qv*) of a shield.

chequée a field comprising a chequered pattern.

cross-patonce a cross with arms that curve.

displayed usually refers to an eagle outstretched.

escallop a shell, often symbolical of pilgrimage.

field the area on the face of a shield.

fleur-de-lis stylised form of the lily used on the French coat-of-arms as a charge.

guardant refers to an animal, usually a lion, looking out from a shield.

helm a helmet sometimes placed on top of an achievement.

label a device resembling an E (sometimes with more than three prongs) turned on its side — used as a cadence (*qv*)

martlet heraldic bird (without feet).

ordinary a shape within a field.

passant refers to an animal, usually a lion, walking across the shield.

rampant an animal standing on its hind legs.

supporters two (rarely one) animals on each side of a shield supporting it.

The royal coats-of-arms of England often appear in stained glass, and it is worth noting when the major changes in these took place:

1190-1340	Three lions passant-guardant in gold on a red field.
1340-1405	The above is quartered with the field of golden fleur-de-lis of the arms of France, over which Edward III proclaimed sovereignty.
1405-1603	The French half was reduced to only three fleur-de-lis.
After 1603	With the ascension to the throne of James VI of Scotland and I of England, the arms of England, Scotland (a red rampant lion on a gold field), and Ireland (the harp) were combined. The French element remained until 1807

THE ICONOGRAPHIC PROGRAMME

Traditionally, the north side of a church or cathedral is associated with the Old Testament. The events and writings that lead towards the central mystery of the Christian faith, the Passion, belong to the east end. The south side is concerned with the New Testament since the events of the Passion, that is, the teachings of Christ and the examples of the saints and martyrs who carry the Word through time. In the west lies the future, which in Christian iconography means the Last Judgement and the end of time.

Within this scheme – which can be seen more or less complete in the glass of Fairford church (Glos) and at King's College Chapel, Cambridge – are placed the central images and tenets of the Faith. These were sometimes set in accordance with what is called a 'typological series' – scenes and incidents (also called 'antetypes') from the Old Testament that seem to foreshadow those of the New are placed next to each other. Parts of such a scheme from the early thirteenth century exist at Canterbury, and from as late as the seventeenth century at Lincoln College, Oxford, as well as the examples at Fairford and King's College Chapel, Cambridge.

Medieval iconography gathered its imagery from a number of sources – the Bible (in those days, the Latin Vulgate) being the most important. In the fourteenth century, copies of the *Biblia pauperum* (or 'Bible of the Poor') began to appear rich with Biblical illustrations reproduced from woodcuts; before then, it had existed in only a few manuscript copies kept at important centres of learning, such as Canterbury Cathedral. Here, typological scenes inspired by it appear in some of the north windows of the apse that date from the early thirteenth century. When printed copies became available, the imagery became much more widely known. In the *Biblia*, for example, the Resurrection is portrayed with two Old Testament scenes, one of Samson Carrying the Gates of Gaza, and the other with Jonah Emerging from the Mouth of the Whale; the illustration of Samson and the Gates is echoed in an English panel in St Martin's Church, Stamford (Lincs) and in a Flemish one now in the Lady Chapel of Exeter Cathedral, both from the fifteenth century. The typological imagery is well illustrated here: Jonah's parallel with Christ's Resurrection is easy to see in his three-day sojourn in the whale out of which he emerged alive and well; Samson likewise emerged when, having been imprisoned in Gaza by the Philistines, he burst open the city's gates one night and deposited them on a mountain top.

At about the same time, there also appeared the printed version of the *Legenda aurea* ('Golden Legend'), filled with stories and legends about the lives of the saints, many of which were illustrated in stained glass (*see next chapter*). A little later came the *Speculum Humanae Salvationis* ('Mirror of Human Salvation'), with its type/antetype scenes – one of each – that were used, for example, as a basis for some of the scenes in stained glass at Malvern Priory (Worcs).

From these sources derived most of the designs of windows, so that those who could not read could at least be reminded of the Bible's stories and the Church's doctrines by these images from, say, the *Biblia*, translated into stained glass. Christ was naturally the central figure of all the iconography, but there were also

Old Testament characters who foreshadowed Him, or the saints who, after their deaths, were seen to be in communion with Him. Naturally the most common scenes are those of the Passion, beginning with the triumphal entry into Jerusalem on Palm Sunday and ending with Pentecost. Each stage of the Passion had its scene, as in great paintings, such that the poses and settings became instantly recognisable — in the Ascension, for example, there are invariably a group of Apostles and the Virgin Mary looking up at a pair of feet disappearing through the clouds, leaving behind an imprint on the mountain top (this latter detail originated in pilgrims' tales of how they had been shown the very footprints on the Mount of Olives when they were in Jerusalem).

Thus we see the sequence of The Washing of Christ's Feet, The Last Supper, The Agony in the Garden, The Betrayal by Judas, The Trial before Pilate, The Scourging, The Mocking of Christ, Christ Portrayed with the Crown of Thorns (*Ecce Homo*), Carrying the Cross (the *Via Crucis*), The Crucifixion, The Taking Down from the Cross (*Depositio*) and The Virgin Holding the Dead Christ (*Mater Dolorosa* or *Pietà*). These are followed by The Resurrection, Mary Magdalene Mistaking Christ as the Gardener (*Noli me Tangere*), The Supper at Emmaus, Thomas's Doubt, the Ascension and Pentecost. Occasionally extra incidents find their way in, such as the Three Marys in the Garden, The 'Harrowing of Hell' and The Nailing to the Cross.

The Virgin Mary and the young St John are nearly always portrayed in the Crucifixion, except when there is space for only the *Crucifixus*; the sun and moon appear in some fifteenth- and sixteenth-century Crucifixions, alluding not only to the eclipse – or darkness – reported in the Gospels, but also to register the cosmic nature of this event central to Christian belief (*see illustration on* p.9). Later (that is, from the sixteenth century onwards), angels are sometimes shown around Christ on the Cross, collecting the Blood of Christ, as at Cotehele House (Cornwall) and at Bowness (Cumbria). In the sixteenth century, the two thieves are also occasionally depicted with an angel and demon above the repentent and unrepentent respectively, for instance, at Fairford (Glos), Hingham (Norfolk), St Margaret's, Westminster, and King's College Chapel, Cambridge. Not to be missed are the rare 'Crucifixion lilies', that is, where the Cross is combined with the lily of the Annunciation, such that either the Crucifixion dominates the scene, as at Westwood (Wilts) (*see illustration opposite*) and St Michael's, Oxford (*see illustration on* p.173), or the lily and the Annunciation dominate, as at York Minster and Long Melford (Suffolk).

Christ appears in Glory or in Judgement, holding the orb of the world and with his hand raised in blessing, sometimes on a rainbow, or Displaying the Wounds, often with angels in attendance waving a censer. Christ is always recognisable by his halo, which is divided into four petal-like sections.

The Virgin Mary has her own cycle that in its entirety is sometimes called 'The Joys and Sorrows of the Virgin'. A complete cycle in stained glass does not seem to have survived, but a fair number of panels from the series do exist. It commences with incidents from The Lives of Anne and Joachim, moves through The

Opposite: Lily Crucifixion and angels with Passion relics; E window of Westwood Church, Wiltshire, C15.

Birth and Childhood of the Virgin, and Teaching the Virgin Mary to Read, to her Betrothal to Joseph, the Annunciation and The Visitation with Elisabeth. It includes The Nativity and its associated scenes of The Adoration of the Magi and of the Shepherds, the Massacre of the Holy Innocents and The Flight into Egypt; it continues with The Circumcision, The Presentation in the Temple, and 'With the Doctors in the Temple' – in other words, all scenes where she is present with Christ, therefore including the Crucifixion and Pietà. Special to the Virgin herself are scenes of The Death of the Virgin, the apocryphal incident of The Funeral of the Virgin (*see* Stanton St John, Oxon), followed by her Assumption, the ever-popular Coronation of the Virgin, and Mary as the Queen of Heaven.

Scenes from the Old and New Testaments outside these cycles are not as common as one might expect. Parables and miracles are common in thirteenth-century glass – for example, at Canterbury and Wilton (the Prodigal Son and the Marriage at Cana, *see illustration on the jacket*), but these are rare from the fourteenth and fifteenth century, although they become more popular in Flemish panels and roundels later. Likewise characters, scenes and stories from the Old Testament can be found outside a typological series, but are not as common as those from the New Testament. However, scenes from The Creation, the story of Adam and Eve and the adventures of Noah, where they do exist, are often magnificent, as at Malvern, Newark, York Minster and St Neot in Cornwall. Prophets with Messianic scrolls can sometimes be seen in association with the Apostles (*see below*), but they appear most often in that most popular Old-to-New Testament theme – the Tree of Jesse; from 1144 to as late as 1924, it has proven an amazingly successful runner.

The Last Judgement and St John's Book of Revelation naturally provided plenty of scope for the medieval mind to exercise its fertile imagination, and in the case of the former, there is plenty of evidence that it certainly did. Remains from Last Judgement scenes – or 'Doom' as it was sometimes called – tend to be found in the tracery lights of large windows, as at Carlisle Cathedral; at Fairford in Gloucestershire, the subject used to take up the whole of the west window, but even those bits that are left (below the transom) are really spectacular (the glass above is nineteenth-century work). One quite unique and fascinating subject related to this is vividly depicted in the window of the 'Last Fifteen Days of the World' at All Saints, North Street, York. Also unique is the 'Dance of Death', in St Andrew's Church, Norwich.

Angels naturally abound in stained glass, particularly in the tracery lights, attending all the momentous occasions and holy personages, often carrying musical instruments (a fabulous set can be seen in St. Mary, Warwickshire, *see illustration on* p.199), or 'instruments of the Passion' (crown of thorns, nails, hammer, cross etc.). The Angelic Hierarchy sometimes appears *en masse*, but more commonly individuals have become separated from the rest of the band by the trials and tribulations of time. Each member was seen to have a duty to perform in the universe: Seraphim, Cherubim and Thrones (the third order of the hierarchy) support and worship the throne of God; Dominations, Virtues and Powers govern the operation of the universe; while Principalities, Archangels and Angels are the messengers by whom God's will is made known to man — hence the popularity of

The Ascension, C15 Norwich School glass; note the holly border and also Christ's footprints (*see* p.30); East Harling, Norfolk.

the archangels Michael and Gabriel, the most frequent intercessors of all. Higher members of the Hierarchy, keeping their ceaseless watch over the affairs of the universe, are often portrayed standing on the wheels of time in the tracery lights and covered with feathers, reminiscent of the way in which people dressed for the parts of angels in the fifteenth-century mystery plays – that is, in feathered tights. At All Saints, North Street, York, they have a further intriguing role to play by leading off different classes of people.

The Four Evangelists are always accompanied by their emblems – the bull (Luke), lion (Mark), man/angel (Matthew), eagle (John) – as described by St John in Revelation and interpreted by The Four Church Fathers – or 'Doctors of the Church' – Sts Jerome, Gregory, Ambrose and Augustine. (When either of the Evangelists John and Matthew appear as one of the Twelve Apostles, they do so barefooted and with different attributes.) The Apostles appear as a group at the Ascension, but identification of them individually can give rise to confusion for, with certain exceptions, their attributes are often changed around or alternative ones are used although Sts John, James the Great, Andrew and Peter are nearly always seen with the same characteristics. The same is true with the 'Creed scrolls' that they sometimes carry: it was believed that each Apostle invented a sentence or phrase of the Apostles' Creed and, generally speaking, the first three are fairly consistently attributed to the same Apostles (in Latin, of course), but the attribution of the remaining nine does seem to be rather unpredictable.

Angels from the angelic hierarchy, allocated to taking care of ordinary mortals, one of whom wears a pair of glasses – an early example of a portrayal of the phenomenon; C15, All Saints, North Street, York.

Extreme Unction from a Seven Sacrament series; Cartmel Fell, Cumbria, C15.

Nevertheless, guidelines of who-holds-what, appearance and who-says-which-phrase could be given as follows:

APOSTLE	ATTRIBUTE/ EMBLEM	PART OF THE CREED (TRANSLATED)
Peter	key(s)	'I believe in God the Father Almighty, Maker of Heaven and earth'
Andrew	saltire cross	'And in Jesus Christ, His only Son, Our Lord'
James the Great	scallop/pilgrim attire	'Who was conceived by the Holy Ghost, born of the Virgin Mary'
John	chalice with dragon	'Suffered under Pontius Pilate, was crucified, dead and buried'
Thomas	spear/T-square	'He descended into Hell; the third day He rose again from the dead'
James the Less	club	'He ascended into Heaven and sitteth on the right hand of God the Father Almighty'
Philip	crozier/ small cross	'From thence He shall come to judge the quick and the dead'
Bartholomew (or Nathanael)	flaying knife	'I believe in the Holy Ghost'
Matthew	money box/purse	'The Holy Catholic Church; the Communion of Saints'
Simon	saw	'The forgiveness of sins'
Jude (Lebbaeus or Thaddaeus)	halberd/lance/boat	'The resurrection of the body'
Matthias	lance	'And the life everlasting'

The Chalice and the Host are also very commonly found in stained glass and, like the Passion instruments, are sometimes portrayed on shields, particularly during the fifteenth century. It was around this time that references to the Church's teachings and litany are seen more often in the iconographic programmes, things such as the *Te Deum*, the Ten Commandments, the *Magnificat*, the *Benedicite*, the 'Seven Works of Mercy' (Feeding the Hungry, Giving Drink to the Thirsty, Clothing the Naked, Housing the Traveller, Visiting Prisoners, Visiting the Sick, and Burying the Dead). Often associated with these 'Works of Mercy' are the Seven Sacraments of the Church (Baptism, Confirmation, Marriage, Communion, Penance, Holy Orders and Last Rites, *see illustration on* p.34). Strangely, the 'Seven Deadly Sins' are only to be seen in glass at Newark, and the 'Four Cardinal Virtues' only at Canterbury (in the twelfth-century north rose window) and the 'Seven Virtues' at Tattershall (Lincs).

The Trinity is generally represented by God the Father holding the crucified son on a small cross beneath his knees, with the dove of the Holy Spirit between the two. Rarely, it is shown as three crowned figures, as at Holy Trinity, Goodramgate in York, in a panel beneath the more usual representation. Christ's earthly relations appear in groups as The Holy Family; complete sets are rare (e.g. at Holy Trinity, Goodramgate, York and Thornhill, W Yorks), but isolated individuals have escaped destruction in places. In its entirety, the Holy Family comprises the three Marys and their relations: the Virgin Mary with Joseph, the Holy Child and Mary's parents, Anne and Joachim; Mary Salome, the mother of the fishermen, James and John, and married to Zebedee; Mary Cleophas, married to Alpheus and mother of Jude, Simeon, James the Less and Joseph Barsabus.

SAINT	ATTRIBUTES/DRESS
Agatha	pincers or shears, sometimes carrying her severed breasts on a plate
Agnes	palm, lamb, sword
Alphege	archbishop's attire, axe
Ambrose	beehive, book(s)
Anne	usually teaching the Virgin Mary to read or with the Holy Family
Anthony	abbot with T-cross, staff, bell, pig (the latter possibly representing the pigs that roamed free at his shrine in France)
Apollonia	pincers and tooth
Augustine of Hippo	book, bishop dressed as 'Church Doctor'
Barbara	tower or castle (in which she was locked to keep away unwanted men); her father killed her for refusing to worship an idol, for which he was struck by lightning, hence her association with artillery and sudden death
Blaise	comb for carding wool
Catherine of Alexandria	wheel, sword; occasionally she is shown with the emperor Maxentius underfoot; sometimes portrayed with St Margaret
Cecilia	crown of roses, musical instrument (organ or bell)
Christopher	carrying the Christ Child across a river; sometimes with a flowering staff
Clement	in papal regalia, and with the anchor with which he was thrown into the sea (according to legend)
Cuthbert	holds Oswald's head that was placed in his coffin during the transfer of relics from Lindisfarne to escape the Vikings
Denis	carries his severed head; dressed as a bishop
Dorothy	crown of roses, basket of flowers
Dunstan	wears the habit of a Benedictine monk – said to have tweaked the devil by the nose!
Edmund	king, carries the arrows of his martyrdom
Edward the Confessor	king, sceptre, sometimes a ring
Elisabeth	with the Virgin at the Annunciation, or in salutation with the angel Gabriel; when alone she carries the infant John the Baptist (who, in turn, carries a lamb and a flag)
Etheldreda	nun's habit; sometimes building a church
Francis	with stigmata
Frideswide	abbess holding the Gospels (common in Oxon)
Gabriel	archangel at Annunciation with lily and spear of divine authority
George	in armour, often on horse and slaying the dragon
Giles (Egidus)	with a hind sometimes pierced with arrows
Gregory	papal regalia, dove hovering, with other 'Doctors of the Church'

The cult of the saints is one of the more colourful aspects of medieval life, demonstrating the fertile imagination of contemporaries ever ready to invent new things when required – particularly new holy days. In fact, the business of introducing more saints, usually of a local variety, into the calendar grew to such an extent that, in 1953, the Council of Trent (a series of meetings attended by the hierarchy of the Catholic Church) felt it necessary to ascertain the authenticity of many of them, and their numbers were severely reduced, but not before a Protestant backlash had taken its toll. Today we are lucky if we find only the heads of saints missing in churches and cathedrals throughout the land.

The whole business of analysing the iconography of the saints is an area where

SYMBOLS AND LEGENDS

SAINT	ATTRIBUTES/DRESS
Helen	holding the true Cross; wears a crown
Hugh (of Lincoln)	Carthusian monk's habit; sometimes with a pet swan
Jerome	cardinal's hat, sometimes with lion
Joachim	basket and two doves for the presentation, or with Anne
John the Baptist	Lamb (*Agnus dei*) on a shield or a lamb and a flag with animal (sometimes a camel) skin (*see* Mark 1:6)
Laurence	gridiron (actually being roasted at York Minster!)
Leonard	chain or manacle, dressed as deacon, often with St Stephen
Lucy	sword or dagger through neck
Luke	usually as Evangelist with eagle, but sometimes as an artist painting the Virgin Mary
Margaret of Antioch	dragon or cross; she burst out of the dragon's belly – hence her association with childbirth!
Mary Magdalene	casket of perfume (with which she washed Christ's feet)
Michael	killing dragon or weighing souls; wings
Nicholas	three children in a tub*
Paul	usually bald and with a sword
Roche	pointing to the plague spot on his leg; sometimes with a dog
Sidwell	scythe
Stephen	stones (usually three), sometimes near his head; often with St Leonard
Thomas à Becket	archbishop, Benedictine, sometimes with his head wounded
Ursula	with other maidens either in a boat or in a sheet – usually only a few of them, although the legend says she saved the honour of no less than 11,000 of them!
Veronica	veil with image of the face of Christ
William of York	archbishop
Zita (or Sitha)	keys, book and/or rosary. She came from Lucca in Tuscany, died a pauper after feeding and clothing the needy from her employer's stock – legend has it that bread turned into flowers when she was caught in the act. This saint suddenly became very popular in England after *c.* 1400.

*This originates from a medieval confusion of imagery rising from four stories becoming fused into one. In one version St Nicholas restored to life three children who had been chopped up and pickled in a tub, but the *three* 'children' are thought to have derived from the *three* money bags that the saint, in another legend, threw on to the beds of some girls to give them dowries and save them from prostitution. The tub comes from his association with baptism, water and the sea and his alleged saving of sailors from a wreck. He is also supposed to have saved *three* men unjustly convicted.

even angels fear to tread, fraught as it is with the ease of misidentification. Apart from the ever-popular twelve Apostles, other saints were seen to look after various aspects of the welfare of mortals still on earth by their intercession, and included Margaret (childbirth), Christopher (travel), Apollonia (toothache), Lucy (the eyes), Andrew (gout and stiff necks), Roche (plague). Patron saints of professions were naturally essential — for instance, Barbara (builders), Blaise (the wool business), Sitha – or – Zita – (housekeepers), Nicholas (sailors), Cecilia (musicians) – as were Catherine (learning) and Leonard (prisoners). Above is a list of those saints most frequently encountered and the attributes or dress by which they can be identified (*see* p.35 for attributes, etc. of the Apostles).

St Margaret about to be boiled in oil – a panel depicting part of the saint's legend, C15, at Combs, Suffolk.

Occasionally the lives of saints were illustrated in a series of panels, some lavishly so, but as is often the case, more often only a few fragmentary panels from such series remain. Some of these were embellished with a kind of poetic licence that added details and events that went well beyond those in the 'Golden Legend' – the main source for such stories – to the point of borrowing incidents from the lives of other saints in order to fill out the space available, or perhaps because the story could do with more incident! A classic example is that of the St George window at St Neot church in Cornwall (*qv*), where events from the life of the obscure St Mercurious have found their way into the account of St George. The legends of various saints or their remains can best be seen at the following places:

SAINT	LOCATION
Andrew	Greystoke (Cumbria); Canterbury Cathedral (Kent)
Anthony	Gresford (Clwydd)
Benedict	Twycross (Leics); Raby Castle (Durham)
Bernard	St Mary's, Shrewsbury (Salop); Marston Bigot (Somerset) (*see illustration on* p.39)
Catherine	Clavering (Essex)
Cuthbert	York Minster
Edward the Confessor	Ludlow (Salop); York Minster
George	St Neot (Cornwall); North Tuddenham (Norfolk)
Helen	Morley (Derbys); Ashton-under-Lyne (Greater Manchester)
John	Madley (Hereford); Burrell Museum, Glasgow; Wells Cathedral (Somerset)
John the Baptist	Gresford (Clwydd); Burrell Museum, Glasgow
Laurence	Ludlow (Salop)
Margaret	Combs (Suffolk) (*see illustration on* p.38)
Martin	Beverley Minster (Humberside); St Martin's, York
Neot	St Neot (Cornwall)
Nicholas	Hillesden (Bucks); Canterbury Cathedral; Lincoln Cathedral
Paul	North Moreton (Oxon)
Peter	York Minster; North Moreton (Oxon)
Robert of Knaresborough	Morley (Derbys)
Stephen	York Minster
Thomas à Becket	Canterbury Cathedral (*see illustration* on p.5)
William of York	York Minster

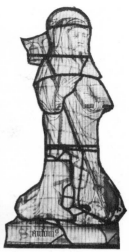

St Catherine, C14, Ely
Stained Glass Museum.

St George, late C15, St
Winnow, Cornwall.

St Christopher, late C15, St
Winnow, Cornwall.

St Anthony, C15, Cartmel
Fell, Cumbria.

St Bernard being dined, c.1500, Marston Bigot, Somerset.

DOMESTIC AND SECULAR STAINED GLASS

Excluding heraldic glass, it would probably be true to say that over 90 per cent of the ancient stained glass that remains today is of religious subjects. It is possible, however, that during the Middle Ages stained glass was at least as common in secular buildings and houses as in churches and cathedrals. Very little of the secular and domestic glass survives *in situ*, notable examples being the nine kings in fifteenth-century glass on the north side of St Mary's Hall in Coventry and the glazing of a similar age in the rectory of Buckland in Gloucestershire, where there are little diamond-shaped pieces of glass called 'quarries' painted with birds and flowers. More of these charming bird quarries can be seen in the Zouche Chapel at York Minster (*see illustration on* p.213) and in the churches at Yarnton (Oxon), and Clothall (Herts) where numerous recognisable species from the English countryside can be seen in the east window (*see illustration on* p.120). The birds in the bird quarries at Yarnton are depicted with little scrolls issuing from their beaks containing remarks such as 'who blayth this ale' and 'ye shall praye for the fox', suggesting that they were originally installed in an inn or a dining room at a college or house.

Trade signs or 'merchant marks' can occasionally be seen in quarries in churches, usually in chapels associated with guilds or benefactors who did not have coats-of-arms: they generally show tools connected with the guild or individual's trade or symbols that, like mason's marks, may have their origins in ancient runes. A number of examples can be seen at Cirencester Church (Glos), and that of the Mercers' Company at Stonefield (Oxon) dating from the sixteenth century. So, too, we find from time to time 'lover's knots' – that is, the initials of the two partners interwoven within a piece of knotted rope. More common are small rebuses, a kind of pictorial pun on a person's name – e.g. the letter K and a bell for the name 'Cable', as seen in glass at Frome in Somerset.

Apart from quarries and the occasional figure panel, a clearly popular domestic form was the roundel painted on to a piece of clear glass and coloured solely with yellow stain. Many of the subjects must have been religious, but one favourite series was that of the 'Labours of the Months' in which, as the title suggests, each month was depicted by some labour or activity connected with that time of the year. In fact, the origin of this series is ecclesiastical: in the thirteenth century, they formed part of what the French medieval scholar Émile Male described as the 'Mirror of Instruction' in which labour was seen to be an essential part of the act of redemption. At Lausanne Cathedral, they appear in stained glass in connection with the signs of the zodiac, where the Labours represent the passing of time on the earth and the zodiac time in the heavens. The twelve scenes were not always represented in exactly the same way throughout the medieval world, although many were.

Fine examples of the Labours from the fifteenth century can be seen at a number of churches and houses in England, although nowhere is there a complete set of all twelve; Norbury Hall (Derbys) and Brandiston Hall both have six. (*See* p.252 for the locations of others.)

A typical series together with variants could be described as shown opposite.

The Labours of the Months

January   Toasting in the New Year, sometimes the two-faced god Janus (or a feast).

February   Warming the hands in front of the fire (almost universal).

March   Pruning vines or fruit trees or sowing seeds.

April   Man holding a small plant (for planting) or branch for scaring away birds.

May   Hunting, cutting grass, hawking or tending flowers.

June   Cutting grass. (Bathing in the courtyard at Brandiston Hall, Norfolk!)

July   Making hay, weeding or building.

August   Reaping the harvest.

September   Grape harvest, fruit picking, threshing the harvest, hunting.

October   Collecting acorns for pigs, sowing, pruning, treading grapes (*see illustration on* p.19).

November   Killing pigs. (Sheltering from the rain at Brandiston Hall.)

December   Wood chopping, feasting, pig killing.

Much more domestic and secular glass, dating from the fifteenth to eighteenth centuries, survives from the Continent, imported into Britain mainly during the first half of the nineteenth century, some of which is now in the Burrell and Victoria & Albert museums. At both of these places can be seen not only examples of the Labours of the Months but hunting, ploughing and other rustic scenes, pageants, roof-tilers, shepherds and dyers at work, windmills, ships and people from all walks of life. Many of these are to be found in the form of roundels with small painted scenes on a central single piece of glass, and the majority came from the Low Countries – in fact, there are now more of them in this country than in the Netherlands! Dr William Cole has done much research into their origins, both in terms of location and the sources of the designs painted on to them, and he has found that, in many cases, they are copies of engravings from the late fifteenth and early sixteenth centuries. He cites, for example, Jacob Cornelius' painting of the Passion in 1514, which can be seen in roundels at Bradford-on-Avon (Wilts), St Andrew's, Waterford (Herts), Nowton (Suffolk) and St James in Norwich, the best of which have a 'delicacy of painting' and show many interesting details of domestic and rural life in the late Middle Ages. At Prittlewell Church (Essex), some of the original designs were by Dürer. Subjects from the Classical world and antiquity are common in those roundels that clearly have their origins in colleges, private houses and halls belonging to the guilds. Many of these are neatly executed in coloured enamel paint.

HISTORY OF STAINED GLASS

STAINED GLASS BEFORE
THE THIRTEENTH CENTURY

The knowledge of how to make and colour glass goes back at least 3000 years to the Egyptians. As is often the case with important discoveries, this one probably first occurred through the fortuitous accident of impurities finding their way into a melt of 'ordinary' glass. It is not clear exactly which colours were discovered when, but by the fifth century AD the Romans knew that colloidal gold dispersed in molten glass produced a result that is ruby-coloured when light shines through it. Pieces of glass recovered from the Venerable Bede's monastery at Jarrow show that, by the seventh century, most colours had been discovered, including the all-important procedure of flashing (*see* p.17).

Although fragments of Anglo Saxon age can be seen at Winchester museum, there is nothing among British remains before the mid-twelfth century to suggest the previous existence of painting on to the surface of glass to give a pictorial coloured window. We do know that the church of St Martin at Tours had coloured glass in the seventh century, and that at St Rémi in Reims, leaded coloured windows were installed in the tenth century, but nothing of these survives. However, in France there is the famous head of Christ from Wissembourg (now at Strasbourg Museum) that dates from the ninth or tenth century, and the magnificent five prophets in Augsburg cathedral in Germany from the late eleventh. In 1134, there was a sufficient quantity of coloured windows in existence for the Cistercians to believe it necessary to issue an edict that allowed only the use of white glass; soon after, they permitted *grisaille* – simple geometric-patterned glass with natural motifs and minimal use of colour. France has some pieces still extant that either pre-date or are contemporary with St Denis (1144), for example, at Le Mans (the exquisite Ascension window), Angers and Vendôme (a beautiful Virgin and Child), and it is from about this time that the first surviving piece of true stained glass made in England dates — the king from the Tree of Jesse at York Minster, similar in most respect to the Trees of St Denis and Chartres of *c*.1150 (*see illustration opposite*).

It should be pointed out, however, that the terms 'made in England' or 'English glass' do not mean precisely what they might suggest: the actual sources of coloured glass throughout the Middle Ages were either Normandy and Burgundy in France or the Lorraine and Hesse districts on the Rhine; the glass reached England via the East Anglian ports, and the glaziers initially were almost certainly all French. In fact, at this early date it is impossible to talk of a national or even

A king from the Tree of Jesse at York Minster, possibly dating from c.1150.

regional style; England and France became inexorably interwoven following the Norman Conquest, and it is not until the late thirteenth and early fourteenth centuries that genuine English-inspired stained glass windows can be said to have appeared, and even then the raw material of coloured glass was still being imported — as was nearly all of it until the seventeenth century.

From the building of Archbishop Rogers' choir at York Minster in 1170-84 and the rebuilding of Canterbury Cathedral (completed by 1184), we have inherited some fine pieces of Romanesque stained glass — in the nave clerestory at the former and in the south transept and west windows at the latter. There is also the remarkable little late twelfth-century winged figure of St Michael at Dalbury (Derbys), which displays early Romanesque characteristics (inherited from the Byzantine style) of large staring eyes and hands held up with palms outwards – very similar, in fact, to the pose of the prophets at Augsburg of a century earlier. At Canterbury, the earliest glass is the north rose window of 1178 with the Four Cardinal Virtues, the Four Major prophets, Moses and the Synagogue at the

43

centre; already we can see a wide palate of colours in use, with a particular emphasis on purple, in addition to the more common red and blue. So too can we see the gentle curve in the long figures at the centre and those characteristically strong Romanesque facial expressions that the stained glass authority Le Couteur elliptically described as being 'the reverse of beautiful' – I personally find them rather endearing!

THE THIRTEENTH CENTURY

By the early thirteenth century, English and French glaziers at places such as York, Lincoln, Canterbury and Chartres were producing windows in a similar style. At Canterbury, for example, the Miracle Windows in the Trinity Chapel of *c.* 1220 (*see illustration on* p.5) are highly reminiscent of Chartres glass in most respects:

— rich colours with sparing use of white glass.

— small pieces of differing colours leaded together within a strong overall geometric pattern, the main division of which are held by an iron armature that follows the main pattern.

— the frequent use of multiple colours in the narrow borders surrounding the scenes, sometimes in conjunction with tiny white circular beading.

— each scene concisely and economically designed to enable a quick 'reading' of what was happening, often in a comic-strip-type sequence (although in the rose windows of this age – the glass of which has been lost in England except for that at Lincoln Cathedral – the scene designs carry on over the stone tracery).

— a simple statement printed in Lombardy-style script on a scroll, either describing events or carrying a statement or a name.

— the contrast between the attempts at realism in figure drawing and the stylised representation of other details such as plants, towns and other landscape features.

In figure design, the poses tend to be rather theatrical, yet are attempts at realistic stances, and the different parts of each figure are differentiated where necessary by colour and with drapery folds, faces, hands and feet all painstakingly painted to impart realism though, strangely, they are often out of proportion. Backgrounds to the figures are usually blue but occasionally red, with the lead lines made as thin as possible. The geometrically defined spaces between scenes are either filled with natural motifs or with mosaic-type patterns.

During this century we also see the extended use of *grisaille*, partly in place of the more expensive coloured glass and partly because Cistercian influence was strongly felt. The huge Five Sisters window at York Minster is the perfect example of *grisaille* from this time. Originally, many *grisaille* windows in Cistercian establishments were arranged in groups of three to emphasise the Trinity, although few examples of this survive intact. Moreover, the repeating flower/leaf patterns painted on to the greenish-white glass were quite permissible in places within the order's sphere of influence – particularly as St Bernard saw in the flower an important symbol of the Resurrection. Towards the end of the century, a style emerged where two layers of *grisaille* enclosed coloured figure panels — a

44

The prophet Hosea in fine C14 glass at Madley, Herefordshire.

fine example of which can be seen at Merton College, Oxford, that dates from the late 1290s. Around 1270, heraldry in stained glass first appeared, for instance, at Chetwode (Bucks) and Salisbury Cathedral.

By 1300, glass painting centres had been established at Oxford, Westminster, Chester, Bath, Chichester, King's Lynn, Lewes (E Sussex) and Southampton, yet apart from the panels at the cathedrals at Canterbury, York and Lincoln, other remains of thirteenth-century glass are rather few and far between; the windows at Madley (Herefs), Westminster Abbey, Salisbury Cathedral and Beverley Minster deserve special mention, as do the Trees of Jesse of this time – or what remains of them – at Nackington (Kent), Kidlington (Oxon) and Westwell (Kent).

THE FOURTEENTH CENTURY

Part of the loss of thirteenth-century glass in England was due to the development of the Decorated style in architecture that began around 1280. Unlike today, it seems that there was little respect for stained glass belonging to a former age and no hesitation in removing a window. Although it is difficult to find clear evidence of this, there were certainly instances where contemporary wall paintings were simply painted over with a new composition, and where a Decorated window was created by knocking an opening right in the middle of a painting as at Little Kimble (Bucks) or Risby (Suffolk). The emergent Decorated windows favoured compositions that broke out of the geometric confines of square, circular or interstitial shapes, a release perhaps prompted in part by the necessity of glazing windows into new curved shapes – the *mouchettes,* etc. – defined by the tracery lights that are such a feature of this period. Nevertheless, figures were still confined within canopies and their sideshafts and, at a later date, with plinths below. Borders, although narrower than in the thirteenth century, remained an integral part of these windows, framing the canopy and sideshafts, and became one of the glories of this era of beautiful English stained glass.

Canopies became a kind of art form in themselves as the century progressed, copying contemporary architectural forms of towers and pinnacles, yet drawn without perspective until the latter part of the century. Sometimes they acquired exotic if not disproportionate heights – for instance, at Gloucester Cathedral and particularly at Tewkesbury Abbey where, complete with flying buttresses, they soar above the figures. Those at the west end of the nave aisles at York Minster are magnificent structures with three tiers that rise like a kind of wedding cake above the figures below.

Drawing was generally an improvement on that of the previous period, figures being larger and more natural, although still some way from the large, realistic, well-portrayed examples of the next century. Indeed, occasional examples are positively weird, as in the case of William of Ufford at Wimpole (Cambs), the Virgin at Fladbury (Worcs) or, for example, some of the strange squinting faces that peer down from a sea of fragments in the windows of the Lady Chapel at Wells Cathedral. Faces were sometimes painted on pale-coloured glass rather than on clear glass as in the previous century, while figures frequently display an endearing gentle S-shaped curve that often imparts a suggestion of motion to the figure; in a strange way, they are reminiscent of some of the early Romanesque stained glass figures drawn with a single gradual curve, as at Rivenhall (Essex) or Le Mans in France.

Colour in fourteenth-century glass was certainly as rich as in that of the thirteenth. Moreover, one often finds schemes that use combinations such as green and yellow, or red and green, but there is a marked fall off in the preponderance of the blue so characteristic of the previous century. During the second half of the fourteenth century, new colours were introduced into the glaziers' stocks of pot-metal glass – a deeper green, more subtle browns, *murrey* (a purple-red) and violet.

However, the most revolutionary discovery at this time was the process of 'yellow staining' (or 'silver staining' as it is sometimes called) a piece of glass – either clear glass to give yellow or a blue piece to give green (*see* p.18). It was probably discovered in the first decade of the century, the earliest example in England being the Peter de Dene window in the north aisle at York Minster that

Opposite: God the Creator with compasses and the celestial sphere of the Universe, C15, Great Malvern, Worcestershire.

dates from *c.* 1310. The technique made possible a number of new effects, such as colouring selected parts of clear glass yellow/gold; for example, the English royal coat-of-arms with its gold lions on a red background ('gules, three lions passant guardant in pale or') could be portrayed by abrading away the flashed-on red and staining the resulting clear glass yellow/gold. (Because flashed blue glass was not generally available until much later, the French coat-of-arms with its gold fleur-de-lis on blue could not be made in this way.) Strangely, this practice of abrading and staining was only slowly adopted, becoming more common during the following century.

Donor figures and heraldry in stained glass became increasingly important at this time. The giving of a window to a church was seen as a way of bettering the donor's chances in the afterlife – a feeling that probably grew in the wake of the Black Death, which so devastated Europe in this century. The donors themselves appear in the windows, often complete with their families, kneeling at the bottom of windows with requests that others should pray for them written on to scrolls incorporated into the design. Heraldry was an additional means of identifying them and is thus a great help in dating such windows.

Fourteenth-century glass can be seen all over the country — there are particularly good examples at Wells Cathedral, York Minster, Tewkesbury, Gloucester Cathedral and Stanford on Avon (Northants). With the Black Death of 1348-50 (and several other epidemics later in the century), when over a third of the population died and the very fabric of life was seriously disrupted, all the crafts naturally took a severe knock and stained glass was no exception. The design and execution of windows were also affected by an evolution in the style of architecture towards the Perpendicular, which could be said to have been born in *c.* 1350, about the time St Stephen's Chapel at Westminster was built (since destroyed) – in other words, just before the great east window of Gloucester Cathedral was glazed in what we now call the Perpendicular style.

The way towards glazing this kind of huge window was, in fact, paved by Master Robert, under whose direction the enormous west window of York Minster was executed in 1337. Twenty years later saw the Gloucester window, a great web of glass and stone that is a masterpiece of design, in which the fourteen main openings carry five rows of figures all set beneath Decorated-style architectural canopies. With its increased use of clear glass and the subsequent reduction of colour, it is a forerunner of most Perpendicular windows of the next 150 years or so. The change can also be seen taking place at Oxford, for example, where the design of the north windows of the Latin Chapel at Christ Church Cathedral of *c.* 1365, with their fine figures in rich green and yellow glass, is decidedly early fourteenth century in style, yet Thomas Glazier's work at nearby New College – only some twenty years later – shows the increased use of clear glass, particularly in connection with the larger and more fantastic canopies, as well as a formalism that tends to lack spontaneity. At Winchester College, however, something of the earlier fourteenth-century richness can be seen in what remains of Thomas's fine, dignified figures of 1393; they also look forward to that other important feature of the fifteenth century, namely more realistic figures and faces, often with fine detail and characterisation in the painting.

THE FIFTEENTH CENTURY

With the increasing wealth and prosperity of fifteenth-century England, it was possibly concern about their lot in the non-commercial afterlife that prompted many of the newly rich to perform some act that was both beneficial to the public, showed gratitude to God for His favour – and displayed what a worthy character the benefactor was. Church building and refurbishing was therefore pursued with a new fervour, and since the prevailing style dictated larger windows, the glaziers were busier than ever. Coloured glass was expensive, even for donors rich from the wool trade, yet each naturally wished to make his contribution as significant as possible. The result was many windows that are still colourful but generally larger and incorporating a higher proportion of clear glass with more painting and yellow stain. The glass was also thinner and more regular in quality than before, so that large clear panes could be cut and fitted between the lead lines. Even John Thornton's great east window at York Minster of 1405-8, which at first sight seems full of colour, uses more clear glass than is immediately obvious to the eye in order to help convey all the elaborate details of its complex subject matter.

At this time, schools of glass painters and glaziers emerged at Norwich and York, which attained new heights in the art with some exquisite figure drawing, as if to compensate for the diminished colour content. Figures were still generally placed under canopies (often with little battlements in the background that are occasionally inhabited by tiny figures), but they appear more realistic as an awareness of perspective becomes more evident in the compositions. Invariably, figures were given a plinth to stand on while, behind them, the naturalistic foliage backgrounds of the fourteenth century were replaced by c. 1380 with a kind of seaweed design painted on to the coloured glass. In some cases, the figures have grown so much that they slightly project from the boxes generated by canopies above, side-shafts, and plinths below – and some even step outside them. Later in the fifteenth century, they are often to be found having broken completely free of canopies and are set against a field of painted quarries, a style that was particularly popular in Somerset and the West Country.

At the Beauchamp Chapel at St Mary's, Warwick – where no expense was spared in procuring the best possible glass – the king's glazier, John Prudde, exploited the exotic technique of creating the effect of jewels in the hems of the garments of the distinguished figures, achieved by drilling holes into a single piece of glass and leading in a small piece of coloured glass. (Compare this with the glass at St Michael Spurriergate, York, where the 'jewels' are stuck on to the surface of the pane rather than leaded in – and, in some cases, have fallen off.) The figure and garment painting at Warwick is, moreover, of the highest standard from the technical point of view, and it results in windows of the most sumptuous quality.

With the close of the fifteenth century, there is something of a reduction in the quality of much stained glass work, evident for example in the *Magnificat* window of Malvern Priory (Worcs) where there seems to be some confusion in presentation as well as rather inferior drawing. In a different sense, there is a kind of decline even in the previously mentioned Beauchamp Chapel windows, which for all their technical splendour house figures that are somewhat lifeless. However, new life was coming into the craft through immigration into the country of German and Flemish glaziers who set up shop, notably, at Southwark, a glass centre since the late thirteenth century. This move was possibly precipitated by the enforced exile in Bruges in 1470-1 of the king, Edward IV, who must have become aware of the changes that the Renaissance, sweeping up from the Mediterranean, was making in art; Henry VII reinforced the invitation in 1485 to glaze chapels at Kings College, Cambridge and, possibly, at Westminster Abbey. Dutch and Flemish art was undergoing a revolution and Edward's return to England was to give these shores an initial taste of it.

THE EARLY SIXTEENTH CENTURY

One of the last products of Edward IV's excursion into the arts was the building of the St George's Chapel at Windsor. Much of the original glazing has, alas, since disappeared, but in the west window, many of the original saints, set very much in the fifteenth-century style, are lined up in the Perpendicular tracery. However, when, some thirty or so years later, King's College Chapel at Cambridge was glazed in the latest style, the requirements of the age resulted in windows that belong to a different artistic era.

The programme for the iconography at King's College Chapel was drawn up by the Bishop of Winchester for an ambitious series of windows that related the framework of events that comprised the Christian faith from the Annunciation to Last Judgement, including all the relevant Old Testament antetypes (i.e. events that seemed to foreshadow those of the New). The execution of this vast project was entrusted to the recently settled Flemish glaziers at Southwark, and the designs were made by Vellert of Amsterdam. To convert them to reality, the leading Southwark glazier, Barnard Flower, and his assistants adopted what was at the time an entirely new approach to stained glass: each scene was spread across individual window lights and the intervening stone mullions as if painted on to one vast canvas across the whole window. The result was to encourage painting on glass. Gradually the design of windows had become less a matter of using lead lines and individually coloured pieces that followed the main features of the subject, and more one of using large pieces of glass on to which a great deal of painting and staining was placed — this can be seen in the windows at King's College Chapel, particularly in the small rectangular panes that comprise much of the background areas. It has to be admitted, however, that the quality of painting here is of the highest order. Great attention has been paid to the realistic portrayals of figures and details, with precise shading to emphasise every facet of characterisation. Gone are the old canopies of the Gothic as the scenes stretch to the limits of the windows, while in the background are the Classical arches, plinths and other architectural features of Rome, painted and coloured with yellow stain across the panes, and distant scenic views beyond.

Other fine examples of Flemish-inspired Tudor glass can be seen at Hengrave

Opposite: God creating the concentric-layered Universe (note the signs of the zodiac), early C16; Hengrave Hall, Suffolk.

Hall (Suffolk), Hillesden (Bucks), Thornhill (W Yorks), the Chapel of The Vyne (Sherborne St John, Hants), Withcote Hall (Leics) and, above all, at Fairford Church (Glos), where there is a virtually unique late medieval church with its original glazing more or less intact. Most of the other examples in Britain from this time originated on the Continent: at St George's Church, Hanover Square in London is a fine Tree of Jesse from Rouen; at St Margaret's, Westminster, there is a rather altered Flemish Crucifixion and an even finer example is at Hingham in Norfolk. In both of these Crucifixion windows, the similarity to the great east window at King's College Chapel is unmistakable.

There was a considerable amount of glazing done in the early sixteenth century that remained relatively unaffected by the Flemish innovations in stained glass design. In North Wales are some splendid examples from the first half of the century, notably in Clwyd at Dyserth, Llanrhaeadr and Gresford where the Tree of Jesse was a favourite theme (*see illustration on* p.16). Down in Cornwall at St Neot and St Winnow, there are also some windows of about this date expounding in some detail on the lives of St George and St Neot, together with the Creation at the former and some charming figures at the latter. New techniques for colouring glass were being developed and applied, notably that of painting enamels on to the glass; flashed blue glass also becomes more common at about this time. Both of these made certain jobs in the craft more easy, particularly the ability to yellow stain abraded areas of flashed blue glass in order to obtain new combinations of colours — a useful technique in depicting the complex quartering involved in some heraldic representations of the time.

In 1536, however, the medieval area was drawing to a close. The Reformation came in the wake of the Renaissance, and the craft was to receive a blow from which it was to take over two centuries to recover.

THE SIXTEENTH
TO THE EIGHTEENTH CENTURIES

The dissolution of the monasteries in 1536-9 signalled times of great trouble for stained glass. As the great abbeys were pulled down, so too went much of their glass. A few pieces were saved and transferred – such as the St Helen series of windows at Morley (Derbys) – but survivors were the exception rather than the rule, regardless of the edicts put forth during Edward VI's reign forbidding such destruction. At this time (1547-53), virtually all the glass at Durham Cathedral was destroyed by its then prelate, Hone of Winchester. After a while, the destruction abated, but it was not until the early seventeenth century that stained glass windows were once again installed, at the instigation of Archbishop Laud. In the meantime, the skills had very largely disappeared – and so too had many of the Continental manufacturers of coloured glass, many of whom where Huguenots who had been forced to flee from France during the anti-Protestant campaign there. Only at Lorraine was glass still made, but in 1633, all that was terminated

Opposite: Sts John the Evangelist and Baptist astride a tree with coats-of-arms of the St John St John Tregoze Family; *c.*1630, van Linge brothers, Lydiard Tregoze, Wilts.

when the armies of Louis XIII began a twenty-six year occupation and the area was devastated. As a result, enamelling and staining were the only ways of colouring windows – with occasional bits of pot-metal glass added to compositions whenever they became available, usually from a second-hand source.

At some time during the second decade of the seventeenth century, the two brothers Abraham and Bernard van Linge were invited from Emden in the Netherlands to England, where both executed a number of windows almost entirely in enamel paints. The best examples of their work are perhaps those at the Oxford colleges of Balliol, Christ Church, Wadham and Lincoln, Peterhouse College at Cambridge, and the strange, almost encyclopaedic windows at Gorhambury (Herts) and Lydiard Tregoze (Wilts) (*see illustration on* p.52). Just prior to the arrival of the van Linge brothers were the achievements of one Robert Rudland who painted a series of windows for Wadham College, the same year (1622) that the Chapel in the Trinity College in Greenwich received its windows, and in the early 1620s, Baptista Sutton executed the windows now in Little Easton church (Essex), as well as those at the Trinity Chapel of the Abbot's Hospital, Guildford (Surrey), with the story of Jacob and Esau. One of the most unusual survivors from this time is the glass at Abbey Dore (Hereford) dating from 1634, which at the time must have been seen as incredibly reactionary with its hybrid fifteenth-century style incorporating pinnacles above canopies, out-of-perspective checked floor patterns and Renaissance arches — unless the exercise was a conscious attempt to create windows in some kind of 'old style'.

The Puritan excesses that took their toll during the 1640s followed a campaign of authorised iconoclasm instigated by the Parliamentarians. Norwich Cathedral was devastated in 1643, and during the next two years, a 'visitor' named William Dowsing wrought his terrible destruction across Suffolk. We know quite a lot about him since (conveniently for historians) he kept a diary of his dirty deeds (*see* p.185), but doubtless there were others like him who did not. Those windows that were not completely destroyed often had the heads of the saints removed or the Crucifixion scenes smashed – mutilations that seemed to satisfy the Parliamentarian 'visitors'. On occasion, the glass was removed and hidden until more favourable times, as was the case at East Harling (Norfolk); at the Chapel of The Vyne in Hampshire, the glass was allegedly hidden in the lake. After a prolonged siege, the city of York struck a bargain with the Parliamentarians that preserved the glass and other religious objects in the churches and the Minster in exchange for the surrender of the city.

After the Restoration in 1660, we hear of Henry Gyles, who was painting heraldic windows in enamels, often elaborate achievements of arms complete with supporters and crowned with angels. He sometimes threw in a free stained glass sundial with a commission, as at University College, Oxford, and Nun Appleton Hall (N Yorks). Also worth mentioning are the splendid pair of heraldic coats-of-arms at Northill (Beds) completed by the heraldic painter John Oliver in 1664 (*see illustration on* p.27).

One of Gyles's pupils, William Price (the Elder), painted the east window at Merton College, Oxford, in 1701-2, which depicts six scenes from the life of Christ (it can now be seen at the stained glass museum at Ely Cathedral); it is an interesting early example of a religious scene in 'stained' glass after the rescinding of the Puritan restrictions. His brother, Joshua, painted fourteen windows in enamels for Lord Chandos, now at Great Witley Church (Worcs), that are typical of their time. The west window of Westminster Abbey dates from 1735 and is by William Price the Younger, who also did the north rose window there. Both of these augment enamel-coloured glass with occasional pieces of a rather starkly coloured, thin pot-metal glass with which various glaziers had been experimenting in the absence of anything better. It was William Peckitt of York, however, who did most of the stained and painted glass work that survives from the second half of the eighteenth century – examples of his can be seen at York Minster, Oriel College, Oxford, and Audley End (Essex). Above all is his extraordinary work in the library at Trinity College, Cambridge, where the Isaac Newton window looks down on readers to remind them of their illustrious former college member and of the spirit of *alma mater*. One exceptional monstrosity from this time is Thomas Jervais' attempt, at New College, Oxford, to transcribe Sir Joshua Reynold's designs of the Virtues into – or, more correctly, *on to* – glass, and the results, although disastrous, remain there to this day.

During the eighteenth century, and particularly towards the end, certain individuals gradually became curious about medieval times and what a later age had described as its 'Gothic' architecture. Sir William Jerningham and Sir Horace Walpole both collected old stained and painted glass which they installed at their homes at Costessy (Norfolk) and the 'Gothick' Strawberry Hill (Twickenham, Middx), but at the same time, James Wyatt and other contemporaries were betraying their feelings about Gothic art by throwing away cartloads of medieval stained glass from Salisbury Cathedral in the name of 'improvement'.

THE NINETEENTH CENTURY

Of windows executed in the late eighteenth and early nineteenth centuries, little remains except for a few isolated examples. Countless others were removed in order to make room for the tens of thousands of later Victorian windows that were to flood into the churches – a deluge that ranges from badly designed and feebly drawn compositions with standardized, sentimental characteristics, often badly fired and executed, to mediocre, yet competent factory-line products, through to the occasional magnificent work.

The course of the development of stained glass during the century is now generally fairly well understood, although much detail remains to be discovered. Martin Harrison's magnificent book, *Victorian Stained Glass,* published in 1980, is a much welcomed and overdue study on the subject. In it, he points out that the main problem has been that the records of many windows made by the firms involved in their production no longer exist – if indeed they ever existed at all. Identification and dating of a particular glazier's work is not always easy – only a few of the firms signed their works and they invariably omitted the designer's name. Some are easily recognised, but the identification of others comes only after much experience of looking at Victorian windows. A great deal of the groundwork of sifting documents, visiting churches and recording findings still remains to be done, but a start has been made by people such as Birkin Haward in East Anglia, Martin Harrison, as well as members of the Victorian Project at Exeter University and of the National Association of Decorative and Fine Arts Societies.

With certain individual exceptions, pictorial painting on glass in the eighteenth-century tradition was very much the order of the day until well into the 1840s. Apart from the ever-popular reproduction of Reynolds' Virtues at New College, Oxford, the subjects of these kinds of windows were often copies or translations-with-artistic-licence of paintings by such popular masters as Raphael or Holbein – some of the early works of the firm Betton & Evans of Shrewsbury are worthy of note and can be seen in a number of churches in Salop and North Wales. In the 1840s, there was a certain popularity for the Nazarene group of German painters, founded by Johann Friedrich Overbeck in 1809, who imitated such masters as Dürer, Raphael and Perugino and became known through the prints of their work that appeared in Britain at this time. However, as mentioned already, Victorian taste later had little time for these early windows, and many were either destroyed or replaced by later glaziers in the wave of church restoration that took a firm grip on the ecclesiastical establishment and architects during the second half of the century. Nevertheless, examples can still be seen at: Brockhampton (Hereford); Hougham (Lincs); Owston Ferry (Humberside); Ewerby (Lincs); Merton and Ditchingham (Norfolk); Newton Purcell (Oxon); St Chad's, St Alkmond and Holy Cross, all in Shrewsbury; Kinlet (Salop); Charlton Mackrell and West Monkton (Somerset); Uppark (W Sussex); St Thomas' Dudley, Tingrith (Beds); and Blacktoft (Humberside). To this list could be added some of the windows by William Raphael Eginton, notably those at Stourhead (Wilts) featuring the School of Athens, one at Stonor (Oxon), the two saints in the south transept of Wells Cathedral and the Resurrection window at Babworth (Notts). Until recently, another superb period piece by William Collins (after John Martin) could be seen at Redbourne (Humberside), but the church is now redundant and the glass has been removed. More idiosyncratic and personal but of some interest is the work of Robert Allen, a former procelain painter at the Lowestoft China Factory, whose bizarre figures and windows of c. 1820 can be seen at Nowton and Lowestoft in Suffolk.

The revival of interest in Gothic art and architecture that began in the latter half of the eighteenth century gradually gained momentum through the first half of the nineteenth – an interest fired to a great extent by glass imported into Britain from the Continent. Much of this became available in the wake of the French Revolution, and appeared at the London auction rooms where it helped to increase public awareness, and whence it was removed to the houses of collectors or, occasionally, to churches. Much of this glass came through one Christopher Hampp who added stained glass to the import-export business that he ran from Norwich — most of the Rouen glass in Britain (of which there is much) passed through his hands. People such as Robert Allen and William Peckitt were engaged to mount and set collections of medieval and Renaissance glass; indeed, the settings, often with elaborate infillings between the antique panels, are worthy of

Opposite: Christ in Glory, by the Irish glazier, O'Connor, 1871; Trent, Dorset.

GRATO·ANCE·DEVO ANIMO·POSCIT ·N·Ð·RECTOR·1871

note in themselves (e.g. at Nowton and Herringfleet in Suffolk).

Inevitably, collections such as those at Costessy and Strawberry Hill (set by Peckitt in 1741) led to a revival of interest in the original medieval techniques. Although Betton & Evans began making facsimiles of medieval glass in enamels and crude pot-metal during the 1820s – often extremely successfully, as in the case of the windows at Winchester College and at St Mary's, Ludlow (Salop) – there were very few people engaged in the stained glass business at this time and none who knew how medieval glass had really been made. The 1831 census lists only three glaziers in the whole country, which even allowing for the inadequacy and incompleteness of such surveys indicates what a low point had been reached.

The leading glazier at this time was Thomas Willement – 'Stained glass artist to Queen Victoria', as he advertised himself, and to William IV before her. Willement's first window dates from about 1812, and until 1824, much of his output was heraldic coats-of-arms. Fine examples of this and later figure work can be seen at St George's Chapel, Windsor and in Hampton Court's Great Hall and Watching Chamber. Through the 1830s and 1840s, with the Gothic revival, more and more glaziers appeared on the scene. Firms and individuals such as Ward & Nixon, Charles and Alexander Gibbs and George Hedgeland (who repaired the medieval glass at St Neot in Cornwall in 1829) emerged to produce a number of windows in the 1830s. Willement's pupil, William Warrington, went into business on his own c. 1833 and produced windows in differing medieval styles. In 1834, James Powell bought up a firm of glaziers situated at Whitefriars that had been in the stained glass business since the seventeenth century, and the new company – James Powell & Sons – remained in operation until as recently as 1973: James Powell himself died in 1844 and was succeeded by Arthur Powell. In Newcastle, the grocer William Wailes turned his hand to stained glass in 1838 and, after working with Augustus Pugin in the early 1840s, became prolific producer of characteristically bright and richly coloured windows.

It was with Pugin, doubtless inspired by his father's book *Specimens of Gothic* in 1821, that the Gothic Revival in church building could be said really to have begun. It was his ideas of a devotional approach to architecture, one that looked to the supposed purity of medieval architecture, that captivated the interest of the Church of England, and by 1850 the neo-Gothic had come of age. Gothic architecture was prescribed as the 'correct' and most pure form of Christian architecture; indeed the Cambridge Camden Society (founded in 1836) went so far as to describe it as 'the only Christian architecture', adding that the fourteenth-century style was the most pure form of all, a view that took hold of the Victorian imagination. All Saints, Margaret Street in London was built to the society's requirements, and as the revival's grip strengthened, the society's organ, *The Ecclesiologist*, judged the varying edifices that appeared — and their glass.

Pugin's first church dates from 1837, and for it, he used William Warrington to execute his windows. One undoubted masterpiece of this collaboration has been singled out by Martin Harrison, namely at St Mary's (R.C.), Sutton Coldfield (W Midlands) of 1838, where Pugin had very quickly grasped the essential components of antique window design – here of the early sixteenth century which he was later to dispense with in favour of the fourteenth. From 1842 he used William

Clayton & Bell, c.1880-85. Note the fairly heavy shading, a feature of their work at this time; St Paul's, Onslow Square, London.

Wailes but was not happy with his work, and finally, in collaboration with John Hardman from 1845, produced some fine windows.

Throughout this period, the quality of the glass had been a major limiting factor to designers. William Peckitt and others had been experimenting with crude forms of pot-metal glass, but it was not until the late 1840s that Charles Winston, a barrister and stained glass enthusiast, together with Medlock and Green of Powell's, produced a range of pot-metal coloured glass that really looked like medieval glass and it was used for the first time, by Ward & Hughes, at the Temple Church (London) where one window still remains. It was not until 1863 that the very best pot-metal glass finally became generally available, the so-called 'antique glass' developed by the firm of Chance Brothers of Smethwick together with J. R. Clayton at the instigation of the architect Sir George Gilbert Scott. John Hardman was the first glazier to use it, and through the 1860s many others became acquainted with its fine properties, notably the newly formed firm of Clayton & Bell.

During the 1850s, architects such as George Gilbert Scott, John L. Pearson, George Edmund Street, William Butterfield, Samuel S. Teulon and George F. Bodley all produced some fine neo-Gothic churches for the Church of England, while Pugin did likewise for the Roman Catholics. Stained glass was required in prodigious quantities. Even by 1851, when no fewer than twenty-four stained glass firms exhibited their wares at the Great Exhibition, a significant industry had come into existence. Apart from Hardman, the leading newcomers to the field during the 1840s were Charles Clutterbuck and Michael O'Connor, and during the 1850s, two important companies came into being: Clayton & Bell and Lavers & Barraud. Numerous alliances and collaborations among architects and glaziers provided the opportunity for the kind of cross-fertilization by which any craft thrives, a process that continued well into the 1860s. For example, Alfred

The Damned from Clayton & Bell's Last Judgement at Hanley Castle, an early masterpiece of theirs of 1860.

Bell joined Scott's studio in 1847 and worked with both Street and Bodley, did some of the designs for James Powell & Sons and, in 1855 at Scott's urging, join-ed up with John Richard Clayton to form Clayton & Bell. Francis Barraud became a partner with Nathaniel Lavers (who initially had gone into business with Alfred Bell three years earlier) to form Lavers & Barraud, and in 1860 they were joined by the scholar-designer Nathaniel Westlake, author of *The History of Design in Painted Glass*. Good Lavers & Barraud windows of this time can be seen at Wrotham (Kent) and St Mary's, Ealing (London).

Clement Heaton from Bradford-on-Avon, who had worked for Holland of War-wick in 1851, was joined by James Butler in 1855 and by Robert Bayne from Clayton & Bell to form Heaton, Butler & Bayne. Michael O'Connor, who had studied heraldic glass with Thomas Willement and had worked for Pugin, went into business on his own in the late 1840s. John Burlison and Thomas Grylls had both trained at Clayton & Bell, and formed Burlison & Grylls in 1868 with Bodley's help; the firm carried on in business until 1953, and particularly good works of theirs can still be seen at Ellesborough (Bucks, *see illustration on* p.78), Edwardstone (Suffolk) and Rowington (Warwicks).

It was during the late 1850s and 1860s, when these main firms had established themselves, that a true nineteenth-century 'style' in stained glass could be said to have come into existence, one that had broken away from the eighteenth-century pictorial tradition and the slavish imitation of medieval panels. After a shaky start when their windows suffered from bad firing, Clayton & Bell's early works from about 1859 to 1865 are a good example of this 'renaissance', where clarity of designs, balance of colour, rich new colours in fine glass and intelligent use of leading combine with simplicity, economy and excellent detail in drawing to give really successful windows. Examples of their best work from this period can be seen at Hanley Castle (Worcs, *see illustration on* p.60), Rochester Cathedral (Kent), St Michael's, Cornhill (London), Howsham (N Yorks), South Dalton (Humberside) and elsewhere. After the mid-1860s, their windows tended to become fussier with too much detail in often overcrowded scenes; what used to be fine areas of colour were later invariably over-painted, sometimes heavily so, and there is much stereotyping of colour, a smaller range with heavy dark reds and browns often appearing. In the 1870s, they moved in factory-type production that even operated a night-shift, and standards inevitably fell. However, by 1880 things improved and some good later works of the 1880s and '90s can be seen at Ely, Truro and Bath.

Heaton, Butler & Bayne shared the same studios as Clayton & Bell *c.* 1859-62 and, not surprisingly, the firms were clearly much influenced by each other. Good examples of Heaton, Butler & Bayne's work can be seen St Mark's, Friday Bridge (Cambs), Malvern Wells (Worcs) and Sculthorpe (Norfolk). All of these show how far the firm had moved since their first window of 1856: the Ascension in a rather Nazarene style (*see* p.56) at All Saints, Hawstead (Suffolk).

During the 1860s and '70s, the stained glass business flourished as at no other time and more firms joined the bandwagon. Frederick Preedy was a notable glazier who had worked for George Rogers at Worcester before moving to London where he set up his own business, and from 1860-8, he was used on a number of occasions by the architect William Butterfield. The Lancashire firm of Shrigley & Hunt was founded in 1874 and is still in business today. From the Continent, too, came windows that clearly belonged to the nineteenth century, yet they originated from a different tradition that is immediately discernible in their style. The works of Capronnier, for example, which can be seen in many parts of Yorkshire in particular, have a pallet of colour that is often almost gaudy (see, for example, St Peter's Church in St Albans, Herts), yet his work was, somewhat surprisingly, much admired by the stained glass authority Charles Winston. This is the same man who, in the 1860s, advised the authorities of Glasgow Cathedral to obtain sixty or so stained glass windows from the Royal Bavarian Glass Studios, at Munich, a choice that turned out to be a complete disaster (*see entry for Glasgow*). The windows of Thomas and Alfred Gérente and A. Lusson, on the other hand, are nearly always of a high standard, which might perhaps be expected from the leading glaziers of the Gothic's natural home, France (in fact, one window by Gérente, now in Sheffield Cathedral, was, until recently, frequently described as 'medieval, Spanish'). At Feltwell (Norfolk), every window is by the French glaziers Didron and Dudinot in an imitation thirteenth-century style, and give us a suggestion of what a church of that age might have looked like.

In 1861, William Morris joined forces with Philip Webb and other Pre-Raphaelite artists. Both Webb and Morris had been working for George Edmund Street, who was something of a scholar as well as being one of the finest architects of his day. He was also a firm believer in the craft aspect of church building and ornamentation – indeed, he is sometimes referred to as being the spiritual godfather of the Arts & Crafts movement – and his strong ideas in connection with stained glass and its function in a church (see *The Ecclesiologist*, 1852) may well have influenced Morris. In 1861, Morris, a dedicated advocate of the concept of fusing art with industry and everyday life, began to put theory into practice by gathering together a number of artists and kindred spirits – Edward Burne-Jones, Ford Maddox Brown, Dante Gabriel Rossetti, C. J. Faulkner and Peter Paul Marshall – and the firm of Morris, Marshall, Faulkner & Co. was founded. Burne-Jones had already designed some windows, his first effort being at the United Reform Church in Maidstone (Kent) in 1857, which was said to have driven John Ruskin 'wild with joy'; others he designed for James Powell & Sons from 1857 to 1861 include those at Bradfield College (Berks), Christ Church Cathedral at Oxford, and at Waltham Abbey (Essex) where, in his rose window above the Tree of Jesse, is a superb Creation. The glass available in 1859 for the Christ Church window was a significant improvement on that of two years earlier; indeed Powell's glass was always used by MOrris's firm after an initial hesitation. From 1861 to 1875 the company produced many fine windows with its excellent team of artists; occasionally they all contributed to a design as at All Saints, Cambridge, but generally one of them designed the main figure or scene while Morris and Webb drew such additional material as background decoration and angels. Morris did, however, design a number of the windows himself during the 1860s, but most of the figure and scene design work was carried out by the others: Rossetti was involved in designing some thirty-six; Ford Maddox Brown, about 130; while the rest were mostly by Burne-Jones. Occasionally other artists were invited – Simeon Simon, Arthur Hughes, Val Princep and Albert Moore all designed at least one window each. In 1874 Philip Webb left the group, and in the following year, the firm was reorganised at Morris's insistence with Burne-Jones as sole designer, an arrangement that continued until the deaths of Morris and Burne-Jones in 1896 and 1898 respectively. The firm itself carried on under John Henry Dearle and W.H. Knight until 1940, when it was finally disbanded.

After Burne-Jones left Powell's in 1861, that firm invited the artist Henry Holiday to become its chief designer, and he did much work for them in his own particular Pre-Raphaelite style, until about 1890. Just as Powell's also took on designers such as Professor Harry E. Wooldridge, Harry Burrow and Charles

Opposite: Two angels with the Ascended Christ, by Sir Edward Burne-Jones, c.1896, Waterford, Hertfordshire.

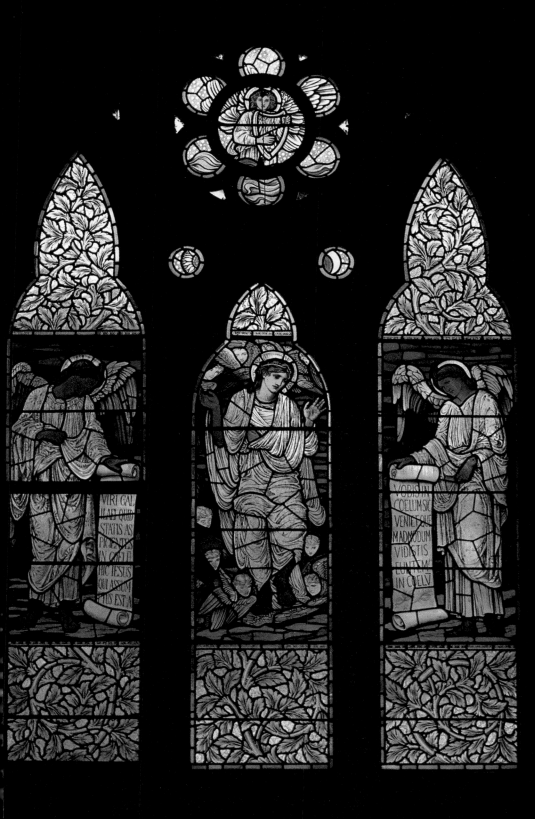

Hardgrave in the 1870s, so too Holiday did some designs for Shrigley & Hunt and Saunders & Co. Fine windows of his can be seen at Mortlake, London (a beautiful Annunciation), at St Clement's, Bournemouth, St Margaret's, Westminster, Amport (Hants) and a host of other places.

Another important glazier at this time was Charles Eamer Kempe. Born in Sussex, he had initially wished to enter the Church but, owing to a speech defect, decided that his talents would be better employed glorifying God through enhancing the beauty of His house. It is reported that, as a child, Kempe underwent something of a mystical experience in Gloucester Cathedral, induced by the setting sun casting its rays through the Cathedral's windows, and that this strengthened his resolve to work with stained glass. Early in his career he became associated with the architect George Frederick Bodley, and subsequently learned his skills with Clayton & Bell under Thomas Baillie. It is possible that his first window was – significantly – for the south choir of Gloucester Cathedral in 1865; in 1867 he helped restore – or, rather, re-create – the saintly fifteenth-century figures at Nettlestead (Kent). As Martin Harrison has pointed out, glass of this age strongly influenced Kempe, particularly its 'subdued colour, intricate detail and use of silver stain'. His own style is particularly strong: his facial drawing is immediately discernible, as is his predilection for pale and dark greens in his compositions, although this emerged during the 1870s and is not a feature of his early work carried out with Baillie in the 1860s (e.g. at Staplefield, W Sussex, and Ovingdean, E Sussex).

In 1869, he founded Kempe & Co., and his prolific, competent though sometimes monotonous work can be seen all round the country (*see illustration on* p.88). After 1900 he used a wheatsheaf as his hallmark, and peacocks' feathers on angels' wings is another clue in recognising his work. He had a number of followers including Ernest Heaseman and Herbert Bryans, but his most notable pupil was Ninian Comper who was to be knighted for his stained glass and other decorative work. Kempe died in 1907, and his successor as chairman of the firm was Walter Tower, who remained there until 1932. Until 1911, Tower superimposed a tower on to the wheatsheaf to underline the continuation of his master's tradition. In fact, many of these 'Tower windows' are by John William Lisle, the firm's chief designer and painter.

THE MODERN PERIOD

In the 1880s, three societies were formed: the Century Guild of Artists (1882), the Art Workers Guild (1884) and the Arts and Crafts Exhibition Society (1888). All three represented a move against the mass-production techniques that had overcome many of the crafts and were threatening the survival of those that remained. The leading lights in this movement included Walter Crane, Selwyn Image, W. R. Lethaby, Nathaniel Westlake, Heywood Sumner, A. H. Mackmurdo, Christopher Whall, Lewis F. Day, J. D. Sedding and, of course, William Morris and Edward Burne-Jones – despite the near assembly-line approach that their own firm had drifted into by this time. The overriding ideal that these people represented was a return to the time when the glazier constantly kept in touch with his product, from commissioning through to the drawing of cartoons, selecting glass, painting, firing, assembling and installing the finished product, so that each job was not only hand-made but nurtured, as it were, by one artist.

In the movement's early days, Selwyn Image was its main exponent, and for a while he produced some forceful windows that are anything but Pre-Raphaelite: in a strange way, his straight, rather priestly, staring figures are reminiscent of the Byzantine Romanesque (e.g. at High Cross in Herts). He used a gentler technique in his window at Waterford (Herts). Walter Crane's most striking work is his 'Sin and Shame' at Stamford Hill, London, of 1897, where the agonised expressions and tortuous twistings of the shapes suggested a whole new world of possibilities to glaziers.

The undisputed leader of the Arts & Crafts movement that emerged in the 1890s, however, was Christopher Whall, who before his death in 1924, was prolific and whose work can be seen in most parts of Britain. He gathered around him a school of followers that initially included Louis Davis and Reginald Hallward, both of whom produced some good designs and windows, particularly Davis, who executed a fine series for Dunblane Cathedral, near Stirling. His style, along with that of another of Whall's followers, Karl Parsons, is unmistakable, and his figure drawing is quite excellent even if it tends at times to be over-sweet. Karl Parsons, on the other hand, displays a distinct predilection for thirteenth-century glass: his windows are almost jewel-like, reminiscent of the work of Harry Clarke, very richly coloured and incorporating all kinds of new techniques, such as acid etching and plating on thin pieces of coloured glass in order to create the desired effect; fine examples can be seen at Bibury (Glos), Waterford (Herts), Tenby (Dyfed) and Porthcawl (Mid Glam).

In 1889, E. S. Prior developed a new kind of glass that became particularly popular in the early days of the Arts & Crafts movement; it was of uneven thickness, had a rough surface and often contained irregularities, flaws and bubbles very much like glass from the thirteenth century, after which it was named – 'Prior's Early English Glass'. In addition, glass of deep and often uneven, streaky colours, which in themselves were quite beautiful, became available and were used to great effect by many of the Arts & Crafts glaziers. Apart from employing these materials, another thing many of the windows of this time had in common was a kind of shimmering effect brought about mainly by using a large number of small pieces of thick glass to make up large areas. Inevitably, much of this was done with clear glass with a kind of speckled surface painting that, in addition to slab glass, imparts a rather gritty appearance and cuts down the overall brightness of a large window, thus enabling glass to display its fine qualities.

In 1897 two glaziers, Mary Lowndes and Alfred Drury, helped set up Christopher Whall in business in London, and in 1906 they built the Glass House in Fulham, which was to become a kind of openhouse workshop for serious-minded Arts & Crafts glaziers. Many passed through its studios and helped spread the gospel abroad, so that a large number of today's practising stained glass artists can, through their teachers – or their teachers' teachers – trace their roots to the Arts & Crafts movement. Many names could be mentioned, but those who come to mind as having windows of merit include Henry Payne (and Edward

Payne his son), Arnold Robinson, Hugh Arnold, Lilian Pocock, Douglas Strachan, R. Anning Bell, Edward Woore, Arild Rosencranz, Margaret Aldrich Rope, Gerald Moira, Caroline Townshend, F. & W. Camm and others (*see the index of artists and firms for examples of work of each of these*).

One vein of development in twentieth-century stained glass that must be mentioned is that which came from Ireland and the neo-Celtic revival of the inter-war years. At the Tower of Glass (*An Tur Gloine*) in Dublin, set up by Sarah Purser and Edward Martyn with the assistance of Christopher Whall's pupil Alfred Child, a modern Irish school of stained glass was established, from which emerged the two notable glaziers, Harry Clarke and Wilhelmina Geddes. Clarke's windows are immensely successful, glowing jewel-like from his finely detailed treatment of designs that have great dignity and inventiveness, while those of Geddes exude a kind of power in their forceful figure drawing set in designs that always seem to impart Celtic overtones; characteristic examples of her work can be seen at Laleham (Surrey), Wallsend (Tyne & Wear), Lampeter (Dyfed) and a more subdued window at Northchapel near Petworth (W Sussex) – all from 1922-30. Also from Ireland came Evie Hone, who, after studying for a while with Geddes, made some very fine windows at Lanercost Priory (Cumbria) (*see illustration on* p.90), Wellingborough (Northants), Eton College Chapel and elsewhere.

It is perhaps too close to look objectively at the stained-glass work of the last fifty years or so. Nothing self-consciously 'modern' in stained glass appeared in Britain until John Piper and Patrick Reyntiens' magnificent windows were created for Oundle School Chapel (Northants) in 1956 (*see illustration on* p.162). Alfred Wolmark's completely abstract and decorative windows for St Mary's, Slough of 1913 are something of an enigma, however: although attractive, they seem to be isolated and not part of a tradition that led artists anywhere, whereas the Piper/Reyntiens work led to Coventry Cathedral and Liverpool Roman Catholic Cathedral. Certain other contemporary stained glass artists stand out through the very strength of their work, such as Laurence Lee, Carl Edwards (who now uses the Lowndes & Drury premises in Fulham) and the Hungarian-born Ervin Bossanyi. Bossanyi's windows are always committed and technically excellent even if his figure drawing does not appeal to all tastes. Quite different, however, are both major windows by Marc Chagall at Tudeley (Kent) and Chichester executed by Charles Marq of Reims; indeed, Marq takes the greatest pains to transfer Chagall's brush strokes to glass, employing complicated and elaborate techniques of aciding, etching and leading (*see illustration* on p.66).

Some glaziers are well known through the large number of windows they have made, whereas others have done much good work yet have received hardly any recognition. Many of these earlier twentieth-century and contemporary stained glass artists whose work can be seen around Britain have not been mentioned in this introductory section. In preparing this book, I asked a number of practising glaziers, who were also members of the Society of Master Glass Painters, to send lists of places where they feel their best work can be seen. The results are found in the gazetteer and readers can judge the merits of the works themselves.

Opposite: Psalm 150 – a recent window by Marc Chagall, made by Charles Marq, Chichester Cathedral.

HOW TO USE THE GAZETTEER

This gazetteer section is ordered by counties as they existed in 1984 with the exception of Worcestershire and Herefordshire which have been separated.

For describing the position of a window in a church, the directions N, S, E and W are used to denote the directions with respect to the altar, which is taken as being at the ecclesiastical E end, even if geographically the church is not orientated with its altar to the east.

Terms such as 'a (or the) N aisle W window' mean a window in the west wall of the N aisle. (1 in diagram.) The westernmost north-facing window in the N aisle is referred to as the 'westernmost window in the N aisle' (2). A window which is north-facing at the western end of the N aisle — but may not be the westernmost window here is referred to as a 'NW window' (3).

In the tables listing places in each county, the location is the parish church unless otherwise stated. The number in the lefthand column (MR) is the map reference number.

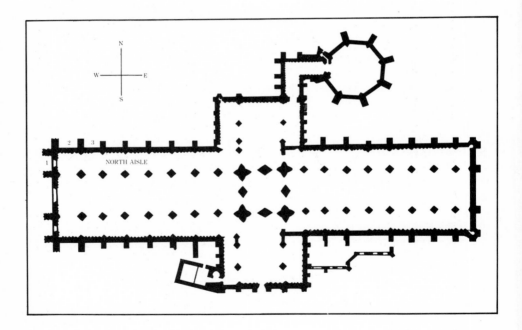

Opposite: Angel from Harry Clarke's window of 1921, Sturminster Newton, Dorset.

PART TWO
THE GAZETTEER

ENGLAND

AVON

'Somerset' glass (*see* p.178) can be seen at a number of locations, notably St Mary Redcliffe and St Catherine's Court, although at both places there has been damage and restoration. Nor is there much left of the C14 'Bristol School' work; fragmentary panels at Bristol Cathedral and Tickenham represent the best examples. Avon is, however, much better off for foreign glass, most of which would have been imported during the last century; St Mark, Bristol has a good collection, much of which came via Beckford's Fonthill Abbey, and the glass at Clevedon is an interesting assortment. C19 glass can, as always, be seen in plenty and the best of this is probably the E window in Bath Abbey.

MR	Place	Centuries									Principal feature(s)
		12	13	14	15	16	17	18	19	20	
1	Acton Turville								*		LBW ws. of the 1870s
2	Banwell			*	+						St Nicholas and child being boiled
3	Bath, Abbey					H	H		*	*	see below
4	– St Bartholomew									*	many ws. by M. Angus, 1980–82
5	Bristol, All Saints									*	fibreglass ws. by RP and Gillespie
6	– Cathedral			+H	*	F			*	*	see below
7	– St Mark				+	F	O				see below
8	– St Mary Redcliffe				*				*	*	see below
9	Burrington				*						part of Seven Sacrament series
10	Chelvey		+		*						Evangelist symbols and figures
11	Chelwood					F					Baptism, Crucifixion, St Stephen
12	Churchill				*						Christ, angels and St Catherine
13	Claverton		F	O	O						C14 (German) Betrayal: Tobit scenes
14	Cleeve								*	*	WM, NC, CEK, HH, 1891–1950
15	Clevedon		F	F		F					see below
16	Clifton, Cathedral									*	see below
17	Dyrham				*						see below
18	Falfield								*		glass by various glaziers 1860–92
19	Hawkesbury				*						St Giles and stag
20	Iron Acton				*						heads of Edward IV, St Ambrose et al.
21	Kelston			*	*	*					see below
22	Keynsham, St Dunston									*	Cross in purple by M.Angus, 1979
23	Locking								*		much of early 1860s, one by Joseph Bell
24	Long Ashton				*						Doctors of the Church and Coronation
25	Portbury		Q								frags. include C14 Qs and border
26	Radstock									*	good early C20 glass by R.A.Bell
27	Rangeworthy									*	ws. by NC, 1919–52
28	St Catherine				*						see below
29	Tickenham			*							Crucifixion, Christ in Majesty
30	Tortworth				+Q						St Margaret, Virgin, Passion shields
31	Weston, St.Mary		F								border possibly from St Remi, Reims
32	Weston-super-Mare, All Saints									*	11 ws. by JP of Whitefriars
33	St Mary			+	+	O					early C16 roundels and English frags.
34	Winscombe			*	*						see below
35	Winterbourne, Downe								*		Pre-Raphaelite glass by J.F. Bentley, c.1876
36	Wraxhall				+				*		much glass by CEK from 1895 and later

See page 280 for table of symbols

BATH, Abbey: A few pieces of medieval glass have been reset into the E window, and some C16 and C17 shields of arms survive in the N aisle, some of which have elaborate quarterings: each is labelled and include the families Windsor, Ley, Russell, St Maur, Speke of Jordans and Rich (Earl of Warwick). The firm Clayton & Bell designed and built the massive E window in c.1873; it was

The head of St Dorothy or Apollonia among C15 fragments at St Mary Redcliffe, Bristol, Avon.

repaired after bomb damage in the last war by Michael Farrar Bell, a descendant of Alfred Bell. The windows with The Healing of the Sick, The Birth of Eve, The Nativity and the long thin S transept windows are all later works by the same firm. Most of the early C20 glass is by James Powell of Whitefriars trying to break away from the rut that most late C19 window design and production had got itself into.

BRISTOL, Cathedral: The Virgin Mary at the centre of the Lady Chapel's Tree of Jesse window is one of the few pieces that survive from the Cathedral's original glazing scheme; most of the rest has gone, although here the shields of arms of the knights who fought at Crécy also belong to the C14. Some medieval fragments have been reset into the E window of the N transept clerestory, where two figures can be made out, and there are some in the N Chapel, in the Berkeley Chapel and in the cloisters. Nell Gwyn is reputed to have given the Cathedral the C16 panels – probably of Continental origin — in the N aisle E window which portray Abraham and Isaac, Jonah and the Whale, Elijah in the Flaming Chariot, and Christ in Gethsemane. High in the S chancel can be seen four early C16 German panels, one of which depicts a notable Annunciation. Most of the C19 glass in the Lady Chapel (and the restored Jesse Tree) is by Bell of Bristol, c.1850. The W rose window is by Hardman to Street's design. Keith New's window in the S Choir aisle is a colourful and dynamic composition of c.1965.

BRISTOL, St Mark: Much of the glass here came from the sale at Fonthill Abbey in 1823. It is well listed in a pamphlet available in the church, but is briefly described here. On the N side of the nave (2nd from W) is French glass from the Château of Écouen, made for Anne de Montmorency and depicting various scenes, some connected with hunting (eg the small panel of the goddess Diana with three interlacing moons); also here are a scene with Christ and one possibly from the *Aeneid*. French glass can also be seen on the S side with Passion scenes, Moses and Elias, the Transfiguration, the Espousal of Mary and Joseph, and Moses Breaking the Tables of the Law. The chancel originally featured C15 English glass, of which only some Passion emblems and part figures of apostles in the tracery lights remain; the main lights now feature (left to right) St Thomas, Tryphon (King of Egypt meeting Jonathan at Bethsan with a scroll cursing all who plot treachery), Catherine, Barbara, a saint holding a head. The Assumption is portrayed below where the Virgin Mary is in prayer and Joseph asleep. In the Jesus Chapel are some good pieces of mixed origin: St Mark's winged lion from Venice, Sts Castor and Castrina above the Abbot John Berendorp and his patron saint Nicholas (glass from Steinfeld Abbey), a kneeling English donor with St John's eagle below and three C15 roundels with birds. In the S Chapel are some twenty-four Flemish Roundels (C16 and C17) with saints, biblical and historical scenes.

BRISTOL, St Mary Redcliffe: In St John the Baptist's Chapel under the W tower are stately figures in C15 'Somerset' glass (*see illustration on this page*), but lacking the usual background of 'Somerset' quarries. In the upper row (left to right) are a bishop, the Virgin and Child both with crowns, a headless archbishop standing on a chequered plinth, and St Laurence with gridiron; below are Sts Michael, Matthias (with halberd), John the Baptist (camel skin and Agnus Dei), and a composite panel with remains that include heads of (?)the Virgin and part of a Trinity panel, with the Cross placed on the globe of the world divided into land, sea and air. The N windows in this chapel have some interesting collages of fascinating C15 fragments and roundels. Vast amounts of C19 glass, by the ubiquitous Clayton & Bell and other firms. Of the early C20 are the Comper windows in the S transept, but more interesting are the post-War set of five compositions with New Testament themes in strong colours in the Lady Chapel by Harry Stammers.

CLEVEDON, Christ Church: In the E window are some interesting panels of imported glass, the centrepiece of which is a C13 king from a Tree of Jesse; also a C14 Virgin Mary from a Coronation scene, two small prophets and part of an angel with a censer. The Risen Christ here is in C16 Flemish glass, as is the upper part of the Virgin Mary being crowned by two angels, part of a Judgement scene, and the unidentified large bearded man walking in the country.

CLIFTON, Cathedral: The excellent walls of coloured glass in the narthex are by Henry Haig, the larger is 'Pentecost', the smaller 'Jubilation'.

DYRHAM, St Peter High up in the tracery lights of the E window are four small but beautiful C15 figures each set with border and under a canopy: St John the Baptist with Agnus Dei, the Virgin Mary as a child holding a book, St Anne and St John the Evangelist (alas with a renewed head) carrying a chalice.

KELSTON, St Nicholas: Good figures in medieval Continental glass in the chancel, St Barbara on the N side carrying a tower (C14 French), and St Anthony with crutched staff, bell and pig (C15 Netherlandish?); in nave N window the part figure of St John Evangelist from a Crucifixion scene in yellow and green and amid fragments, and an angel — formerly supporting the Virgin at the Assumption? — (C14 French). In the tower W window is a fine early C16 (Flemish?) Baptism of Jesus in the River Jordan.

ST CATHERINE, St Catherine's Court: The E window here is a much restored late C15 Crucifixion with the Virgin Mary,

St John and St Peter set against Somerset quarries; beneath are shields of arms and the donor Prior Cantlow in supplication to the Virgin. There is little pot metal glass used, most of the colouring resulting from yellow staining. The Edward IV sunburst emblem in the tracery light suggests a late C15 date.

WINSCOMBE, St James Some of the best glass in Somerset/Avon, notably in the N Chapel where the E window has a Crucifixion with St Mary, St John and St Anthony, the latter portrayed with his pig peeping out from under his cloak; all the figures are beautifully drawn and set against characteristic 'Somerset' quarries. Beneath are four pairs of donors and, above, angels carrying shields with Instruments of the Passion, roses, pomegranates, and Edward IV's sunburst emblem indicating a late C15 date. On the S side is St Catherine (similar to the Virgin of the N Chapel's E window), part of the Virgin and Child, and St James with book, pilgrim's staff and scallop. In the S aisle is the youthful figure of a bishop giving blessing, St James again with Passion shield below and an archbishop. In the S chancel are parts of figures of St Catherine and St Mary Magdalene, both with emblems. The N Chapel has the later 'Peter Carslegh Window' of c.1535, named after its donor and depicting the three St Peters — Apostle, Deacon and Exorcist — in a yellow stain which has become rather hot in tone — note that the Renaissance type of grotesques begin to appear in this otherwise late Gothic glass. In the long thin lancets of the E end is fine richly coloured Pre-Raphaelite glass which Martin Harrison has identified as being an early masterpiece by Fred Weeks for Saunders & Co., dating from 1873.

BEDFORDSHIRE

Bedfordshire is, alas, not very well endowed with ancient stained glass. However, what little there is often has great charm particularly the C14 glass at Cockayne Hatley, although it originates from Yorkshire. The C17 panels at Northill are a splendid sight, and there are some interesting works of the C20 by Christopher Whall, Alan Younger, John Piper and John Hayward.

MR	Place	Centuries									Principal feature(s)
		12	13	14	15	16	17	18	19	20	
1	Barton-le-Clay			+							Evangelist symbols in rectory
2	Bedford, Museum			+							some remains from Chicksands Priory
3	– St Paul								*		by HH, JP, CEK, SH
4	Bushmead Priory			+		+					C14 head of (?)Christ
5	Chicksands Priory				+	+					glass sundial; see also Audley End

MR	Place	Centuries								Principal feature(s)
		12	13	14	15	16	17	18	19	20	
6	Cockayne Hatley			*	*						see below
7	Dean				*						donors (Lyeset), monk, St Catherine
8	Dunstable									*	post-War glass by J.Hayward
9	Edworth		G	*	*			*			see below
10	Eyeworth			H							arms of Adam Francis, c.1370, S a. E w.
11	Houghton Conquest				H						arms of Ludlow, St Amand, Mowbray
12	Leighton Buzzard								*	*	good glass by CEK over period 1887–1905
13	Linslade			*							in the W w.
14	Luton, St Mary				*					*	see below
15	Maulden								*		an early work by CB, 1858
16	Northill						H		*		see below
17	Odell			+	*						seraphim, bishop, Evangelist symbols
18	Old Warden				*						St Margaret, donor Walter de Clifton, angels
19	Potsgrove				*						Evangelist symbols
20	Tingrith								*		early Victorian glass of the 1840s
21	Totterhoe									*	see below
22	Turvey									*	an early w. by JH, 1854
23	Wilden				*	*					Sts James, Laurence by Thos Glazier School?

See page 280 for table of symbols

COCKAYNE HATLEY, St John the Baptist:
In the N aisle E window are four good C14 figures, each placed under C14 canopies, and then in pairs again under C15 canopies. They are the northern saints Edward, Oswald, Ethelbad and Dunstan (the glass is believed to have come originally from Yorkshire in the early C19 and contains some C13 fragments in characteristic deep red and blue, *see illustration on* p.7). In the tracery lights above are three restored C15 figures set on chequered floors (and one not very good imitation figure) — St Mary Magdalene is good, as is the seraphim on a wheel and carrying a banner. The E window with New Testament scenes is an imitation of Flemish glass, formerly at Wilbraham Church but now missing. The Netherlandish-styled E window here is by Willement, 1829, who also did the armorial glass, c.1839.

EDWORTH, Church:
In the S chancel is some C13 *grisaille* against which is set the C14 figure of St Edmund carrying the arrows of his martyrdom (he was an East Anglian king, killed by the Danes for refusing to renounce Christianity, c.870, *see illustration*); above Edmund under a canopy is another C14 saintly figure (head modern), and above that fragments that suggest the figure of St George. In the S clerestory is a C15 figure of St James set against quarries. There is an unusual painting on glass in the S aisle in brown and blue enamels, possibly of the eighteenth century.

LUTON, St Mary:
The Perpendicular E window has an assortment of C15 glass, gathered from various windows, and includes angels with harps and gitterns, the Virgin Mary and Child,

The saint-king Edmund carrying the arrows of his martyrdom, C14, Edworth, Bedfordshire.

St John the Baptist, Sir John Wenlock and various bits, one of which has the words 'Hola' — Sir John's battle-cry! The 1979 'Magnificat Window' in the S transept is by Alan Younger who stresses the 'revolutionary venom' contained in his readings of the Magnificat: it certainly suggests Mary's 'explosion of Happiness' as the artist describes it.

NORTHILL, St Mary:
In the S nave are two huge panels of glass painted by John Oliver c.1664, with elaborate heraldic achievements. One has the arms of the Grocers' Company with its spice-bearing camel atop and the escutcheon of Lady Margaret Slaney (*see illustration on* p.27); the other, those of Charles II. The ubiquitous C.E. Kempe & Co. has windows of 1891 at the E end of

the N wall and of 1906 in the SE chancel – his usual competent work. A number of windows by Clayton & Bell, notably at the aisles' W end and the tower.

TOTTERNHOE, Parish Church: The E window here with the Tree of Life is by John Piper and Patrick Reyntiens and dates from 1970-71. It uses predominantly blue and gold 'antique' glass, that is glass which is non-machine-made, being muff or crown as made in medieval times (*see* Chapter 3, p.15). There are also some C15 remains here reset into a S window.

BERKSHIRE

Good modern glass can be seen at Eton College Chapel, at St Mary, Slough, and at Wargrave, and early Burne-Jones at Bradfield College (for Powell's), and Cranbourne. There are plenty of Victorian windows of varying quality, but ancient glass is rather thinly spread throughout the county. Aldermaston has some superb C13 medallions, and the C14 and C15 glass at Binfield and Stratfield Mortimer is well worth seeing. Unfortunately it is not possible for the public to see the superb C15 armorial panels at Ockwells Manor, but the early C16 array of figures at St George's Chapel, Windsor, may compensate for this!

MR	Place	Centuries									Principal feature(s)
		12	13	14	15	16	17	18	19	20	
1	Aldermaston		*								see below
2	Avington								*		early HH w. of 1867 in chancel
3	Binfield			*	*						see below
4	Bradfield, College								*		see below
5	Bucklebury						*				see below
6	Cookham Dean								*		2 early ws. by Westlake for Lavers, 1860s
7	Cranbourne								*		see below
8	Easthampstead								*		Last Judgement *et al* by B-J/WM
9	East Ilsley		Q								vine leaf quarries
10	East Shefford				*						Annunciation scene
11	Eton, College									*	see below
12	Greenham						F				Netherlandish Tree of Jesse, *c.*1618
13	Inkpen		Q								early C14 grisaille
14	Knowl Hill								*		3 early ws. by JH, *c.*1854
15	Lambourn				*						St John
16	Langley Marish			*		*	H				good remains and heraldic panel
17	Ockwells Manor				H						outstanding heraldic achievements
18	Pangbourne,										
	Purley Hall						*				sundial and arms by JR, *c.*1734
19	Shottesbrooke		Q+								some grotesques and arms for Neville
20	Slough, Methodist Ch.									*	d-d-v ws. by Fourmaintreaux/JP, 1965
21	– St Mary								*	*	see below
22	Stratfield Mortimer			*	*	*H					portrait of William of Wykeham
23	Tilehurst								*	*	WM, 1869; Farrar Bell, 1970; Wailes ws.
24	Warfield			H*	*				*	*	angels, bishop, arms of Edward III
25	Wargrave									*	ws. by JHY (1962) and Jane Gray (1980)
26	Wasing					F	F				some C15 and C16 pieces
27	Windsor, Guildhall								*		panels by Royal Windsor Glass Works, *c.*1880
28	– St George's				*				*	*	see below

See page 280 for table of symbols

ALDERMASTON, St Mary: On the N side of the chancel are two C13 medallions in quatrefoil shape and with rich colours portraying the Coronation of the Virgin and the Annunciation; note the scroll in the latter window bearing the words 'Ave Maria Grat' in Lombardic script (generally easier to read than the later Black Letter variety). These panels are not indigenous to the church.

BINFIELD, All Saints: Some C14 glass and good C15 figures on the S side of the church. St George is accompanied — as is often the case in medieval glass — by a somewhat theatrical dragon; St Paul has his sword; and both figures are placed beneath canopies. Also here are St Peter with keys and book, The Annunciation and St John bearing the cup from which the dragon was said to have emerged when someone tried to poison him.

BRADFIELD College Chapel: The E window here is Sir Edward Burne-Jones's second work in stained glass (Maidstone was the first) for James Powell and Sons. He did a number of windows for Powell between 1857 and 1861 before joining William Morris's firm.

BUCKLEBURY, St Mary: A stained glass sundial can be seen here. It is dated 1649 and bears the inscription 'S S me fecit'. Such sundials were popular during the second half of the seventeenth century — some glaziers gave them away free to customers who had commissioned whole windows.

CRANBOURNE, St Peter: The S Chapel here has the first window by the newly formed company of Morris, Marshall, Faulkner & Co. The subject, which Morris himself designed, is a child being blessed. In the W window of a year later, also by the firm, the design of Christ Setting a Child in the Midst of the People is by Ford Maddox Brown, whilst the Marriage at Cana is by Morris. Other windows are by John Hardman (nave), Clayton & Bell (S Chapel E window), O'Connor (Chapel W window) and Selwyn Image for Powell & Sons (the window with St Peter and St Cornelius).

ETON Chapel: The E window is Evie Hone's fine work of 1952 with the Crucifixion above the Last Supper, with Melchisedek on the left (representing the priest/king of the Old Dispensation) and the sacrifice of Isaac on the right (symbolising the first offer of sacrifice): rich colours and powerful figure drawings characteristic of the C20 Irish 'School' of stained glass design. Of quite a different flavour are the more abstract but equally engaging Miracle and Parable windows at the eastern end of

the nave, designed and executed by John Piper and Patrick Reyntiens, 1959-64. The four Miracle (N side) are The Miraculous Draught of Fishes, The Feeding of the Five Thousand, The Stilling of the Waves, and The Raising of Lazarus — The Miraculous Draught is a truly inspired work. The Parables opposite are the Wheat and the Tares, The Lost Sheep, The House Built on Rock and the Light Under a Bushel.

SLOUGH, St Mary: The four lancets of the W window — the Ellerman Memorial — with their semi-abstract and geometrical patterns were something of a landmark in the evolution of stained glass; although they date from 1915, nothing like them appeared again in England until after the Second World War. They were designed by Alfred Wolmark (and Robert Anning Bell?) and made by Arthur Dix. Far more conventional and conservative are G.E.R. Smith's later windows with figures of saints set against clear glass. Also a number of windows by the prolific Kempe & Co., some of which are by Tower/Lisle; Christ in Glory in the S Chapel is an early Kempe, c. 1877.

WINDSOR, St George's Chapel: Much of the old glass here has disappeared. However, the great W window has some seventy-five or so early C16 figures that are reputed to include some twenty-nine royal figures, eight archbishops, two bishops, twenty-four popes, ten saints and two ordinary mortals, one of whom is the master mason William Vertue carrying his hammer and chisel. The E window is a rather fussy composition by Clayton & Bell of 1863 with The Nativity, Last Judgement and The Resurrection as the main scenes; beneath are fifteen panels depicting incidents in the life of Prince Albert. The Choir aisle windows and those of the Beaufort Chapel are of note, portraying various kings and their queens by Willement over the period 1841-65 — also the six stately early C19 figures in the Urswick Chantry Chapel (NW corner). A relief from all this formality is the abstract Piper-Reyntiens window of 1969.

BUCKINGHAMSHIRE

A reasonable amount of English and Continental ancient glass can be seen around the county and, of course, plenty from the last two centuries. Addington, Drayton Beauchamp and Hillesden are a must to visit; also the C14 glass at Hitcham: although it is not of the best quality, yet it is interesting from the point of view of its arrangement in the chancel. The hobby horse drawn on a C17 piece of glass in Stoke Poges Church is an interesting and unique subject in stained glass.

MR	Place	12	13	14	15	16	17	18	19	20	Principal feature(s)
1	Addington				O	O					see below
2	Amersham						*				12 apostles, but much is C20 facsimile
3	Aston Sandford		*								darkened fig. of Christ, c.1290
4	Aylesbury, Kings Head				H						royal arms include those of Anjou
5	– St Mary								*		ws. by TW, Gibbs, OC, Oliphant, 1855–75
6	Beaconsfield								*		Gladstone and Lord Salisbury with King Saul!
7	Bledlow			H							arms of Henry of Lanc., Bohun, Edward III
8	Bletchley								*		HH w. for JP in S a., 1868
9	Chenies					*					donor fig.
10	Chesham Bois				+	*					reset frags. include Flemish Crucifixion
11	Chetwode		*	*					*		see below
12	Clifton Reynes			q	*						frags. include fig. of a bishop
13	Dorney								*		portrait of King Charles I in C19 glass
14	Drayton Beauchamp				*						see below
15	Edlesborough				*						St James with scallop shell
16	Ellesborough				*				*		fine BG, 1875 (see illustration on p.78)
17	Fenny Stratford						H				nine coats-of-arms, all labelled
18	Fingest								*		E w. by F.Barraud for JP, 1849
19	Flackwell Heath									*	rose w. by RP, 1962
20	Frieth								*		see below
21	Fulmer				O						Petrarch Triumphs, Love Fame Death Chast.
22	Haddenham				*						t.l. figs. of apostles
23	Hillesden					*			*		see below
24	Hitcham			*							see below
25	Horton								*		good CEK, 1882-3: his Milton Window
26	Ickford									*	three ws. by NC, 1919–45
27	Long Crendon									*	24 ws. in slab/concrete by GG, 1970
28	Lower Winchendon				*	O					C15 St Peter; C17 Susanna and the Elders
29	Maids Moreton				*						four saints in tower w.
30	Marlow								*	*	see below
31	Monks Risborough			*							delightful tiny Virgin and Child
32	New Bradwell								*	*	ws. by G.Webb, H.Stammers, G.Moira
33	Olney								*	*	early C19 by Holland; new ws. by JC
34	Radclive			*							Virgin and Child
35	Soulbury									*	three-light w. by M.Farrar Bell, 1956
36	Stoke Hammond				*						bishop, archbishop, four prophets
37	Stoke Poges					H	*		*		see below
38	Waddesdon, Manor				*	FH					English and Swiss coats-of-arms
39	Wavendon								*		many ws. by OC
40	Weston Turville			H	*						Virgin, royal arms and Thos Earl of Lancaster
41	Weston Underwood			*							see below
42	West Wycombe				O	O					many Biblical scenes
43	Wing			H*							Coronation of the Virgin
44	Wotton Underwood								*		heraldry by FE, 1800 (set in 1868)

See page 280 for table of symbols

ADDINGTON, St Mary: A fine collection of C16 and C17 Flemish roundels and other panels in ten windows around the church. Most of the subjects are self-explanatory — a detailed study, recently carried out by Dr William Cole, is available in the church. In traditional manner, the subjects are placed around the church such that the Old Testament subjects are on the N side (along with one or two pagan pieces!), New Testament episodes and the Evangelists in the chancel, Passion scenes in the S Chapel E window, and other New Testament subjects in the S windows. Particularly delightful is the rather dozy lion at the feet of a thoughtful St Mark.

CHETWODE, St Mary: In the chancel are two long lancet windows with medallions set in them; the S side has C13 and C14 panels, whereas the E window is an 1842 imitation of its neighbour. The left panel of this S window has (top to bottom) a roundel of *grisaille,* a predominantly green-coloured Crucifixion scene (both C13), then a C14 saint under a canopy; the centre lancet has glass of c.1260 with St John the Baptist (with Agnus Dei) in an oval vesica, a bishop and, at the bottom, an early example of a coat-of-arms in stained glass (arms of Henry III); the right lancet has a Crucifixion, the Virgin, St (?)Peter and a bishop with 'amicus dei Nicholas' C14 (in Lombardic writing).

Tracery light panels in yellow stain from the Decorated/Perpendicular transition period in the late C14, Weston Underwood, Bucks.

DRAYTON BEAUCHAMP, St Mary: Some of the finest glass in Buckinghamshire in the E window where ten of the apostles are portrayed in C15 glass (Sts Luke and Barnabas are missing). Each is labelled on the base of the chequered plinth upon which they stand and carries a scroll with a sentence from the Creed. These depart from the norm (*see* p.35) in several places — the figure labelled St Thomas, for example, carries the sentence which translates into 'From thence He shall come to judge the quick and the dead', more usually associated with St Philip. In the S chancel are the C14 arms of the Cheyne family set above a C15 figure of the Virgin, possibly from a Crucifixion, set against an unusual but handsome background of blue and white diaper. There are possibly some C15 fragments in the C19 W window which imitates the fine C15 glass in the E window of the church.

FRIETH, St Peter: The E window here is a Pugin design made by John Hardman in 1849 — conservative and imitation Gothic as usual, but undoubtedly successful. Pugin, who had strong ideas about what stained glass should look like, was often at odds with his glaziers; 'the glaziers will shorten my days,' he is once reputed to have said despairingly. Yet he established a working relationship with John Hardman & Co. — one in which he played the dominant part — and together they produced many fine windows in the 1850s.

(Another of their works of *c.*1845 can be seen locally at St Peter's, Marlow.) Also in the church are windows by Hudson of Pentonville (the W window) and two by Kempe & Co. with St John (1880) and St David (1901).

HILLESDEN, All Saints: The chancel E window has medieval remains of figures of popes, bishops and saints in the tracery lights, but the main attraction in this church is in the S transept E window where eight early C16 panels depict scenes from the Legend of St Nicholas, as related by the Golden Legend: thus we can see the saint reviving a boy who had been strangled by the devil disguised as a pilgrim, the boy and the chalice, the grain ships at Myra, and the conversion of a rich Jew. All the scenes are very picturesque and the Flemish influence is obvious — indeed some of the near-grotesque faces are positively Breughel-like. Note Burlison & Grylls' good imitation of the style in the 1875 window next door, however lacking the charm and humour of the C16 glass.

HITCHAM, St Mary: In the symmetrically arranged chancel with its nine windows are C14 remains of a complete set of The Nine Orders Of The Angelic Hierarchy, together with three of the four Evangelists in the quatrefoils of the N and S windows. High up in the E window tracery lights is a rather patchy panel of Christ in Majesty with the four Evangelists again.

MARLOW, All Saints: Much of the glass here is by Burlison & Grylls of 1876, a time when much of their output was of a generally high quality. In the S aisle the archangels are by the Lancastrian firm Shrigley & Hunt. Lilian Pocock's St Christopher Window of 1915 is a good example of Arts & Crafts work at this time.

STOKE POGES, St Giles: There is much C16–C18 heraldic glass in the two windows of the Hastings Chapel, some of which might originally have come from the Manor House. So, too, the Lady Chapel E window has four C16 heraldic achievements executed mostly in enamel paint; one has elaborate quartering. Possibly the most interesting piece of glass in the church is the C17 portrayal of a hobby horse, forerunner of the bicycle, which can be seen amongst the reset quarries in the W window. Of the C19 glass the most interesting is the very painted Raphaelesque representation of Mary, Queen of Heaven, in the Italian Cinquecento style, a striking if somewhat sentimental work by Mayer & Co. of 1871.

WESTON UNDERWOOD, St Laurence: Amongst the best ancient glass in Buckinghamshire. In the tracery lights of the E window are nine little C14 figures, mostly painted and in silver stain set against a colour: they comprise a bishop, Sts Peter with a key (a rather darkened panel), John Baptist with lamb and flag, John Evangelist with chalice and dragon, Laurence with gridiron (also darkened), and Paul with a sword; above is Christ Ascending with two censing angels, all c.1380 (*see illustration on* p.77).

One of the three very fine Archangels from an early window by Burlison & Grylls, 1875, in the south aisle at Ellesborough, Buckinghamshire.

CAMBRIDGESHIRE

Much good glass from C14 to the present day at a number of places throughout the county, eg the C14 heraldic glass at Wimpole Church, good C15 windows at Landwade and Leverington, the magnificent early C16 glass at King's College, Cambridge, the bizarre C18 Isaac Newton window at Trinity College. C15 and C16 Continental glass can be seen at Thorney, Diddington and Wisbech St Mary, and plenty of Victorian windows at Cambridge and of the C20 in the colleges.

MR	Place	12	13	14	15	16	17	18	19	20	Principal feature(s)
					Centuries						
1	Bar Hill, Shared Ch.									*	'New Life' w. by Ray Bradley, 1972
2	Barnack								*		C19 w. by former rector, M.Argyles
3	Buckden				*						Coronation and Annunciation
4	Burghley House				*						see below
5	Cambridge, All Saints								*		see below
6	– Christ's Col.				*						Henry VI, VII, Elizabeth of York

MR	Place	12	13	14	15	16	17	18	19	20	Principal feature(s)
7	– Corpus Christi Col.				F						Death of the Virgin
8	– Fitzwilliam Mus.				F						wild man and woman, Triumph of Bacchus
9	– Holy Sepulchre								*		C19 glass by TW and Jones & Willis
10	– Jesus Col.								*		see below
11	– King's Col.			*	*				*		see below
12	– Magdalene Col.Lib.				*						Sts Laurence, Edmund, angel and king
13	– Peterhouse Col.								*		see below
14	– Robinson Col.									*	good recent glass by PR
15	– St Botolph									*	Arts & Crafts E w. by Rachael Hancock
16	– St John's Col.								*		CB for Scott, 1863–9; also JH, Wailes
17	– St Mary's								*		ws. by JH, JP and J. Hogan
18	– Trinity Col. Lib.							*			see below
19	– Westminster Col.									*	13 ws. by DS on Benedicite, Law, Love
20	Coton		Q+	Q+							Qs and frags.
21	Diddington				F	F					see below
22	Doddington								*		see below
23	Eaton Socon				*						St Nicholas and three boys in a tub
24	Ely, Cathedral			*	*		*	*	*		see below
25	Fordham			*							roundel with St Thomas Becket
26	Fowlmere								*		fine CB w. of 1862
27	Godmanchester								*		virtues by B-J/WM, ws. by GG, CEK
28	Great Staughton			H	H						St Mary Magdalene?
29	Hilton				*						rose w. has C15 panel
30	Huntingdon								*	*	see below
31	Keyston				*						many remains include St Barbara
32	Kimbolton			Q*					*		see below
33	Kirtling					F					Swiss Crucifixion scene in W w.
34	Landwade				*		*				see below
35	Leverington				*				*	*	see below
36	Madingley				*	*					see below
37	Maxey				*						St Paul and Virgin Mary
38	Meldreth			*							St John the Baptist
39	Peakirk								*		Overbeck's 'Christ at the Door' by JP, 1856
40	Peterborough								*	*	see below
41	St Neots				*						Sts Stephen, Laurence, angel, arms
42	Sawtry				+	Q+					many interesting frags.
43	Spaldwick					*					two small panels in S a. E w.
44	Thorney				F				*		see below
45	Toft						*				Moses, Daniel, David, Ezekiel
46	Trumpington		+	H*							Sts Peter and Paul, Trumpington arms
47	Upwood				*						small figs. in canopy tops
48	Waresley								*		good glass by HBB (1865) and GG
49	Wimpole			H*							see below
50	Wisbech				*						Apostles
51	Wisbech St Mary			*	F	F					see below
52	Wistow				*						Annunciation and Resurrection

See page 280 for table of symbols

BURGHLEY: In the two six-light windows of the Hall is some interesting C15 glass originally at Tattershall (Lincs) and moved here in 1757 when other related panels were moved to St Martin's Church at Stamford. In one window are four panels set above C16 coats-of-arms and modern glass with scenes of Christ Preaching to the Souls in Hell, Joseph Cast into the Pit, the Mocking of Elijah (?), and a crowd scene — note the toothy grotesque atop! In the other window are numerous reset fragments that include a head of Christ, strangely reminiscent of that at Melbury Bubb in Dorset.

CAMBRIDGE, All Saints: The fine five-light E window here by Morris & Co. of 1866 portrays various figures of the Old and New Testaments — all conveniently labelled. Burne-Jones designed many of the figures. Abraham and Isaac, Noah and Edward the Confessor are all by F.M. Brown, whilst St Catherine and St Peter are by Morris himself (St Peter, incidentally, looks remarkably like W.M.!). On the N side are some rather staid windows by Kempe & Co. and one by the Arts & Crafts Scottish glazier Douglas Strachan evoking 'womanhood' that dates from 1944.

CAMBRIDGE, Jesus College Chapel: The E window here is a Pugin–Hardman collaboration of 1849-50 based on medallions at Chartres, such that the fifteen or so Passion scenes are contained within C13-styled vesicas. They also did four of the lancets on the N wall. Most of the rest of the glass in the chapel is by Morris & Co., the earliest being in the nave SW (1872) with Moses, David, Solomon and scenes from their lives, designed by Burne-Jones, who was also responsible for the big S transept window with the Angelic Hierarchy (1873) and a number of others dating from the period 1872-7. Ford Maddox Brown was responsible for the S transept W window with St Mark, the Phrygian and Libyan Sibyls above the Resurrection, and also for the Passion scenes in the E wall here, below Burne-Jones's St Luke and two other Sibyls.

CAMBRIDGE, Kings College: As full descriptions of these remarkable early C16 windows have already been made in a number of books and pamphlets, only a summary is given here. Nearly all of the twenty-six windows in the main chapel date from the period 1515-30, marking the overlap of Gothic and Renaissance styles; thus the fan vaulting and the somewhat heavy Classical architecture portrayed in the windows have to live comfortably together under the same roof. Henry VII instructed that the windows should portray the Old Law and the New Law which they do, with the scenes sometimes spread across more than one light; the scale is one of large canvasses, and the style unmistakably influenced by Dutch and Flemish paintings of the time. The programme was drawn up by the then Bishop of Winchester, the designs entrusted to Vellert of Antwerp and executed by Dutch and English glaziers resident at Southwark; initially this team was led by Barnard Flower but he died after completing four windows, the work thereafter being done by Galyon Hone together with James Nicholson, Francis Williamson, Richard Bond, Thomas Reves and Symond Symonds. The figures and scenes reveal in their style and design new efforts to achieve realism — look for example at the face of the Unrepentant Thief in the E window: it is quite different from anything seen before in English glass (yet can be seen in the Flemish-inspired windows at, say, Hillesden, Bucks). Unfortunately the legibility of these big scenes, set across stone mullions and within the mosaic of little rectangular panels, does not always aid immediate recognition of what exactly is being portrayed. The windows follow a 'type–antetype' scheme, that is, they portray

incidents of the Old Testament in conjunction with those of the New that they seem to foreshadow or prefigure (*see* p. 29). Each is divided into four sections: upper left and right, lower left and right, with angels or prophets in each central lancet carrying a label. There are twelve windows down each side and the starting point is the N window in the NW corner where all four sections are given over to the birth of the Virgin Mary and events in the lives of her parents, Anne and Joachim, that prelude the event. Thereafter, moving eastwards, the windows describe Christ's birth, childhood, Baptism and life (together with their Old Testament counterparts) up to the Passion which is spread across the wider E window. The easternmost southern window is in fact a C19 work by Hedgeland in the style of the other windows and after Rubens, while the rest of the S windows recount the Resurrection, Ascension and incidents from the life of St Paul, ending with the Assumption and Coronation of the Virgin Mary. Clayton & Bell did the huge W window in 1879, a notable effort in imitation of the rest of the chapel's glass.

If one has any energy left after surveying this splendid display, a visit should be made to the easternmost N and two westernmost chapels where there are many fragments of C15 glass.

CAMBRIDGE, Peterhouse College: In the Chapel the Crucifixion window is by Bernard van Linge of *c.*1632, typical of its time and with much enamel painting. It is flanked by a series of colourful — almost gaudy — windows by Max Ainmuller of Munich, 1855-8. In the Hall bay window of 1870-71 are Ford Maddox Brown's portraits of Homer, Aristotle, Cicero and other worthies, including the college's founder, Hugo de Balsham. He also did a number of the other figures here, Burne-Jones being responsible for St George and Hugo de Balsham. Chaucer's heroines and figures from history and literature in the **SENIOR COMBINATION ROOM** are again by Burne-Jones of the early 1870s and again include the ubiquitous Hugo.

CAMBRIDGE, Trinity College Library: On the S side of the library is the fabulous C18 Alma Mater Window by William Peckitt after Giovanni Battista Cipriani. Alma Mater — the Spirit of Cambridge — presents Sir Isaac Newton to George III. Sir Francis Bacon in Chancellor's robes records the grand occasion; Minerva stands behind the throne, Britannia takes her place beside the king, whilst Fame flies amid the clouds proclaiming the news abroad. In a N window there is a more mundane heraldic coat-of-arms of Queen Anne by Henry Gyles, *c.*1704.

DIDDINGTON, St Laurence: A rather mixed bag of late medieval Continental and English glass, the latter being found in the S chapel where in the right hand window are reconstructed figures of St Margaret and St Catherine (the latter with a new head); between them is Christ resurrecting and the head of St James with a beaver hat; below are three figures (C14?), one with a scroll suggesting he is either St Matthew or Mathias. In the left window are some interesting Continental secular fragments and Flemish roundels with secular and familiar sacred subjects.

DODDINGTON, St Mary: The Crucifixion window in the N aisle is an early (1865) work by Morris, Marshall, Faulkner & Co., originally installed in the church at Langton Green in Kent. Its design was a co-operative effort by members of the firm, Rossetti being responsible for the Crucifixion, Morris for St Peter, and Ford Maddox Brown for St Paul.

ELY Cathedral: Of the original ancient glass at Ely little survives — a few canopy tops in the Lady Chapel and numerous reassembled fragments set into the E window of St Dunstan's Chapel in the SE transept (included here is a roundel of St Etheldreda, founding abbess of the Cathedral). At the W end can be seen some C16 glass originally from St John's church, Rouen, to which was added in the early C19 complementary scenes: the original glass depicts Christ Before Pilate and the Via Dolorosa, and two panels below from a series of the Legend of St John — the saint with Cassiodorus and with St Clement (related panels from Rouen can also be seen at Wells Cathedral and in the Burrell collection). Other fragments can be seen in the cloisters. Very much of its period is the figure of St Peter in the N triforium by James Pearson, 1769, which for a while was part of the E window. In the N tribune (over the N aisle) is the **Ely Stained Glass Museum,** opened in 1979 'to rescue and preserve fine stained glass from redundant churches and other buildings which might otherwise have been lost to posterity ...'; it includes a fine but much-restored Annunciation of *c.*1340 formerly in Hadzor (Worcs), a beautiful head of Christ from Little Brington (Northants), four charming little C14 yellow stain figures (*see illustration*) from the

Small C14 figures under canopies from the Ely Cathedral's Lady Chapel, now in the Ely Stained Glass Museum, Cambridgeshire.

A pair of donor figures, C15, Leverington, Cambs.

Essex). Also here is a good Flemish roundel of the Crucifixion.

HUNTINGDON, All Saints: Clayton & Bell glass of 1860 in the clerestory when the firm was in its prime. Of about the same time is their Te Deum window in which can be seen such diverse people as Queen Victoria, William of Wykeham, Isaac Newton, Béde, Cranmer, Handel and the Duke of Wellington. The W window is by Kempe of 1900 and the E by his successor, Walter Tower, together with J.W. Lisle, 1920.

KIMBOLTON, St Andrew: In the S chapel is a sole C15 tracery light figure with the name 'Symon'. Next door is a rather fussy but fascinating window of 1902 by Tiffany portraying Christ with little children, given by the Cuban Consuelo Yznaga as a memorial to her two daughters, Lady Alice and Lady Jacqueline who so it is believed – appear among the children. Note the characteristic Tiffany thick chunky moulded glass that imparts an almost three dimensional effect. The figure painting is rather disappointing – and is flaking off in places. Also in the S aisle is a good window by Lavers, Barraud & Westlake from sometime after 1868.

LANDWADE, St Nicholas: A remarkable array of saints and apostles of c.1450, the latter carrying Creed scrolls: Sts Matthew, Simon and Bartholomew (N nave); Margaret, the Virgin and Etheldreda (born at nearby Exning); Mark, Luke and two other female figures in N windows; Peter and Andrew in the S transept. On the S side of the nave are the C17 arms of the Cotton family and their alliances.

LEVERINGTON, St Leonard: In the N aisle E window is a highly unusual C15 Tree of Jesse with sixty-one small figures spread across five lights: of these, thirteen are original, seventeen restored and the remainder are modern. The colour of the window is predominantly blue, although each of the figures is painted with pigment and yellow stain on white glass and set against a pot metal coloured background. The disposition of the thirty-one prophets and twenty-seven kings suggests, says Mr Kirby, that the Jesse Tree ideal has been completely misunderstood here: for example, the figures look at one another and not at the Virgin Mary who is even below some of them; prophets have even invaded the central lights 'which has hitherto been inviolate'. Nevertheless, it is a splendid sight. In

Lady Chapel and two excellent C14 figures of St Catherine (*see illustration on* p.39), and St Laurence formerly at Woodwalton (Cambs). There are also a number of modern panels. Ely Cathedral is, as Dr Pevsner describes it, 'an inexhaustible mine of Victorian glass', although some would disagree with his attitude that the study of it amounts to 'somewhat morbid curiosity'. A good booklet prepared by the Cathedral authorities on the sixty-three or so windows is sold in the Cathedral: it lists the many makers, both English and French. Glass particularly worthy of mention is Wailes' E window, those in the octagon and in the N transept also by him. So too, of stylistic rather than aesthetic interest, is the large Clayton & Bell window in the S choir, a good example of the firm's less successful early-to-middle period (the mid-1860s) when yellows and browns became more popular in their designs and the scenes become more crowded. Martin Harrison, an authority on C19 glass and first curator of the stained glass museum here, has suggested that Warrington's window of 1849 and Gibbs' in the S nave are both good examples of the Cathedral's C19 glass; the Gerente window at the eastern end of the S aisle — exhibited at the 1851 Great Exhibition — should be added. Finally there is the **Prior Cauden's Chapel** where the E window is a much-restored Flemish work of c.1800 (related to the glass at Brightlingsea,

the S Chapel E window are two pairs of C15 donor figures (*see illustration* on p.82), including Sir Laurence Everard and Dame Margaret Colville, and a rather restored Pieta, all C15. Something of a mystery is the window in the S chancel that says it was 'restored by T. Curtis, 1924', and portraying six prophets in the late C15 style, reminiscent of the glass at Nettlestead in Kent where Curtis also did some restoration work; this window does contain a few pieces of C15 glass, but is mostly Curtis. The E window is by Daniels & Fricker in the style prevailing in 1920.

MADINGLEY, St Mary Magdalene: Numerous C15 and C16 fragments and part figures, notably in the S chancel window where there is a half-figure of St Bartholomew (with knife), St Mary Magdalene (with casket of precious ointment) and others; next door is an early C16 Crucifixion with Sts Mary and John, and Jerusalem in the background; also here are fragmentary figures of the Virgin and Child and of St John Baptist with Agnus Dei. Some interesting C15 quarries with initials 'IC' (for John Cuts of Childerley Hall?) and a bird and scroll for Bishop Alcock of Ely.

PETERBOROUGH, Cathedral: All that remains of medieval glass are fragments patched up into the upper parts of some apse windows and in some tracery lights in the retrochoir. Some of the C19 glass, however, is good, notably The Agony and Betrayal by Heaton, Butler & Bayne of 1864 in the N transept. Excellent also are Rossetti's Sacrifice of Abraham and Joseph in the Pit, both in the S transept and of 1862. Other windows are by Wailes, Clayton & Bell, Cox & Son, Gibbs and O'Connor.

In the BISHOP'S PALACE nearby are three small early windows by Patrick Reyntiens from around 1960.

THORNEY, Abbey Church of St Mary and St Botolph: There are six splendid panels of late C15 glass depicting the Passion from Cologne (obtained as long ago as 1638, probably by the fourth Earl of Bedford, when many Continental people settled in Thorney). On the S side are St. Peter's Denial, The Supper at Emmaus, the Pieta; on the N side, The Mocking of Christ, The Holy Women Approach the Sepulchre, and The Harrowing of Hell. One name can be identified, Godart Hauser, a distinguished councillor of Cologne at the end of C15. The E window here has some fine C19 glass based on the windows in the Trinity Chapel aisle at Canterbury Cathedral.

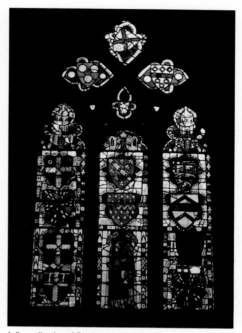

A fine collection of C14 heraldry and the figure of, possibly, William of Ufford, Wimpole, Cambs.

WIMPOLE, St Andrew: A fine display of C14 heraldic glass in the N Chapel, set into three lights and traceries of a N window. The fourteen shields include the arms of England, France, the Prince of Wales and the Ufford, Engaine, Bohum, Tiptoft, Bassingbourne and Avenell families. Also here is the figure, possibly of William of Ufford, pictured as a Compostello pilgrim with staff and cockle shell (*see illustration above*). Much less spectacular are the shields of the Yorke family in the W gallery, painted round the outer rims of the two windows by William Peckitt. (Other shields by Peckitt formerly here have been transferred to the chapel at Erddig in north Wales.)

WISBECH ST MARY: A rather mixed collection of English and Continental glass spread through the church. Bought by the incumbent in the 1920s, the English pieces are rather fragmentary and can be seen mostly in the N aisle windows — they include a charming top-half figure of St Sitha with enormous key, royal coats-of-arms, an angel and C14 roundel. There are some fine heads amongst the Continental glass on the S side of the chancel as well as some good enamel-painted and pot metal coats-of-arms with wreathed surrounds.

CHESHIRE

Some fine C14 glass, that can be related by style to work at Shotwick and Gawsworth, can be seen at Grappenhall. Otherwise Cheshire is rather poorly endowed with old glass. There is, however, an unusual early C17 painted window at Farndon, late medieval Continental windows at Disley, and representative examples of early C20 glass at a number of places.

MR	Place	Centuries									Principal feature(s)
		12	13	14	15	16	17	18	19	20	
1	Alderley Edge								*		B-J and FMB designed glass for WM, 1874
2	Astbury			+	*				*		see below
3	Chester, Cathedral								*		see below
4	– St Mary				*						Passion emblems, C15 saint with wheatsheaf
5	Crewe									*	see below
6	Daresbury									*	see below
7	Disley				*	F					see below
8	Farndon						*				see below
9	Gawsworth			*	+						St Andrew?, Passion emblem, canopy
10	Grappenhall			*					*		see below
11	Great Budworth									*	A. Fisher and Fourmaintreaux ws. for JP
12	Hulme						*				w. by William Peckitt, 1769
13	Malpas					F	F				Presentation of Christ
14	Mobberley	Q	H	H	H	H					C14 arms for de Mobberley, et al.
15	Nantwich			+		H			*	*	see below
16	Over Peover				+						parts of Sts Mary, Christopher et al.
17	Pott Shrigley				*						St John the Baptist, bishop, canopies
18	Prestbury			*							fig. with Saltair cross (cf. Gawsworth)
19	Shotwick			*							a good Annunciation
20	Tattenhall			*					*		see below
21	Warrington						H*	*			hunting scenes: C17 coats-of-arms
22	Wilmslow									*	see below
23	Worleston								*	*	early CEK (1872–82); H.Dearle/WM

See page 280 for table of symbols

ASTBURY, St Mary: Some C14 remains in a S window, but of more interest are the C15 part figures of St Anne Teaching The Virgin Mary, and a Virgin and Child; in some tracery lights of the S aisle are the remains of an Apostle series, censing and musical angels. C19 glass by O'Connor (1871), Ward & Hughes (1872) and Warrington (c.1860).

CHESTER, Cathedral: A fine display of C19 glass, the best perhaps being O'Connor's E window of 1857 in the N choir chapel, and Heaton, Butler & Bayne's E window in the Chapter House. An unusual window of 1961 by W.T. Carter Shapland which Pevsner enigmatically describes as being 'a work that will please many but can also please the few'!

CREWE, St John the Baptist: A splendid rose window in the Arts & Crafts tradition with Christ Amid Angels by A.J. Davis and the Bromsgrove Guild, 1929. Davies was taught by Henry Payne of the Birmingham School of Art who in turn had worked with Christopher Whall, reviver of the Arts & Crafts tradition in c.1900.

DARESBURY, All Saints: The Alice in Wonderland window by Geoffrey Webb of 1932 marked the centenary of Lewis Carroll's birth; it follows the style of Tenniel who did the original illustrations for the book.

DISLEY, St Mary: Some good glass from a variety of sources. The best is possibly in the E window where the C16 panels with Passion scenes come from Steynfrit and date from 1535: above are scenes from the Life of St Elisabeth of Hungary. Over the chancel arch is a panel with Christ among the Doctors of the Church, also C16. In the easternmost window on the S wall is a small C15 window with Christ at The Resurrection with St Mary Magdalene. Nearby are four enamel painted panels of later date with scenes of Adam and Eve in the Garden of Eden with a variety of animals including an elephant and a dromedary!

Fine C14 glass at Grappenhall, Cheshire, with Apostles and St Mary Magdalene, c.1335.

FARNDON, St Chad: The small Gamul Window in the N chapel is a memorial to those who supported Charles I at the siege of Chester in the Civil War; some nineteen figures are painted on to the small panel, five of which are Royalists who distinguished themselves, the rest soldiers and musicians. Portrayed complete with military equipment, they include Richard Grosvenor, Sir William Mainwaring and Sir Francis Gamul, attendant to the king. Maurice Rushworth has pointed out that some of these figures are in fact copies of figures by Abraham Bosse, although the window was probably executed by French artists. Most of the rest of the glass is by James Powell of Whitefriars of the late 1920s/early 1930s, and three by T.M. Cox, c.1962.

GRAPPENHALL, St Wilfred: Very fine glass of c.1335 in the easternmost window on the S side where some of the eight reset figures originally set as quatrefoils include Sts Thomas, John the Baptist with camel skin in the centre beneath a canopy, James with pilgrim's hat and scallop shell, Peter and Bartholomew (here portrayed carrying his own flayed flesh over his arm — a vivid example of medieval realism if ever there was one!). In the tracery lights above are an odd small figure pointing skywards, Sts Philip and Mary Magdalene. Note the neat roses that accompany many of the figures. Of the C19 glass here, the most interesting is Shrigley & Hunt's Adoration of the Lamb in the N aisle of c.1890, an unusual design with equally unusual colouring (*see illustration above*).

NANTWICH, St Mary: In the Chapel of the Virgin Mary the Kempe restored (1876) wheel-traceried window has Nativity scenes and a Tree of Jesse that includes some medieval material. Numerous C14 fragments in chancel windows — one fine piece with St John expelling the demon from the chalice; also the arms for Rope (pre-1572). There are three more good early Kempe windows of 1876 in the N transept, as well as two by Hardman (1862 and 1864); those in the S transept are by Wailes, c.1858. Clayton & Bell did the W window (Christ in the Temple) in 1875, the E window a year later and the Old Testament figures in the N aisle. One C20 rarity is Harry Clarke's rich expressionist window in the S aisle with St Cecilia, the Virgin and Child, and St Richard amid numerous birds. His style is reminiscent of Aubrey Beardsley's.

TATTENHALL, St Alban: Two much-restored C14 figures in the chancel of Sts Stephen and Alban. Also here is an early window by Lavers & Westlake, c.1870.

WILMSLOW, Pownall Hall: In the Hall is some interesting glass with the Signs of the Zodiac and the Four Winds by Shrigley & Hunt of c.1890, designed by artists of the recently formed Century Guild (founded in 1882).

CLEVELAND

MR Place	Centuries									Principal feature(s)
	12	13	14	15	16	17	18	19	20	
1 Guisborough					*					Christ in Judgement, St John the Baptist
2 Hartlepool								*		ws. in W Gallery by DS, 1920s
3 Redcar							*			B-J/WM ws. 1878–99
4 Stockton-on-Tees								*		N.T. S w. by Paul Quail
5 Yarm						*				portly Moses in S w. by Peckitt, 1763

See page 280 for table of symbols

CORNWALL

Very fine late C15/early C16 glass at St Neot which – from the iconographic point of view — is some of the most interesting in Britain. At St Kew and St Winnow are some lovely C15 windows and remains. Lesser amounts of C15 glass can be seen at a number of places throughout the county. Truro Cathedral has a splendid display of C19 glass by Clayton & Bell, the largest job they undertook. It includes three fine rose windows.

MR Place	Centuries									Principal feature(s)
	12	13	14	15	16	17	18	19	20	
1 Blisland								*		late C19 ws. by F.C. Eden
2 Cothele House					*					see below
3 Davidstowe				+H						in tower w.
4 Egloskerry				*						part of a Trinity panel
5 Falmouth					F					Italian Ascension, Sts Philip, John, Matthew
6 Golant				*						Sts Sampson and Anthony
7 Ladock								*		see below
8 Laneast				+						Crucifixion, Sts Christopher, Gulval
9 Lanteglos-by-Camelford				*						a few very corroded t.l. remains
10 Lanteglos-by-Fowey				*				*	*	*see illustration* on p.88, *in situ* C15
11 Liskeard									*	a recent w. by Osmond Caine
12 Lostwithiel								*		Faith, Hope, Charity by TW
13 Mount St Michael				*	F	+				some interesting reset panels
14 Quethiock								*		see below
15 St Germans								*	*	late C19 B-J/WM ws. and later ws. by WM
16 St Ives								*		notable w. by Sir E.Poynter for JP
17 St John			G		O	+				C14 leaf *grisaille*, frags. and roundels

MR	Place	Centuries									Principal feature(s)
		12	13	14	15	16	17	18	19	20	
18	St Kew				*				*		see below
19	St Michael Penkevil								*		early B-J/WM of 1866
20	St Neot				*	*			*		see below
21	St Teath				*	H					Passion emblems; Arundel alliances
22	St Winnow				*	*					see below
23	Sheviock					*			*		female saint; E w. by Wailes for Street
24	Sithney				*						in S a. S w. a bearded figure
25	Truro				+				*		see below

See pages 280 for table of symbols

COTEHELE House: In the Chapel E window is a large early C16 Crucifixion with the Virgin Mary and St John, and above a charming Annunciation. Made for the house, it was restored in the C19: the figure of St John, however, remains almost unaltered. The S window of the same date has St Anne with the Virgin Mary, and St Catherine, again with some restoration. This glass is thought to be contemporary with the windows at Kings College, Cambridge, and Fairford (Glos) and executed by the Anglo-Flemish glaziers at Southwark (*see illustration below*).

St Anne Teaching the Virgin, *c.*1500, Cotehele, Cornwall.

LADOCK, St Ladoca: Early glass by Morris, Marshall, Faulkner & Co. of 1863 where the three Marys are accompanied by the local saint, Ladoca (designed by Morris); also here is The Washing of Christ's Feet and, in the rosette above, Christ Enthroned (both by Burne-Jones). Also by the same firm are two windows of a later date where most of the designing is again by Burne-Jones, except for the figure of St Luke which is by Ford Maddox Brown.

QUETHIOCK, St Hugh: Unusual glass, to say the least, in the W window where the Last Judgement was designed by the incumbent in 1880; he got his own back on his flock by picturing some of them amongst the damned and rewarding others, so it is said, by placing them with the elect!

ST KEW, St James: Fine C15 panels and fragments, of which the best can be seen in the E window of the N chapel with nine scenes from the Passion: the Entry to Jerusalem, the Washing of the Disciples' feet, the Last Supper, the Agony in the Garden, the Betrayal (with St Peter and the High Priest), the Scourging, Judgement Before Pilate, the Via Dolorosa, Crucifixion, Entombment, Harrowing of Hell; below are groups of donors and their families. Over in the SE chapel are the remains of a Tree of Jesse with part figures of David, Solomon, the Virgin Mary and Jesse's head. Broken bits in the E window include St Michael and St Laurence. Of the C19 glass here, the Ascension in the N chancel is clearly influenced by Morris and Co. and there are four fine saints by Kempe & Co. opposite.

ST NEOT, St Anietus: Remarkable glass contemporary with Fairford (Glos) *c.*1500, restored extensively in 1830 but still retaining its late C15 character. Starting in the NW corner is the St George Window which recounts the gory details of events in the saint's legendary life — some of these are unique in that they are not recorded anywhere else in any form; the panels have faded

Shepherds at the Nativity; detail from a window by Charles Kempe of 1905; Lanteglos-by-Fowey, Cornwall.

somewhat, but we can see the saint fighting, killing the dragon, being beheaded by the Gauls, being thrown into molten lead, tortured in a number of novel ways and even being ridden, horse-like, by the king's son! Next door is the less dramatic Legend of St Neot who seemed to suffer nothing more unpleasant than the theft of his oxen; we see how he lived off one fish a day from an inexhaustible well — that is until his servant thought he could do with a good square meal and served up two fish in one day, much to the saint's horror, for such an action rendered the well sterile. However, he returned both fish to the well and miraculously they came back to life, so all was well again. Eastwards down the N aisle, we pass three windows with figures: first Sts Cleer, Manacus of Lanreath, and God holding souls of the saved in a sheet — the conventional medieval representation of the Bosom of Abraham (cf. the W rose windows at Chartres and Nantes); then come St Mabena, the Pieta, Christ at the Resurrection, St Mewbred of Cardinham and, below, the donors — twenty wives from the parish. Next door is the Harys Window, with Sts John, Gregory, Leonard, Andrew and the Harys family below. Behind the organ are two C19 windows by Hedgeland, as is also the main E window. In the E window of the S aisle is the best glass in the church, fifteen scenes that relate events from the Creation up to the time of Noah's Ark according to the Bible, with legendary embellishment. Thus, starting in the top left corner, we see: (1) God planning the creation of the world with a pair of compasses; (2) the division of land and water; (3) the creation of fish and birds; (4) the creation of man and (5) woman; (6) Adam being forbidden to eat the fruit; (7) the temptation by the serpent (note its human head); (8) the expulsion; (9) Adam and Eve at work; (10) Cain and Abel's offerings; (11) Cain kills Abel; (12) Cain sentenced; (13) Cain shot by Lamech (according to Jewish legend); (14) the death of Adam (Seth plants seeds in his mouth to produce the Tree of Knowledge from which the Cross will be hewn); (15) God orders Noah to build the Ark — Noah concurs by lifting his cap politely! In the tracery lights above are a full complement of angels — the complete hierarchy:

Top Row

Seraphim	four wings, blowing trumpets and treading in fire
Thrones	seated, four wings and cross diadem
Cherubim	two wings, diadem and book

Bottom row

Angels	staff and harp
Dominations	gold bottle and mace
Virtues	carrying censers and blowing on the embers
Powers	shield, sword, dragon underfoot
Principalities	princely with banners and orb
Archangels	crowns and sceptres

At the E end of the S aisle we see Noah building and embarking upon the Ark, the dove, Noah's drunkenness and his death. Moving down the S aisle are a series that mirror those in the N aisle. First is the Borlasse Window with Sts Christopher, Neot, Leonard and Catherine; then the Virgin and Child, the Crucifixion, Sts John, Stephen and donors (Martyn) below; next are the four Evangelists with donors (Motton), followed by the Callaway Window with Sts Lalluwy (patron saint of Menheniot), German, John, Stephen and in the tracery lights The Resurrection with St John. Finally at the W end of this S aisle is the Tubbe Window with Sts Paul, Peter, Christ the King and James with Tubbe and Callaway arms below — above is an Annunciation.

ST WINNOW, St Winnow: In this fine and beautiful church with its lovely screen, bench ends, and setting by the riverside there is glass to match. The S aisle E window has late C15 glass with two rows of saints alternating with kneeling donors (*see illustrations on* p.39 *for two of the saints*); they include St George killing the dragon, the Virgin and Child, Sts Christopher and Michael in the first row, and Sts Winnow, the Virgin Mary, Mary Magdalene and Leonard in the second. Each figure is set against flower quarries within a fine border of shields; the traceries have shields, quarries and little borders. The E window's Crucifixion is less satisfying.

TRURO Cathedral: This was the largest job that Clayton & Bell undertook, glazing the newly built Cathedral in the late 1880s. The scheme begins with the Creation and carries on through to the accession of Queen Victoria and the founding of Truro Cathedral (both of which can be seen in the westernmost window in the N aisle). Most spectacular are the main E window and the three great rose windows which portray the Genealogy of Christ (N), The Holy Spirit (S) and the Creation (W). The windows in St Mary's aisle — which is in fact the old parish church — contain glass by William Warrington of *c.*1850, and at the W end a few medieval fragments.

CUMBRIA

A fair amount of medieval glass in the county, particularly in the south. The glass at Greystoke is interesting, if only to see the extraordinary adventures of St Matthew and St Andrew in the City of Dogs! There is also plenty of C19 glass; Henry Holiday's pre-Raphaelite inspired windows seem to have been particularly popular here; they can be seen at the places noted below and Ambleside (1881–91), Bootle (1899), Calderbridge (1877), Grasmere (1891), Keswick (1879, 1889), Ponsonby (1893), Rydal (1891) and Windermere (1905–8).

MR	Place	Centuries									Principal feature(s)
		12	13	14	15	16	17	18	19	20	
1	Alston								*		E w. by Prof. Wooldridge for JP
2	Beck Side			*							Christ giving blessing (S chancel)
3	Bowness-on-W'mere		*	*	*				*		see below
4	Brampton								*	*	see below
5	Brough				*						St John the Baptist (a. N w.)
6	Brougham			*	*						Resurrection, Virgin and Child (E ws.)
7	Carlisle			*					*		see below
8	Cartmel Fell				*						see below
9	Cartmel Priory			*	*						see below
10	Clifton				*						Virgin and St John
11	Cockermouth								*		good E w. by JH, 1853; also CEK, 1897
12	Coniston (R.C.)								*		notable JH w. of 1886
13	Crosthwaite				*						see below
14	Edenhall			*							King (?) Coolwyn and St Cuthbert (E w.)
15	Gilcrux								*		copy of Da Vinci's Last Supper by Chance
16	Greystoke				*				*		see below
17	Haverthwaite				*H						Crucifixion and Virgin and Child (W w.)
18	Kendal									*	Virgin amid Roses, by M.A.Scott for SH, 1922
19	Lanercost Priory								*	*	see below
20	Levenshall Hall					H	H				arms with Bellingham alliances
21	Martindale								*		15 contemporary ws. by Jane Gray
22	Orton								*		unusual w. by Campbell, Smith & Co., 1880
23	Sedbergh								*		General Gordon at Khartoum *et al.* by CEK
24	Shap				*						part fig. of St John (N w.)
25	Staveley								*		good WM of 1881 in E w.
26	Troutbeck								*		see below
27	Wetheral				*						2 saints and kneeling donor (W w.)
28	Whitehaven									*	Virgin and Child by R.F.Ashmead, 1970
29	Witherslack					H	+				arms by Henry Gyles, 1670

See page 280 for table of symbols

St Cecilia by Evie Hone, *c.*1950; Lanercost Priory, Cumbria.

BOWNESS-ON-WINDERMERE, St Martin: The E window has a formidable quantity of C14 and C15 glass. It possibly originated from Cartmel Priory and comprises a partly restored late C15 Crucifixion on Golgatha attended by angels, St Mary and St John who have strange red ribbons that weave about them; to the N are Sts George and Barbara (the latter mostly restoration), whilst to the S is St Catherine and a jumble of C14 fragments that form a quartet of saints, amongst whom can be seen the inseparable Sts Laurence and Stephen; below are excellent though rather restored donor figures — clerics and three gentlemen/knights with their ladies — their coats-of-arms and fragmentary labels; in the tracery lights are some twenty C14 and C15 shields of arms of old Furniss families and C13/C14 fragmentary scenes and pieces, eg the Virgin and Child of *c.*1260, the Entry to Jerusalem and The Resurrection. At the top of the third light from the right are the coats-of-arms of John Washington, twelfth ancestor of George Washington. In the N aisle is a C16 Merchant's Mark of the Lead Carriers. The C19 glass here includes windows by Ward & Hughes and Shrigley & Hunt.

BRAMPTON, St Martin: In this rather unattractive church designed by Philip Webb there is an outstanding collection of windows by Morris & Co., nearly all of which were designed by Burne-Jones. The earliest (1878) is the Adam and Eve Window on the N side amid the numerous labelled figures; the latest is in the NE corner of the chapel dating from 1920 — made over twenty years after the deaths of William Morris and Burne-Jones – that utilises their designs. Burne-Jones himself described his rich and deeply coloured E window of 1880 with Christ as the Good Shepherd as 'a capo d'opera of conception' and charged Morris £200!

CARLISLE Cathedral: The magnificent E window has in its tracery some fine, recently restored C14 glass depicting scenes from the Last Judgement – a pair of binoculars reveal some lively incidents. Below in the main lights is a huge and successful window by John Hardman, *c.*1850.

CARTMEL FELL, St Andrew: Some fine C14 and C15 (?)York School glass in the five-light E window. Christ on the Cross is surrounded by fragment of five of the Seven Sacraments in three inner lights — Communion and Extreme Unction (left) (*see illustration on* p.34), Penance (centre), Confirmation and Marriage (right). In the outer lights are

St Anthony with pig and bell (*see illustration on* p.39), a female donor, and St Leonard dragging his chain; above are canopies and a female donor figure; interspersed with this are fragments of saints, kings, queens (eg St John the Baptist's Lamb and Flag). In a N window some good remains of the Crucifixion, an 'Ecce Homo', and a bishop with Patriarchal Cross.

CARTMEL Priory: Fine remains of a Tree of Jesse in the S aisle E window of *c.*1340 whose figures (one king and six prophets) are reminiscent of those at Madley (Herefs) — one wishes that there was more of this beautiful glass! The angel Gabriel in the tracery light above suggests the former presence of a series of Christ's Childhood, rather than the Doom that usually appears above such Trees in glass of this age (eg at Wells; Carlisle; All Saints, York). On the S side of this Chapel are some reset fragments and panels, notably the angelic trumpeters and the charming figure of an abbess. In the main E window are the large but fragmentary C15 figures of an arch-bishop, the Virgin and Child and St John the Baptist; above them are many saints inhabiting little niches in the numerous tracery lights that seem to go on for ever, although the window is so vast that their number seems diminutive — Andrew, Bartholomew and Matthias can easily be seen, but binoculars reveal many more.

CROSTHWAITE, St Kentigern: In the N aisle is part of an unusual portrayal of St Anthony in C15 glass with his traditional attributes of a crutch, book and pig; his head is encircled by a golden (yellow stained) nimbus, whilst on his scapula there is a tau cross.

GREYSTOKE, St Andrew: A unique subject can be seen in the bottom panels of the E window of *c.*1520 (restored in 1848); it relates the adventures of Sts Matthew and Andrew in Wronden, the City of Dogs, according to an apocryphal legend: Matthew, visiting the City, is imprisoned by its inhabitants; Christ promises to send St Andrew, and St Anthony disguised as a sailor; they reach the city, free Matthew and proceed to a mountain-top where they meet St Peter; the cannibalistic citizens prepare to eat one of their own number in reprisal, but Andrew prevents this by allowing himself to be tortured; he has a vision of trees bear-ing fruit and is miraculously healed; the city is flooded, recovers, is converted to Christianity, and erects a church. Of this we see Andrew outside the city, Christ with Peter and Andrew, Andrew in

St Matthew in prison: the Gothic script seems to read 'Long tyme were set cryst wyght gyfts Mathew here his foly'; *c.*1520, Greystoke, Cumbria.

front of the church, Christ in the boat, Andrew baptising the inhabitants, Matthew in prison, and other composite panels (*see illustration above*). There are other miscellaneous panels that include figures of Christ, St Catherine, the Virgin Mary, St Oswald, St Thomas Becket, a mitred bishop and donor figures (a mother and daughter). The angels in the tracery lights are older, belonging to the previous century. On the S side of the chancel are nine ?C15 roundels with delightful portrayals of birds and animals. A very pictorial Kempe window by the organ, *c.*1901.

LANERCOST Priory: A charming St Cecilia window by Evie Hone — the Cecilia Maude Robert Memorial — of *c.*1848 (*see illustration on* p.90). Three windows by Morris & Co. on the N side: the Evangelist St Luke with a small healing scene below (designed by Burne-Jones), the Burial of Moses (*c.*1902), and (the best of them) Burne-Jones's Annunciation to the Shepherds of *c.*1890, brilliantly set into the long thin lancet at the W end.

TROUTBECK, Church of Jesus: Morris & Co. glass yet again, this time of 1873 where the E window is nearly all designed by Burne-Jones (the Supper at Emmaus by Ford Maddox Brown); amid the angels in the tracery lights is Christ and Mary Magdalene by Burne-Jones, concerning which he said to Morris: "The latter perfectly lovely (the former I grant a failure as usual) but how can I lift myself to the adequate contempla-tion of such a theme at the wretched price of £8 the pair!" (quote from C. Sewter)

DERBYSHIRE

Good medieval glass in the county, eg of the C12 at Dalbury, the C13 at Ashbourne, of the C14 at a number of places – some clearly being by the Nottinghamshire Lenton School (*see* Dronfield) – and excellent C15 glass at Haddon Hall, Morley and Norbury. There is a fair amount of C19 and C20 glass throughout the county.

MR	Place	Centuries									Principal feature(s)
		12	13	14	15	16	17	18	19	20	
1	Ashbourne		*						*	*	see below
2	Ault Hucknall				*						Crucifixion, St Ursula, donors (S a.)
3	Bakewell								*		ws. by JH, 1859–92; also HH, 1893
4	Bamford								*		E w. by Preedy of Worcester, 1860
5	Birchover									*	5-light w. by Brian Clarke, 1971
6	Borrowash									*	Arts & Crafts by A.J.Davies
7	Buxton									*	2 N ws. by Joseph Nuttgens, c.1947
8	Chesterfield, St Bart.								*	*	Nuttgens w. of 1959; WM, 1915
9	– St Mary								*		see below
10	Cubley			*							St Catherine (a. S w.)
11	Dalbury	*									see below
12	Darley Dale								*		good early B-J/WM/Philip Webb, 1862–3
13	Derby, Cathedral									*	2 abstract ws. by Ceri Richards/RP
14	Dronfield			+							see below
15	Egginton			*							Crucifixion, canopies, border
16	Haddon Hall				*						see below
17	Killamarsh			*					*		Virgin and Child (S chancel); Warrington, 1845
18	Matlock									*	HBB chancel w. 1920, LL's E w., 1969
19	Morley				*						see below
20	Netherseal			*							grotesques etc. from Lenton School
21	Norbury, Hall			H	*						Labours of the Month (Jan. and June)
22	– St Mary			H	*				*		see below
23	Ockbrook				*					*	Evangelists in E w., c.1500; E.Payne, 1968
24	Sandiacre			Q+							grotesques etc.
25	Staveley			+		H					Frenchville arms (Gyles); Lenton frags?
26	Swanwick									*	see below
27	Tideswell								*		good E w. by HBB, 1875; W w. by JH
28	West Hallam				*						see below
29	Whitwell			*							Lenton School border (E ws.)
30	Wilne						*				possibly a van Linge w.
31	Youlgreave								*		Salvator Mundi by B-J, 1876; also WM, 1897

See page 280 for table of symbols

ASHBOURNE, St Oswald: Small but fine C13 medallions — always a joy to see — in quatrefoils in the N transept W window set against *grisaille.* The subjects clearly belong to a Nativity cycle: Herod issuing Orders to Massacre the Innocents; the Presentation in the Temple; the Adoration of the Kings; the Kings before Herod; the Angels with the Shepherds. In the N window here are some C14 fragments which include a small Crucifixion painted in yellow stain. Ten C14 coats-of-arms in the E clerestory windows. There is much C19 and early C20 glass of which Warrington's SW lancets of *c.*1857 are notable, as is Kempe's E window of 1896, Burlison & Grylls' W window and one of Christopher Whall's best pieces of 1905 in the S aisle.

CHESTERFIELD, St Mary: A collection of C19 and C20 glass of interest, notably by John Hardman in the S transept of 1875, Heaton, Butler & Bayne of 1890 in the N wall, and by Warrington in the Lady Chapel and St Katherine's Chapel. Margaret Aldrich Rope, who trained at the Birmingham School of Art, has a window in the A & C tradition in the St Peter's Chapel. There are also three early C20 works by Christopher Webb.

DALBURY, Parish Church: A superb mid C12 figure of St Michael with wings and portrayed in the full frontal Romanesque 'orans' positions with both hands held with the palms facing outwards and characteristic staring eyes.

DRONFIELD, St John the Baptist: Although there are no complete stained glass figure panels or scenes in this church, there are some interesting fragments in addition to some fascinating details among border pieces in the S chancel windows: these include the bizarre baboons, and drolleries characteristic of the C14 Lenton School of glaziers who came from the town of the same name in Nottinghamshire. Instrumental angels and saints can also be seen, eg St Cecilia playing the organ and in a SE window parts of figures, one of which is St John the Baptist — all fine drawing in rich C14 colours.

HADDON Hall, Chapel: There is some good glass of 1427 in three windows, although there appears to have been some rearrangement following the disappearance of much glass from the S window during the last century. In a N window is St Michael trampling on the devil, St Anne teaching the Virgin Mary to read and St George spearing the dragon; in the tracery lights are apostles with traditional attributes. The E window has the Crucifixion accompanied by angels carrying chalices, the Virgin Mary and St John the Baptist; above is an Annunciation scene, St Helen, three other fragmentary figures and a royal coat-of-arms.

MORLEY, St Matthew: Splendid glass of *c.*1480, originally from Dale Abbey, purchased in 1539 after the Dissolution. Much restored in 1847 by Warrington, it depicts the Legend of St Helen and fills ten of the twelve panels in the easternmost window in the N chapel; starting top left is: (1) the Making of the Cross: (2) Christ being Crucified; (3) the Burial of the Cross; (4) its whereabouts revealed to Helen; (5) its discovery in AD 326; (6) its efficacy put to the test on a dead body; (7) Chosroes who removed the Cross and refused to be baptised is executed; (8) Chosroes' son accepts baptism; (9) Heraclius finds the city walled up; (10) exultation of the Holy Cross on '18 Kal Oct', ie 14 September; (fragments and composite donor figures fill the other two panels). The next-door window tells in seven of its panels a more mundane yet delightful tale about the local saint, Robert Knaresborough, who: (1) shoots a deer whilst trespassing in a neighbouring park; (2) the gamekeepers complain about him to the king; (3) the saint defends himself to the king; (4) the king tells him to put the deer into a pen, which he does; (5) the keepers again plead with the king; (6) the king announces that he will give the saint as much land as he can plough in a day; (7) using a deer to pull the plough he does so (the eighth panel here is something of a mystery). In the S chapel we return to more conventional subjects, albeit one of them is comparatively rare, ie the window with St Ursula of Cologne and her 11,000 martyred maiden companions represented here as eleven figures in an angel-borne sheet; also here are a Virgin and Child, St Mary Magdalene and the unusual subject of the Te Deum with the Holy Church represented by a pope, cardinal and bishop, together with twelve apostles and thirteen martyrs. The S chapel E window has St Elizabeth and St Peter and below them is set a charming group of donors' children.

NORBURY, St Mary: A fine collection of C14 and C15 glass (some was being repaired and cleaned at the time of writing). The glass in the E window has been assembled from around the church and includes some fine late C15 figures of the apostles, each carrying a Creed scroll, as well as some other (as yet unidentified) saints and heraldic panels; also here at the head of the centre light is an early C16 Trinity panel. The eight side-windows in the chancel contain a splendid display of heraldry, most of which dates from the first half of the C14 — a full list of the coats-of-arms is given in the church — it includes the arms of England, France, Warrenne, Poynings, Fitzherbert and Lancaster. The Fitzherberts appear as donors in the C15 S Chapel E window where the main lights contain St Anne teaching the Virgin Mary to read with St Sitha (with keys) and St Winifred; above them are three other figures, St Barlok (to whom the church is dedicated) flanked by St Anthony and St John the Baptist. In the Lady Chapel are stained glass windows by J.E. Nuttgens.

SWANWICK, St Andrew: The E window is an early work by Martin Travers in the Arts & Crafts tradition and dating from 1923: Travers studied under Sir Ninian Comper and was teaching at the Royal College of Art at about the time he did this window. It was probably executed by J.E. Nuttgens who also did the W window in this church in 1953.

WEST HALLAM, St Wilfred: In a S clerestory window is the C15 figure of St James the Less with a club, possibly originating from Dale Abbey. In the S chancel are some quarries with birds painted and yellow stained onto them. The quarries probably came from old West Hallam Hall.

DEVON

There is much old glass in Devon, but it is fairly widely dispersed around the huge county. The early and late C14 glass at Exeter Cathedral is good, but more intimate are the windows at Bere Ferrers. A visit to Doddiscombsleigh is a must; nor should Torbryan be missed. There is a massive amount of C19 glass in the county which is at present being studied at Exeter University. Of the C20, the Piper/Reyntiens windows at St Andrew in Plymouth are rewarding. The local contemporary glazier, Roy Coomber, has a number of windows installed with Wippells of Exeter. Apart from Woodbury, they can be seen at Budleigh Salterton, East Charlton, Newquay, Blundell's College and James Patterson's are at Appledore, Ashburton, Bideford, Churston Ferrers and St Peter's, Plymouth.

MR	Place	Centuries									Principal feature(s)
		12	13	14	15	16	17	18	19	20	
1	Abbots Bickington			+	*						Sts Christopher, Anthony, Nicholas, Christ
2	Alfington								*		Pugin-designed glass made by JH, 1852
3	Ashcombe				F						Passion scenes
4	Ashton-on-Teign			H+							parts of an Annunciation, figs. etc.
5	Awliscombe					*					Sts Catherine, Barbara, Anne, M.Magdalene
6	Bampton					*					rather jumbled scenes and figs.
7	Bere Ferrers			*							see below
8	Bondleigh				*						Annunciation
9	Bridford				*						Sts Mary Magdalene, John, Catherine
10	Broadwood-Kelly					*					Virgin and Child and donors, c.1523
11	Buckland Monachorum								*		CEK's portraits of Missionaries, c.1910
12	Burlescombe								*		Good w. by JP of c.1858
13	Cadbury				*						Christ, from Seven Sacraments series
14	Calverleigh				F						Crucifixion scene (from Brittany)
15	Cockington			*	*						C15 apostle figs; C14 St Paul
16	Combe Martin								*		N a. E w. by LB
17	Cullompton								*		late WM w., and one by Drake, 1892
18	Doddiscombsleigh				*						see below
19	Dunsford				*						see below
20	East Buckland								*		Crucifixion by Beer of Exeter
21	Exeter, Cathedral			*	F				*		see below
22	– Royal Clarence Htl.					O	O				see below
23	Gittisham					O	O				some Flemish roundels
24	Haccombe			*	F						bishop, archbishop and Virgin
25	Hatherleigh				F						St Peter, Crucifixion (Flemish/German?)
26	Horwood				*						figs. of the apostles
27	Ilfracombe								*		see below
28	Ipplepen				*					*	see below
29	Kelly				*						see below
30	Kenn								*		various ws. by JH, eg the E w. of 1868
31	Littleham				*						Christ, Sts Roche, Michael and the dragon
32	Littlehempston				*						Sts Christopher, Stephen and donors
33	Loddiswell				H						arms of Ferrers, Fortesque, Courtenay
34	Lustleigh				+						Sts Margaret, Catherine, the Virgin et al.
35	Manaton				*						Sts Peter, Andrew, James, John
36	Merton				*						Sts Edward the Conf., Margaret, Christopher
37	Northleigh				*						Sts Peter, Paul, (?)Giles
38	North Tawton				H						arms of Hankforth, Valletort, Bouchier
39	Ottery St Mary								*		see below
40	Pancrasweek				*						Sts Pancras and John the Baptist, and Christ
41	Payhembury				*						see below
42	Plymouth, St Andrew									*	see below
43	Plymstock								*		Te Deum by Fouracre & Watson, 1880
44	Sampford Courtenay				*						Virgin and cherubs in Renaissance style

MR	Place	Centuries									Principal feature(s)
		12	13	14	15	16	17	18	19	20	
45	Shobrooke								*		Shelley Mem. by BG, 1869; Dixon w., 1881
46	Sidmouth				*						Sts Michael, Mary Magdalene, Sidwell, Virgin
47	Tavistock							*		*	see below
48	Torbryan				*						see below
49	Torquay								*		see below
50	Weare Giffard				*						top half of a Tree of Jesse
51	– Hall				*						instrumental musician figs.
52	Woodbury					*				*	parts of donors figs. and bishop; w. by RC
53	Yarcombe				*						some t.l. figs.
54	Yarnscombe			*							angel carrying a shield

See page 280 for table of symbols

BERE FERRERS, St Andrew: Early C14 glass reminiscent of the panels at Eaton Bishop (Herefs) with fine figures of Christ on a rainbow between the donors (de Ferrers); also St James, St Anne teaching the Virgin Mary, another saint and the coats-of-arms of the Carminow and de Ferrers families (*see illustration below*).

DODDISCOMBSLEIGH, St Michael: Magnificent glass of *c.*1450 in the E and four N aisle windows, possibly executed by glaziers from Somerset. The church was reopened in 1879 after years of neglect: Clayton & Bell were responsible for the restoration of the glass. In the E window the Sacraments surround Christ (alas, modern): Eucharist, Matrimony and Confirmation to his left; Holy Orders, Baptism and Extreme Unction (*see illustration on* p.96) to his right, and Penitence below; above are the four saints, Stephen, Laurence, Blaize and one carrying three pots. The array of figures down the N aisle has some interesting portrayals: starting at the E end is St James the Great, the Trinity as three figures and a C19 St Edward; then St Patrick tramples on snakes, St George on the dragon, and St Andrew with saltire cross; next door are a modern St John, the Virgin Mary and St Paul with his hand over his eye; then St Christopher carrying the Christ Child, St Michael and a modern St Peter.

DUNSFORD, St Mary: Above the main lights on the S side are some charming tracery lights with C15 glass reminiscent of the work at Doddiscombsleigh but, as it were, of the glaziers' cheaper line; in one set are four rather unusual-looking figures, possibly the Doctors of the Church; next door are some rather heavy yellow stained angels. The traceries on the N side house some better-drawn and charming figures of the female saints Margaret, Barbara and Catherine.

EXETER Cathedral: The great E window here with its C14 glass was restored by Frederick Drake

in 1884 and is (at the time of writing) undergoing further cleaning. It contains glass that belongs to two main phases of glazing in the C14, by Lyen (*c.*1390) and Walter (*c.*1303) — finalisation of the details of what glass belongs to which phase has still to be ascertained — and added to this are Peckitt's C18 additions. However, there are fine figures of Sts Margaret, Catherine, Mary Magdalene, the Virgin Mary, Martin, Peter, Paul and

Lady Isota de Ferrers and coat-of-arms against strapwork and quarries, early C14, Bere Ferrers, Devon.

95

Sacrament of Extreme Unction, C15, Doddiscombsleigh, Devon.

Andrew all in the bottom row; above them are St Sidwell with a huge scythe and St Helen with the Cross, Sts Michael, Gabriel and Catherine and the two saint/kings Edward and Edmund; in the top row are Abraham, Moses and Isaiah. The white borders to each light in this window makes it shine with great force in the morning sun. To the right on the N wall are four more C14 figures, amongst whom is St Philip. The Lady Chapel has a fine collection of C15 Flemish and French panels set against white glass in the S windows: they came to Exeter from the Costessy collection and include scenes from a type–antetype series: eg Samson at the gates of Gaza, Joab slaying Amasa, Elisha and the Shunamite woman, Judas accepting the bribe, Doubting Thomas, the Virgin Mary with Christ and St Anne. Other C15 remains and fragments can be seen in various chapels, notably the kneeling donors in the NE St John Chapel, and part of a Crucifixion in St Gabriel's Chapel.

Most of the C19 glass was destroyed in the Second World War: some has been repaired, e.g. Clayton & Bell's Boer War Memorial and Burlison & Grylls 'Tanner Window', both in the S aisle. Of the C20 is Marion Grant's 'Triumph of Right over Wrong' in the Lady Chapel, as well as three windows by A.F. Erridge and one each by Sir Ninian Comper and Hugh Easton (in the St Andrew's and St James' Chapels).

EXETER, Royal Clarence Hotel (Orchard's Carvery Café): A nice bonus for stained glass hunters seeking refreshment, for in the windows are some thirty interesting sacred and secular panels of Continental C16-C18 glass, some in colour, some in monochrome; amongst them are fine depictions of Jonah and the Whale, St Cyril, St Giles, Baalam and the Flagellation of Christ.

ILFRACOMBE, Holy Trinity: An above-average, interesting collection of C19 glass: eg the Stubb Memorial Window in the N aisle by Ballantine of 1866 (his windows are comparatively rare outside Scotland); John Hardman's E window of 1861; Willement (S aisle); O'Connor (N aisle); and Kempe & Co. (N aisle), by the tower (1896).

IPPLEPEN, St Andrew: Behind the beautiful C15 fan-vaulted screen is Kempe's not over-obtrusive Venite E window; in the tracery lights are some fine figures and coats-of-arms for Henry VII, Bishop Grandison (1327-70) and Bishop Lacy (1420–56) held, as it were, by hands from heaven. The figure with a red hat is probably Cardinal Beaufort — for whom an obit of remembrance was ordered in 1473. Also here are the C15 figures of St(?)Dorothy with roses in her hair, St John the Baptist and St Thomas. Other early C20 windows by Kempe & Co., and one by Drake of Exeter.

KELLY, St Mary: In the E window of the N aisle is a fine large – but much restored – C15 Crucifixion window where Sts Mary and John are joined by St Edward the Confessor, all set against quarries and within a beautiful border; above and below are the arms of Kelly and Tremayne.

OTTERY ST MARY, St Mary: An interesting collection of glass from the early 1850s in a number of windows around the church. Typical of that time is the huge W window of the N aisle where Wailes' 'Glorious company of the Apostles' is drawn in a style that has evolved only slightly from the C18. More advanced is the small Hardman window of c.1850 with the Stoning of St Stephen, as well as Warrington's Transfiguration and scenes from the disciples' lives window.

PAYHEMBURY, St Mary: Some nice little C15 tracery light figures can be seen here, particularly in the second window from the W in the N aisle; on deep colours and well drawn are Sts Blaise (with comb), Laurence, Stephen and Vincent (with two cruets). Next door, only the delightful figure of St Apollonia (*see illustration on this page*) with a pair of pincers and elephantine-sized tooth is medieval, the rest are obviously modern. Also arms of Malherbe, Ferrers, Courtenay and Wotton.

PLYMOUTH, St Andrew: Six splendid large windows of the 1960s by John Piper and Patrick Reyntiens in their colourful and symbolic style: Instruments of the Passion and St Andrew's Cross can be seen in the W window (the Astor Memorial) of 1962, the Four Elements (1963) in the E window, Symbols of the Virgin Mary (in the Lady Chapel), St Catherine's Wheel and the Four Evangelists, all of 1965-6, the symbols of the Creation, of the Trinity and the golden coloured Music Window in the transepts. One cannot help but wonder what the whole church would look like, filled with their glass!

TAVISTOCK, St Eustachius: A huge amount of Victorian and early C20 glass by numerous firms, some of which is pleasing. Unmistakable is the N aisle E window designed mostly by Burne-Jones (angels by Morris) with Old and New Testament figures and scenes from Christ's childhood and life. In the S aisle, between Mayer's and Clayton & Bell's windows is a work by Percy Bacon.

TORBRYAN, Holy Trinity: The E window here has some good C15 figures of female saints, some of which are also painted on to the fine fan-vaulted screen of about the same age. Sts Dorothy and Catherine, for example, appear on both with the same attributes in both portrayals. The window also depicts Sts Anastasia, Bridget and Sidwell (or Sitha — she carries keys and a scythe!) whereas the figures of Margaret, Martha and Apollonia are new. In the S chancel are the four Doctors of the Church, Sts Gregory, Jerome,

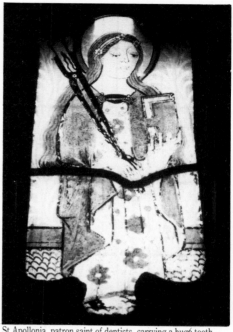

St Apollonia, patron saint of dentists, carrying a hugé tooth, C15, Payhembury, Devon.

Augustine and Ambrose, with their names written on to scrolls. Most of the seraphim that process round the church through most of the tracery lights are in modern glass, although there are old fragments in some of them.

TORQUAY, St John the Evangelist: The five-light E window with its rose above is a splendid affair by Morris, Marshall, Faulkner & Co., dating from 1865, with saints, angels and Old Testament figures designed by Burne-Jones; he was paid £5 per figure and 23 shillings for the angels — 'What a price for such figures,' he lamented in a letter to Morris (quote from C. Sewter; see Bibliography). The W window of 1890 is also by the firm.

DORSET

Dorset must once have been particularly rich in C15 glass for there are many places with fragmentary remains and a few panels; but, apart from the window in Sherborne almshouses chapel, large displays are, alas, virtually non-existent. C19 glass abounds, as always, and at Sturminster Newton it is particularly good, together with some interesting windows by C20 artists, notably Harry Clarke, Isobel Gloag and Mary Lowndes.

MR	Place	Centuries									Principal feature(s)
		12	13	14	15	16	17	18	19	20	
1	Abbotsbury			G+							various figs., scenes; *grisaille*
2	Almer					F	F				N.T. scenes in Swiss glass
3	Bournemouth, Mus.									*	see below
4	– St Peter								*		see below
5	– St Stephen								*		see below
6	Bourton								*		two early ws. by CEK of c.1878
7	Bradford Abbas				*		FH				an angel and St John
8	Bradford Peverell				*						see below
9	Cattistock								*	*	see below
10	Cerne Abbas			H							many fine coats-of-arms
11	Christchurch, Priory								*		Te Deum by LB, 1861; also by OC, 1875
12	Creech Heath								*		pictorial w. by TW, 1849
13	Dorchester, Cemetery								*		early w. by C.Whall, c.1890
14	– Museum				*						St Edmund
15	Ibberton				*						some rather faded figs.
16	Kingston								*		CB glass in Lausanne-like rose w., c.1890
17	Langton Long								*		HBB w., 1862, for T.T.Wyatt
18	Loders				*						Sts Barbara, Dorothy, (?)Leonard
19	Lydlinch				*						4 feathered angels
20	Lyme Regis								*		Westlake's E w. of 1882
21	Lytchett Matravers				*						Sts Anne, Thomas and (?)Denis
22	Mapperton					O					saints, N.T. scenes, arms
23	Marnhull			Q							some C14 Qs
24	Melbury Bubb				*						see below
25	Melbury Sampford				H						heraldic glass formerly at Melbury House
26	Melcombe Horsey				*						Christ, Christopher and the Four Doctors
27	Milton Abbas				H	H	H				arms of Anglo-Saxon King Athelstan
28	Monkton Wyld								*		five good ws. by JP, 1875
29	Poole									*	see below
30	Portland									*	Avalanche Mem. with 106 lenses for lives lost
31	Sandford Orcas			H	H	H					various remains of C14 to C17
32	Sherborne, Abbey				+				*		see below
33	– Almshouses				*						see below
34	Silton								*		Wise and Foolish Virgin by A.Bell, c.1880
35	South Perrott			G			*				roundels of Last Supper and Crucifixion
36	Stinsford									*	Thomas Hardy Mem. by D.Strachan
37	Stour Provost									*	Jasper and Molly Kettlewell w. of 1960
38	Sturminster Newton								*	*	see below
39	Symondsbury								*		rare w. by W.R.Lethaby, 1880
40	Tarrant Gunville					H					arms of Henry VIII with the Catherines
41	Thornford			Q*							bird Qs, St Stephen
42	Trent				*	F	F				see below
43	Westbourne				*					*	19 modern ws. by JH
44	Wimborne Minster				*				*		see below
45	Wimborne St Giles				F						donor with St Andrew; Entry into Jerusalem

See page 280 for table of symbols

BOURNEMOUTH, Russell-Coates Art Gallery and Museum:

There is a large amount of *in situ* glass here, dating presumably from when the museum was built in 1894. There are many natural subjects in the windows — swallows, leaves, flowers, berries, radiant suns etc. — all rather Art Nouveau-ish in flavour. The skylight (25′ × 10′) in the main hall is dull, to say the least — far more interesting is the smaller dome-shaped window above the staircase.

BOURNEMOUTH, St Peter:

In this church by Street there is some fine glass dating from the second half of the C19, eg Burne-Jones' early window with the Miracles of Christ (1864) in the S Chapel. Clayton & Bell has some good work here, more pictorial and on a smaller scale than at St Stephen's Church close by (qv); they did the E window (1866), scenes from St John's Revelation in the window on the N side of the nave (1874), the W tower window, and the Te Deum window in the S transept, where John Keeble is said to be portrayed amongst those praising God. The windows in the aisle are by Wailes (1852–7) and at the W end of the S aisle is Percy Bacon's Nativity Window of 1896, verging on Art Nouveau.

BOURNEMOUTH, St Stephen: Sumptuously rich and glowing glass by Clayton & Bell for Pearson, possibly rather on the heavy side, but very much of its date (1881–98) and reminiscent of Truro Cathedral. The clerestory has been left with clear glass, otherwise it would be almost impossible for people to see their way around — as is the case in Chartres immediately after entering on a sunny day. A fine nine-petal rose window with archangels below in the N transept.

BRADFORD PEVERELL, St Mary: In a N chancel window there is a delightful C15 Coronation of the Virgin and Annunciation scene, somewhat restored, together with interesting quarries and orange/brown silver stained border. The E window is a powerful and richly coloured imitation of C14 glass at New College, Oxford, that does in fact contain some old fragments. In the nave can be seen William of Wykeham's coat-of-arms and motto 'manare makythe man', again much restored.

CATTISTOCK, St Peter and St Paul: Some interesting C19 and C20 windows in a number of places. The Morris & Co. window with angels amongst the stars is very rich and satisfying (St Michael and the angel-musician by Burne-Jones *see illustration,* and the rest by Morris). In the W window is a Tree of Jesse, said to be by Clayton & Bell, 1858. The St Dorothy window on the N side is very much of the Arts & Crafts tradition and is by Robert Anning Bell, *c.*1920; opposite is an Annunciation by Tower of 1916; both are well executed but neither seems to inspire.

MELBURY BUBB, St Mary: Late C15 glass in a number of windows, some of it of high quality. The centrepiece is in the N aisle where there is a fine figure of Christ Displaying the Wounds in what one could describe as a 'west country style': the face with small eyes and halo are very similar to portrayals at Crudwell (Wilts), East Brent (Somerset) and Sherborne Abbey. Clearly there was a Seven Sacrament Series here once as at Crudwell, although only Holy Orders survives now (*see illustration on* p.100). Above in the traceries is a beautiful Annunciation with the two figures of the Virgin and the angel Gabriel on chequered floors: also here is a rare representation of the Wise and Foolish Virgins — four of them. The main W window has a splendid display in the tracery lights, with God the Father, the Dove of the Holy Spirit and eleven of the twelve

Angel-musician by Burne-Jones for William Morris & Co., 1882, Cattistock, Dorset.

Apostles all depicted in yellow stain and dark pigment. Shields of arms in the E window for Warre and Maltravers are accompanied by symbols of the Evangelists and the date 1466.

POOLE, St Osmond, Parkestone: A rather dull, heavy building with equally dull, heavy rose windows, yet the glasswork in them — an arrangement of thick chunks of glass — is rather successful. It is by the architect, Professor Prior Cant, and dates from 1913-16.

SHERBORNE Abbey: Very little old glass survives   what there is has been assembled in the St Catherine and St Mary-le-Bow chapels. The fragments include a tiny head of Christ with the Cruciform halo, reminiscent of that at Crudwell (Wilts), some labelled prophet figures, St Thomas, a Pelican-in-her-Piety and some coats-of-arms. The S window of the S transept has John Hardman's huge Te Deum window of 1851-2; designed by Pugin, it houses ninety-six figures, all labelled and neatly arranged in pairs;

Opposite: The Sacrament of Confirmation, C15, St Mary, Melbury Bubb, Dorset.

some of the faces are beginning to fade, unfortunately. The W window is also by Pugin/Hardman. More interesting are the (rather difficult to see) choir clerestory figures of early church worthies, well drawn and in rich colours, an early work of Clayton & Bell (*c.*1857). Christopher Webb's Annunciation and Nativity in the Lady Chapel is typical of the artist's work.

SHERBORNE, Almshouses Chapel: The S window here has three fine mid C15 figures of the Somerset school that have somehow survived the test of time. It depicts the Virgin Mary and the two St Johns, with Evangelists' symbols and an Agnus Dei in the tracery lights above and Passion shields below.

STURMINSTER NEWTON, St Mary: The Roma Spencer Smith Memorial of 1921 is one of the few windows in England by Harry Clarke of Dublin — and very good it is too. With his unique style, rich palette of colours and exotic figure-drawing he depicts St Elisabeth of Hungary, the Virgin and Child, and St Barbara in the main lights, and two kneeling angels (*see illustration on* p.69) embracing a scene of the shepherds watching over their flocks by night. The E window is a very cosmic effort by Hardman of 1865 with the Acts of Mercy; whilst the very stern Arts & Crafts three-light window of 1901 in the S chapel is by Mary Lowndes and Isobel Gloag — the former founded the firm Lowndes & Drury whose

premises in Fulham have been used by many glaziers, from Christopher Whall and his school at the turn of the century until the present day, thus perpetuating the spirit and tradition of the Arts & Crafts ideals.

TRENT, St Andrew: Behind the beautiful C15 fan-vaulted screen carved by the monks of Glastonbury is the E window with its fine display of C16 and C17 Swiss and German panels. Of the many pieces of assorted shapes and sizes assembled in the C19 is a large scene of Christ as the Gardener in Gethsemane, a Crucifixion, St Margaret, an Ascension and Mary, Queen of Heaven. Many of them are enamel painted, and the heraldry and writing suggest that some come from St Gallen, Wettingen, Lucerne and Cologne. Of quite a different pedigree are the twelve Apostles in the chancel windows by Wailes (1843) representing the Turner Memorial, and there are other windows by him of the same age in the nave. O'Connor's pleasing window of 1871 in the S transept shows well his very individual approach to colouring and canopy design (*see illustration on* p.57).

WIMBORNE Minster: In the E window is the remains of an early C16 Tree of Jesse originally from the Low Countries; it has a number of complete figures, including the Virgin and Child, and King David. The W window is a notable early work by Heaton, Butler & Bayne of 1857, and in the N aisle some colourful small compositions of 1859 are said to be by Gibbs, but look more like Clayton & Bell.

DURHAM

Only a few panels and fragments of indigenous glass survive from medieval times at Durham Cathedral, Lanchester, and Wycliffe. There are, however, some fine, recently identified pieces from St Denis at Raby Castle.

MR	Place	Centuries									Principal feature(s)
		12	13	14	15	16	17	18	19	20	
1	Barnard Castle					F	F	F			many uncatalogued German/Flemish panels
2	Darlington, Hospital									*	complete d-d-v scheme by A. Fisher, 1980
3	Durham, Castle								*		much glass by CEK of the 1880s
4	– Cathedral			*	*			*			see below
5	– St Oswald								*		see below
6	Lanchester		*								see below
7	Raby Castle	F	F			F					see below
8	Staindrop				H	H			*		arms of Neville, Gifford, Greystock, Percy
9	Ushaw								*		see below
10	Wycliffe		*	*							see below

See page 280 for table of symbols

DURHAM Cathedral: Much glass has been lost here through the familiar combination of Puritan destruction, alteration and discarding of unfashionable 'old' glass, neglect, fire and tempest; but here it had also to contend with bored Scottish prisoners locked into the Cathedral: inevitably they took pot shots at the windows to help pass the time and make their protest. Recently a study by Jeremy Haselock and David O'Connor has attempted to elucidate the original glazing programme and catalogue the comparatively few remains that exist. There is a pale coloured mosaic of fragments in a S chancel window, but the more interesting remains are in the S transept and Galilee Chapel. In the former place there is a St Leonard of c.1345 in the E window, and in some S tracery lights eight figures of saints above Clayton & Bell's window, two of which are Benedictine monks. On the S and W sides of the Galilee Chapel are windows with reset pieces of old glass, some indigenous and some imported; of the four on the W wall the southernmost window has a scene of the sacrament of Matrimony (c.1435), the top half of a fine C14 panel with a bishop under a canopy, the arms of Ravenscroft impaling Mountford and Passion emblems on shields. Next door the numerous reset pieces include the composite figures of two saints, one a Benedictine and the other St Bede, c.1430; also some parts of a late C14 Tree of Jesse, a C15 censing angel and the arms of Greystock and Percy. The central W window has more fragments, including a tonsured donor and small C15 dragon; the tracery lights include a fragmentary panel with the Flight Into Egypt and a group around the Virgin and Child. The right-hand window here has some Flemish and French panels (bought in 1957), in addition to a superb Crucifixion fragment placed between the sun and moon set against quarries (*see illustration on* p.9). In the Chapter House are delightful bird quarries, a saint trampling on a devil and St Christopher with the Christ Child, late C15, Gartered royal arms, St John the Baptist, Henry VII's crown in a hawthorn and other bits.

There is inevitably much glass of the C19, notably by Clayton & Bell whose fine Tree of Jesse adorns the W window; their glass in the Chapel of The Nine Altars beneath their fine rose window – although darkening in places – does help generate a real atmosphere in the NE corner of the Cathedral. Other glass includes C20 windows by Hugh Easton (three at the W end of the nave), and by Pugin and Alan Younger in the Galilee Chapel, the latter commemorating the 1,300th anniversary of the Venerable Bede's birthday in 1973. Most

recent of all is Mark Angus's 'Daily Bread' Window in the N aisle, with strong symbolical colouring (blue for heaven, green/earth, purple/God) and thirteen symbols within the shape of life's table.

DURHAM, St Oswald: The W window here has a fine window by Morris, Marshall & Faulkner, c.1865, with incidents from the life of St Oswald — some of the scenes were designed by Ford Maddox Brown.

LANCHESTER, All Saints: Three fine panels of early C13 glass from a Nativity series with The Annunciation to the Shepherds, The Adoration of the Magi and The Flight into Egypt, all with fine scrollwork and Lombardic lettering.

RABY Castle Chapel: Recent cleaning and restoration of the glass by Peter Gibson and the York Glaziers' Trust has led to the virtual rediscovery of some very significant C12 and C13 glass; indeed Dr Peter Newton and David O'Connor have identified portions of three figure panels and four border pieces as originating from St Denis near Paris that probably found their way into the chapel via Christopher Hampp (*see* p.56) in the early C19; in a S window tracery light are the fine remains of a panel from the St Denis Infancy Window of c.1144 depicting the three kings, one of whom is being warned of Herod's intentions; two heart-shaped border panels and the figure of Isaiah holding a scroll saying 'Ecce Virgo', also from the Infancy Window; part of a panel of a tonsured monk in simple habit with a red nimbus and seated before a lectern, identified as being part of the St Benedict's Window at St Denis (part of which is also at Wilton and Twycross); in a neighbouring window are two more remains from St Denis. In a N wall window is the standing figure of a female saint with martyr's palm (c.1280) and a tonsured monk in a brownish pink robe and holding a book (c.1250), both probably French. Also in the chapel are two Flemish roundels with the Sacrifice of Isaac, The Presentation, The Holy Family and Passion emblems; ecclesiastical saints and armorials of Renaissance age probably from a German Cistercian abbey, and an early C16 panel of a kneeling king (from an Adoration of the Magi?).

USHAW, St Cuthbert's College Chapel: The W window is a fine Hardman/Pugin collaboration of 1847, 'their undoubted masterpiece', says Martin Harrison. The E window in the Chapel of St Joseph is also by them.

WYCLIFFE, St Mary: In the tracery lights of some S chancel windows are panels with a Mercy Seat Trinity, The Virgin and Child (twice), musician angels, Christ in Majesty with two angels, St John the Baptist, angels and instruments of the Passion — also some remnants of apostles and a deacon under "perspective' canopies, *c.*1375. In the N chancel are some armorials set against *grisaille, c.*1300, and the rather darkened panel of a prophet, *c.*1290.

ESSEX

There is much fine stained glass in Essex, ranging from some of the earliest panels in Britain at Rivenhall (of C12), through some good work of the C15 at Clavering and Margaretting, of C16 at Prittlewell Church/Museum and of C17 at Messing, to interesting early work by Burne-Jones at Waltham Abbey and of C20 at Thundersley and Harlow New Town. Fragments of old glass can be found in many of the charming little churches scattered throughout the county.

MR	Place	Centuries									Principal feature(s)
		12	13	14	15	16	17	18	19	20	
1	Abbess Roding				*						St Margaret and St (?)Edmund
2	Alphamstone			G*							frag. fig. in S a.; *grisaille* in chancel
3	Arkesden				H						arms of Fox/Bigwood, Arundel/Warenne
4	Audley End, House				+		*				Last Supper by Peckitt; Chicksands' frags.
5	– St Marks			Q*							Virgin and Child; bird Qs
6	Belchamp Walter			*							small Virgin and Child
7	Brightlingsea				+		F				St Paul; Life of the Virgin, 1982
8	Broomfield									*	N.T. scenes by Rosemary Rutherford, 1951-6
9	Chelmsford, Mus.			*							May and October from the Month's Labours
10	Chigwell, School									*	recent glass by Paul Quail
11	Clavering				*						see below
12	Coggeshall									*	St Catherine and Peace ws. by LCE, 1975
13	Colchester, Mus.			+	F		H				C17 heraldics; some French ws.
14	Easthorpe				F						scene with Christ preaching (Swiss?)
15	Eastwood									*	former vicar/geographer memorial by FS
16	Frinton-on-Sea								*		early WM & Co. w. designed by B-J
17	Gestingthorpe				*						Virgin and Child
18	Great Bardfield			*							see below
19	Great Dunmow			+	+	O					Trinity emblems, canopy bits; many roundels
20	Harlow, NT (R.C.)									*	good ws. by Goalen of Buckfast Abbey
21	– St Mary			*	*	*	H*	*			see below
22	Hatfield Peverel				F	O					numerous Continental panels – German?
23	Heybridge		*								late C13 fig. of a saint
24	Lambourne						F				see below
25	Layer Marney			H	HF						St Peter
26	Leigh-on-Sea									*	see below
27	Lindsell		G	*	*	*					C15 Virgin and Child; C16 donor figs.
28	Liston				*						Sts Marg.,Anne,Mary,George,M.Magdalene
29	Little Baddow			*							Sts Michael and (?)George
30	Little Easton				*						see below
31	Maldon				H	*					3 N.T. scenes; arms of Henry VIII
32	Manningtree					F					3 panels with Sts Paul, John and Jerome
33	Margaretting				*						see below
34	Mashbury			*							unidentified saint with a book
35	Messing						*				see below
36	Newport			*					*		Sts Margaret & Catherine; Elijah by CB
37	Prittlewell					F				*	see below
38	Rivenhall	F	F		FO						see below
39	Roxwell						F				N.T. subjects and Virtues, *c.*1600
40	Saffron Walden								*		much C19 glass by JP and LBW
41	Sheering			*							see below
42	South Shoebury								*		early w. by JP, 1858

MR Place	Centuries									Principal feature(s)
	12	13	14	15	16	17	18	19	20	
43 South Weald				F		*				2 Flemish O.T. scenes
44 Stambourne					*					donor figs. (McWilliam)
45 Stapleford Abbotts			*							St Edward the Confessor
46 Stisted					F					Flemish panels set into E lancets
47 Thaxted			*	*						see below
48 Thundersley									*	good vast St Peter ws. by RB, 1966
49 Toppesfield				*						small scene of Coronation of the Virgin
50 Twinstead								*		good early w. by JH, c.1860
51 Waltham Abbey								*	*	see below
52 White Notley			*		*	+				St Etheldreda
53 Widdington			H			*				sundial dated 1664

See page 280 for table of symbols

CLAVERING, St Mary and St Clement:
Some glass from the Norwich School in the N aisle
E window — i.e. of the highest quality — depicting
scenes from the life of St Catherine in four panels;
she can be seen disputing with the four of the fifty
philosophers in one panel: they are then committed
to the flames for failing to answer her questions —
yet their souls ascend to God the Father in a tracery
light; St Catherine is then seen with the emperor
Maxentius; she is taken to prison for refusing to
marry him. More C15 remains can also be seen in
four sets of N tracery lights: Gabriel, angels and
fragments; part of another St Catherine scene,
angels; part figure of St Michael and Christ;
Sts Apollonia with pincers, Petronilla, the Virgin
Mary and Christ, Sitha with basket and Cecilia. In
the S aisle E window are parts of the figures of
angels and St Erasmus praying.

GREAT BARDFIELD, St Mary: In the
easternmost quatrefoils of the N window are three
small late C14 figures set in a border of ring and
dot: St Laurence, St Stephen and the Crucifixion;
St Stephen appears again next door along with a
mainly modern Trinity panel. In the N aisle W
window are various royal shields of arms, two of
which impale the arms of Mortimer (husband of
Edward III's granddaughter Philippa), fine heraldic work that utilises the technique of producing
green by yellow staining blue glass.

HARLOW, St Mary and St Hugh: A beautiful C14 Virgin and Child in the vestry with vine-leaf
border and set on quarries of oak leaves and
flowers. The N transept houses an assemblage of
pieces that span C14 to C18: the two crowned
wreaths with roses, portcullis and the initials
'H.R.' are early C16; slightly later is the Crown and
Garter and shields of royal arms. In round panels
(dated 1563) are incidents in the life of Solomon,
decidedly Renaissance in style. There are also
other royal C17 coats-of-arms and portraits of King

Charles I and Queen Anne from the C18. Note
King Charles I's martyr's crown.

LAMBOURNE, St Mary and All Saints:
Five German (or possibly Swiss) C17 panels, some
dated: The Choice Between Good and Evil, 1630;
Adoration of the Magi, 1637; The Incredulity of
St Thomas; Christ Walking on the Water, 1631;
Adoration of the Shepherds. Each has a shield of
arms and above them are the Annunciation, The
Apocalypse and St Christopher.

**LEIGH-ON-SEA, the churches of
St Clement and St Margaret:** Both of these
churches have modern glass by Francis Stephens.
The earlier of the two is at ST MARGARET'S where
the Epiphany in the Lady Chapel E window dates
from 1950, 'obviously by a disciple of Martin
Travers,' he confesses. At ST CLEMENT'S is his
Madonna and Child window of 1971.

LITTLE EASTON, St Mary: Six panels in
two S windows have C17 German glass painted by
Batista Sutton. Originally in the chapel of Easton
Lodge and given to the church in 1857, they
portray five Passion scenes and – somewhat out of
place, it would seem – The Adoration of the Shepherds. The style is similar to that of the windows in
the chapel of the Trinity Hospital at Guildford and
to glass at St Leonard's, Apethorpe (Northants).

MARGARETTING, St Margaret: The
much restored but fine Tree of Jesse dates from
c.1460 and was made by the King's glazier John
Prudde (see his *chef d'oeuvre* at the Beauchamp
Chapel at Warwick). Originally in the N wall, it has
three lights with four panels in each: a huge Jesse
at the base has pairs of kings and prophets in the
encircling branches above, and the Virgin and
Child at the top. The figures are all conveniently
labelled and include such personalities as Abraham
and Isaac, not usually found in Jesse Trees.

104

MESSING, All Saints: Six of the Seven Works of Mercy are in the E window, a work that is attributed to Abraham van Linge, c.1640, with Faith, Hope and Charity in the tracery lights.

PRITTLEWELL, St Mary: The glass in the Jesus Chapel E wall has an interesting history. It was originally 'salvaged' from a SW window in the church of St Ouen, Rouen, soon after the French Revolution; it was purchased by an Englishman soon after and subsequently sat forgotten in a packing case until the 1880s when it was given to the church by the Neave family. Reset by the A. K. Nicholson studios, these twelve early C16 panels are particularly interesting in that the hand of Albrecht Dürer can be seen in the design of some of them. The twelve scenes are: Elijah's Sacrifice on Mount Carmel, Jesse asleep under a canopy becomes the root of the Tree (note David with his harp in its branches), Elisha Raising the Shunamite Woman's Daughter, the Virgin and Child, Jesus being led bound from Annas to Caiaphas, and to the Crucifixion, St John the Baptist meets Jesus, The Offer of Fish and Honey to Jesus after the Crucifixion, the Temptation in the Wilderness, the Rebuilding of Jerusalem, the Death of David and Crowning of Solomon, and the Burning Fiery Furnace. Evidence of Dürer's involvement is suggested by the strange hand-signal given by one of the people in the panel with Jesus being led to the Crucifixion, by Jesse's beard, and by the Nuremberg towers in the Elisha panel.

There are also some interesting C19 and C20 panels here, notably the flamboyant P. C. Bacon's window with Sir Galahad, King Arthur, St George and St Michael in the porch of c.1922, and his Crucifixion (nave S) and Annunciation (chancel), c.1929. In the S wall of the Jesus Chapel is a work by the Misses Townsend and Howson. The rest of the windows are by the A. K. Nicholson studios, of which the St Francis window portraying the twelve months is perhaps the best.

RIVENHALL, St Mary and All Saints: Some really beautiful late C12 and C13 panels in the E window, purchased by a vicar during the last century from the church of St Martin at La Chenu near Tours in France. The four circular panels date from c.1170 and portray Christ in Majesty, a most intimate Virgin and Child (*see illustration on this page*), the Annunciation (with the characteristic curve of C12 figures), and the Entombment of the Virgin Mary. They are flanked by two large figures of bishops (or abbots) beneath semi-circular topped canopies; their date

Virgin and Child in French glass, c.1170; Rivenhall, Essex.

is c.1200. Below right is a yellow and brown figure on horseback, Robert Lemaine. At the top is a very fragmentary Adoration of the Magi and at the bottom a bishop, both early C16. Also in the church are some Flemish roundels, one of which depicts Veronica's handkerchief with the face of Christ.

SHEERING, St Mary: In the E window is a complete late C14 Coronation of the Virgin Mary with two censing angels, and eight of the nine angels from the Orders of Angels.

THAXTED, St John the Baptist: There are substantial remains of C15 glass in the N chapel, but it is, alas, rather fragmentary; in the second window from the E the headless figures include St Christopher with the Christ Child (note the watermill and ship in the background), St Edmund (with arrow) and a donor below, St Michael with a coat of arms for England/France below, then St George. Next door are Sts Catherine, Elizabeth and Nicholas, a bishop and donors below. In the S aisle are four somewhat fragmentary C15 panels from a Fall of Man series, Adam and Eve in the Garden of Eden, the Temptation, Expulsion and parts of Adam digging and Eve spinning; St Ursula is in the tracery lights with two bishops, an archbishop and three angels. The oldest glass here is to be found in the N transept, a C14 knight with the arms of Mortimer and a spear, probably from a genealogical series, also here is a mainly modern panel of Abraham within an old border.

105

WALTHAM Abbey: The E window with its rose above is an early work by Burne-Jones for Powells, *c.*1860. In the main lights is a Tree of Jesse with Patriarchs (left) and Prophets (right), and Jesse accompanied by David, Solomon, Jonas and Hezekiah in the centre; in the rose above are the Seven Days of Creation, a fine colourful composition. The E window of the N aisle commemorates the 900th anniversary of the foundation of the Church by King Harold: it is a colourful window designed and executed by Francis Stephens in 1966 with a rather Byzantine Crucifixion that symbolises the famous Rood, or Waltham Cross. The E window of the S aisle with Christ in Glory dates from 1864 and is also by Burne-Jones, but after he had joined Morris when his style of stained glass design had evolved considerably. Also here are two windows by A. K. Nicholson and G. E. R. Smith of 1929-46, not, alas, as inspiring as the Burne-Jones work.

GLOUCESTERSHIRE

With Gloucester Cathedral, Fairford, Tewkesbury, Bledington, Buckland and Cirencester all within its boundaries, Gloucestershire must rate as one of the best counties for seeing medieval stained glass. Indeed, it is rich in examples from the C14 and C15. Nor does it lack good work from the C19 and early C20, notably by Henry and Edward Payne. In addition to the places listed below, Henry Payne's work can be seen at Box, Cherington, Elkstone and Turkdean; Edward Payne's at Birdlip, Box, Chalford, Cheltenham, (St Paul), Clearwell, France Lych, Minchinghampton, and Stonehouse.

MR	Place	Centuries									Principal feature(s)
		12	13	14	15	16	17	18	19	20	
1	Alstone				*						Christ, saints, pope (and Mass of St Gregory?)
2	Arlingham			*	+						see below
3	Bagendon				*						frags. incl. a lovely fig. of the Virgin Mary
4	Bibury		G					*		*	see below
5	Blaisdon			H						*	N a.w. by AJD/Bromsgrove Guild, 1920
6	Bledington				*						see below
7	Bourton-on-the-Hill				*						rather decayed donor figs. (N a.E w.)
8	Bromsberrow			+	+	H	*				C14 t.l. arms of Lanthorny Priory
9	Buckland				*						see below
10	Chaceley			*							early C14 Crucifixion, frags., Qs.
11	Chedworth				+						unusual panel with the 'man-in-the-moon'
12	Cheltenham							*			see below
13	Chipping Campden							*		*	ws. by JH, 1878, and Henry Payne, 1920
14	Cirencester				*				*		see below
15	– Agric. College									*	'Benedicite Omnia Opera' Paul Quail, 1963
16	Cleeve Hill					*					Crucifixion within a rainbow
17	Coln Rogers				*						St Margaret and her dragon (in a N w.)
18	Daylesford							*			see below
19	Deerhurst			*	*						see below
20	Driffield							*			complete scheme of mid-1860s by Gibbs
21	Dursley							*		*	good BG in E w.; other by GW and Tower
22	Dymock				*						Annunc. plus two fine dogs (in porch)
23	Eastington				*						St Matthew with money box (nave N)
24	Edgeworth			*							archbishop, *c.*1390 (base and canopy modern)
25	Fairford				*						see below
26	Forthampton							*			good glass by CB, 1862
27	Frampton-on-Severn				*						St Veronica, donors, Seven Sacrament frags.
28	Gloucester, Cathedral		*	*	*			*	*		see below
29	Hailes				*						9 of the apostles plus Creed scrolls (E w.)
30	Hartbury			+							Trinity and Crucifixion remains (N nave)
31	Hatherop							*			ws. by OC, 1850s, later C19 by LBW
32	Highnam							*			ws. of 1850s by CB, Pugin/JH, Wailes
33	Kempsford				*						St Anne teaching the Virgin (N chancel)
34	Longlevens					*	*O				see below

MR	Place	Centuries									Principal feature(s)
		12	13	14	15	16	17	18	19	20	
35	Matson House						*				figs. by Wm Peckitt (in the Oratory)
36	Meysey Hampton			*							St Michael and other kneeling figs.
37	North Cerney				*					*	see below
38	Northleach				*						Sts Laurence, Stephen and Christ Child
39	Notgrove			*							early C14 Virgin and Child (in vestry)
40	Ozleworth				F						figs. of the Evangelists (Flemish?)
41	Pauntley			H*							angel; arms and alliances of D.Whittington
42	Preston (nr Dymock)			*							C14 Crucifixion plus Sts Mary and John
43	Prinknash					*				*	9 angels from the Hierarchy (nave); d-d-v
44	Rendcombe				*						see below
45	Saintbury			*							2 saints under canopies plus Edward I border
46	Selsley								*		see below
47	South Cerney			*							Christ in Majesty (chancel S)
48	Stanton				*					*	Sts Bartholomew, John, angels; Comper w.
49	Stroud								*	*	ws. by HBB, 1868; LB,WH and Bewsey (1913)
50	Sudeley, Castle								*		modern glass that copies the former collection
51	– St Mary		*		*					*	see below
52	Syde				*						St James of Compostello in roundel
53	Temple Guiting				*						Virgin, St James Less and Mary Magdalene
54	Tewkesbury			*						*	see below
55	Toddington, Manor			H	*						Last Judgement (collection sold in 1911)
56	Upper Slaughter								*		CB, 1869-82
57	Wick Rissington			*							Crucifixion between sun and moon (in a S w.)
58	Willersey				*						St Mary Magdalene; grazing stag (in qtfl.)
59	Woodchester								*		3 good ws. by Preedy for LB

See page 280 for table of symbols

ARLINGHAM, St Mary: Fine mid C14 figures in a N nave window include St John and the Virgin from a Crucifixion and St Catherine in a tracery light; next door has St Margaret with a double-headed dragon underfoot and a saint (perhaps Barbara). In the chancel S windows and in a nave tracery light can be seen C15 remains of an Apostle series with Creed scrolls – eg St John's cup, St Jude's ship, St Philip with Cross and scroll and St James Less with a club.

BIBURY, St Mary: A fine panel of C13 *grisaille* can be seen in the S chancel, reminiscent of that at Brabourne in Kent with its pieces of pot metal coloured pieces inserted like jewels at key points in the window's geometry. The E window is a fine work by Willement of 1855, but Karl Parsons' N window with the Virgin and Child and Caritas of 1927 with its rich jewel-like texture is stunning and a much better companion piece to the *grisaille* opposite.

BLEDINGTON, St Leonard: Fine glass reminiscent of Prudde's work at Warwick of c.1470 in the chancel S tracery lights, with a Coronation of the Virgin and six apostles with traditional attributes: John, Bartholomew, Matthew, James, Matthias, Andrew. In a N clerestory window are figures of St Mary Magdalene kneeling and with a border of crowns, a Pietà

with a kneeling donor below, and St George in plate armour spearing the dragon beneath him; also two pairs of donors. In a nave window is the fine top half of a figure of St Christopher with the Christ Child amid fragments and quarries; also a much restored Virgin Mary with sceptre and rosary – note the angels in the canopy and its fine finial amid the stars; in tracery lights are the Evangelists' symbols and suns *ensoleille*.

BUCKLAND, St Michael: Fine panels (c.1490) in the E window with three of the Seven Sacraments: Baptism, Confirmation and Matrimony, each with canopies (one with a band of 'jewels', another with angels) that seem to be made of a kind of fluid that pours down gracefully from above. Arms of Gloucester Abbey and other remains in the S chancel. In the Hall of the **RECTORY** just down the road is some fine C15 *in situ* glass, mainly quarries with birds.

CHELTENHAM, St Mary: A good collection of C19 glass, where all twenty-six windows date from the thirty-year period, c.1870-1900. A number of good windows by Lavers and Westlake, eg their painterly and pictorial Last Supper window in the S aisle W end, although their Ascension (N aisle W window) and E windows are better works: stained and coloured glass, as opposed to painting-on-glass. The beautiful huge

C14 rose window has no old glass – what is there is by Wailes of 1876.

CIRENCESTER, St John: A pair of binoculars will be useful for examining the huge wall of glass at the W end of the S aisle where some of the C15 panels exhibit the rarely used technique of 'placing jewels on glass', ie sticking small pieces of coloured glass on to the panels. At the top are three of the Church's four Doctors, Sts Jerome, Gregory and Ambrose; beneath them are Sts John of Beverley, William of York, Zita and Bathild and, in the lowest row, donor figures. The glass in the E window originally came from Siddington: it has the Virgin and Child, Sts Catherine and Christopher while below are the donors (Langley) – note how the women have 'butterfly' head-dresses fashionable in Edward IV's time. Also here are angels, seraphim, a beautiful Virgin and shields of arms (Garstang). In the Trinity Chapel E windows, reset fragments include the head of the Duke of York, and in the tracery lights some seraphim in a rather hot yellow stain that has gone orange in places. The Lady Chapel has some fine canopies with figures, c.1450, and at the E end (N side) are three large rather fragmentary figures, some of which have jewelled borders to their garments – ie late C15 work of high quality; also here is a beautiful Annunciation in the bottom left and right panels with scrolls and the words 'ave' and 'plena' in Gothic script. There are some C19 windows by Hardman: the St Catherine Chapel E window, however, is by Warrington.

DAYLESFORD, St Peter: A Pearson church of 1860 with glass by Wailes in the E and W windows, but the best is by Clayton & Bell in the form of neat C13-like medallions that nevertheless belong very much to the C19 and to the firm's newly emerged style. Also some glass of 1816 from the previous church.

DEERHURST, St Mary: In the W window of the S side below suns *ensoleille* and set between four groups of donors is the charming figure of St Catherine, c.1335, with characteristic C14 S-shaped curve and the larger C15 composite figure of St Alphege; in the tracery lights are the coat-of-arms of de Clare.

FAIRFORD, St Mary: A rare opportunity to see a parish church with most of its original glazing still intact. The twenty-eight late C15 windows were given by the wool merchant John Tame and

The Mouth of Hell: note the abraded flashed ruby glass that create the teeth; c.1500, Fairford, Glos.

date from just before those at Kings College, Cambridge, ie 1497-1500. The work is interesting in that it is truly of its time, when artists were moving away from the 'set pieces' of medieval design towards attempts at portraying scenes set within realistic perspective-controlled settings. Most of the windows have four lights in each and a single row of traceries above; some have faded, probably due to under-firing, which at the time of manufacture helped preserve the subtle details in the glass by means of light washes of pigment that the artists wished to impart. Nevertheless, many of the windows are still full of incident and details which are a joy to discover, eg the lovely face of the Virgin in the Presentation scene. The sequence of subjects is not quite as logical here as that at King's; it starts with Adam and Eve in the N aisle at the window by the door to the Lady Chapel and moves clockwise round the church to window (20) which is to the left of (1), although the natural culmination of the series – Last Judgement – is (15), the W window. (1) has a rather pale Eve portrayed with the Tree and serpent, followed by Moses and the Burning Bush, Gideon kneeling with his fleece, and the Queen of Sheba offering a casket to

Solomon; (2) has Joachim, the Birth of the Virgin Mary, the Presentation of Mary in the Temple, and her marriage to Joseph; (3) the Annunciation, Nativity, Adoration of the Magi and Presentation of Christ in the Temple. The Lady Chapel E window (4) has five lights, the Flight into Egypt covering two of them, the Assumption of the Virgin in the centre, and Christ with the doctors in the Temple on the right. The main E window (5) features the Crucifixion with Christ between two thieves (as at King's) – note the angel and demon above the penitent and unrepentant thieves respectively (cf. Hingham, Norfolk); below the transom are scenes from Passion Week. The S side of the chancel (6) portrays the Descent from the Cross, the Entombment, and Proclamation of the Good News to imprisoned spirits (while demons are jostled!); the S Chapel E window (7) has the Transfiguration attended by the usual Peter, James, John, Moses and Elijah, flanked by the apocryphal scene of Christ's appearance to his mother (left) and the Holy Woman with Christ (right) – note the interesting background drawing with the churches in differing styles; (8) depicts the Supper at Emmaus and the Doubting Thomas; (9) the Miraculous Draught of Fishes (New Jerusalem above), the Ascension and Pentecost (here, incidentally, are some of the best tracery light figures); (10) has the first of Twelve Apostles, each carrying a Creed scroll: Sts Peter, Andrew, James the Great, John; (11) Thomas, James the Less, Philip, Bartholomew; (12) Matthew, Simon, Jude (Thaddeus), Mathias (mostly modern); (13) in the SW corner of the church, has the Doctors of the Church: Jerome, Gregory, Ambrose and Augustine (with Monica's Heart); (14) fragmentary pieces suggest the Judgement Hall of David (and Veronica's Handkerchief); (15) the great W window was badly damaged by a storm in the C19 and all the glass above the transom is new; below are many original pieces which portray the souls divided at Last Judgement by St Michael, a scene that is dominated by a particularly vivid Mouth of Hell on Satan's body, a terrifying figure all in red glass with effective abrasion of the flashed ruby glass to give vicious white teeth! (*See illustration opposite.*) (16) depicts the Judgement Hall of Solomon; at the W end of the N aisle are the Evangelists (17); whilst the next three windows (18-20) portray the twelve prophets corresponding to the Twelve Apostles, each carrying a prophetic scroll and with a label on its plinth. Up in the clerestory, more windows depict martyrs and confessors of the Church on the S side and its persecutors (with a gallery of devils) on the N.

GLOUCESTER Cathedral: The great E window (72' × 38') was built to commemorate the Battle of Crécy and completed in *c*.1357. Red and blue predominate, together with much white glass and a little pot metal yellow. The figures – restored and swapped around somewhat – are set beneath canopies and focus to the top where Christ crowns the Virgin Mary beneath the topmost tracery lights, flanked by apostles, saints and kings (at the very top there is, strangely, a later inserted C15 figure of St Clement that replaces a flaming star); in the row below are fourteen saints and martyrs including Cecily, George, Canute, Margaret, Laurence and Catherine; kings and ecclesiastics inhabit the next row, whilst at the bottom the shields of arms identify the Crécy knights, Edward I and III, the Duke of York and others. There is a little old glass at the heads of some choir clerestory windows and in two N windows where C15 remains include figures of Sts John the Baptist and Margaret in the tracery lights and Patrick, Oswald and James the Great in the main lights; two windows to the right have Thomas and Catherine above and Dorothy, George, Thomas and three angels below. In the Lady Chapel the E window has a rather confused assembly of C14-C16 glass in the midst of which are scenes from the Legend of the Virgin Mary by Barnard Flower (of King's, Cambridge, fame); three earlier C15 scenes and some apostles (including St Simon with a saw) can also be seen here, and fragments and kings from a C14 Tree of Jesse, as well as Christ standing over the mouth of Hell. In the cloisters are some fine C16 heraldic panels that include the arms of Catherine of Aragon.

C20 glass in the cloisters is mostly by Hardman, in addition to one each by Ballantine and Clayton & Bell. Christopher Whall did the fine Arts & Crafts windows in the Lady Chapel in conjunction with his daughter Veronica and son, C. W. Jr. In the Cathedral itself, the best C19 glass is perhaps the 1870 glass with musician angels by Burlison & Grylls in the St Paul's Chapel, and that by Kempe & Co. in the ambulatory (it was in this Cathedral that Charles Kempe as a youth claimed to have found his vocation to be a glazier). Other windows here are by Joseph Bell (S aisle second from W), Preedy (E end of N aisle), Rogers of Worcester (E end S aisle), Heaton, Butler & Bayne (S aisle – also Warrington here), Hardman and Clayton & Bell.

LONGLEVENS, Holy Trinity: Glass formerly at St Luke's, Gloucester, includes C16–C17 roundels of Christ being shown to the crowd, and one from the life of St Catherine; also early C16

St Catherine, the Virgin Mary and St Dorothy in mid C15 glass in a north window at North Cerney, Glos. Note how each figure is drawn from the same cartoon, although in one case the cartoon was reversed in order to impart variety to the composition.

panels of Sts Andrew and Peter with donors, and Sts Gregory and Augustine.

NORTH CERNEY, All Saints: The N transept has good mid C15 glass with a Crucifixion group and the donor John Eycote in the E window; equally interesting is the trio of female saints on the N side, all drawn from the same cartoon: Catherine, the Virgin Mary and (?)Dorothy, the latter figure being depicted as a mirror image of the other two (*see illustration above*). Over in the S chapel E window are two ecclesiastics – Sts Martin and Urban (portrayed with a papal tiara, mistaking the saint for the Pope!) – and the Virgin Mary again, with flaming sun and Yorkist badges, ie late C15; note the 'jewels' in the border of the Virgin's gown. There are two C20 windows by F. C. Eden in the sacristy and gallery, one with St Nicholas and the other with the Wine-press.

RENDCOMBE, St·Peter: Unusual late medieval glass here of *c.*1520 related to that at Fairford but later and more Renaissance in character – despite the lack of perspective in the chequered floor patterns. These remains are strongly suggestive of there originally being a type-antetype scheme. In the N aisle E window are much restored figures of Sts James and John, Christ, Peter and Paul (and angels with musical instruments and Passion relics above). In a N aisle window are three lights: a large early C16 figure of (?)Jacob set amid fragments and C19 pieces, and painted panels of St Anne with the Virgin, and Gabriel (Sts Clement and Apollonia above); next door are two windows with early C16 panels and C14 fragments set astride C19 Jesse Trees (scenes include the Crucifixion, Salome, the Ascension, a feast scene – the

Virgin and Child and St Christopher above; then the Brazen Serpent, the Sacrifice of Isaac, St Peter and a saint).

SELSLEY, All Saints: One of Morris, Marshall, Faulkner & Co's first commissions (by Bodley) in 1861. The apse windows with Crucifixion, Resurrection and Adoration were designed by Philip Webb and Burne-Jones; the Sermon on the Mount in the S aisle is by Rossetti. Burne-Jones did The Creation in the W rose window and Adam and Eve in the S chancel: Ford Maddox Brown designed the other figures here – his style is unmistakable. Note Webb's fine drawing of animals which inhabit some of the windows.

SUDELEY, St Mary: In a N aisle window are two C13 martyrdom scenes involving knights in richly coloured Canterbury-style glass; they were given to the church by a collector. In the E window of the chapel is the C14 figure of a bishop giving blessing and a kneeling donor lady in Tudor costume with her six daughters. In a side light is (?)Swiss C17 glass containing an extraordinary figure with feathered hat, musket and powder flask confronting what looks like a dragon. Most of the C19 glass here is by Preedy of Birmingham.

TEWKESBURY, The Abbey Church of St Mary: Seven good windows of glass with fine figures dating from *c.*1375 in the chancel clerestory; some of the figures are drawn from the same cartoon which is sometimes either completely or partially reversed. From N to S, (1) has from left to right Robert Earl of Gloucester, Gilbert de Clare, Hugh Despenser, Robert Fitzhamon; (2) Old Testament figures, of which Aaron and David are easily recognisable; (3) Jeremiah, Solomon, Joel and Daniel; (4) is the E window with Last Judgement below the apostles, the Virgin Mary offering her breast to Christ, St Michael and Christ, whilst the donor (Lady Eleanor de Clare – correctly naked for the occasion) can be seen, below right; (5) has more Old Testament figures (eg Reheboam); (6) Samuel, Abijah and others; (7) William Lord Zouche of Mortimer, Richard, the Gilberts (Earls of Gloucester). In the rose window above is the Coronation of the Virgin attended by musical angels. Fragments of a C14 Tree of Jesse can be seen in the vestry with figures of Amos, Joel and Jonas. Much of the C19 glass is by Hardman, eg in the aisles and W window; the Historical Window of 1879 in the St Nicholas Chapel is by Swaine & Bourne, and Geoffrey Webb's work can be seen in the St Faith Chapel.

GREATER MANCHESTER

Fine medieval glass can be seen at Ashton-under-Lyne and Middleton (and some interesting Arts & Crafts windows at the latter place), but there is little else of that age apart from the C15 fragments at Denton and some heraldic work at Bramhall Hall. William Morris's firm is well represented at Marple, Farnworth and Wigan – and an interesting project in C20 glass at Manchester Cathedral.

MR	Place	Centuries									Principal feature(s)
		12	13	14	15	16	17	18	19	20	
1	Ashton-in-Makerfield									*	w. by Harry Clarke, 1930
2	Ashton-under-Lyne,										
	Albion (Cong.)							*			see below
3	– St Michael				*				*		see below
4	Birtles				F	F					much Swiss and Netherlandish glass
5	Bramhall Hall				H	*					Crucifixion scene with 3 small figs.
6	Davyhulme									*	d-d-v by K.G. Bunton, 1969
7	Denton				H+						St Laurence, angels, frags. LBW, 1872
8	Eccles					F					Triumphal Entry into Jerusalem (Flemish)
9	Farnworth									*	Burning Fiery Furnace by B-J/WM, 1868
10	Manchester, Cathedral									*	see below
11	– St Anne							*			3 large figs. of apostles by Peckitt
12	– Synagogue									*	see below
13	Marple								*		see below
14	Middleton					*				*	see below
15	Millbrook (R.C.)									*	d-d-v by Pierre Fourmaintreaux, 1963
16	Pendlebury								*		good BG ws. for Bodley, 1871–4
17	Rochdale, St Peter								*		much glass by Capronnier, 1888–90
18	– Town Hall								*		rose ws. with Queen Victoria and Albert
19	Stalybridge, St Raphael									*	d-d-v by Pierre Fourmaintreaux
20	Stretford									*	dynamic Trinity w. by G.Clarke, 1961
21	Swinton								*		WM ws. c.1900; also CEK ws., 1872
22	Wigan								*		Wailes' E w., 1874; B-J/WM in S a., 1868

See page 280 for table of symbols

ASHTON-UNDER-LYNE, Albion Congregational Church: Morris & Co. windows from the height of their career, 1893-6, all designed by Burne-Jones – notably the massive seven-light E window depicting saints and Virtues, the Crucifixion scene with the Evangelists and St Stephen in the N transept window, the Old Testament characters in the S transept, and the further group of O.T. people with apostles in the transept clerestory windows.

ASHTON-UNDER-LYNE, St Michael: In the S aisle are the remaining panels of c.1500 from the seven-light E window end – originally there were twenty-one; this fine glass (well restored in c.1913 by Caldwell) has recently been reset and cleaned by Keith Barlow and features a sequence of scenes from the legend of the Life of St Helen, mother of the emperor Constantine, who was believed to have found a fragment of the Cross (cf. the glass at Morley, Derbys); the scenes move from her birth to her entry into a convent, her betrothal and marriage to Constantine, the defeat of the emperor Maxentius, Constantine's birth, baptism, the Council of Nicaea, Helen in the Holy Land, her questioning of Judas concerning the Cross, she finds it, two scenes of the magician Zanbury killing the bull, its revival, Helen's conversion whilst digging for the three crosses, finding the True Cross at Jerusalem, and finally the founding of the Church of the Holy Sepulchre; at the base of the window are the kneeling members of the donor's family (the 'Asshetons'). In a N aisle window are the three large C15 figures of saintly kings: Edmund, Edward the Confessor (*see illustration on* p.112) and Henry VI (who enjoyed an unofficial and temporary promotion to sainthood by cult followers after his death); further down the aisle is another window with reset C15 fragments that include figures of St (?)Elizabeth, the Virgin, a bishop and St Anne wearing a huge and unusual hat. The E window of 1872 is by Ballantine of Edinburgh and it is possible to see some weird faces amongst the figures.

St Edward Confessor with the ring, set against quarries, C15,
St Michael, Ashton-under-Lyne, Greater Manchester.

MANCHESTER Cathedral: Much of the modern glass here is by Antony Hollaway, which he describes as being part of a plan 'formulated so as to control the colour scheme and light entering the building so that the architectural intentions of the C15 builders may once more be realised'. Progress to date towards completing this ambitious scheme includes windows in the inner SW aisle with St George and the dragon of 1972, St Denys of 1976, and the W window with the Virgin 1981, honouring the patron saints of the building.

MANCHESTER, Whitefields Synagogue: Twelve windows portraying the tribes of Israel by Roy Young of The Modern Art Glass Co., dating from 1969-70. Also a window by Abbot & Co. in abstract symbolism designed by R.F. Ashmead in 1975 and entitled 'the Resurrection and Redemption of the Jews in World War II', illustrated by the Warsaw ghetto.

MARPLE, St Martin: Good representative glass by Morris & Co., of c.1870, designed by William Morris, Burne-Jones, Ford Maddox Brown and Dante Gabriel Rossetti: the E window has the Crucifixion, Nativity and the twelve apostles, mostly designed by W.M. and B.-J., although St Andrew is by F.M.B. and St Jude by D.G.R. In the S chancel is W.M.'s Annunciation and Presentation and St Elizabeth with St John by F.M.B. The W and SW windows are by Kempe's pupil Herbert Bryans, all of the early C20.

MIDDLETON, St Leonard: In the S chancel below other fragments are the figures of seventeen kneeling archers, each with their name and bow, and traditionally held to represent Sir Edward Stanley's contingent that fought at the Battle of Flodden Field in 1513; they kneel on a chequered floor like donor figures, together with Sir Richard Assheton who appears with his wife and chaplain, Henry Tayler; since the window mentions a date of 1505 (ie seven years before the Battle of Flodden Field) it seems more likely that it was Sir Stanley's own troop of archers who gave the window to the church (*see illustration on* p.24). There are also two interesting Arts & Crafts by Christopher Whall, one with Faith, Hope and Love in the N aisle, the other with the Ascension (S chapel E window) — both display the artist's clever use of streaky glass; also windows by Nicholson and Burlison & Grylls (the Boer War Memorial).

HAMPSHIRE

With the exception of Winchester College and Sherborne St John, Hampshire has a rather thin representation of medieval stained glass. C13 pieces recovered from Salibury Cathedral have found their way into the churches at Grateley, East Tytherley and Headley; C15 glass can be seen at Mottisfont and in the chapel at St Cross Hospital, Winchester, whilst the chapel of The Vyne has some good early C16 Continental-inspired windows, and there is a formidable collection of Flemish roundels at Rownhams. Stained glass enthusiasts on holiday on the Isle of Wight should not miss the opportunity of seeing the good Morris & Co. glass at Bonchurch and Gatcombe – nor heraldry enthusiastics the display of royal arms at Froyle.

MR	Place	12	13	14	15	16	17	18	19	20	Principal feature(s)
1	Ampfield								*		Wailes' ws., 1850s; K. Mem. by Butterfield.
2	Basing									*	J.Hayward w. 'angel of peace and dove'
3	Basingstoke				+						frags. from demolished Holy Ghost Chapel
4	Bentley			.*							Annunciation plus angel (E w. t.l.)
5	Boldre									*	E w. is a choice work of A.Younger, 1967
6	Bramley			+	*	F					7 small figs., some plus music instruments
7	Dean					*					St (?)Barbara (in porch w.)
8	East Tytherley		*	*							bishops, St (?)Peter from Salisbury
9	Fareham						*				copies of Reynolds' ws., New Col., Oxford
10	Froyle			H							see below
11	Funtley								*		Nativity and Ascension designed by J.Ruskin
12	Grateley		*								Martyrdom of St Stephen – from Salisbury
13	Harbridge				O	O					many Flemish roundels
14	Havant								*		the ubiquitous CB – here of the 1870s
15	Headley		*								death of female saint — from Salisbury
16	Hinton Ampner									*	glass by RP (also at Hound)
17	Hursley								*		see below
18	Lyndhurst								*	*	see below
19	Milford-on-Sea									*	choice w. of BB, Sts Francis and Anthony
20	Mottisfont				*					*	see below
21	Oakley				H*						arms of Archbishop Wareham & Canterbury
22	Portsdown, Christch.									*	10 post-War ws. by M.Farrar Bell
23	Portsmouth, Cathedral									*	choice w. by Carl Edwards (Ramsey Mem.)
24	– St Cuthbert									*	choice w. by Osmond Caine
25	Romsey				F						"Salvation" from Soul Pilgrimage, in nave S
26	Rownhams				O	O					52 roundels, given by Mrs Colt in C19
27	Sherborne St John					*	*				see below
28	Sherfield English								*		ws. by CB & BG, 1868-1900; Art Nouveau ws.
29	Sherfield on Loddon				H	*					St George slaying the dragon
30	Southampton, All Sts									*	Christ as Alpha and Omega by G.Loire
31	– Ascen. Ch., Bittern									*	much glass by A.K. Nicholson
32	Stoke Charity					*					restored saints, c.1470, E w. and N
33	The Vyne					*	*				see below
34	Winchester, Cathedral			+	+				*	*	see below
35	– City Musum		+	+	H+	H+					see below
36	– College			*	*				*		see below
37	– St Cross Hospital				*						figs. of Virgin, Sts John, Catherine et al.
38	Winslade				*						Sts Margaret of Antioch (S w.); Popham arms
39	Wymering								*		a suite of ws. by CB at their peak in 1861
Isle of Wight											
40	Bonchurch								*		see below
41	Gatcombe								*		see below

See page 280 for table of symbols

FROYLE, St Mary of the Assumption: Good glass for those interested in heraldry (*see section on heraldry,* pp.26-8). Lt. Col. J. F. Wilcocks has made a study of the C14 coats-of-arms in the E window. At the top are the arms of Edward the Confessor (azure a cross-patonce between four martlets or); in the second row are the arms of England 1198-1340 (gules three lions passant guardant in pale or); and to the right those of the heir apparent (England with a label of five pieces azure); in the third row are de Bohun (left), England (centre), Warenne (right – checky or and azure); in the fourth row (left to right) are England, France ancient, Chastleton, and Brotherton (England with label of five pieces argent).

HURSLEY, All Saints: The glass here is interesting in that the plan for the windows was drawn up for the Revd Keble and based on the late medieval scheme at Fairford (qv). It was executed by Wailes mostly in 1858, although the N aisle E window is of 1842.

LYNDHURST, St Michael and All Angels: Fine early glass by Morris, Marshall, Faulkner & Co. of 1862-3 in the E window (including the rose) and in the S transept where Burne-Jones designed the figures. Compare these with their contemporaries' work here: Clayton & Bell's Te Deum (N transept), Kempe's W window and Powell's in the N aisle.

The Mocking of Christ, C16, Sherborne St John, Hampshire.

MOTTISFONT, St Andrew: Good C15 glass in the E window of which the main light has a much restored Crucifixion with the Virgin Mary and St John, Sts Peter and Andrew in side lights; in the tracery lights is a Coronation of the Virgin with Sts John the Baptist and Catherine and two seraphim standing on wheels. More remains of C15 figures in the S chancel – Sts Michael and Catherine, a bishop and one other – mainly in yellow stain. A sun *ensoleille* in the N chancel suggests a late C15 date. 'Consider the Lilies' in the S nave is by Powell of Whitefriars, 1931.

SHERBORNE ST JOHN, St Andrew: Three early C16 and C17 panels can be seen in the de Brocas Chapel E window: Zacharias and the Angel in the Temple, the Soldiers Mocking Jesus, and Dagon Dismembered Before the Ark (as in I Samuel 5:4). Also a figure of St Laurence and an elaborately quartered coat-of-arms for Pexsall.

THE VYNE, Sherborne St John: In the Chapel is a fine display of early C16 Dutch-Flemish-inspired glass executed by a 'group of itinerant glass painters engaged in Calais by Lord Sandys', says Woodforde (1952, p.6). The subjects are the Via Crucis and Veronica with the Handkerchief (S window), the Crucifixion (E window), and Resurrection with Henry VIII, Catherine of Aragon and Queen Margaret of Scotland (the King's sister), together with their pet dogs; behind each of them is their patron saint. In the upper lights of the Antechapel are fragments of glass

from the same school of painting, although these were transferred from the Chapel of the Holy Ghost at Basingstoke before it became derelict. In the Tomb Chamber is an Adoration of the Shepherds after Van Dyck by John Rowell, 1731 – the small oval window with the same subject is also his of a year earlier.

WINCHESTER Cathedral: Numerous small fragments of medieval age in a number of windows but hardly any figure panels or scenes; the W window has a mass of them, amongst which some heads can be spotted. There are plenty of C19 and C20 windows, however; moving clockwise round the cathedral, the first ten windows of the N nave have glass mostly by David Evans of c.1850: the monotony is only slightly relieved by Hugh Easton's glass (No. 5) and by No. 8, the Jane Austen Memorial of 1901 with St Augustine. Then follows a window by Kempe & Co. that date from after the deaths of Morris and Burne-Jones – the Visitation window was designed by Henry Dearle, whilst the rest are re-used designs of Burne-Jones. The E window is David Evans again of 1852 and, in the Lady Chapel, Kempe yet again (note Queen Victoria and the Mayor of Winchester in one of these). Kempe yet again of 1899 in the SE (Langton) Chapel. Powell of Whitefriars did the large figures in the S chancel aisle, c.1880, as well as the Izaak Walton window in the Silkstead Chapel, 1914, where the author of the *Compleat Angler* is portrayed by the river Itchin. In the S aisle are windows by Evans, Easton (1938) and at the W end a notable work by Gibbs of 1857.

WINCHESTER, City Museum: Several thousand pieces of excavated fragments of glass that date from the C7 to C16, including some blue and green Anglo-Saxon pieces and others from the old Minster. On display are some fine medieval fragments, notably with the heads of Christ and the Virgin Mary. Some C15 and C16 coats-of-arms in the Westgate Museum.

WINCHESTER College Chapel: The remains of a Tree of Jesse in the large E window made by Thomas Glazier in 1393 were removed in the last century and replaced by Betton & Evans' replica, but this too has recently been removed. Parts of the original C14 work were supposed to have been so corroded that they were disposed of. Some were sold and are now in America, but a sizeable portion went to Ettington church (Warwicks), but these have now been returned to Winchester and were reset after restoration by Dennis King in the 1950s in the Thurburn Chantry W window. The style of Glazier's drawing will be immediately recognisable to those who have seen the companion figures of St John, St James and Ezekiel now in the Victoria & Albert Museum; here most of the twelve figures in the main lights are prophets and kings, all labelled except for the Virgin and Child (bottom left) and Christ with a kneeling king (bottom right). In the tracery lights are St Peter at the heavenly gate, a mitred soul from the General Resurrection, another charming Virgin with suckling Child and two adoring saints. The S window here has C15 figures in the main lights. Sts Mary Magdalene, Helen, the Trinity, Anne with the Virgin, and Catherine with donors kneeling below; in the tracery lights, below an Annunciation, are some female saints, including the rarely seen St Ursula with her 11,000 maidens in a boat (actually only half-a-dozen here!), St Agatha with pincers and St Agnes with her lamb. More C14 fragments in two windows to the right.

In the **Fromond Chancery** in the cloisters is more of Thomas Glazier's work, reset into the E window. They comprise mostly more prophets and kings from the Tree – two of the figures were recovered from Coleorton church – although the resetting had to create composite rather than complete figures, which is why some of them look almost comical.

ISLE OF WIGHT, BONCHURCH, St Laurence: The W wall has glass by Morris & Co. formerly in Ventnor Hospital chapel; it is of 1873 with Burne-Jones' design for Peter, Ford Maddox Brown's for St Luke and St John – other scenes are by Morris, except the window with the Woman with an Issue of Blood, now set in a light box on the N wall and by F. M. Brown. Also from Ventnor are Sir William Reynolds-Stephens' very Art Nouveau row of angels above a frieze of intertwined daffodils and two medical scenes (in memory of Dr G. J. Shaw), now in the W window.

ISLE OF WIGHT, GATCOMBE, St Olave: A good early Morris, Marshall Faulkner & Co. window of c.1865 in the chancel where Rossetti designed the Crucifixion, Ford Maddox Brown did The Entombment, Burne-Jones designed the Baptism and angels, and the rest are by Morris.

HEREFORDSHIRE

Herefordshire has some magnificent glass of the early C14 that naturally links with contemporary glass in Worcestershire and Gloucestershire. There are fine figure drawings at Brinsop, Credenhill, Hereford Cathedral, Madley and particularly at Eaton Bishop. The characteristic deep colours – invariably in combinations of red and green or yellow/gold and green, occasionally brown, and with sparing use of white glass – combine with compact simple designs and strong figure drawing to make this glass perhaps the most appealing in Britain. Smaller remains can be seen at a number of places. Quite unique is the glass at Abbey Dore, a rare survivor from the second quarter of the seventeenth century.

Please note that Worcestershire locations are listed separately.

MR	Place	Centuries								Principal feature(s)
		12	13	14	15	16	17	18	19	20	
1	Abbey Dore				+		*				see below
2	Aconbury		G								in N E qtfl ws.
3	Allensmore			*							frags. of Annunc. plus Crucifixion (E w.)
4	Bishopstone					F					St John the Baptist, Christ, Prodigal Son
5	Bridge Sollers								*		good glass by JP in E w., 1871
6	Brinsop			*						*	see below
7	Brockhampton (B'yard)						*				rare w. of c.1800 with fig. of Christ
8	Brockhampton(Ross)									*	see below
9	Canon Frome						*				fine E rose w. with Christ, c.1860
10	Clehonger			Q+							diaper Qs, border, 2 dragons N,W ws.
11	Credenhill			*							see below
12	Dilwyn			*							2 censing angels (chancel S)

MR	Place	Centuries									Principal feature(s)
		12	13	14	15	16	17	18	19	20	
13	Eaton Bishop			*							see below
14	Foy						*				E w. is a 1675 copy of the Sellack E w.
15	Goodrich				*						Passion relics; arms of Thos Cantilupe
16	Hereford, Cathedral	*	*				*				see below
17	– Holy Trinity									*	Joseph the Carpenter by R.Coomber, 1979
18	Kentchurch									*	2 ws. on N side, 1 on S by AJD
19	– Court				F						13 Swiss panels — 4 are coats-of-arms
20	Kilpeck							*			apse glass by Pugin
21	Kingsland		*								see below
22	Ledbury		*	+				*	*		see below
23	Llanwarne				O	O					see below
24	Madley		*	*	*						see below
25	Moccas			*							early C14 canopies with small figures
26	Much Marcle					H		*			arms of Charles I, 1628 (Chapel E w.), CEK
27	Norton Canon		G								late C13 grisaille in N tspt and S a.
28	Pembridge			*							frags. of Sts Laurence, Stephen, Christopher
29	Pixley							*			early glass by WM & Co., 1864 (E w.)
30	Pudleston							*			angels and Apostles by Pugin, c.1850
31	Richards Castle			*							Coronation scene (N Chapel E w.)
32	Ross-on-Wye				*						see below
33	St Weonards				*				*		see below
34	Sarnesfield		*	+							figs. of angels, saint and man plus zither
35	Sellack		+	*	+	*					see below
36	Thruxton			*							Crucifixion, Qs with covered cups
37	Ullingswick				*						Virgin and Child (in E w.)
38	Weobley				/*						Seraphim plus Passion Instruments, c.1400
39	Weston under Penyard								*		choice w. of Basil Barber in S nave
40	Wormbridge				*						many frag. figs. of saints in chancel ws.

See page 280 for table of symbols

ABBEY DORE, St Mary: Set into the three noble Cistercian/Early English lancets of the E wall is glass given to the church by John Scudamore in 1634. It features the Ascension with eleven of the apostles and cherubs amid the clouds overhead: the figures stand on chequered floors, as in many C15 designs, although here perspective has been brought into the composition; Sts Matthew, Mark, Peter and Andrew are in the N light, John the Baptist and Moses in the centre, and Sts Luke with John the Evangelist, James and John the Apostle on the S side. In the E window of the Ambulatory the right window has fragments that include a Carwarden achievement of arms with supporters and two wild men. Numerous other remains of rich glass have been reset into the SE chapel window to give composite figures of a bishop in one light and a kneeling woman in the other; also some quarries and many border pieces.

BRINSOP, St George: C14 glass reminiscent of the fine rich work at Eaton Bishop in the E window, notably St George with shield and spear under a trefoiled canopy edged with a border of fleur-de-lis; also the figure of the Virgin and coats-of-arms for Chandos (left) and Dauncey (right). In a NW window is Christ in Majesty against a red background. Recent glass includes the First World War memorial and St Francis windows in the S wall by Sir Ninian Comper, 1920-8; also two that relate to William Wordsworth's visit to Brinsop, one in the S chancel and the other, the St Edith window, in memory of his sister Dorothy, his wife Mary (formerly Mary Hutchinson of Brinsop Court) and his daughter Dora.

BROCKHAMPTON BY ROSS, All Saints: In this temple of the Arts & Crafts by Lethaby (1901-2) the E window is by Christopher Whall, put in when the building was erected. His W and S transept windows are of later date.

CREDENHILL, St Mary: In a S chancel window, two figures of c.1330 with St Thomas of Canterbury and St Thomas of Cantelupe of Hereford (a bishop who died in 1282; he had been an adviser to Edward I, and miracles were alleged to have occurred at his tomb in Hereford Cathedral): both figures here are set against fine quarry backgrounds and have borders of fleur-de-lis and castles for Edward II (his mother being Eleanor of Castile). Amongst the tracery light fragments in a nave NE window is a part figure of the Virgin and Child and the arms of the Talbot family.

EATON BISHOP, St Michael and All Angels: The magnificent E window here is filled with early C14 glass donated by Adam de Muirimouth, Canon of Hereford and Canon of Exeter in 1328. From left to right can be seen fine figures of the Virgin and Child (*see illustration*) with a kneeling priest below them; then the splendid St Michael holding a pair of scales with a canopy and super-canopy above that, another donor priest below and the words 'Magister Ade EC'; the Crucifixion with Sts Mary and John occupies the centre light with a bishop below and priest below him; then the archangel Gabriel with a palm and the donor Adam de Muirimouth again; in the right light is the head of Christ under a canopy and a kneeling sainted woman below. Two windows on the N side carry on this good C14 work: a small Crucifixion is in one whilst the other has Christ in Majesty in the tracery light and four reset panels together with another Crucifixion, an angel and two charming kneeling figures, all with the strong colours and concise and compact design associated with glass of this age.

HEREFORD Cathedral: Some fine panels of *c.*1300 from (?)Munich in the Lady Chapel with figures set against rather darkened *grisaille*: Christ in Majesty – one hand raised in blessing, the other on the orb of the world – is at the top, portrayed in a vesica and with the four symbols of the Evangelists also in little vesicas; then a Crucifixion with Sts Mary and John, the Three Marys at the Sepulchre, and Christ Carrying the Cross. In the S chancel aisle are four good C14 figures beneath large canopies of Sts Mary Magdalene (with scroll), Ethelbert (church and sword), Augustine (crozier) and George (in armour). In the NE transept, only the canopies are C14, the figures being by Warrington, whereas in the N transept W window reset fragments include a number of female saints, eg St Dorothy with flowers in her hair, St Elizabeth with the child St John – and the Virgin Mary below. Elements from a scene of Joseph's Dream – such as the sun, moon, stars and wheat-sheaves bowing to him – and Joseph in the pit are amid C14 fragments in a S aisle window.

There is much C19 glass of variable quality in the Cathedral, notably imitation C13 glass by Charles A. Gibbs of 1852 and 1867 in the Lady Chapel windows. At the top of the E window is Hardman glass of 1871 – other good work of his can be seen in the N transept (N side), 1864. Warrington has windows in the SE transept (1863), the N chancel aisle E (1862) and the Zacharias window in the N aisle; also windows by Clayton & Bell and Heaton,

The Virgin and Child — the latter carrying a bird — in early C14 glass at Eaton Bishop, Herefs.

Butler & Bayne (theirs is the Transfiguration in the N aisle). In the Stanbury Chapel are some Arts & Crafts windows by A. J. Davies of the Bromsgrove Guild that date from 1923.

KINGSLAND, St Michael: C14 glass can be seen in the tracery lights of the E window with Christ in Glory and a Coronation of the Virgin. All four archangels together (something of a rarity in old stained glass) inhabit the main lights: Raphael is with Tobias and the fish, Gabriel at the Annunciation, Michael with the dragon (mainly modern work), and Uriel teaching Esdras. In a N window there is an archbishop and (?)St Helen.

LEDBURY, St Michael: Most of the glass here belongs to the late C19 and early C20, but there are some medieval fragments worked into Kempe's E and S chancel windows, as well as some heraldic remains in the NE chapel, whilst the W window of the outer N chapel – surrounded, incidentally, by a beautiful stone ball-flower decoration – contains C13 pieces of a Flight into Egypt scene and a figure said to be King Canute. In the S aisle all the windows are by Kempe, 1895-1904, as are those in the chancel – with the exception of the late Morris &

Co.'s window (by H. Dearle, 1912) with the Shepherds and the Nativity, and the small St Martin window on the S side by Veronica Whall of 1950. Her father, Christopher, did the window in the N aisle with the unusual assemblage of St Michael, Prudence, Fortitude and the Soul's Journey. Next door is another late Morris & Co. work of 1913 that re-uses a cartoon of Sts Raphael and Gabriel, Christ the Good Shepherd and the Annunciation by Burne-Jones. Also here is a Faith, Hope and Charity window of c.1830 based on the figures of the Virtues by Joshua Reynolds at New College, Oxford; the 'Virtuous Woman' window at the W end of the S aisle is by C. Cotterill, 1893.

LLANWARNE, St John the Baptist: In two nave windows are a collection of Flemish roundels with biblical scenes and saints; most of them date from the C16 and C17. They vary widely in quality; some have faded, others are rather crudely drawn; but a few are superb, such as the scene of Justice; Joseph's Dream is also a pleasing composition.

MADLEY, Church of the Nativity of the Virgin: A magnificent E window with C13 medallions, C14 panels of a king and prophets from a Tree of Jesse and C15 fragments. In the N lancet are C13 scenes from the Legend of St John, the Death of St John and the saint with Aristodemus: below them is the beautifully drawn C14 figure of the prophet Hosea (see illustration on p.45); in the centre lancet C13 scenes of the Three Holy Women at the Sepulchre, St John on Christ's Breast at the Last Supper and the C14 prophet Ezekiel below; in the right lancet a C13 Presentation in the Temple, Adoration of the Magi and a C14 Jesse Tree king; above the lancets are the C14 arms of Bohun and

Warenne and some *in situ* foliage at the apex. Amongst the reset C14 fragments in NE and SE apse windows are parts of Sts Luke and Mark's symbols, two bishops and some heads from the Jesse Tree that continue the fine drawing.

ROSS-ON-WYE, St Mary: Four fine C15 figures with some restoration in the E window that came from the Bishop of Hereford's house during the C19: Edward the Confessor, St Anne Teaching the Virgin to read, St Joachim and St Thomas Cantilupe of Hereford (see Credenhill, above).

ST WEONARDS, St Weonard: The N Chapel E window is a combination of C15 and C19 glass (the latter by Baillie and Mayer) with large figures of St Catherine, St John the Baptist (the head is old), a Crucifixion with the Virgin Mary and St John (mostly modern), and St Weonard (all modern); in the tracery lights are Christ with the Five Wounds and (left to right) a female saint, St Margaret, a female saint, priest saint, kneeling donor, empress saint (modern), St Helen and St Leonard. In a N window is an early German or Flemish panel with The Calling of St Peter and Christ Walking on the Water.

SELLACK, St Fesiliog: The E window is a c.1630 assembly of C15, C16 and C17 glass; the Crucifixion in the tracery light is C17, the border and foliage of c.1400 and the figures and scenes of the Virgin and Child, the Three Magi, a stable and ass all from a Nativity scene, St Joseph, St Mary Magdalene and St Catherine are a mixture of C16 and C17 work – at the bottom are the initials R. S. for Richard Scudamore (John Scudamore gave the glass at Abbey Dore in 1634). In a nave SE window the part of a Trinity is C15, and the head of Christ in a N chapel E window C14.

HERTFORDSHIRE

Little medieval glass in any quantity in the county – Hunsdon and Much Hadham have the best of it, and there are some nice pieces at Barkway. The C15 bird quarries at Clothall are a sheer delight, and there are fine C16 Continental panels at Wyddial and good English C17 glass at Gorhambury House and Hatfield House. High Cross has really excellent turn-of-the-century glass by Selwyn Image, as well as an early Kempe work; so, too, Waterford has not only fine Morris & Co. glass but also works by Image and Karl Parsons. There is much from the C19 and C20 at St Albans Cathedral, and Alfred Fisher's modern glass at Cuffley is an interesting experiment in fused glass, carried out in the early 1970s and until recently was unique.

MR Place		Centuries									Principal feature(s)
		12	13	14	15	16	17	18	19	20	
1	Aldbury				+	F					German Pieta plus Crucifixion; C15 canopies
2	Barkway			*	*						see below
3	Barley			+	*	+					C14 Crucifixion, C15 Sts Chris., Stephen
4	Bourne End								*		apse ws. by Alfred Bell, 1854, ie before CB
5	Bovingdon								*	*	see below
6	Clothall			+	Q						see below
7	Cuffley									*	see below
8	Datchworth								*		good w. by SH
9	Furneux Pelham								*		2 ws. by WM and B-J in S a., 1867
10	Gorhambury					*					see below
11	Great Offley				*O	O	O				Tudor remains
12	Hatfield, House					*					see below
13	– Marychurch									*	glass by Norris of Buckfast Abbey
14	– St Etheldreda								*		C19 glass by WM, 1894; CB, 1870–72, BG
15	Hemel Hempstead								*		CB glass of 1859, also ws. by Gibbs and OC
16	Hertford, Mus.					O		Q			roundel of Moses on Sinai, Tudor roses et al.
17	High Cross							*	*		see below
18	Hunsdon				*						see below
19	Little Hadham			H	*						St Laurence (S nave); Braybook arms (N w.)
20	London Colney									*	see below
21	Much Hadham				*			*			see below
22	Newnham				Q						Qs in S a. W w. and S clsty
23	Royston			*	+						6-winged seraphim (N w.); C15 canopies
24	St Albans, Cathedral			H				*	*		see below
25	– St Peter			+	+			*			see below
26	St Paul's Walden			*							Virgin and Child in tower w.
27	Sandon				+						charming little angel in N nave t.l.
28	South Mimms					*					donors and families (Fransys and Frowyks)
29	Tewin								*	*	ws. by JP, 1874; and RP, 1965
30	Wallington			H*							6 female saints plus arms of John Pryset
31	Ware							*	*		see below
32	Waterford							*	*		see below
33	Watford, Nazarene Ch.									*	circular w., a choice work by AF, 1984
34	Watton-at-Stone						*				Clutterbuck's N.T. scenes of 1849
35	Welwyn Garden City									*	2 favourite works by the Kettlewells, 1963
36	Wyddial				F						8 late C16 Flemish of Passion scenes

See page 280 for table of symbols

BARKWAY, St Mary Magdalene: The E window of the S aisle has a fine restored C14 Tree of Jesse with four kings and some splendid musical angels overhead; in the lancets to each side and amid C15 fragments are the figures of four saints – one a female (possibly St Sitha) carrying a book and two keys, a fine St Roche pointing at his plague spot, St John and St (?)Petronella.

BOVINGDON, St Laurence: A recent (1984) small two-light window by Alfred Fisher with the symbol of St Laurence and the Cross of St Alban (and with depictions of the church and St Albans Abbey). The E window of 1856 with The Resurrection was made by Lavers and, says Martin Harrison, designed by the painter Charles West Cope.

CLOTHALL, St Mary: Late C14 heads of Christ, the Virgin Mary and saints, in roundels, much restored and set against most delightful C15

quarries in the E window. These quarries portray numerous birds in the English countryside – and one or two that might puzzle the modern ornithologist! (*See illustration on* p.120.)

CUFFLEY, St Andrew: A unique major installation of windows made up from 'fused glass' that date from the late 1960s; this technique was developed by Whitefriars Studios and enabled true pot-metal colours to be overlapped, often with dramatic effect; Alf Fisher did the designs (this is a choice work of his) and the theme of the set is 'The Earth is the Lord's and all that therein is'. (The firm closed down in 1972, but an interest is being shown again in this technique.) On the S side is a later window, suggestive of the Tree of Life.

GORHAMBURY House: In the entrance hall to this house (built in 1770) are two windows with a mixed assemblage of glass panels and fragments

119

Some of the charming C15 bird quarries at Clothall, Herts.

arranged into the present designs earlier this century. Michael Archer has shown that there are three distinct groups of glass, the earliest probably being the 'patch-worked' sections at the heads of the windows surrounding the coats-of-arms, with a bizarre assortment of figures and pictures of fish, birds, gods, Eskimos and Indians; in fact they are copies of prints of Marcus Gheeraerdt the Elder's 'Continents and Elements' of c.1580. It seems that they were copied on to glass at the instigation of Sir Francis Bacon, probably by Lewis Dolphin and Richard Butler in c.1610 (they also did the glass in Hatfield House, qv). The coats-of-arms are those of Harbottle Grimston and date from after 1652. Finally there are the numerous rectangular panels of enamel painted birds, beasts and flowers arranged like postage stamps and each surrounded by a scroll-like pattern; these are similar to the work at Lydiard Park (qv) and were probably by Abraham van Linge.

HATFIELD House Chapel: Above the altar are twelve panels: eleven by Lewis Dolphin and Richard Butler of Southwark of 1610-20, one, the Resurrection panel, is by Warrington of 1835. As with the Southwark glaziers who did King's College Chapel at Cambridge and Fairford parish church, the subject matter is based on a type-antetype set of scenes: here the scenes are labelled and Biblical references are given.

HIGH CROSS, St John the Evangelist: Kempe's four-light E window – 'Noli Tangere' – is an early work of 1876 that makes much use of silver staining, some very cleverly. The W window of c.1893 with the three powerful figures of Christ, St Mary and St John is a fine work by Selwyn Image, a founder member of the Century Guild of Artists who got together in 1882 to 'do something about' the production-line state of affairs that most stained glass glazing had got into – and that included Morris & Co., which had been founded on high ideals. Much inspired by the early windows of Morris, Burne-Jones and, particularly, Ford Maddox Brown, Selwyn Image started producing Arts & Crafts windows in c.1890; the Pre-Raphaelite influence is strong in these works.

HUNSDON, St Dunston: Much glass of c.1460 in a number of windows; in the chancel E above the Holy City of 1910 are some panels with the Annunciation (the Virgin in a far right light and Gabriel far left), the Ascension and Resurrection, flanked by delightful little angels; the chancel N and S windows have reset pieces that include a York rose and quarries. In the tracery lights of the nave are figures of Sts Peter, Paul, Thomas, Andrew and John the Evangelist on the N side, but rather darkened with corrosion. Of these, St John is the best. On the S side at the W end are both a bishop and an abbot.

LONDON COLNEY, All Saints Pastoral Centre: Sir Ninian Comper did much of the decoration in this church, notably the Tree of Jesse in the E window; the W rose window is by Sebastian Comper, 1964.

MUCH HADHAM, St Andrew: Fine *in situ* C15 figures of female saints in the second row of the E window tracery lights that include the Virgin of Pity, St Margaret with dragon, a female saint with a book, Sts Catherine, Barbara, Mary Magdalene; above is St Andrew, the Evangelists and one other saint (the figure of Christ at the top is C19). In the S aisle is a Transfiguration, 1882, in deep colours with heavy features, but excellently drawn and reminiscent of S. Image's work.

ST ALBANS Cathedral: There is very little old glass in the Cathedral but much of the C19 and C20: on the E side of the N transept are some medieval quarries, fragments and the coats-of-arms of Edward III, the Black Prince, John of Gaunt and Lionel, Duke of Clarence; the lamb and the flag, an angel carrying St Andrew's cross and two (?)phoenix birds can be seen in N nave tracery lights. The vast W window spread across nine lights represents the Bedfordshire and Hertfordshire War Memorial of 1924 by Sir Ninian Comper, featuring the Crucifixion in a very Renaissance setting: warriors and the flags of many nations surround Christ. In the N aisle, at the W end, are two windows by C. Webb with Annunciation and New Testament scenes, then two of four lights each by Burlison & Grylls; they also did two opposite in the S aisle. There are two works by Kempe in the Lady Chapel, by Clayton & Bell in the S transept of 1876 and by Burlison & Grylls on the E side with Sts Catherine and Mary. In fact Burlison & Grylls' late C19 and early C20 windows can be seen in a number of other places – eg the Fathers of the Church in the N transept, the Livery Companies' Lady Chapel E, as well as some of the N and S windows here, in the Chapel of the Four Tapers, and in the E window of St Michael's Chapel with saints and archangels, 1914. But their best work is the forceful and colourful window with musician angels high up in the Saints' Chapel of 1907. Finally it should be mentioned that Francis Skeat and Christopher Webb both have panels set against clear glass in the St Ambulatory and in St Michael's Chapel. The N late C19 rose window with its holes of varying sizes for the coins of the realm is an abomination and, thankfully, has no glass!

St Cecilia — a *tour de force* of stained glass work by Karl Parsons, 1929, Waterford, Herts.

ST ALBANS, St Peter: In the N aisle are some C14 pieces reassembled to make up scenes, one of which would seem to be a martyrdom and the other a procession, both within horseshoe-shaped borders: there are some good heads among fragments. The seven-fold rose window — reminiscent of that at Cheltenham — has a few C14 pieces in it. The brightly coloured windows filling the S side are by Capronnier of Belgium. Another includes a portrait of John of Wheathampstead, thirty-third abbot of St Albans.

WARE, St Mary: Pre-Raphaelite-inspired glass with groups of New Testament scenes by Shrigley & Hunt in the S aisle of 1885; by Christopher Whall in the N aisle of 1905 and in the N transept of 1910. The earlier E and W windows of 1845-50 by Wailes would seem to be inspired by the Nazarene artists.

WATERFORD, St Michael: Some beautiful C19 and C20 glass here; all the chancel windows are by William Morris or Burne-Jones of 1872: the E window with angels and the Nativity (B-J), St Michael on the N side, and the large and striking Annunciation on the S (both designed by Morris). More of Morris & Co. in the W windows where the single figures of Sts Philip and John the Baptist were designed by Philip Webb, Noah by Ford Maddox Brown, and the St Peter in the nave is by Burne-Jones, c.1876. The Wise Virgins also in a more animated Pre-Raphaelite style is by Selwyn Image for Clayton & Bell. Truly remarkable is the St Cecilia window of Karl Parsons of 1929, a *tour de force* of glazing that uses techniques such as aciding, plating and etching in addition to traditional methods, in order to obtain the required textures and many colours often found on a single pane (*see illustration on* p.121).

HUMBERSIDE

Beverley Minster's huge E window alone contains most of the old glass to be seen in Humberside, although a few C14 remains can be seen at Leaconfield, Barnoldby-le-Beck and Barton-upon-Humber. At South Dalton there is exceptionally fine C19 glass by Clayton & Bell, whilst that at Owston Ferry is something of a rarity.

MR	Place	Centuries									Principal feature(s)
		12	13	14	15	16	17	18	19	20	
1	Barnoldby-le-Beck			*							Crucifixion, Sts Mary and John (S a. E w.)
2	Barton-upon-Humber			*	H						Sts James and George plus fish border in E w.
3	Beverley, Minster		*	*	*				*		see below
4	St Mary								*		see below
5	Boynton							*			heraldic and mosaic work by Peckitt, 1768
6	Brigg									*	E w. by FS, Risen Christ and local scenes
7	Bubwith			H+							arms of Ross and Warenne
8	Burton Agnes						H*				Roger de Somerville plus arms by Peckitt
9	Burton Constable				*		*				glass by William Peckitt in the Chapel
10	Burton upon Stather						*				Christ as Ruler of the World by Pearson
11	Cottingham							*			much glass by the Belgian, Capronnier
12	Harpham						H*				St Quentin family plus arms by Peckitt, 1771
13	Hayton				F						Flemish glass in the E w.
14	Hedon							*	*		ws. by Wailes (1878) in S a.; Stammers (1951)
15	Hotham								*		some ws. by D. Strachan, 1938
16	Howden							*			Capronnier ws. (1862–88) and HS, 1953
17	Kingston-upon-Hull					H*			*		see below
18	Leconfield			H*	+						Virgin, angel, arms of Neville and Percy
19	Messingham			*	*	*					St Thomas, Harrowing of Hell, Virgin
20	Middleton-on-the-Wolds							*	*		good w. by LBW of 1872; and by AY, 1981
21	Owston Ferry							*			see below
22	Redbourne						*				see below
23	Roos			Q	+	H					bird Qs, Gabriel plus scroll, Royal arms
24	Scorborough							*			a fine early CB, 1859
25	South Dalton							*			see below
26	Welton							*			fine WM & Co, and Capronnier
27	Wold Newton					F					some C17 Netherlandish panels

See page 280 for table of symbols

BEVERLEY Minster: In 1725 all the old glass in the Minster was assembled in the E window and later rearranged by the firm of Shrigley & Hunt, although that above the transom is very largely original to the window but not *in situ*. With a pair of binoculars one can admire the sixty or so panels of the tracery lights which house a great Te Deum; descending from the summit where God the Father rules over all below, we encounter the angels of the Hierarchy, the Cherubim and Seraphim that 'continually cry Holy, Holy, Holy...', and are duly followed by the Noble Army of Martyrs, the Goodly Fellowship of the Apostles, not to mention the Holy Church all above the transom; beneath them but still above it are nine stately figures which are (left to right): Henry VI (possibly a portrait), St Peter, another saint, a bishop, the prophet Joel, Sts Leonard, Paul (with sword), James Less and Andrew with traditional emblems, some of whom carry Creed scrolls. Below the transom are C14 and C15 canopies with five very reconstructed figures made up from lavish fragments of C14 glass, of which the Virgin Mary and St Laurence can be easily identified. To either side of these figures are some twenty panels of C13 glass, mostly depicting scenes from the life of St Martin. The unusual Tree of Jesse in three lancets in the S transept is by John Hardman, *c*.1860, whose firm also built the S windows here; Hardman also did a number of windows in the S aisle and the good glass in the NE transept (designed by Dunstan Powell).

At **St Mary's Church** (just down the road), the great window is a Hardman/Pugin composition.

KINGSTON-UPON-HULL, Holy Trinity: In the vestry there are some places of mostly Continental glass, one of which is possibly of Lot escaping from Sodom; another has Solomon Pronouncing Judgement, all C17; also the arms of Percy impaling Lucy with a Garter. Two windows in the church are by Walter Crane and J. Silvester Sparrow of 1897 and 1907.

OWSTON FERRY, St Martin: Three stately figures of Christ, St Peter and St Paul under canopies can be seen in an early window by Ward & Nixon of 1836, where the very Georgian-style poses are supplemented by attempts at leading in addition to just painting on thin rectangular pieces of glass, which had characterised the craft during the previous century. The S aisle E window is of some twenty-five years later by the same firm (Ward & Hughes as it was called by then), when the Victorian revival had led to creating windows with coloured glass and utilised methods more akin to medieval techniques.

REDBOURNE, Church: Removed pending a decision on the Church's future is the late C18 window (probably painted by William Collins) of John Martin's 'Opening of the Sixth Seal' – Martin worked for Collins. It is interesting to see how people react to this kind of work: 'skilfully executed in enamels', says the Norwich glazier Dennis King; 'Horrific', said Sir John Betjeman!

SOUTH DALTON, St Mary: A brilliant portrayal of the Last Judgement in the E window by Clayton & Bell of 1861 which, like the glass at Howsham that dates from about the same time, represents work put out by this firm when it was at its peak. The rose above it with Christ dominating all else is magnificent. Also theirs are the W and the S transept W windows: these were all done for the architect Pearson.

KENT

Kent must once have been exceedingly rich in medieval glass: there are over 140 places where remains and fragments can still be seen, some of which make an interesting display. At Brabourne is the earliest example in a church of a complete *in situ* window that dates from the C12; Canterbury Cathedral contains the best C13 glass in the country and many noble C12 figures. There are occasional C13 panels to be seen at a number of locations, as well as rich early C14 pieces at others: of the late C14 are the fine tracery lights at Boughton Aluph. C15 glass is not so common, the best pieces being found at Nettlestead and Great Chart. Interesting collections of painted foreign glass are at Temple Ewell and Patrixbourne, and fine C20 glass at Canterbury Cathedral (by Bossanyi) and Tudeley (by Chagall). Not to be missed is the splendid Art Nouveau composition at Wickhambreaux.

MR	Place	Centuries									Principal feature(s)
		12	13	14	15	16	17	18	19	20	
1	Bearsted									*	see below
2	Bethersden				*						some good canopies
3	Bicknor								*		good CB glass of 1861
4	Biddenden				*						3 roundels of Labours of the Month
5	Bilsington			*							Virgin and Child, Trinity, c.1400 (nave N)
6	Birchington									*	Rossetti Mem. by F.J.Shields, 1925
7	Bishopsbourne			*		H	FH				C14 angels, Dutch oval scenes (chancel)
8	Blean								*		an early HH w., Pre-Raphaelite style
9	Boughton Aluph		\	*							see below
10	Brabourne	G									see below
11	Canterbury, Cathedral	*	*	*	*	*	*		*	*	see below
12	– St Mildred				*						fig. of St Mildred in S Chapel
13	Challock Lees				H						arms of Apuldrefold, Etchingham et al.
14	Chartham		G*								see below
15	Cheriton			*							Trinity panel
16	Chevening									*	choice w. by Moira Forsyth, 1950s
17	Chilham				*						Sts Cath., Leonard, Clement, Greg.; Virgin
18	Cliffe-at-Hoo			*	+						C14 Virgin and Child in N a.
19	Cobham								*	*	see below
20	Cranbrook				*	*					Sts Cath., George, James the Great et al. (N a.)
21	Crundale			*	Q+						Virgin Coronation, c.1300 (chancel S)
22	Doddington		*								Flight Into Egypt in E w.
23	Eastling								*		Presentation of Christ, by JP, 1863
24	East Malling			*	*						C14 angels; C15 Coronation plus canopies
25	East Peckham				Q+						Qs and canopy tops in S and N ws.
26	East Sutton				*	H					frags. of Sts Peter, (?)Paul, and bishop (W w.)
27	Elham				*	O		*			see below
28	Farningham								*	*	see below
29	Faversham									*	Joseph of Arimathaea by W.H. Geddes
30	Fawkham		+	*	+						St Anne Teaching (in chancel S)
31	Fordwich			*	*						C14 figs. on S side; C15 in N qtfls
32	Goodnestone			*	*						C14 St Michael, bishop; C15 bishop (N w.)
33	Great Chart				*						see below
34	Harbledown			*							2 C14 Ascension scenes plus other frags.
35	Hastingleigh		G								geometric grisaille (on N side)
36	Headcorn				*						canopies, Sts Stephen and Laurence (N ws.)
37	Hever Castle		F								see below
38	Higham								*		E w. by R. Bayne of HBB, 1863
39	Ightham					*					Henry VII plus his queen (Dutch style glass)
40	Iwade					*					Early C16 Crucifixion: S Chapel
41	Kemsing		*		*					*	see below
42	Kilndown								*		mid C19 period pieces by FXE of Munich
43	Kingsnorth				*						good St Michael and dragon in nave w.
44	Langton Green								*		early WM with FMB, 1862; E w. by CEK
45	Leigh			*							Virgin and Child in a N qtfl
46	Lullingstone			*	*	F	*				see below
47	Maidstone ·								*		see below
48	Mersham				*						see below
49	Minster-in-Thanet								*		good w. by TW in chancel, 1861
50	Molash			*	*						C15 Coronation, St Peter; in situ C14 t.l.s.
51	Nackington		*								see below
52	Nettlestead				*				*		see below
53	Nonington				*						donor and family (N a.w.)
54	Otford						F				fine St Michael and dragon (N w.)
55	Patrixbourne					F	F				see below
56	Penshurst						H		*	*	see below
57	Preston		G								grisaille in N chancel
58	Ramsgate, St August.								*		see below
59	– The Grange								*		see below
60	Rochester, Cathedral								*		see below
61	Ruckinge			G*							St Michael and dragon, early C14. (N a. E w.)
62	Sandhurst				*						Sts Michael, George, Anthony, (?)Etheldreda

MR	Place	Centuries									Principal feature(s)
		12	13	14	15	16	17	18	19	20	
63	Seal				*	F					Flemish panel of the Resurrection (E w.)
64	Sellindge				*						St Michael (S chancel)
65	Selling	H*							*		see below
66	Sevenoaks							*			CB rose w.; chancel ws. by HBB, c.1880
67	Sevington			*				*			fine Virgin and Child; Evang. symbols; JW
68	Southfleet							*			S w. is an early exuberant OC, 1857
69	Snodland			*	Q*						14 Evang. symbols; C15 St James the Great
70	Speldhurst							*			CEK W w., 1878; CB & WM ws. of 1870s
71	Stockbury		Q		+						red and blue bands in *grisaille* of c.1250
72	Stowting			*	*						see below
73	Sutton at Hone				F						O.T. and N.T. scenes (nave ws.)
74	Swanscombe									*	N a. E w. by Christopher Whall
75	Temple Ewell		+		+	F	F				see below
76	Teynham				H*						remains of an Apocalypse scene? (N tspt)
77	Tonbridge								*		see below
78	Trottiscliffe			*							good Trinity panel, c.1330 (N nave)
79	Tudeley								*		see below
80	Tunbridge Wells								*		see below
81	Upchurch			*							frag. figs. include St John the Baptist (N a.)
82	Upper Hardres			*					*		see below
83	Warehorne		*	+							C13 roundels, one with mythical monster
84	Westerham							*			HH ws., 1864 & 1882; CEK, 1890; JP, 1867
85	West Kingdown			*							Virgin and Child, Christ in Glory in qtfls
86	Westwell		*	H	*						see below
87	Wickhambreaux								*		see below
88	Willesborough			G*							2 C14 saints (John the Baptist); C15 Virgin
89	Woodchurch		*			O	O				C13 Entombment of the Virgin (S a.)
90	Wormshill			*							late C14 Coronation in E w.
91	Wrotham							*			S a.E w. by J.M.Allen/LB, 1861
92	Wye, College			H*							St John; arms of John Kempe, Henry VII

See page 280 for table of symbols

BEARSTED, Holy Cross: Three early C20 windows of no great artistic merit, but interesting due to the fact that the faces of the saints are based on people associated with the church: St Augustine is modelled on the Revd Albert Alexander (a pioneer missionary in New Guinea and assistant curate at Bearsted, 1888-9); St Andrew bears the features of Canon John Scarth (vicar 1884–1902 and founder of St Andrew's Waterside Church Mission); St Louis of France has a portrait of Maj-Gen Lewis Edward Knight (a great-nephew of Jane Austen).

BOUGHTON ALUPH, All Saints: The E window tracery lights house a number of excellent figures of c.1380; at the head are a king and queen – possibly intended to be a Coronation of the Virgin – flanked by lesser kings, a bishop, a nun, part of a St Michael panel, two angels playing a regal and St Christopher. Over in the N transept are shields of arms for Pembridge, Bohun, England, (?)Paveley, Hoo and Mortimer, set amid fragments. Note the fine stone tracery work here. Note also the tracery of the W window, which contains some old *grisaille*.

BRABOURNE Church: A unique patterned window of *in situ* C12 glass on the N side of the chancel that is in effect a forerunner of *grisaille*; note the four repeating geometric designs in white and coloured pieces of glass and the little flowers in the gaps formed between them.

CANTERBURY Cathedral
The Old Glass
Looking at the splendid glass in the **Trinity Chapel** that embraces the former site of Thomas Becket's tomb, one may be forgiven for thinking for a moment that one is in Chartres Cathedral. Indeed the design and features of style in these Trinity Chapel windows of c.1220 – notably the prominantly red and blue glass making up the scenes and figures set into the strongly geometric patterns of lead and iron that form the substructure of the window – have close affinity with Chartres, St Denis or even Bourges. This is hardly surprising, since the source of the uncut and unpainted coloured glass was the Ile de France and most of the glaziers would probably have been either French or French-trained. The subject matter here, however, is decidedly English; numbering

125

Pilgrims on their way to St Thomas Becket's tomb at Canterbury, C13, Trinity Chapel, Canterbury Cathedral.

the windows I–XII starting at the W end on the N side, I has the Life of St Thomas Becket and III–VII, XI and XII have scenes of miracles associated with his tomb (*see, for example illustrations on* p.5 *and above*). IX has two medallions of pilgrims going to Canterbury. Of the same age are the beautiful panels in the **N choir aisle** where the scenes are arranged typologically, ie with Old and New Testament scenes juxtaposed. In one of the two windows here are scenes of the Nativity and Christ's Childhood: The Wise Men being guided by the Star, Herod receiving them, the Magi and Shepherds adoring the Child, the Magi being warned in a dream of Herod's intentions (note how they are pictured in bed with their crowns on!), and the Presentation of Christ in the Temple. Next to each of these are characters, eg Baalam, Isaiah, Pharaoh and Moses, Joseph and his Brethren, Lot,

Samuel and Eli, representing Old Testament anticipations of New Testament events. The sequence continues in the next window, but before moving there we must consider the seven lower panels in this first window. They contain scenes of Christ teaching, representations of some of the parables, notably that of the Sower, and the Church with the three sons of Noah and the three 'blameless estates' – ie Virginity, Continence and Marriage. Incidents from Christ's Life then continue in the next-door window: Christ Among the Doctors (paralleled by Moses, Jethro, and Daniel and the Elders) and the Marriage at Cana with the six wine vessels reflecting the Six Ages of the World (personified here in Adam, Noah, Abraham, David, Jeconias and Christ with the Gospels); the third roundel depicts The Miraculous Draught of Fishes, and other related scenes.

Progressing clockwise round the Cathedral from this point we see three windows associated with the shrines of Sts Alphege and Dunstan which they formerly overlooked: these are scenes from their lives. In the modern E window of the **NE transept** are some C13 borders and a scene of St Martin Dividing his Cloak. The high circular window here – not a true rose window – contains the oldest glass in the Cathedral, dating from *c.*1178, ie contemporary with the building under its first master mason, William of Sens. The window features Moses and the Old Dispensation symbolised in the blindfolded figure of the Synagogue, surrounded by the four Virtues, four prophets (Ezekiel, Isaiah, Jeremiah and Daniel) and with minor prophets round the perimeter. In the clerestory above, some of the C12 genealogical windows survive amongst the replicas, notably Shem and Isaac: they are large portrayals of prophets, kings and patriarchs, each seated on a throne and set against blue glass and beneath a frame which in some cases amounts to a canopy, and with a label behind him. This sequence continues in the **choir clerestory** where all except eight of the panels are copies (there were originally eighty or so of these fine figures at the clerestory level of which only about half now remain, most having been moved to the W and S transept windows). The Trinity Chapel with its Thomas Becket windows has already been mentioned, but in addition there is here the **Corona** with five scenes (the Crucifixion, Entombment, Resurrection, Ascension and Pentecost), each of which is surrounded by four Old Testament 'antetype' scenes. The left window here has some panels from a late C12 Tree of Jesse with Josiah and the Virgin Mary, whilst its neighbour is a C19 reconstruction to give an impression of what the original would have looked like. To the extreme right, beyond the C19 panel, is a C13 panel (from Pethan Church) of Christ Giving Blessing and the Evangelist symbols. In the **south triforium** are three windows with C13 scenes: one is from the legend of the Virgin Mary, another from the Crucifixion, and the third from the Nativity and Childhood of Christ. The **south choir aisle** has windows with C13 panels from the Hearst collection of St Donat's Castle, four of which have scenes from the life of St Andrew. The S window of the **south transept** has a great display of old glass with some of the best C12 genealogical windows from the clerestory windows, together with later shields of arms and C13 glass in the tracery lights. The nave W window is under repair at the time of writing, but usually houses C14 apostles and kings

set above eight sovereigns – all that remain from twenty-one made by (?)John Prudde of *c.*1450; beneath them are saints and apostles of the same age of which only St Peter and St Paul (with key and sword) can be positively identified; at the bottom are seven more of the C12 genealogical figures. The **nave N aisle** has on its W wall a C15 St Edward the Confessor with cross and church. In the **NW transept** is the heavily laden 'Royal Window' by the king's glazier William Neve of 1476 with eight prophets at the top leading to the twelve apostles with their usual attributes and fourteen saints; in the main lights are kneeling royal personages, the little murdered princes, Edward IV with St George and dragon, (?)Charlemagne, with queens, princesses and duchesses. On the W side there is an Annunciation and three shields of arms. More C13 panels with Christ and various saints can be seen in the **water tower**, together with some C15 and C16 coats-of-arms. In the chapels of the **crypt** are yet more C13 panels, St Mary Magdalene Washing Christ's Feet, scenes from St Nicholas' life, and a Virgin and Child in the E window.

C19 and C20 Glass

Of recent glass in the Cathedral, the replica C13 Tree of Jesse in the **Corona** by George Austin is interesting, as is Clayton & Bell's imitation C13 medallion in the second window of the Trinity Chapel (II in the above numbering scheme); they also did the W window in the NE transept. Those in the apse of the **SE transept** are by George Austin Jr, in 1852: his, also, is the rose window here based on the C12 rose opposite; the four modern windows here are by Bossanyi and date from 1956 with Peace (left) and Salvation (right) in the large lights, whilst in the smaller lights are Christ Walking on The Water, and St Christopher. Glass by Harry Stammers of 1959 in **St Anselm's Chapel**, by Sir Ninian Comper of 1959 in the **NW transept** with the Annunciation, heraldic glass by William Wilson in the Warriors' Chapel of St Michael, whilst the W window of the **S transept** has characteristic Arts & Crafts work of Christopher Whall, 1903.

CHARTHAM, St Mary: Some rather restored but interesting *grisaille* windows in the chancel of *c.*1300 with coloured border of buds, hop and passion flower leaves, tracery fillings and geometric design; also in the chancel on the N side is a Coronation of the Virgin in a tracery light quatrefoil and, opposite, Christ in Majesty with the four Evangelists, also *c.*1300.

COBHAM, St Mary Magdalene: There is an Arts & Crafts window here of 1902 by Reginald Hallward, an artist/colleague of Christopher Whall and a designer of children's books. The E window is a notable work of Lavers & Barraud, dating from 1863. Christ the Healer in a post-war window by Brian Thomas is a memorial to a doctor.

ELHAM, St Mary: In the N chapel are two C16 Flemish roundels with Nativity-related scenes, and the C15 arms of Hammond and Eustace Janulies; in the chancel is a panel of *c.*1490 with St Thomas Becket. Two unusual and amusing windows of the late 1880s in the chancel, one by Samuel Caldwell of Canterbury in which the then vicar is portrayed as King David; the other was made by the vicar's brother, Frank Wood-house, at the vicarage; it shows Gladstone and Disraeli and three of Queen Victoria's daughters with Saul and David – whose faces are portraits of Thomas Carlyle and Adelina Patti the singer.

FARNINGHAM, St Peter and St Paul: The window above the choir-stalls was designed and partially executed by the vicar's son, Charles Winston, in 1832 when he was only eighteen years old – it has the coats-of-arms of the Mildert and Winston families. Winston later became a barrister, but his devotion to stained glass led him into studies of how medieval stained glass was originally made; these discoveries were put to the test and yielded glass the like of which had not been seen new for many hundreds of years (*see* p.59). The E window here is a later work of his in C15 style, whilst the W window contains what is believed to be the first portrait of the present Queen together with Charles I: it is by Faith Craft-works and was made in 1954.

GREAT CHART, St Mary: Rearranged C15 glass in a S aisle window with Sts Michael, George, and angel and two part figures; also in the S chancel E window are donors kneeling before the mainly modern figure of a sainted bishop, with C15 angels in the tracery lights and shields of arms for Goldwell and the See of Norwich.

HEVER Castle: In the small oratory off Henry VIII's room are C13 French panels of the Trinity, The Virgin Mary and St John.

KEMSING, St Mary: The remains here include a C13 roundel of the Virgin and Child in a nave S window and some assorted fragments on the N side. In the S chancel is part of a C15 scene

St Christopher with the Christ Child on his shoulder, C15, Mersham, Kent.

with St Anne Teaching the Virgin Mary. Of the C20 are various windows by Comper (E and W windows of *c.*1902), the W window of the N aisle by Douglas Strachan, 1935, and one by Christopher Whall in the nave, of 1905.

LULLINGSTONE, St Botolph: Some interesting glass of C14 to C18, gifts of the lords of the manor; in the N chapel are two small C14 bishops; in the chancel E window is St Anne Teaching the Virgin Mary to read, *c.*1500, together with St Agnes (left) in blue and St Elizabeth (right) crowned and in violet; on the S side of the nave is some heraldic glass and C16 (?)French panels, depicting (left) the martyrdom of St Stephen, (centre) St John the Baptist and (right) St George spearing a spotted dragon while Princess Cleolinda looks on; in a N nave window are two C18 panels with St Luke and St Botolph.

MAIDSTONE, United Reform Church: The Good Shepherd window of 1857 was Burne-Jones's first stained glass window, made by Powell's of Whitefriars; it is reputed to have driven Ruskin 'wild with joy'.

MERSHAM, St John the Baptist: In the splendid C15 tracery of the W window are the remains of what was once a Last Judgement, although there is now much alien glass included; just above the transom are two Evangelist symbols and two soldiers resurrecting at the sound of the Last Trumpet; below it are twelve quatrefoils with musician-angels with viol, harp, horns, regal, trumpet and psaltery; in the twelve large openings below (originally housing the apostles) are now only the remains of three with Creed scrolls – St Bartholomew with a knife, St Matthew and St Thomas with a lance. At the very bottom are fragments of heraldic glass – and two charming little green frogs! In a chancel N window are substantial C15 remains of St Christopher and the Christ Child (*see illustration opposite*), St George spearing the dragon and Edmund Rich, Archbishop of Canterbury.

NACKINGTON, St Mary: Partly restored panels of *c.*1220, probably originating from Canterbury Cathedral, in the lancets of the N chancel contain the top of a Tree of Jesse with the crowned Virgin Mary seated and in prayer, with David (plus harp), Solomon and Moses. In the next window is a panel with the Marriage at Cana, probably original to the building, and beneath it a panel of St Thomas Becket with a blue chasuble, richly jewelled and with a pallium – on either side of him is a head, possibly of Henry II and Louis VII.

NETTLESTEAD Church: The nave here was designed with the display of stained glass very much in mind, the glass being given by John Pympe in *c.*1465. Numbering the windows clockwise round the church and starting in the NW corner (1), (2) and (3) are on the north side of the nave; (4), (5) and (6) in the chancel; (7), (8) and (9) on the S side of the nave. Only (2) and (4) are in anything like their original state; (1) has fragments and a scene from the life/legend of St Thomas Becket; (2) houses the stately figures of Sts Thomas, Bartholomew and Matthew beneath huge canopies; (3) is a clever imitation by Curtis, Ward and Hughes of 1894; (4) has Sts Stephen and Laurence, St John's eagle in the tracery lights and the small figure of a monk praying; (5) is the Crucifixion with Sts Mary and John with much restoration; (6) is C19; and the originals of (7), (8) and (9) were all destroyed in a storm in 1763. The heraldry is mostly concerned with the de Pympes; note also the suns-in-splendour, which are emblems of Edward IV.

PATRIXBOURNE, St Mary: A collection of some eighteen Swiss panels dating from 1538 to 1670, most with arms for families in the Cantons. The eight in the S window of the Biffon Chapel are (left to right, top to bottom): the Crucifixion, Peter Gisler of Burglen, St John the Baptist on the River Jordan, the Raising of Lazarus, the Standard-Bearer of the Levantina Valley, Pyramus and Thisbe, the Murder of St Meinrad, and the Adoration of the Shepherds. In the E window of the

chancel is Christ's Agony in Gethsemane, the Crucifixion, Samson in the left light; Jacob Wirtz (a knight), a Roman Soldier/Allegory of war, the Magi, St John Evangelist and Elisabeth of Hungary in the centre light; a knight in armour, Christ's Agony (again), and Samson slaying the lion – a copy of a woodcut by Dürer (as in another window connected with Dürer, at Prittlewell in Essex, Dürer's home town of Nuremberg is portrayed in the background). There are some good imitation C13 medallions in the N aisle E windows by George Austin Jr, who did the same kind of work at Canterbury Cathedral.

PENSHURST, St John the Baptist: In the tower W window there is a good heraldic shield of arms of 1627. In the two clerestory windows above the chancel crossing is glass by Henry Holiday for Powell's, *c.*1884. At the W end of the S aisle is the Becket window, commissioned to celebrate the parish's 800th anniversary (Becket installed the first priest in Penshurst in 1170, the year of his death). The artist, Laurence Lee, says he designed the window with, amongst other things, T. S. Eliot's *Murder in the Cathedral* in mind.

RAMSGATE, St Augustine: Built and financed by Pugin, the church has glass by Hardman; in the S transept Pugin himself appears as a Benedictine monk kneeling before his saint and holding a model of his church in the traditional medieval manner; with him are his three wives who kneel before their saints.

RAMSGATE, The Grange: Pugin's own house, with glass by John Hardman that portrays the owner and his family. In the dining room are some C16 roundels of Continental glass.

ROCHESTER Cathedral: Good early glass by Clayton & Bell of 1858-9 in the upper windows of the N transept; they are a near copy of the Chartres C13 style, with tall stately figures under exotic canopies and with small scenes below each – a pair of binoculars will reveal the very fine figure and drapery drawing. The W window has sixteen panels also by Clayton & Bell, which use much clear glass in order to offset the highly coloured scenes.

SELLING, St Mary: Some fine panels in the E window date from *c.*1300 with figures set against *grisaille*, beneath a simple triangular canopy and between a pair of stylised plants (common in C13 scenes) and with a coat-of-arms below each. On the left is St John the Evangelist and the arms of Gilbert de Clare; then St Mary Magdalene holding the vase of precious ointment and with the arms of León and Castile quarterly; the Virgin and Child with the arms of England; St Margaret with cross-staff and dragon, and the arms of Margaret of France (second wife of Edward I); on the right, St John the Baptist and the arms of Warenne; white roses in the tracery lights. On the N side is Goddard & Gibbs' Benedicite Window, depicting the life and scenery of Kent; it was designed by Arthur Buss in 1970.

STOWTING, St Mary: A beautiful early C14 Virgin and Child in a nave N window, showing the characteristic S-shape common in early C14 figures: she has a green mantle and crown of gold. In the S aisle is a complete three-light C15 window with three large figures and donors below: St James the Great as a pilgrim with staff and slouched hat, St John the Baptist in the centre carrying the Agnus Dei, and St Augustine of Canterbury (right) with jewel-studded mitre; below are Richard Stowtin and his family.

TEMPLE EWELL, St Peter and St Paul: Some C17 Swiss panels similar to those at Patrixbourne (qv): on the S side of the chancel are episodes from the life of the patriarch Joseph: Pharaoh's Dream, Jacob's Sons, Receiving his Brethren and The Butler Before Pharaoh. In the N aisle are four more in a rather strange arrangement of thirteen shields, representing the Swiss Federation as it was 1351–1798, the arms of Austria in the centre and an Adoration of the Shepherds at the Nativity, all set with C13 fragments and C15 roundels of birds and stags; a panel of the Madonna of Loreto with St Bartholomew and Bishop Theodule (patron saint of Valais Canton) at the top of which is an Adoration of the Magi and the arms of Wolfenchiessen; a Coronation of the Virgin with Annunciation above and a village scene in the foreground (Wolfenchiessen); in the lower right is the best panel with a Flight into Egypt, probably in German glass.

TONBRIDGE, St Stephen: An interesting modern ' E window by Leonard Walker that utilises only streaked coloured glasses and no paint whatever in order to achieve its design. Also here are many late windows by Morris & Co., 1910-13, some of which are designed by Henry Dearle (eg the Road to Emmaus in the N aisle and

the archangels at the Ascension) and others are re-used cartoons of Burne-Jones.

TUDELEY, All Saints: Chagall's first stained glass work in this country is in the E window, a memorial to Sarah d'Avigdor-Goldsmid who was drowned in a sailing accident. It incorporates a vision of Christ and a girl in the waves amid predominantly blue glass – a beautiful and successful window. The rest of the glass in the church is also by him: the yellow abstract windows on the S side – the side of the sun – contrast with the quieter blues and purples in the N windows. Chagall's windows are made by Charles Marq at Reims.

TUNBRIDGE WELLS, School Chapel (formerly the Convent of the Sacred Heart, Pembury Road): A number of abstract windows by Paul Quail, 1967, two dalle-de-verre: the one in the Sacred Heart Chapel evokes Christ's Love for Mankind; two appliqué windows in the Lady Chapel depict the Sorrowful and Joyful Mysteries. There is also work here by J. Nuttgens and Keith New.

UPPER HARDRES, St Peter and St Paul: The E window of the chancel has eight C14 panels originally from Stelling: in the N lancet is the Virgin Mary, St Edmund with an arrow, the Salutation of Mary and Elizabeth and a shield for Haut; in the S lancet St John (from a Crucifixion?), Archbishop Edmund Rich, St Anne Teaching the Virgin and a shield for Hardres. (The W window had three C13 panels which were destroyed in a recent fire.) The 1971 Annunciation in the Lady Chapel by Francis Stephens was inspired by a C13 window in Chartres.

WESTWELL, St Mary: The top half of the C13 Tree of Jesse now in the E window was rediscovered after the last war; it has the Virgin, Christ and the dove of the Holy Spirit at the top, somewhat corroded and set on blue glass: there are also two prophets with their scrolls – the bottom two panels are C19. In the nave aisle N windows are impaled shields of arms of Edward the Confessor with Richard II, for Anne of Bohemia and of the Confessor with his wife Edith, 1397. The E window of the N aisle has a C15 angel in a tracery light.

WICKHAMBREAUX, St Andrew: The 1896 E window is indeed 'a real stunner', as Dr Pevsner described it, by Arild Rosencrantz in full-blown Art Nouveau style; it portrays the

Annunciation with the Virgin in a field of lilies, over-looked by a crowd of saints and angels, all beneath a fascinating sky – it was given by Count Gallatin of New York and made by John la Farge in America. The window in the S aisle by Gibbs of 1884, stands up to it remarkably, perhaps by providing something of a contrast. In the E window of the S aisle is a gory C14 scene of the beheading of St John the Baptist, surmounted by an elaborate canopy.

LANCASHIRE

Lancashire – or what is left of it after large slices have gone to Greater Manchester and Merseyside – has some interesting C19 and C20 glass, but very little from medieval times, the best perhaps being the Netherlandish work at Tunstall. The complete scheme of glass by Patrick Reyntiens at St Mary's, Leyland, (R.C.) is well worth seeing.

MR	Place	Centuries									Principal feature(s)
		12	13	14	15	16	17	18	19	20	
1	Blackburn, Cathedral								*	*	see below
2	– Turton Tower				F	F					see below
3	Bracewell									*	d-d-v by Pierre Fourmaintreaux for JP, 1960s
4	Burnley, Holy Trinity								*		ws. by FMB,PW & B-J for WM, 1875-7
5	– St Peter								*	*	some CEK; 'New Life' by FRA, 1962
6	Chipping									*	w. by Alfred Fisher for SH, 1962
7	Colne								*	*	E w. by LB, 1863; 3 by J & MK, 1973
8	Earby									*	E and W ws. choice works by AF, 1979
9	Eccleston								*		a full set by BG, 1890s
10	Gisburn			*							2 figs., one a weeping saint
11	Habergham									*	one of the best of Brian Clarke's ws., 1976
12	Halsall		Q+								*grisaille*, Qs and bits (S a.E w.)
13	Hoghton									*	Jordan Baptism by H.Harvey for SH, 1971
14	Leyland									*	see below
15	Lytham								*		late C19 ws. by B-J/WM, JH, CB, Capronnier
16	Nelson									*	WM&Co. ws. by HD (re-used B-J), 1919–45
17	Penwortham			+							Trinity panel (in chancel)
18	Scarisbrick Hall								*		staircase w. with Pugin and his patron (by JH?)
19	Tunstall				F	F					see below
20	Whalley								*		Pugin/JH w., 1847

See page 280 for table of symbols

BLACKBURN Cathedral: The splendid 56-light Thompson Lantern here is glass appliqué work by John Hayward of 1967. His also are the four-light E window of the St Martin Chapel, almost entirely executed in stain on pale greens and white glass, and the large ten-light S transept window, mainly made up of Victorian fragments in 1968. In the transepts are the Morris, Marshall, Faulkner & Co. windows of *c.*1880 and 1889 with Faith, Hope and Charity in one and Enoch, Paul and Elijah in the other. Both of the windows were designed by Burne-Jones.

BLACKBURN, Turton Tower: The corridor has C16 and C17 Swiss panels with scenes painted in enamels, one with an angel holding the Tablets of the Law, another with the figure of God making a pact with Justice, and eleven shields with coats-of-arms. In the bay window are five more scenes, one of which is of William Tell shooting the apple off his son's head: also a royal Gartered coat-of-arms and some other shields.

LEYLAND, St Mary (R.C.): The glazing scheme for the whole church is by Patrick Reyntiens, a rare opportunity for a glazier to create a unified scheme which here has been successfully achieved in dalle-de-verre (*see* p.19), 1964–5.

TUNSTALL, St John the Baptist: In the E window are some Netherlandish panels bought by Richard North some time before 1853; they include a late C15 figure of the Virgin Mary and Christ and St Peter of the early C16. The two-light memorial window with symbols and emblems of the Church is by Jane Gray, 1979.

LEICESTERSHIRE

Leicestershire is fairly well-endowed with C14 and C15 glass, although it is spread rather thinly throughout the county. Nevertheless, at Laude Priory, North Luffenham and Stockerston there are reasonable amounts to be seen. The C16 windows at Withcote Hall are a fine collection that have somehow survived from late medieval times. Leicestershire's *pièce de résistance* is, however, the C12 and C13 French glass at Twycross. There is also a fine collection of C15 and C16 panels at the City museums in Leicester and a good display of C19 glass at Melton Mowbray.

MR	Place	Centuries									Principal feature(s)
		12	13	14	15	16	17	18	19	20	
1	Appleby Magna			*							good figs. of female saints in N a.t.l.
2	Ashby de la Zouch				HF	O					Swiss glass and Flemish roundels
3	Ayston			*							see below
4	Bagworth			*							see below
5	Barrowden									*	choice w. of Caroline Swash, 1980
6	Breedon-on-the-Hill			*							small fig. of Christ Crucified (NE w.)
7	Clipsham				Q						lovely bird Qs in E w., one with a fox
8	Cosby			*							Crucifixion with the Virgin
9	Empingham				H*						angels, saints, coats-of-arms (N tspt)
10	Frolesworth			G	*						C15 Sts Peter, Andrew; C14 angel, canopy
11	Garthorpe			*							early C14 figs. of saints in yellow stain
12	Goadby-Marwood			H	+	+	+				parts of figs. include (?)Charles I, saints
13	Hallaton								*		see below
14	Kegworth			*		*					frag. Sts Mary and John from a Crucifixion
15	Langham									*	early C20 ws. by NC in S tspt and chancel
16	Laude Priory				*						see below
17	Leicester, Castle Rock									*	at this school is a glass by M. Traherne
18	– Cathedral									*	C.Whall's E w. by Harry Payne
19	– Mus.				*	*					see below
20	– St Andrew									*	powerful Arts & Crafts E w. by H. Payne
21	Lockington			*							Trinity panel remains c.1320 (S Chapel)
22	Loughborough								*	*	ws. by WH, 1864; and HH, 1907
23	Market Harborough									*	The Annunciation by Celtic Studios, 1967
24	Melton Mowbray								*		C19 ws. of variable quality – good Wailes
25	North Luffenham			*						*	see below
26	Noseley			H*							remains of saints, angels, foliage, canopy
27	Peckleton			*							figs. of an abbess and St Michael (chancel)
28	Preston								*	*	mid C19 w. by Gerente; 'Nativity' by RR
29	Ratcliffe on the Wreake			G							early C14 *grisaille* with coloured border
30	Sheepy								*		figs. by B-J/WM; 2 side ws. by CEK
31	Skeffington				*						Virgin, donor figs. (N chapel E w.)
32	Stockerston				*						see below
33	Theddingworth				*						Evangelist symbols (clsty)
34	Thornton			*							see below
35	Thurcaston		+	+	*						donor (J.Meresdon); frags. of angels
36	Tixover				+	+	F				St Catherine (from Lucerne, 1646)
37	Tur Langton								*		some good ws. by HBB of 1866 and 1878
38	Twycross	*	*								see below
39	Whitwell			G*							early C14 Crucifixion plus canopy (chancel)
40	Withcote Hall					*					see below
41	Witherley				G*						Virgin and Child; royal arms in t.l. (S w.)

See page 280 for table of symbols

AYSTON, St Mary: A S aisle window has a rather restored but beautiful C15 scene of the Crucifixion with Sts Mary and John, as well as two saint-bishops and the Virgin with Child below. Other fragments and roundels include an Adoration of the Magi, a Presentation in the Temple the head of a friar and the coat-of-arms of the Brudenell family.

BAGWORTH, Parish Church: At the heads of the intersection tracery lights are some C14 fragments and three scenes from a Nativity series which show the Flight into Egypt, the Three Kings, and the Virgin and Child.

HALLATON, St Michael: Much high Victorian glass by C. E. Kempe & Co. His generally high quality work and personal style of figure drawing are nearly always immediately recognisable: so too his predilection for depicting angels' wings with peacocks' feathers – as in the musical angels here in the S chancel and the archangels in the E window of the S aisle.

LAUNDE Priory: In the E window are three large well-drawn C15 figures of the Annunciation angel, St John the Baptist and St Catherine; above in the tracery lights are Tudor roses and six saints, including St Roche and St Margaret. In the tracery lights of some S windows are about twenty smaller C15 figures, mainly of saints and fathers of the church, some named.

LEICESTER Museums: At both Jewry Wall and Newarke House museums is a substantial collection of stained glass of which the most important part is the glass from Wygston's House. The twenty-nine C15 panels in yellow stain and dark paint in the JEWRY WALL museum are well documented in the official pamphlet and feature the Life and Joys of Mary from the Nativity to the Assumption, fourteen scenes of the Seven Sacraments and Seven Acts of Mercy. At NEWARKE HOUSE are early C16 scenes with figures of Sts Margaret, Christopher, Catherine and George, and the Nativity.

NORTH LUFFENHAM, St John the Baptist: A triple light in the N wall has a fine display of C14 glass. Beneath tall canopies and sandwiched between three layers of mid C14 shields of arms are three (fairly heavily restored) early C14 figures of St Mary Magdalene, Barbara and Edward (all with new heads); the double border of vine stems framing the cups of Galacia and towers of Castile is probably not original to the figures. In a window next door are more fragments and a number of shields of arms. Of the C19 glass perhaps most notable is C. E. Kempe's five-light E window of *c*.1892, a memorial to a former rector, the Revd Gretton Dennis.

STOCKERSTON, St Peter: Fragments of late C15 glass from a workshop that operated in the Stamford-Peterborough area can be seen in the N aisle; they include figures of a bishop (possibly St Clement), St Christopher, two kneeling donors and a Crucifixion.

THORNTON, St Peter: Recently one of the S aisle windows has been reset and cleaned to reveal three early C14 Nativity cycle scenes: the Magi, a king offering a crown to the Virgin and Child, and the Flight into Egypt. These scenes are set within borders of castles and under battlement canopies.

TWYCROSS, St James: Remarkable C12 and C13 panels in the E window from the Ste Chapelle (*c*.1245), St Dennis (*c*.1140), Le Mans (*c*.1100-1135) and other English and Flemish work, some *'atrocement mutilées',* says Louis Grodecki, in order to fit them into this window. Using the abbreviations SD for St Denis, SC for the Ste Chapelle, and LM for Le Mans, the various panels can be identified and allocated as follows: the left lancet has (top to bottom) a scene from the life of St Benedict (SD), a kneeling saint, the people before Moses (SC), and St John (SC). In the centre a Resurrection of *c*.1200, the Presentation in the Temple (SD), an exquisite Deposition from the Cross wth Sts Mary and John (SC), and The Spies with the Grapes (SC). On the right is another St Benedict panel (SD), a C14 kneeling woman (LM), Moses and the Ten Commandments (SC), and the emperor Domitian (SC) linked to the St John panel. Work is in progress to find the precise provenance and location of these panels, which are clearly related to some of the glass at Raby Castle in Durham (qv) and at Wilton parish church in Wiltshire (qv).

WITHCOTE Hall, Chapel: Eight apostles and ten prophets all strongly coloured and each carrying a scroll with a prophecy or part of the Creed line the N and S sides of the chapel. They are similar in style to the glass at King's College, Cambridge, and probably by Galyon Hone who worked at King's – the heraldry for Jane Seymour suggests a date of 1536-7. From E to W the figures are Sts Peter, Andrew, John; then James the Less, Philip and Bartholomew; Thomas, Jude and Zachariah. On the opposite side are Isaiah, Jeremiah and Ezekiel; Daniel, Hosea and Joel; then Amos, Micah and (?)Zephania. There are also coats-of-arms for Ratcliffe, Ashby, Smith as well as royal coats-of-arms. Also see the small scenes of Christ Crucified between two thieves and Sts Mary and John from another Crucifixion.

LINCOLNSHIRE

There is plenty of medieval glass in the county, especially of the C15, and there are good examples at a number of places; indeed, one could spend days in Stamford alone digesting the glass in all its churches. Lincoln Cathedral is a treasure house of C13 glass, much of which is at present (1984) being cleaned and releaded, and – for those who have acquired a taste for it – there is plenty of C19 glass.

MR	Place	Centuries									Principal feature(s)
		12	13	14	15	16	17	18	19	20	
1	Addlethorpe				*						see below
2	Boston, Guildhall Mus.				*						see below
3	Brant Broughton								*		see below
4	Carlton Scroop			*							t.l. figs. of a knight and other donor
5	Corby Glen				*						figs. of St John and the Virgin
6	Corringham								*		2 good ws. by Wailes; Tree of Jesse by CEK
7	Edenham				*						4 musical angels W w; St Catherine (N w.)
8	Gedney			*	+						see below
9	Glentham									*	Arts & Crafts w. by C.Whall, c.1915
10	Grantham								*	*	see below
11	Hackthorn								*		early work by HH for JP, 1861
12	Heydour			*	*						see below
13	Kelstern									*	3 late ws. by NC, 1954–8
14	Kingerby				G*						a beautiful St Catherine (S a. E w.)
15	Lea			*	*						C14 figs.; C15 Crucifixion
16	Leadenham					F					Christ and angels in Flemish glass (E w.)
17	Lincoln, Cathedral	+	*					*	*	*	see below
18	Locksley Hall			*	*	H	H				2 C14 panels from Norwich; C15 saint
19	Long Sutton			*	*						see below
20	Metheringham				*						C15 apostles (clsty)
21	Nettleham								*	*	St Francis by CEK, 1883; w. by JHY
22	North Thoresby				*						3 small figs. (N a.)
23	Pinchbeck			+	*						C15 figs. (N a. E w.)
24	Raithby					F*					C16 German panels
25	Sleaford								*		mid C19 ws. by Holland of Warwick and JH
26	South Ormsby				*	O*					see below
27	Stamfd., Brown's Hos.				*						see below
28	– St George				Q*						200 Garter motto Qs.; Sts Anne and Cath.
29	– St John the Baptist				*			*			see below
30	– St Martin				*	*	*				see below
31	– St Mary				*				*		see below
32	Tattershall				*						see below
33	Thorpe Tilney, Hall									*	recent semi-circular w. by PR
34	Willoughby-by-Alford									*	John Smith Mem. by FS, 1974
35	Wrangle				*						see below

See page 280 for table of symbols

ADDLETHORPE, St Nicholas: In four N nave sets of tracery lights are some charming little C15 figures of saints: Stephen with three stones set on ruby glass (and trumpeting angels); then Zita carrying a book, keys and rosary; Lucy with a sword through her neck; and St Mary of Antioch; next door are some feathered seraphim, whilst in the fourth set of lights is St Stephen again, with St Laurence as an archbishop.

BOSTON, Guildhall Museum: In the front gable can be seen eleven mid-C15 figures, angels (one a left-handed flute-player!), eagles and mythical creatures that include a part archer/bird/lion; the figures are an unusual combination: St Mary, (?)Christ or Joseph, Sts Matthew, Bartholomew, John, Philip, Simon, Peter, Mathias, Paul and Jacob.

BRANT BROUGHTON, St Helen: The E window here is a fine work by Burlison & Grylls of c.1876 for the architect Bodley. The rest of the C19 glass, however, was designed by Canon Frederick Heathcote Sutton, a sometime incumbent: eg the three Doctors of the Church in a N window of c.1876. In this instance his windows were made for him by Kempe & Co.; but the Canon was a serious amateur glazier and on other occasions made the windows himself using his own kiln; examples of his work can be seen in other Lincolnshire churches (eg Grace Dieu and Ketton) and in Lincoln Cathedral.

GEDNEY, St Mary: The E window of the N aisle has fine C14 remains comprising the top half of a Tree of Jesse with six near-complete figures and many names, some of which are attached to the figures: note the grapes in the Tree and the different types of border – castles, cups, vine and oak-leaf all characteristic of the mid C14 (*see illustration on* p.21). There are also some C15 remains in the traceries of the clerestory on the N side with monograms, and some fine *in situ* tracery lights on the N side of the nave with complete plants, (this is very typical of the C14).

GRANTHAM, St Wulfram: Kempe & Co. glass of the 1890s in the N aisle, of the 1880s in the S aisle; whereas in the E and SE windows it is by the firm when under Walter Tower in the 1920s and early 1930s and therefore probably designed by Lisle. Clayton & Bell's glass of 1875 can be seen in the S chapel and S aisle, and Wailes's of the mid 1850s at the W end of the church. Of 1962 is St Michael Triumphant over Evil by H. W. Harvey of York and Laurence Bond. On the S side is a semi-abstract representation of the Seven Sacraments and, on the N, St Peter walking on the water, both post-war works by John Hayward.

HEYDOUR, St Michael: In two N aisle windows are some well-preserved figures in the tracery lights: Sts Edward, George and Edmund in one are of c.1380 and have shields of England and Scrope below; Sts Vincent, Laurence and Stephen with saw, gridiron and stones are in another – two of the C15, but Laurence is C14; there are strange grotesques of dragons and bagpipe-playing centaur-women below.

LINCOLN Cathedral: The splendid C13 glass here has suffered somewhat over the centuries from iconoclasm, gunfire (in C16 and C17), and insensitive restoration in the C18 in addition to the ravages of time and present-day pollution. The panels and fragments that remain have been moved about somewhat and possibly added to with extraneous material, such that what remains is rather confusing. The **Dean's Eye** (the N rose

window) contains about fifty per cent of its original glass of c.1210-20; enough remains to deduce that the main theme was that of the Last Judgement into which over the years have been interpolated scenes from the life of St Hugh as well as incidents from the legend of the Life of the Virgin Mary, bishops and even Adam and Eve. Here is the layout of the glass now:

1 Christ in Majesty, 2 Jesus among the doctors, 3 The foolish virgins, 4 Four men standing back to back, 5 The blessed in adoration, 6 An emtombment scene, 7 The blessed in adoration, 8 The blessed in adoration, 9 Joseph is chosen as Mary's husband, 10 The blessed in adoration, 11 The blessed in adoration, 12 The blessed in adoration, 13 St Hugh's body being carried to Lincoln, 14 Men carrying a coffin, 15 The blessed in adoration, 16 The blessed in adoration, 17 The blessed in adoration, 18 Censing angels, 19 Censing angels, 20 Censing angel, 21 Censing angel, 22 Christ as Judge, 23 Two angels with a spear, 24 Two with the crown of thorns, 25 Seven seated apostles, 26 Two angels with trumpets, 27 Adam delving, Eve spinning, 28 A bishop, 29 An archbishop, 30 A bishop, 31 An archbishop, 32 A bishop, 33 A fragment, 34 Resurrection of the dead, 35 Two angels with trumpets, 36 The Virgin and apostles, 37 Angels with nail and censer, 38 The Cross

Opposite this magnificent window is the more dramatic Bishop's Eye of the **S transept** with its filigree tracery that dates from c.1330; it is filled with fragments of C14 glass that seem to suggest the former presence of a Last Judgement scene. These two 'orbiculae' as the C13 Metrical Life of St Hugh describes them, 'are the two eyes of the church: rightly the greater is the bishop, the lesser the dean. For on the north is the devil, to the south the Holy Ghost: towards these the two eyes look. For the

The Nativity – in a domestic setting with midwife! C16 Flemish (?); South Ormsby, Lincolnshire.

bishop faces south that he may receive the one: the dean the north that he may avoid the other; one looks to be saved, the other lest he perish. The front of the church is the lantern of heaven, and with these eyes surveys the gloom of Lethe.' Beneath the Bishop's Eye are four lancets with C13 glass; the easternmost has five scenes related to the Temple worship that are (top to bottom) three figures entering the Temple, 'sprinkling the people with blood', Giving the Law (note the strange whorls of cloud around Moses), the shew-bread and lamb sacrifice; the second has two angels in green, children in front of an altar, three boys in bed (part of the St Nicholas story – note the man with an axe about to chop off the boys' heads: see p.37 for the confusions attached to this story!), a saint with three figures behind, St Nicholas on a ship (note his name inscribed here), the Virgin Mary before a lectern learning of her forthcoming death and Assumption; in the third are two little angels, the arms of Beaumont impaling de Vere, the Bosom of Abraham (souls in a cloth, as in the W rose window at Chartres), Solomon and Sheba(?), The Feast of the Return of the Prodigal Son, David Feigning Madness (by standing on his hands!); the fourth has two figures of Christ, an angel appearing to a shepherd, three Magi sent by Herod, Christ appearing to the disciples, a part-figure of God with manna set in a vesica. Yet more C13 glass can be seen in the three-light E window of the **S choir aisle**, some of which are related to the previously mentioned panels: the first has Isaac, the Calling of St Matthew, St John in boiling oil, an execution scene, St Thomas Becket being received into heaven; the second light has a Virgin and Child and a Jesse Tree king (both

C12), a bishop, Barabbas, another Jesse king; in the third are St Paul, the Ark, figures, St John preaching, Moses reading the Law. In the equivalent position in the **N choir aisle** is another Jesse king, Moses and the destruction of Pharaoh's hosts, Theophilus of Adana (who sold his soul for glory in the world instead of accepting a bishopric), the Virgin receiving Theophilus' deed; the second has various saints; in the third is yet another Jesse king, a man in a grave, the (?)'wine-press' of Revelation, two figures and a censing angel, people with the Virgin Mary, and a panel from the story of the Jewish glassmaker at Bourges. In the **N transept** underneath the Dean's Eye is some C13 *grisaille*, and in a window by the Dean's doorway are five C14 musician-angels. At the N end of the **NE transept** are some geometrical drawings by W. Peckitt of 1762.

Much of the C19 glass here is imitation C13, notably the E window with numerous roundels by Ward & Hughes of 1855, which firm also did the glass in the N aisle; that in the S windows of the S transept is by Hedgeland, whilst much of the glass in the nave, S aisle, W window and W rose is by the Revds Frederick and Auguste Sutton (see Brent Broughton). The window over the Russell Chantry is by Francis Skeat.

LONG SUTTON, St Mary: Many C14 and C15 remains in tracery lights around the church, the centrepiece of which is a fairly complete C14 figure of St George in the S choir aisle (not John of Gaunt – a mistaken tradition brought about by a misplaced coat-of-arms); above him are C15 fragments and panels of St Apollonia, the Virgin, donor figures, a psaltery-playing angel and a dragon probably from a St Michael window; in the Eastern-most set of tracery lights here is the figure of St Ursula and a few of her 11,000 maidens, various heads and fragments. On the N side of the chancel seven windows have tracery remains, some of which house tiny figures under canopies.

SOUTH ORMSBY, St Leonard: A two-light S window has some interesting pieces of old glass: at the head is a reconstructed Crucifixion scene, set with two female heads (the Marys?). Below left are some eight Flemish roundels that include the execution of a Dominican, St John as bishop, St Nicholas with three children in a tub, the Via Crucis, Gethsemane, the Betrayal, an Annunciation and an Old Testament prophet; right, are the Jordan

Baptism, Good Samaritan, St Margaret, Stoning of two saints, Nativity, an archbishop and St John.

STAMFORD, Brown's Hospital Chapel: High quality glass of 1475 in the chapel, reminiscent of that in the Beauchamp Chapel, Warwick. Above the transom of the S wall window can be seen the figures of St James as a pilgrim, St John the Baptist with camel-skin and Agnus Dei, a Stoke-rebus of a stork rising from its nest, a complete Trinity panel (with Father, Son and Dove) and St Edmund; below the transom are a number of different representations of the Virgin Mary within interesting canopies, borders and niches and inscriptions to William and Margaret Brown; also on the S wall a portrayal of St Michael with the devil amid other remains; a third window here has a merchant's mark, a shield of arms for Browne, another of the same impaling Elmes, a stork rebus again. Not to be missed on the S side is the Audit Room with the figures of St Paul and two St Davids with arms of the Elmes family: also King Solomon – and a male saint with the name 'Seneca' on a scroll!

STAMFORD, St John the Baptist: In the tracery lights of the aisles are some figures of varying quality of saints and Virtues; in the N aisle (E to W) are Sts Augustine, Ambro and parts of angels; then Giles, Botolph, Blaise, Leonard, Peter the Martyr and saints with mitres; next door, the Virgin Mary with God holding souls in a sheet, embraced by the Four Cardinal Virtues: Spes, Fides, Caritas, Sapiencia. Over in the S aisle (E to W) are Sts Mark, (?), Christopher, George (plus dragon), Matthew, John; the westernmost has Sts Petronilla, Mary Magdalene, Ethelreda, Catherine and two others. The Vestry E window has St Elisabeth in the tracery lights, reset pieces that include St Oswald's head, prophets, donors, a small phoenix, angels and a lion. All the glass here dates from c.1451. The huge C19 window with the Adoration of the Magi is by Oliphant, c.1878.

STAMFORD, St Martin: Much of the mid C15 glass here was removed to and then returned from Tattershall, together with some of its glass, and reinstalled by William Peckitt in 1757–9. In the large and splendid E window are four saints in the central row with God in the centre, four large angels and the royal arms above, C16 shields below and various panels of

David slaying Goliath, C15; St Martin, Stamford, Lincolnshire.

reset fragments and geometric arrangements filling the spaces in between; in the tracery lights can be seen an Annunciation in the centre. On the S side of the chancel is another Peckitt arrangement that includes musician angels in the heads of the lights, various reset heads and three composite saintly figures in the bottom row. The S chapel E window has three saints, two with mitres and one with cross-staff (and extraneous female head!); C16 shield of arms in the tracery lights. The S window has two angels in the outer lights above the transom and a pair (from a Trinity?) between them; below the transom are three rather composite figures. The best glass in the church can be seen in the S aisle where three Old Testament scenes are set above three from the New — clearly panels from a type–antetype series (based on the *Biblium Pauperum*) which was originally at Tattershall: Moses striking the rock, Samson carrying the gates of Gaza, and David slaying Goliath (*see illustration above*). The Crucifixion, the three

137

Marys at the tomb, and the Resurrection are below; also shields of Goldsborough, (?) Marmyon, Russell and Grey of Rotherfield.

STAMFORD, St Mary: In the E window the Lady Chapel is Christopher Whall's first window of *c.*1890 with the Virgin and Child, Adam and Eve and St Michael with angels.

TATTERSHALL, Holy Trinity: We have here the unfortunate aesthetic clash between the freshness of a spacious Perpendicular church well illuminated by clear glass, and its interesting ancient glass at one end (in the E window of the Chapel) that loses its impact due to too much light on its inside surface. As it happens, at the time of writing, the glass was in a poor state of repair, but the potential quality of it is quite outstanding; companion panels can be seen at St Martin's, Stamford (qv) and Burghley House (Northants, qv). Some was lost through a barbarous act in 1754, yet there remain twenty panels dating from *c.*1481–83, mostly scenes from a series of the Corporeal Acts of Mercy and of the Seven Sacraments, interspersed with all sorts of bits and pieces. Starting with the left lancet we can see (top to bottom): (1) Clothing The Naked, angels on a wheel with a shield, Confirmation, angels (possibly part of an Annunciation); (2) fragments and interesting roundels, St Luke's Ox, the Virgin and Child with Sts James the Great behind and four angels; (3) angels identical to those in the left light, the Virtues Misericordia and Pax with organ and Yorkist badge above, Sts James the Great and Paul, Pieta, a broken panel and the Resurrection; (4) various fragments, Baptism from the

Sacrament series, more fragments; (5) the same pair of angels as before, Veritas, Sts Peter and John (with chalice and serpent), two musician angels and a dragon above; (6) roundels, feathered and musican angels; (7) Feeding the Hungry from the series, arms of Cromwell impaling Tattershall, an odd-shaped rose *ensoleille,* a scene from the legend of a saint and the same pair of angels.

WRANGLE, Sts Mary and Nicholas: Some fine glass in the N aisle, particularly in the E window where the main lights house (beneath C15 canopies) C14-C15 pieces that include part of a Scourging scene, part of what might be a Marriage at Cana scene, the Nativity and part of an Annunciation below, the Resurrection and the best panel of all — the Assumption with the Virgin Mary placed in a vesica of radiant light and surrounded by six angels. Above in the tracery lights are figures from a genealogy of Christ series that include the prophets and kings David, Solomon, Jeremiah, Osia, Joash, Isaiah, Ezekiel, Josias, Hezekiah, Amos, Joel, Reboas and Jonas. In the tracery lights of three N windows are many good C15 figures, not all indigenous: (E to W) we can see in (1) Sts Perpetua (with palm), Alban and George above Cecilia (with organ), June, Obeth, a king and (?)Agnes (or Lucy with a dagger through the neck), Abiram and Sitha (with key); (2) an Annunciation above fine figures of Sts Barbara (with tower), Stephen, Edmund, a king, Laurence and (?)Lucy, all with attributes; (3) Sts Peter and John above a female saint, Margaret and six prophets (rather decayed), some of which may have come from a Tree of Jesse.

LONDON

London has much interesting stained glass although – with the exception of the Victoria & Albert Museum – hardly any of it is of medieval age. The V & A has a splendid collection of glass of all ages and from most parts of Europe: in fact anyone looking for a crash course in stained glass recognition could gain much by visiting it at frequent intervals. There is some heraldic glass, mostly of the C17 in the City; West Wickham, Bromley has some good C15 windows. St Mary's, Wimbledon, in Merton, possesses a fine *in situ* C14 tracery light panel with St George and the dragon, and there are a few C15 panels given to All Saints, Margaret Street, City of Westminster. For C19 and C20 glass, London is particularly rich: examples from just about every decade over the past 150 years and by numerous different glaziers can be found; the main problem is getting into locked churches to see the glass there.

MR Place	Centuries								Principal feature(s)
	13	14	15	16	17	18	19	20	
Barnet									
1 St Mary, East Barnet			+	+					some remains on the N side
2 St Joseph, Mill Hill								*	rich abstract glass by GG, c.1973
Bexley									
3 The Red House							*		see below
Brent									
4 All Souls, Harlesden								*	early C20 glass by Selwyn Image
5 St Andrew, Kingsbury							*		see below
6 St Augustine, Kilburn							*		see below
7 St Gabriel, Cricklewood								*	ws. on N side by M. Travers and J. Nuttgens
8 St Francis, Gladstone Park								*	Arts & Crafts w. by MAR, 1920
Bromley									
9 St John the Baptist, West Wickham			*				*		see below
10 St Martin, Chelsfield								*	E w. by M.Forsyth; 2 ws. by C.Whall, 1925
11 St Mary, Downe								*	see below
12 St Nicholas, Chiselhurst							*		rose and other ws. by J.Brook and Hardman
Camden									
13 Christ Church, Albany Rd							*		see below
14 Church of Christ the King								*	see below
15 Lincoln's Inn Chapel					*				see below
16 St Andrew, Frognal Lane								*	much glass by D. Strachan, 1922–5
17 St John, Hampstead						*			CB semi-circular ws.; E w. by Wooldridge
18 St John, Kentish Town							*		see below
19 St Luke, Kentish Town							*	*	see below
20 St Mark, Regent's Park Rd								*	ws. by B.Thomas, J.Hayward, GG, and NC
21 St Pancras, Euston Sq.							*		excellent CB of 1860-62 behind altar
City of London									
22 Baker's Hall								*	3 ws. by J.Piper for rebuilding of 1968–9
23 Baltic Exchange								*	unusual ws. by J. D. Forsyth, 1922
24 St Andrew, Undershaft				*			*		see below
25 St Botolph, Aldersgate						*	*		see below
26 St Dunstan-in-West							*		Kempe's Izaac Walton w. based on 'Lives'
27 St Ethelburga				H					arms of Mercers, Sadlers, Vintners, City
28 St Helen, Bishopsgate				H					arms of Leathersellers, J.Crosby, Lumley
29 St Katherine Kree				+H		*	*		see below
30 St Magnus the Martyr				H					arms of the City and the Plumbers
31 St Michael, Cornhill							*		see below
32 St Michael, Paternoster Royal								*	Dick Whittington and E ws. by J.Hayward
33 St Nicholas, Cole Abbey								*	Keith New's E w.: Church as a Ship, 1962
34 St Peter, Cornhill							*		E w. by Gibbs, 1872; 2 by H.Easton in N a.
35 St Sepulchre-without-Newgate								*	see below
36 St Vedast								*	Conversion of Clovis, B.Thomas, 1961
37 Selection Trust Building								*	Carl Edward's 'Mirror Window'
38 Temple Church							*	*	see below
39 Tower of London		FH	FH	F	F				see below
City of Westminster									
40 All Saints, Margaret St			*				*		see below
41 Immaculate Conception, Farm St								*	Assumption & rose ws. by Evie Hone, 1953
42 Houses of Parliament							*	*	The Lords: C. Edwards and Pugin ws.
43 St Barnabas, Pimlico							*	*	Christ and Children by HH, 1901; w. by NC
44 St George, Hanover Sq.				F					see below
45 St James, Sussex Gardens							*	*	C19 ws. by WW and CB; C20 Te Deum by AB
46 St Margaret, Westminster				F			*	*	see below
47 St Mary Magdalene							*		see below
48 St Paul's, Knightsbridge							*		Crypt and Jesse Tree by LBW
49 St Peter's, Vere St							*		late C19 colourful ws. by B-J for WM
50 St Stephen, Rochester Row							*		glass by WM; also by Wailes (c.1850)
51 Savoy Chapel			+	+					2 donor figs. Qs and *grisaille*

MR Place	Centuries								Principal feature(s)
	13	14	15	16	17	18	19	20	
52 Synagogue,									
Great Portland St								*	symbolism in glass by Roman Halter
53 Westminster Abbey	*		*			*	*	*	see below
Croydon									
54 St John, Upper Norwood							*	*	N rose by NC (this was his church); CB ws.
55 St Matthew								*	see below
Ealing									
56 Holy Cross, Greenford			H*						see below
57 St Anselm, Southall								*	the 1971 E w. is by RP
58 St Hugh, Northolt								*	d-d-v by Pierre Fourmaintreaux/JP, 1970
59 St John Fisher								*	10 ws. by GG
60 St Mary, Ealing						*			The Temptation of Eve is a good early LB w.
61 St Nicholas, Perivale			+						2 half-figs. of the Virgin and St John
Enfield									
62 Christchurch, Southgate						*			see below
63 St Andrew, Enfield			H +						Thomas Roos' Gartered arms; figs. of nuns
Greenwich									
64 Morden College Chapel			*						figs. of c.1600
65 Queen Elizabeth									
Almshouses			F						N.T. scenes in Flemish glass
66 St Luke, Charlton								*	a choice w. of Laurence Lee
67 St Peter, Woolwich					*	H			fig. in E w. dated 1639
68 Trinity Hospital Chapel							*		ws. design by Pugin, made by Wailes, c.1850
Hackney									
69 Ch. of the Good Shepherd						*			see below
70 St Mary,									
Stoke Newington (old)			H+	H					in low part of E w. figs. and arms
71 St Mary,									
Stoke Newington (new)							*		apse w. by Francis Skeat, 1957–8
72 St Paul, Shoreditch						*			some good glass by HH, 1887–8
Hammersmith and Fulham									
73 All Saints, Fulham				H	H	*			much competent glass by HBB of the 1880s
74 Charing Cross Hosp.				H	H		*		see below
75 Public Library				+	+				various remains from Strawberry Hill
Haringey									
76 All Hallows, Tottenham				F	F				Evangelists, David, Isaiah, Jeremiah
77 Queens Hotel, Crouch End								*	Cakebread, Robey & Co's Art Nouveau ws.
78 St Anne's, Highgate							*		Acts of Mercy w., early LBW, 1865
79 St Mary, Hornsey Rise							*		good C19 glass; eg Westlake's Tree of Jesse
80 St Michael							*	*	see below
81 St Paul, Wood Green								*	'Mary, Queen of Heaven' by Moira Forsyth
Harrow									
82 Harrow School Chapel							*		ws. by Lusson of Paris, CB, JH, Warrington
83 Pinner, Parish Church								*	A. Fisher w., 1981, after Chartres Virgin
84 St Anselm, Hatch End								*	see below
Havering									
85 St Andrew, Hornchurch			*						Crucifixion (plus Virgin's head interpolated)
86 St Mary, N.Ockendon	*		H*						see below
87 St Thomas, Noak Hill				F	HF				see below
Hillingdon									
88 Hillingdon Hospital								*	see below
89 St Gregory, Ruislip								*	P. Quail w.
90 St Mary, Harefield				*					roundels with Christ, priests, Revelation
91 St Peter and Paul						*			early CEK glass in E w., 1873
92 Uxbridge Civic Centre								*	in Marriage Room, recent glass by J.Gray
93 Uxbridge Underground Sta.								*	see below
Hounslow									
94 St George, Hanworth			*		H				2 seraphim, columbine Qs
95 St Mary, Norwood Green				F	O				see below
Islington									
96 St Andrew, Whitehall Park				*					Sts James and Simon
97 Holy Trinity						*			the fig. of R.Cloudesley by TW of the 1820s

MR Place	13	14	15	16	17	18	19	20	Principal feature(s)
98 Moorfields Hosp.								*	Celtic Cross by R.Rutherford, 1971
99 St Mark								*	'The Ascension' by A.Buss for GG
100 St Saviours, Aberdeen Park							*		a notable w. by N.Westlake of 1865
Kensington and Chelsea									
101 Chelsea Old Church			F	O					4 Flemish fig. panels, donors
102 Holy Trinity, Brompton Road							*		E w. by Warrington, 1845; the rest are by JP
103 Holy Trinity, Sloane St							*	*	see below
104 St Columba, Pont St								*	E rose w. by M. Forsyth, 1955
105 St Mary Abbots							*	*	much CB glass, JP rose w., 2 by A.Fisher
106 St Paul's Onslow Sq.			*				*	*	CB ws.; St Cecilia by A. Rosencranz, 1930
107 St Simon Zelotes							*		E w. is a notable early w. of LB
108 Victoria & Albert Museum	*	*	*	*	*		*		see below
Kingston									
109 All Saints, Kingston							*		see below
110 Christchurch, Surbiton							*		HBB E w. of 1865; B-J/LB in N a., 1871
111 Public Lib. and Museum			H						arms of James I, Charles I, Anne of Denmark
Lambeth									
112 Christchurch, Streatham							*	*	see below
113 Lambeth Palace			+H	+H				*	see below
114 St John, Vassal Rd								*	rich post-war glass by T.Carter Shapland
115 St Mary, Lambeth								*	see below
Lewisham									
116 St Andrew's, Catford								*	Robson's Art Nouveau w., M. Travers w.
117 St George, Perry Hill							*		see below
118 St Margaret, Lee Terrace							*		good CB glass
119 St Mildred, Lee								*	see below
120 St Stephens, Lewisham							*		CB medallions, 1865; J.Nuttgens ws.
121 Sacred Heart Convent								*	6 richly coloured ws. by AF, 1985
Merton									
122 St Mary, Wimbledon		*	H						St George and dragon; arms of Thomas Cecil
123 St Laurence, Morden				*					Moses and Aaron (van Linge school?)
Redbridge									
124 Ilford Hospital Chapel			H						late C16 arms of (?)John Gresham
125 St Mary, Little Ilford			H	F	+				in N chapel frag. remains
Richmond									
126 Hampton Court Palace							*		C19 ws. by TW replace C16 (see Earsdon)
127 St John, Kew Rd								*	Chapel E w. by CW, 1912; 1 by Mabel Esplin
128 St Margaret (R.C.) Twickenham								*	'Christ Breaking Into the World' by RP
129 Strawberry Hill			O	FO	F				see below
Southwark									
130 All Saints, West Dulwich								*	four lights by Basil Barber — a choice work
131 Glaziers' Hall								*	Glaziers coat-of-arms by A. Fisher
132 James Allen School								*	Gustav Holst Mem. by M.Farrar Bell, 1969
133 St George's Cathedral (R.C.)								*	rich E & W ws. by H. Clarke Studios
134 St Giles, Camberwell							*		see below
135 St John, Meeting House Lane								*	ws. by S. Johnson, 1960s
136 St Luke, Peckham								*	ws. by Marion Grant and R. Hendra
137 St Peter's, Walworth								*	colourful E w. by Clare Dawson
138 Southwark Cathedral			H				*	*	see below
Sutton									
139 All Saints, Benhilton								*	Kettlewells' E w., 1965; ws. by JH
Tower Hamlets									
140 St Anne, Limehouse							*		The Crucifixion by Clutterbuck, 1853
Waltham Forest									
141 William Morris Gallery							*		good collection of cartoons by WM & Co.
Wandsworth									
142 All Saints, Putney							*	*	see below
143 Ch. of The Ascension							*		see below

MR Place	Centuries								Principal feature(s)
	13	14	15	16	17	18	19	20	
144 Our Lady of Victories							*		Pugin-designed glass for JH, 1850-53
145 St Mary, Battersea					*			*	see below
146 Whitelands, Col., Putney							*		B-j/WM ws. of female saints, 1885-93

See page 280 for table of symbols

BEXLEY, The Red House, Bexley Heath: Built for Wiliam Morris by Philip Webb in 1858, the house has some small windows of *c.* 1861 by Morris in the lower corridor and on the stairs, as well as some find bird quarries designed by Philip Webb.

BRENT, St Andrew, Kingsbury: The E window is a late collaboration by Pugin and Hardman that dates from *c.* 1862. The rest of the windows are by Clayton & Bell of 1868 and 1877. Of particular note is the magnificent five-lancet W window with Christ in Glory surrounded by many saints.

BRENT, St Augustine, Kilburn: Competent and sumptuous glass of the high Victorian era by Clayton & Bell for Pearson, notably the huge W rose window with subjects from Genesis. Note the highly coloured angels in the small SE apse windows. Adam and male saints are along the S aisle, and Eve with the females down the N.

BROMLEY, St John the Baptist, West Wickham: In the N chapel is some late C15/early C16 glass; the figures are large and generally well drawn, but some of the yellow staining has darkened to a rather ugly shade of orange. The E window has St Christopher with the Christ Child (note the fish under his feet and the tiny trees in the background); beneath is a kneeling skeleton with a coat-of-arms for the donor Heydon of *c.* 1480, who bequeathed the window to the church in his will; also here are figures of St Anne teaching the Virgin to read, and the Virgin again with the Christ Child, the latter holding a bird. On the N side is another St Christopher, but headless this time, St Catherine with the emperor at her feet, St Dorothy with the infant Christ and the Virgin as the Mother of Sorrows. The C19 glass here is by Kempe & Co.

BROMLEY, St Mary, Downe: A fine window with the Crucifixion by the Irish stained glass artist Evie Hone, a theme she also used at Eton College Chapel. Keith Coleborne's sanctuary window of 1973 commemorates a world voyage.

CAMDEN, Christ Church, Albany Street: Some fine glass by Clayton & Bell in a number of windows dating over the period *c.* 1867-1908, notably in the galleries; their best window, however, is possibly the three-light Crucifixion in the S aisle in their characteristic style of the mid 1860s. Next to it is a charming small group of three windows by D.G. Rossetti of *c.* 1870 for Morris & Co., depicting the Sermon on the Mount, in which the faces of Mary and Mary Magdalene are said to be modelled on Christina Rossetti and Jane Morris.

CAMDEN, Church of Christ the King, Woburn Square: In the Lady Chapel the splendid Arts & Crafts E window is by Lilian Pocock, a pupil of Christopher Whall, *c.* 1930. On the N and S sides here are windows of 1954 by John Weatherley for Goddard & Gibbs, with Creation and Redemption.

CAMDEN, Lincoln's Inn Chapel: The original glazing here dates from 1623 by Bernard van Linge, but much was damaged in an air raid in the First World War; only the S window with the Apostles Sts James, Simon and Matthias remain with some restoration; the rest of the windows are good modern imitations.

CAMDEN, St John, Highgate Road, Kentish Town: Fine early windows by Morris, Marshall, Faulkner & Co. of 1862-3, designed mainly by Burne-Jones. The windows depict Noah building the Ark, Christ with disciples, and the Building of the Temple. The Baptism of Christ of 1845 is by Wailes.

CAMDEN, St Luke, Caversham Road, Kentish Town: Morris & Co. glass of *c.* 1910 in the clerestory windows with the figures of Sts Alphege, Edward the Confessor, Thomas Becket and Hugh of Lincoln; the cartoon for the figure of St Alphege, originally drawn by Burne-Jones, was in fact first used for the figure of Bishop Alcock at Jesus College, Cambridge, in 1873. Henry Holiday designed the apse windows (for Heaton, Butler & Bayne) and the Six Days of Creation in a circular window of *c.* 1868.

CITY OF LONDON, St Andrew Under-shaft, St Mary Axe St: The W window has the figures of Edward VI, Elizabeth I, James I and Charles I that date from *c.*1637. The figure of William III is obviously of a later date. All have been restored following a fire in 1976. The massive Crucifixion and Ascension window is by Heaton, Butler & Bayne.

CITY OF LONDON, St Botolph, Alder-sgate: The Agony in the Garden at the E end resembles a painting rather than a window, due to the strange lighting inside the church: it was in fact painted on to glass by James Pearson in 1788 to designs by Nathaniel Clarkson. Of *c.* 1886 are the picturesque windows in the N aisle by Ward & Hughes; those in the S aisle are of recent date by M.C. Farrar Bell.

CITY OF LONDON, St Katherine Kree, Leadenhall St: The E rose window of 1630 with abstract patterns in glass was probably inspired by the rose that used to adorn the E end of the old St Paul's Cathedral; it was repaired by Pearson in 1777 and may still contain some pieces of that era. In two S aisle and one N aisle windows are reassembled C17 fragments that incorporate shields – that in the NE corner has Cordwainers' arms. In the S aisle the window of Christ walking on the Water is by M.C. Farrar Bell (1963), a memorial to those who drowned in the sinking of the ship *Lancastria*. In the N aisle is a Transfiguration by Kempe & Co., *c.* 1890.

CITY OF LONDON, St Michael, Cornhill: Outstanding early glass by Clayton & Bell of 1859 with New Testament scenes; note the brilliant colour and gorgeous robes of the Magi in a nave S window, also the foliage and the palm tree (a detail that often occurs in their early windows). The round E window with Christ in Glory of the same date is also by them, possibly inspired by the round windows in Florence Cathedral.

CITY OF LONDON, St Sepulchre-without-Newgate: A number of post-war windows, notably Brian Thomas's memorials to John Ireland and Dane Nellie Melba in the N chapel, A.K. Nicholson's Walter Carroll Memorial and St Bernard window, and Francis Skeat's John Smith window. There is also the notorious Musicians' Window with Bach, Handel, St Cecilia and Sir Henry Wood playing the organ: it is by Gerald Smith, who, having worked with A.K. Nicholson, did his Memorial here.

St John the Baptist taking leave of his parents, C16 from Rouen; now in the Victoria & Albert Museum in London.

CITY OF LONDON, The Temple Chur-ch: Of the pre-war glass little remains – some Willement pieces of 1842 are reset in the S aisle and there is an interesting survivor of Winston's 'new' glass (*see* p.59) in a window by Ward & Nixon at the W end. Carl Edwards' E window is a fine work and very much in tune with the medieval surroundings: it depicts Christ as Judge over London during the blitz and includes Knights Templar on horseback.

CITY OF LONDON, The Tower of London, Chapel in the White Tower: A number of pieces of the C15-C18 formerly at Walpole's Strawberry Hill include Henry VIII's coat-of-arms as well as those of the Duke of Norfolk, Hastings

(Gartered) and a Dudley coat in the E window quartered sixteen times. On the S side are some enamel painted scenes that include the anointing of King David, Esau seeking Isaac's Blessing, Charles V as emperor and a large (?) Flemish panel with a soldier on one knee. Other panels include Walpole's arms, a very broken C17 Dutch scene of the expulsion of Adam and Eve, and a C18 portrayal of The Creation.

CITY OF WESTMINSTER, All Saints, Margaret St: In the W window of the S aisle are nine reset panels that include C15 figures of St John, an English angel, St Mark's lion, Christ with a chalice (Austrian glass), and two C16 French pieces. The ten saints in C19 glass on the S side are by Gibbs, replacing the original Gérente windows; the S aisle E window is by O'Connor. The fine Tree of Jesse with sixteen figures is a much altered window, originally by Gérente and modelled on the Wells Cathedral Tree, but drastically altered by Gibbs in *c.* 1877, giving rise to the present window; in fact, much of the original was transferred to Sheffield Cathedral where it was thought until recently to be a C14 Spanish work! Original Gérente glass in the N aisle W window.

CITY OF WESTMINSTER, St George, Hanover Square: The E window of *c.* 1525 was originally made by Arnoult de Nijmegen for a Carmelite church in Antwerp (its companion is in Lichfield Cathedral, qv). Primarily it is a Tree of Jesse into which have intruded medallions with St George, Victory and Isabella of Portugal (the latter at the head of Jesse's throne). To the left are Aaron and Esaias, to right Moses and Eli; above and to the left of the Virgin Mary are Josaphat with Osias, and Manasseh and Jechonias to her right; other side figures include David, Rehoboam, Solomon, Joram *et al.* Unfortunately, God the Father, intended for the summit, could not fit in and was relegated to Wilton Parish Church where the panel changed mysteriously so that God became St Nicholas!

CITY OF WESTMINSTER, St Margaret, Westminster: The E window here of *c.* 1502 was originally intended for Henry VII's Chapel at the Abbey, but it found its way to St Margaret's after residing successively at Waltham Abbey, Boreham New Hall and Copt Hall in Essex. It depicts the Crucifixion in Gothic-Renaissance transitional style, together with portraits of Prince Arthur and Catherine of Aragon; in the tracery lights are angels by William Price (the younger).

The quiet abstract modern glass on the S side, mostly in greys and blues, is by John Piper and Patrick Reyntiens, 1966, evoking the idea of 'Spring in London'. Clayton & Bell did the W window with its stately figures (1882) and the Milton window in the N aisle (1888). The S aisle W window is by Henry Holiday for Powell's, 1882, and there are two by Edward Frampton in the N aisle.

CITY OF WESTMINSTER, St Mary Magdalene, Woodchester St, Paddington: Henry Holiday's designs of 1895 for Heaton, Butler & Bayne (commissioned by G.E. Street) in the N apse include the Te Deum. In the crypt is glass by Ninian Comper.

CITY OF WESTMINSTER, Westminster Abbey: The oldest glass in the Abbey is in the Jerusalem Chamber where six C13 medallions depict the Ascension, Pentecost, the martyrdoms of Sts John the Baptist and Stephen, the Massacre of the Holy Innocents, and St Nicholas with the boy and golden cup in a boat; also of the C13 is the Resurrection window in the Muniment Room: all this is possibly by William le Verrer, mentioned in a charter of 1272. Much of the rest of the glass in the Abbey is frankly rather dull: there is a somewhat fragmentary C15 figure of St George, fragments of *c.* 1400 made up into a figure in a window under the W tower, and in the Henry VII Chapel some C16 angels and initials of Henry VII and Elizabeth of York. Joshua Price did the huge W window in 1735 in addition to the N rose window with its sixteen figures designed by Thornhill, whereas the S rose has Burlison & Grylls' glass of 1902 to Bodley's designs; but neither is particularly pleasing.

Of the C19 and C20 there is the Brunel Memorial in the S aisle by Henry Holiday for Heaton, Butler & Bayne with six Temple scenes and allegorical female figures (1886); also in the S aisle are a window by Burlison & Grylls (1922) and one by J. Dudley Forsyth of 1921, (cf. his dome window in the Baltic Exchange). Hugh Easton's famous Battle of Britain window in the Henry VII Chapel is one of his better pieces and is certainly better and more exciting than those in the Benedict and Abbot Islip Chapels. There are no fewer than seven windows by Ninian Comper in the N aisle, the most interesting of which are the Bunyan Memorial and perhaps the window to Sir Henry Royce; the Trevithick window here is of 1883 by Burlison & Grylls. In the Chapter House much of the glass is by Clayton & Bell with some post-war work by Joan Howson.

144

Sts George, Paul and Cecilia by Arild Rosencrantz, *c.*1930; St Paul's, Onslow Sq., Kensington and Chelsea, London.

CROYDON, St Matthew: The six large windows on the S side depict the Images of the Kingdom of Heaven according to St Matthew's Gospel and incorporate glass from the old church, abstract designs by John Hayward 'deliberately in dark glass', he says, that moves from 'the Treasure Buried in the Field, through that of The Sower, the Net of Fish and the Pearl of Great Price to the Leaven in the Lump'.

EALING, Holy Cross, Greenford: Heraldic glass and a few other early C16 pieces possibly from King's College, Cambridge, in a number of windows. In the E window are the arms of Henry VIII impaling those of Catherine of Aragon, quarries with harts, a stag's head, flowers and the arms for the Grocers' Company and a quaint roundel with a windmill. In a N window are a Tudor coat-of-arms and the arms of England

145

St Mark by Ford Maddox Brown, 1862; Southgate, London.

illustration); and in the nave SW the figure of St James as Bishop of Jerusalem is by Burne-Jones and St Jude by D.G. Rossetti. Other windows are mostly by Burne-Jones, some from after his death re-using old cartoons; but the excellent E and W windows with New Testament scenes are by Clayton and Bell, *c.* 1860.

HACKNEY, Church of the Good Shepherd (and of the Agapemone), Rockwood Rd, Stamford Hill: A remarkable series of expressionist windows by Walter Crane and Silvester Sparrow of *c.* 1897, notably the S aisle W window with its blazing sun and four angels. In the N aisle are the tormented figures of Adam and Even portraying the 'Cosmic Shame' of The Fall, a window that contrasts with the calmness of the stained glass lily plant next door – there are more flowers in the porches.

HAMMERSMITH AND FULHAM, Charing Cross Hospital, Chapel: Two windows by John Piper and Patrick Reyntiens at the entrance; the two on either side of the altar, with the themes 'Life on Earth' and 'Life after Death', are choice works by Alfred Fisher, 1976.

HARINGEY, St Michael: The E window is one of the few windows by the Irish stained glass artist Evie Hone whose work is always stimulating – see Eton College, Downe, Farm Street and Wellingborough for other examples. Those at the E end of the aisles are by Kempe.

HARROW, St Anselm, Hatch End: Some Arts & Crafts glass by the illustrator Selwyn Image, notably the W window with an Adoration of the Magi and Shepherds, with his rather unearthly figures; also the Pentecost and Blake Memorial windows in the NE chapel. Other windows here by Louis Davis, all *c.*1915.

HAVERING, St Mary, North Ockendon: In the N chapel is an early C14 figure of a female saint with a book and cross, possibly St Helen under a canopy of later date. Also a C15 figure of St Mary Magdalene with traditional casket of perfume, and shields for Clare, Warenne, Old England, Old France, *et al.* in tower W window.

HAVERING, St Thomas, Noak Hill: Much of this collection of medieval and later glass came from the Continent, e.g. the large Crucifixion with the Virgin Mary and two soldiers, formerly in the

quartering France, while a S window has those of the colleges at King's, Cambridge, and Eton.

ENFIELD, Christchurch, Southgate: Important glass from Morris & Co.'s second year (1862); in the Lady Chapel are three Evangelists by Morris – St Mark is by Ford Maddox Brown – under C14-styled canopies (*see*

church of Notre Dame du Lac, Tirlemont, Belgium. Below are figures of the Virgin Mary, St Elizabeth, Zacharias and St John the Baptist from a church in Rouen. On the N side are C16 and C17 shields of arms and badges for Jane Seymour, France quartering England, the Duchy of Lorraine, Barre and a panel of Doeg before Saul. On the S side are medallions of French heraldry, three of which are crowned and wreathed: below are three C17 panels with the Incredulity of St Thomas, the Scourging, The Agony in the Garden and two other coats-of-arms.

HILLINGDON, Hillingdon Hospital, Chapel: Twenty-six colourful abstract windows, many strongly geometrical, by Jane Gray, in glass and epoxy resin, 1968-73. On the N side the themes are described by the artist as 'Christ enters the world of man, the Spark of Faith, a Hawk, Dove and other symbols'; on the S side is St John's Revelation 'with God spreading the Word from Alpha to Omega'.

HILLINGDON, Uxbridge Underground Station: Characteristic glass with civic heraldry by Ervin Bossanyi, a Hungarian artist who came to England from Germany in 1934. He has few works in England – York Minister, Port Sunlight in Merseyside, St John's College, Oxford. Possibly his best are at Canterbury Cathedral.

HOUNSLOW, St Mary, Norwood Green: In the easternmost S nave window are some rather restored foreign panels and fragments of c. 1600 that include an unusual representation of the Virgin with the Christ Child playing with a windmill, St John the Baptist and a head of the Virgin Mary. Three C17 roundels in the W window depict Christ in Gethsemane, an eagle, foliage and design work.

KENSINGTON AND CHELSEA, Holy Trinity, Sloane St: The massive twelve-lancet E window by Morris & Co. of 1894-5 was mostly designed by Burne-Jones and was the firm's largest, yet '. . . not their greatest work', says Charles Sewter, the authority of Morris & Co.'s glass. At the top are the Apostles, then Old Testament characters, two layers of saints and (in the tracery light) scenes of the Crucifixion, Ascension, Annunciation, and Acts of Mercy, together with musician angels. Also some Arts & Crafts glass by Christopher Whall and, notably, in the N aisle three of the few windows by Sir William Blake Richmond.

The Annunciation, French glass from Normandy, c.1525; Victoria & Albert Museum, London.

KENSINGTON AND CHELSEA, Victoria & Albert Museum: A fine collection of glass from all over Europe that spans 800 years. There are five main areas of display: (1) On the ground floor (temporarily removed at the time of writing) are some good English and French C13 and C14 pieces, including some magnificent Jesse Tree panels of c. 1250, and the three superb figures formerly at Winchester College Chapel of 1399. (2) Large C15 Netherlandish and Cologne School panels with scenes of Constantine and his mother Helen, Maximilian of Austria and his wife, Philip le Beau, St Ursula and the 'thousand maidens' and a Crucifixion. (3) The large main display has ten windows filled with glass of all ages, all well-labelled and comprising English and French C12 and C13 glass, C14 and C15 English, heraldic examples, glass from Morris & Co., German C14 and C15, C16 Netherlandish and French (some from Rouen). (4) Room 116 has many subject and figure panels in C16 German glass from the Cistercian Abbey of Mariawald. (5) Room 117 is a fine collection from Steinfeld Abbey near Cologne, with many fine biblical scenes; opposite are more Cologne pieces, notably a charming panel of Tobias and Sarah asleep in bed. Also in the Museum is the unusual C17 'Betley Window' portraying May Day celebrations in Staffordshire; and in the C20 galleries a circular panel by Roger Fry and the Omega workshops of 1914. Also a large window by Francis Stephens (from c.1965) in a light box – an opportunity to see etched flashed glass at close quarters.

147

'Weep Not' by Walter Crane, *c.*1891, Christchurch, Streatham, Lambeth, London.

and juxtaposing of colours; the E windows of the gallery have two sets of small New Testament scenes designed by J.F. Bentley for Lavers, Barraud & Westlake. In the N aisle are two works by Walter Crane dating from the turn of the century, 'Feed My Sheep' and 'Weep Not' (*see illustration*), with his characteristic facial expressions, particularly in the agonised weeping figure. At the W end of this aisle is a colourful modern work by John Hayward: his also are both the E window here with Christ and The Instruments of The Passion, and the one in the S aisle with St Michael. The nine apse windows are by Laurence Lee.

LAMBETH, Lambeth Palace: C16-C19 glass displaced during the last war has been reset into the windows of the Archbishop's Hall. In the Chapel the new glass is by Carl Edwards and Hugh Powell, with the theme of The Redemption of the World by Christ presented typologically with Old Testament incidents being set alongside those of the New which they seem to foreshadow – e.g. Elijah Raising the Widow's Son is next to Lazarus' Resurrection from the Dead (and next to Elisha raising the Shunamite's son); Christ's Ascension is opposite those of Elijah and Enoch.

LAMBETH, St Mary, Lambeth: In the N aisle is Laurence Lee's recent Tradescent Window based on John Smith's quotation, 'Adam and Eve did first begin this innocent worke, to plant the earth and to remain to posteritie, but not without labour, trouble and industrie.' The E window of 1953 by Francis Stephens has the figures of Sts Thomas of Canterbury, George, Edward, Nicholas and Christopher, 'obviously by a pupil of Martin Travers', confesses the artist; the pedlar and his dog are also by him.

KINGSTON, All Saints, Church St, Kingston: An extraordinary W window of 1863 by Lavers & Barraud of the Te Deum with kings playing harps and apostles adoring; some of the figures are said to be portraits of local personalities at the time – Christ supposedly being modelled on 'the man from the waterworks', St Matthew on the then vicar, and St John on the curate!

LAMBETH, Christchurch, Streatham: Many of the windows here were lost during the war, but of C19 origin are the figures in the gallery by O'Connor with his unusual choice

LEWISHAM, St George, Perry Hill: The large bold C19 W rose window is structurally very much in the high Gothic style of those at, say, Notre Dame in Paris; the glass, however, is very much Henry Holiday of *c.* 1900 with figures radiating out from the centre. The nave and aisle windows are by Percy Bacon and R. Corbould of Hemming & Co.

LEWISHAM, St Mildred, Lee: A powerful and expressive window by Wilhelmina Geddes with the Virgin and Child of 1952 displaying her characteristic figure drawing, although there is still much of the Arts & Crafts tradition about the style and choice of colour. Also a ten-light window by Frederick Cole of 1953.

RICHMOND, Strawberry Hill (St Mary's College: Most of Horace Walpole's medieval stained glass collected in the eighteenth century was dispersed earlier this century (some can be seen at the Tower of London, in Bexhill and Hammersmith Public Library), but a number of pieces remain. The fifty or so panels are spread through a number of rooms, hallways and staircases; they are mostly Dutch roundels and paintings on glass of C16-C18, some of sacred subjects, others of secular origin – particularly from Inns – and settings of coats-of-arms; some are still in their original settings by William Peckitt. In the tiny Chapel in the Wood (of 1772 and designed to house Walpole's collection of stained glass) is a three light window by Harry Clarke, more sober than usual, but still distinctly his work. Gabriel Loire of Chartres executed the dalle-de-verre lights in the main Chapel which explore the Mysteries of the Rosary in the abstract glass with its Chartres-like colours.

SOUTHWARK, St Giles, Camberwell: Some late C13 *grisaille*, possibly of German origin, was incorporated at the time of building in the mid C19. Unique to the building is a sole surviving window designed by Ruskin, namely the Chartres-styled left lancet of the E window in C13 style depicting Noah's sacrifice, the Expulsion from Eden, and Cain slaying Abel: the rest of the window is by Ward & Hughes to Oldfield's design. Other less interesting windows here include one by Ninian Comper and some rather faded Lavers & Barraud work.

SOUTHWARK, Southwark Cathedral: Much modern glass here – only the reassembled wreathed and gartered C16 royal arms are pre C19. At the W end is Henry Holiday's fine Creation window of 1893, and the E window by Ninian Comper is more appealing than much of his other work; also a good window by Laurence Lee in the S choir (the Rider Memorial). The glass in the American Chapel from earlier this century is appropriately by an American, John LaFarge – and the Shakespeare Window in the S aisle is by an Englishman, Christopher Webb, 1954.

WANDSWORTH, All Saints, Putney: One of the best collections of glass by Morris & Co. in London: Burne-Jones's hand in many of the designs is prominent, e.g. in the saints of the 1878 E window (St Catherine is by Morris), in the figures of the 1883 W window, in the angels by the organ and the charming windows in the Baptistry, both of 1877; also much work by the firm over the period 1883-98 and, after Morris and Burne-Jones's deaths, up to 1929.

WANDSWORTH, Church of The Ascension, Lavender Hill: In this fine church by James Brooks the glass is by Kempe and, as always, of high quality; his later windows were done in association with his nephew, Walter Tower (and J.W. Lisle?); these include Christ in Glory in the E window and the Presentation in the Temple (1881 and 1891), Christ with the Virgin Mary and Elizabeth (1896), Daniel and Malachi (1897), the Visitation (1900) and Annunciation (1904). After 1900 Kempe & Co. began using the wheatsheaf symbol as a kind of trademark – it can usually be seen in the border.

WANDSWORTH, St Mary, Battersea: Interesting glass of *c.* 1621 in the E window, transferred from the earlier church on the site by Bernard van Linge who did the related window in the church at Lydiard Tregoze (Wilts); as in Wiltshire, the glass portrays the coats-of-arms and alliances of the family of Sir John St John Lydiard Tregoze: here they include those of Henry VII, Elizabeth of York and Margaret Beauchamp with their portraits. The lamb and the dove in the circular window is by James Pearson, 1796. In the nave the C20 windows by John Hayward depict people connected with the church's past and include William Blake, the artist Turner and Benedict Arnold.

MERSEYSIDE

Both cathedrals in Liverpool have interesting windows, the collection at the Roman Catholic Cathedral being possibly the more inspiring. Morris & Co.'s glass seems to have been particularly popular in the area for, in addition to the places mentioned in the table, it can also be seen at Bidston, Gateacre, Halewood, Oxton, Prescot, Wallasey, Whiston and Woolton, as well as in a number of Liverpool churches – e.g. Knotty Ash, New Ferry and Edgehill.

MR	Place	Centuries									Principal feature(s)
		12	13	14	15	16	17	18	19	20	
1	Allerton								*		good WM glass; also by HBB
2	Bebington								*		HH ws. in S tspt 1881 and 1886; also Wailes
3	Caldy									*	early C20 ws. by A.J. Davies
4	Claughton									*	ws. by C. Whall, 1906; SH on N side
5	Frankby								*		C19 glass by WM, CEK, CB
6	Kirby								*		HH ws. 1872–97
7	Liverpool Cathedral									*	see below
8	– (R.C.)									*	see below
9	– Mus.									*	23 ws. in slab glass and conrete by JH
10	– Mossley Hill									*	E and W ws. by Carl Edwards
11	– St Christopher									*	contemplative panels by RP
12	New Ferry								*		a series of ws. by WM; and HH, c.1950
13	Port Sunlight									*	2 ws. by E. Bossanyi, c.1950
14	St Helens		+		+				+	*	see below
15	Sefton					Q+					Qs with Passion instruments
16	Speke, Hall		?	?	?	?	?				Philip Nelson's uncatalogued collection
17	West Kirby								*	*	see below
18	Woodchurch					F					some (?)Flemish glass

See page 280 for table of symbols

LIVERPOOL Cathedral (Anglican):

A huge amount of glass in the spirit of the first half of the C20, mainly by James Hogan and J.W. Brown for James Powell of Whitefriars, Carl Edwards and H. Hendried (referred to in this entry, as J.H., J.W.B., C.E., H.H., respectively). The only exception is C.E.'s later masterly 53-foot-high W window of 1979, a vast area of colourful abstract glass expressing the theme of the Benedicite 'as Creation, God the Creator, Christ the Worker for all mankind, and finally man the worker'. It is complementary to J.W.B.'s Te Deum in the E window which has in its four lights The Glorious Company of The Apostles, The Fellowship of The Prophets, The Army of Martyrs, The Holy Church Throughout All the World. The nave windows feature people connected with the Church of England since the Reformation, dividing them into Musicians, Hymnologists and Scholars on the N side (by C.E.) and Bishops (by W. Wilson), Parsons (C.E.) and Laymen (H.H.). H.H. also did the NW transept glass featuring The Church in England, and J.H. the main windows in the SE transept with Christ's Blessing to All Humanity. In the choir, the Four Evangelist windows are by J.W.B. and the glass under the tower is by J.H. with the Old Testament on the N side and the New on the S.

The Chapter House has late glass by Morris & Co. of 1916-23, some of which is designed by Henry Dearle, with Old Testament subjects: Faith, Hope, Charity and Justice. The saints of the Church's Calendar in the Lady Chapel are by J.H., and the female saints connected with national and local history are by Carl Edwards.

LIVERPOOL Cathedral (R.C.):

The centrepiece of the stained glass work here is the magnificent central Lantern over the nave, by John Piper and Patrick Reyntiens of 1965-7, 12,500 square feet of glass contained in 156 panels of slab glass set in concrete and epoxy resin. The theme of the composition is The Trinity, expressed in colour as bursts of light amid the circular cycle of the spectrum, with yellow, red and blue acting as the points of focus. Piper and Reyntiens also did the nave lights that define the various bays of the Cathedral; the predominant colour is blue, dissolving into purples and mauve, with patches of green and red. Margaret Traherne did the 30-foot windows in the St Paul Chapel where reds dissolve into rose, the colours of fire and martyrdom; she also did the gentle glass in the Lady Chapel with its graduations of colour from a milky white to amber in special German glass, some of which was thinly flashed in opalescent white; it is held together by oak tracery. The glass in the **Chapel of the Blessed Sacrament** is by Reyntiens in conjunction with Ceri Richards: and with John Piper he did the red and green windows of the Chapel's entrance, in addition to the glass in the **Chapels of St Anne and St George**. David Atkins did the rose range of colours in the **Chapel of St Thomas**, the glass in the Baptistry and the twenty-three small windows in crimson and purple in **St Columba's Chapel**.

ST HELENS, Pilkington Glass Museum:

There is a good display of stained glass here and an account of the differing characteristics of glass of each age. Fragments can be examined more closely than is generally possible in churches, and there is some useful information on the technical aspects of the craft. The oldest examples are C8-C9 window glass, also some specimens from Dennis King's collection, and replicas of well-known medieval windows.

WEST KIRBY, St Bridget: A set of windows by C.E. Kempe that span nearly his whole working career, from 1870 (in chancel S) up to the dormer window of *c.* 1906, the year before he died. Those in the aisles date from 1882 and 1890. (See also the entry for the Church of the Ascension, Wandsworth, London.

NORFOLK

The wealth of C15 Norfolk expressed in its many fine Perpendicular churches is also reflected in the quantity and quality of the stained glass that filled them; remains and panels can be seen at nearly 200 places although, thanks to the zeal of Puritan iconoclasts, much of this has been reduced to only a few fragments. The Norwich school of glass painting and glazing that emerged at this time to meet the demand consistently produced work of the highest quality, of which the best examples can be seen in the churches of East Harling and St Peter Mancroft in Norwich; lesser displays remain at Martham, Salle, Bale, Harpley, Ketteringham, Mulbarton, Stody, Warham, Wiggenhall and Wighton, to name but a few. Mileham and Pulham both have examples of C14 glass which is otherwise comparatively rare in Norfolk, and Saxlingham Nethergate possesses some C13 pieces. Norfolk is also rich in Continental panels, being on the doorstep of one Christopher Hampp who managed to import large quantities of glass, particularly from France: Hingham has a magnificent piece in the E window and lesser specimens can be seen at Aylsham, Chedgrave, Erpingham, Felbrigg Hall, Hevingham, Langley, *et al*. Birkin Haward of Ipswich has visited virtually every church in Norfolk and Suffolk and has found some fine glass from the beginning to the end of the C19.

MR	Place	Centuries									Principal feature(s)
		12	13	14	15	16	17	18	19	20	
1	Acle								*		good E w. by HBB, 1867
2	Antingham								*		see below
3	Ashill				*						3 of the Church Doctors (no St Ambrose)
4	Attleborough			*							angels and Annunciation (W w.)
5	Aylsham				+	*			*		see below
6	Bale			*	*						see below
7	Banham								*		see below
8	Banningham			*	*						late C14 seraphim, cherubim, St John; angels
9	Bawburgh			*	*						see below
10	Bedingham				*		*				saints include Catherine, Paul, Stephen
11	Blickling							*			good E w. by JH for Butterfield, 1850
12	Brisley							*			dramatic E w. of 1855 by Clutterbuck
13	Brundall				O						St Laurence
14	Burnham Deepdale				*						good Trinity panel; frags. of St (?)Ursula
15	Buxton							*			ws. by TW, 1858; Clutterbuck, 1858
16	Caister									*	Arts & Crafts E w. by Paul Woodroffe, 1901
17	Carleton Rode		*								seated fig. (S chancel)
18	Castle Acre			*							St George in S a. E w., Jesse frags., *c.* 1390
19	Chedgrave					F	F				see below
20	Cley			*							see below
21	Cromer							*	*	WM in S a., E w. by JH, 1875, W w. by AW
22	Denton			*				*	*		see below
23	Dunston			*		*					C14 Sts Christopher, Remigius, donor, Qs

MR	Place	Centuries									Principal feature(s)
		12	13	14	15	16	17	18	19	20	
24	Dunton								*		good E w. by HBB of 1863
25	East Barsham				*						angel musicians and St Elizabeth (N w.)
26	East Dereham								*		good E w. by HBB, 1863 (cf. Dunton)
27	East Harling				*						see below
28	Elsing			*	*						early C14 Virgin; 3 late C14 apostles
29	Emneth				*						Sts Cuthbert, Scytha, Virgin (N a.)
30	Erpingham				F	F					see below
31	Felbrigg, Hall				*	F					see below
32	Feltwell								F		see below
33	Field Dalling				*				*		see below
34	Foulsham				O	O					September; 'Nine Worthy Conquerors'
35	Framingham Earl				*						figs. of Sts Catherine and Margaret
36	Gaywood									*	'Harvest Parable' E w. by RR, 1966
37	Great Massingham				*						apostles in chancel ws.
38	Great Snoring				*						Thrones, Dominations, Powers, Cherubim
39	Great Yarmouth, Mus.				*	*					see below
40	– St John								*		WH glass of the 1860s
41	Griston				*						St Catherine, prophets and angels
42	Guestwick				*						Norwch school figs. Sts Lucy, Catherine *et al.*
43	Gunthorpe								*		4 Preedy ws., 1860s; E w. by WW, 1854
44	Haddiscoe									*	Martin Travers w. of 1931
45	Halvergate			*							early C14 St Christopher in a N w.
46	Harpley				*						see below
47	Hevingham					F					see below
48	Hingham					F			*		see below
49	Holkham							H			arms by Peckitt, 1769
50	Hopton								*		E w. by B-J/WM, 1882; also later WM ws.
51	Houghton								*		St Giles w. by A.Booker in nave S, 1891
52	Hunstanton, St Mary								*	*	2 ws. by Preedy; Annunciation by PQ
53	Kelling				*						Sts Etheldreda, Withburga, Helen
54	Ketteringham Hall				O	O					some Flemish roundels
55	– St Peter				*	O					see below
56	Kimberley			*		*F					see below
57	Langley					F			*		see below
58	Long Stratton				F	O					French panel of Christ's Baptism (E w.)
59	Martham				*						see below
60	Mautby			*							good C14 canopies in yellow & green (N w.)
61	Merton			*	+	H	H		*		saints *c.*1325 in chancel; rare glass of 1830s
62	Methwold								*		early w. by HH for JP, 1866
63	Mileham			*	*						see below
64	Mulbarton				*	F					see below
65	Necton								F		French C19 glass by La Roche, *c.*1842
66	Nordelph								*		see below
67	North Pickenham								*		see below
68	North Tuddenham				*						see below
69	Norwich, Cathedral				*	HF	H		*	*	see below
70	– Guildhall				*	*					see below
71	– St Andrews				H*						unique 'Dance of Death' panel; St Michael
72	– St Peter Hungate				*	*					see below
73	– St Peter Mancroft				*					*	see below
74	– Union Building						*				2 oval panels by Henry Gyles, 1699
75	Old Buckenham				*						angels & shields: Sts Botolph, Leonard
76	Ormesby								*		some ws. by HH, 1898–1902
77	Outwell					*					St Laurence, 2 royal and 1 female saints
78	Oxborough, Hall		F	*	*	*					C13 roundel; C14 figs.; C15 St Sebastian
79	Poringland				*						donor, saint, Christ displaying wounds (E w.)
80	Pulham			*	*·						see below
81	Reepham								*		E w. a characteristic work by OC, 1867
82	Reymerston					F					large C16 figs. of Christ, Sts Peter and John
83	Ringland				*						Annunciation, Virgin, The Baptism, Trinity
84	Saham Toney,								*		early Wailes w. with The Last Supper, 1845
85	Salle				*						see below

MR	Place	Centuries									Principal feature(s)
		12	13	14	15	16	17	18	19	20	
86	Sandringham				*						East Anglian saints in some ws.; c.1500
87	Saxlingham										
	Nethergate		*	*	*						see below
88	Scole								*		E.Woore's Arts & Crafts w. in S a.; RP E w.
89	Sculthorpe							*			see below
90	Shelton				H*						donors (Sheltons), Annunciation; C16 Virgin
91	Shropham								*		Arts & Crafts Nativity, 1898, by M.Lowndes
92	South Acre		G	*	+						interesting *grisaille*; C14 Coronation S w.
93	Southburgh								*		glass by Leonard Walker, 1935
94	South Creake			+	*						Trinity, saints, unusual Crucifixion
95	Stockton				H*						Virgin and Child
96	Stody				*						see below
97	Stradsettt					F					Magi Adoration, Crucifixion, angels(German)
98	Stratton Strawless				*	F					Virgin; C15 Coronation and Annunciation
99	Sustead				*				*		St Catherine; musical angels; C. Whall ws.
100	Swardeston								*		Edith Cavell Mem. by Bryans & Heaseman
101	Taverham				*						Crucifixion panel (Norwich school) (N w.)
102	Thetford							*			notable WH ws. of 1860 and 1868
103	Thursford							*			good JP ws., c.1862, by AM and Wooldridge
104	Thurton				*	F	F	F			C15 Trinity panel
105	Warham			*	*						see below
106	Weasenham				*						delightful little figures — St Margaret (N a.)
107	West Barsham								*		glass by Margaret Tarrant, 1953
108	West Bradenham							*			good E w. *et al* by Wailes; and BG, 1893
109	Weston Longville				*						Sts James, John, Philip and musical angels
110	West Rudham				*						see below
111	Wiggenhall				*						see below
112	Wighton				*						see below
113	Witton							*			good coloured E w. by CB of 1859
114	Woodton			*							Sts Margaret and Catherine (S a. E w.)
115	Wramplingham				*						remains of the 12 apostles (chancel t.l.)

See page 280 for table of symbols

ANTINGHAM, St Mary: Good glass of the 1860s by J. & J. King of Norwich in the E window, and by Morris, Marshall, Faulkner & Co. of 1865 in the S chancel with the Virgin Mary by Burne-Jones and Martha by Rossetti. The nave N window tracery light angels with bells are also by Burne-Jones.

AYLSHAM, St Michael: A few remains of old glass in some chancel windows and a C16 German/Flemish figure of St John in the S aisle. The rest is C19, two of which are by Clutterbuck in the S chapel of c. 1855-7, two by Clayton & Bell from 1858 and 1860 (a good time for them), and five by Yarington of Norwich c.1850.

BALE, All Saints: A magnificent window in the S nave with Norwich glass of c. 1450-80 where the remains of no less than four Annunciations can be seen, the angel Gabriel missing from two of them; it also includes panels with feathered angels, parts of the Trinity (the Crucified Son), of St Etheldreda, the risen Christ, canopies as well as the 'seaweed' diaper, border and ears of wheat that characterise C15 Norwich glass;

note also the neatly abraded flashed ruby in one of the Virgin's dresses. There are also two C14 apostles carrying Messianic scrolls.

BANHAM, St Mary: In the N aisle is a panel with the Virgin and Child in medieval glass, possibly of French origin. The E window of 1857 has patterned glass in five lights by James Powell and a fine Crucifixion medallion said to have been designed by J.R. Clayton. The E window of the S aisle with Christ's Birth, Baptism and Ascension is a good early design by Henry Holiday for Powell's dating from 1864; the two in the N chancel are also by Powell.

BAWBURGH, Church: A fine C15 figure of St Barbara with palm and castle in a S window, Gabriel and the Virgin Mary (next door) from an Annunciation. In a N window are remains of the four Church Doctors and C14 censing angels.

CHEDGRAVE, All Saints: In the three-light E window is much C16 and C17 Continental glass bought in 1802 by Lady Beauchamp Proctor. It probably came from Rouen and is a bizarre assemblage, for in the left light is a 'merman' riding a many-headed hydra, set above a sainted figure which in turn is above the Virgin Mary from a Coronation scene; in the centre light is a left-handed fiddling angel above the Virgin and Child with an adoring Evangelist and Sts Peter, Paul and a young nimbed figure at the top; in the right light is another hydra with the label 'MACVLANONEST', an angel trumpeting and a kneeling donor at the base.

CLEY, St Margaret: In the tracery lights of a S aisle window to the left of the main door are some good C15 figures of female saints: an immodest Agatha, Sita, one with a sword, Petronella, Barbara, Faith, Apollonia and Cecilia, the latter portrayed with flowers rather than the more usual organ or harp.

DENTON, St Mary Magdalene: Joshua Price's arrangement of the glass in 1716-19 includes C15 figures and roundels, some with charming subjects such as two birds playing a musical instrument, Sts Christopher, John and Edmund and the Virgin Mary. In the S chancel is November from a series of the months, here depicted as The Killing of the Ox. Some good early windows by Ward & Hughes of 1855-60.

EAST HARLING, St Peter and St Paul: The E window here has twenty magnificent panels of *c.* 1480 reminiscent of the glass at St Peter Mancroft, Norwich; it survived the iconoclasm of the Puritans by being hidden until more favourable times. Given by the Wingfield and Chamberlain families, the central theme is the Life of the Virgin Mary in fifteen panels (see the diagram for the key to the arrangement). In (1) is the Annunciation; (2) the Visitation; (3) the Nativity – note the two midwives; (4) the Adoration of the Shepherds, and (5) of the Magi; (6) Presentation in the Temple; (7) Christ with the Doctors; (8) the Wedding at Cana; (9) the Betrayal – note the unusual detail of the cutting off of the High Priest's ear; (10) the Crucifixion with Mary, John, Pilate and Longinius the centurion; (11) the Pieta; (12) the Resurrection; (13) the Ascension; (14) Pentecost – note how the cartoon is that of the Ascension, but reversed so that the Spirit descends from where Christ has ascended; (15) the Assumption. Panels (16) and (17) have the donors, Sir Robert Wingfield and Sir William Chamberlain; (18) St Mary Magdalene; (19) an angel with a text from the Te Deum; (20) has a collection of fragments including the

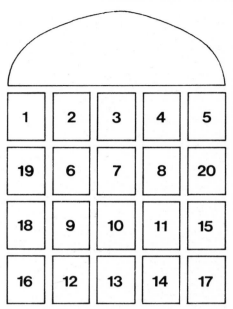

E window, East Harling, Norfolk.

head of St Gregory and Anne Harling's mantle. In the tracery lights here and in the N clerestory are some fine Norwich school angels. (*See illustration opposite and on* p.33.)

ERPINGHAM, St Mary: Many good panels from the Continent collected in the C19 into the E window originally at Blickling Hall. The top four lights have glass from the monastery at Mariawald, yet each is of a different age and origin, i.e. Susanna and the Elders (French C16), the Presentation of the Virgin Mary, Joachim and St Anne (both late C15 French) and the Massacre of the Holy Innocents (German). In the eight lights below are panels from Steinfeld, part of the same series of thirty-eight at the Victoria & Albert Museum, probably acquired by Hampp (see p.56); the scenes include the Adoration of the Shepherds, Doubting Thomas, Christ and the three Marys, the Flight into Egypt, two scenes from the martyrdom of St Quirinius, Sts Paul and Norbert, the Virgin Mary and St Potentius. The trumpet-blowing angels in the S aisle E window is probably indigenous.

FELBRIGG Hall: A fairly large collection of foreign glass as well as some from St Peter Mancroft, Norwich (and some copies of other glass at St Peter's by John Dixon of Norwich who installed the glass in 1840). Six of the foreign panels

The Assumption, fine glass of c.1480; East Harling, Norfolk.

kitchen, various roundels and hexagonal panels oversee the cooking, with the head of a bishop, a lion devouring a man, two rather Raphaelesque figures, Christ on the Cross, and two saints in a landscape. In the corridor are some Flemish panels of fishing and sailing scenes, and on the stairway a C15 English figure of St George and the dragon, and coats-of-arms held by angels.

HARPLEY, St Laurence: The W window has a fine array of C15 scenes and figures in the tracery lights. Sts Edmund and Edward the Confessor sit beneath an Annunciation, flanked Sts John and James, whilst the outer parts of the traceries have Sts Wilfred, Laurence, (?)Vincent and Leger on the left and Sts Thomas of Canterbury, Martin, Stephen and Blaise on the right. The lowest layer of lights houses angels.

HEVINGHAM, St Botolph: A few English fragments; but the main interest here is the collection of remains of C16 scenes (originally from Steinfeld) set into a S nave window; they include two of the Magi, the Spies and the Grapes, Naaman Washing in the Jordan, two scenes with Abraham, David crossing the Cadron, St Mark fleeing Gethsemane, the Sacrifice of Isaac.

HINGHAM, St Andrew: The magnificent E window has glass of c. 1500 from (?) Cologne spread through its seven lights, given to the church by Lord Wodehouse in 1813; the centrepiece is St Anne teaching the Virgin with the Christ Child and St Thomas with T-square, whilst four large scenes surround them: the Crucifixion (note the angel and demon over the head of the repentant and unrepentant thieves, as at King's College, Cambridge), Deposition, Ascension and Resurrection, in the background of which are four smaller scenes of the Harrowing in Hell, Christ and the three Marys, the Appearance to Peter, and Thomas's Incredulity; in the traceries are two donors and a saint with a book. The S aisle has a fine early window by Lavers & Barraud, c. 1859, and there is a rich Kempe Resurrection in the tower W window.

KETTERINGHAM, St Peter: In the E window is a good C15 assemblage with the Coronation of the Virgin attended by two angels as the centrepiece and Sts Edmund, John the Baptist, Margaret, Catherine, George and Michael below. Also some Flemish roundels that include portrayals of various saints and King David playing the psaltery.

are Swiss; one has the names and date: Jacob Schmyter and Elsbett Lochmanin, 1571. Flemish roundels include a scene with Abraham and Isaac, and St Jerome from the Doctors of the Church series.

FELTWELL, St Mary: Interesting C19 glass since all the glazing is of the C13 style and was installed over a short period (1859-63). The glaziers were French: Adolphe Napoléon Didron and Eugène Oudinot; they give us something of the flavour of what a fully glazed medieval French/English church might have looked like.

FIELD DALLING, St Andrew: In some S nave tracery lights are small, rather faded C15 figures of female saints whom David King identifies as being Sts Mary Magdalene, Catherine, Agnes and Cecilia; next door are eight apostles with their attributes, and in a third window Sts (?) Etheldreda and (?) Leger. More remains of apostles' and prophets' figures with Creed and prophecy scrolls in some N tracery lights. The C19 glass is by Warrington, c. 1855.

GREAT YARMOUTH, Elizabethan House Museum: Bought-in and indigenous glass contemporary with the house (1569); in the

The Pedlar's Window, C15; Mileham, Norfolk.

KIMBERLEY, St Peter: The E window has some fine but rather darkened reset glass, mostly of the C14 but with some C16 pieces, notably two splendid angels: there are both figures and fragments, of which St Margaret under a canopy and spearing the dragon is particularly fine; some figures originate from tracery lights and mingle with composite figures, angels and other fragments in the main lights, while in the tracery lights is a Crucifixion and Christ in Glory. In the S chancel are early C16 figures that include two splendid angels with scrolls, the (?)Virgin, and two scenes in the ubiquitous Steinfeld glass, the paint of which is fading somewhat – Christ expelling the Moneychangers (note the large word 'DOMUS' in its Renaissance-type vaults) and the General Resurrection.

LANGLEY, St Michael: Glass from Rouen in the E window bought by Lady Proctor (see also Chedgrave) and installed in c. 1803 characteristically by Yarington of Norwich (cf. Herringswell, Suffolk); it shows scenes of the Nativity, St George and St Gregory. Various roundels and medallions in the W window include a scene of Moses receiving the Law; the three Evangelists and various other demi-figures date from c. 1823 and are the work of Robert Allen, a porcelain painter from Lowestoft turned glass painter (see also Lowestoft, Suffolk).

MARTHAM, St Mary: Some fine reset C15 panels in the E windows of the aisles; on the N side is the Crucifixion at Golgotha, the Mocking of Christ (decidedly Flemish in style), the Presentation in the Temple, the Ascension, part of an Annunciation, and down the sides the Apostles at the Ascension, the Resurrection with sleeping soldiers, and a number of figures that include Sts Edmund, Margaret, Juliana (with quaint little chained devil), Agnes (with a lamb), Edward III and Queen Philippa. Over in the S aisle is a fine St Michael and a panel of Eve spinning (from a series of which other pieces can be seen in Mulbarton Church), Sts Margaret (with dragon), John, James the Great, and angels; in the tracery lights are some musical angels and a Coronation of the Virgin.

MILEHAM, St John the Baptist: The near-complete C14 W window has fine decorative glass in the tracery lights and splendid figures in the main lights under large canopies: Sts Catherine, John the Baptist and Margaret all date from c. 1350; the castle and fleur-de-lis borders confirm the mid C14 date – the donor, Lord Richard Fitzalan, Earl of Arundel, was related by marriage in 1345 to one of the members of the royal house of Lancaster, which might explain why such high quality glass is here; below the figures there would originally have been heraldry associated with the family, but this would have been removed during the Civil War; now there are fragments from other parts of the Church that include the C15 figures of St Barbara and St Margaret again and a C14 figure (with C15 head) between them. The chancel S window has an odd C15 panel – the 'Pedlar's Window' – with a scene involving two horses, donors and the name 'Brown' (there was a vicar by that name in the C15). The E window was removed in 1983, and after cleaning and restoration will probably be replaced there: it has three very composite figures (*see illustration*).

MULBARTON, St Mary Magdalene: The two panels with the Expulsion of Adam and Eve and of Adam Delving came from Martham (qv), as did the Powers from the Angelic Hierarchy, possibly the figure in armour and the bishop. David King suggests a connection between this glass and that at St Peter Norwich Mancroft, (qv). In the 1815 setting of glass in the S chancel are C15 English panels with King Solomon, St Anne teaching the Virgin Mary, a Patriarch and C16 Flemish panels with a nun and monk.

NORDELPH, Holy Trinity: The E window of c. 1865 is an outstanding work by Heaton, Butler & Bayne 'at their best. One of the finest in East Anglia,' says Birkin Haward.

NORTH PICKENHAM, St Andrew: A fine W window by Henry Holiday for Powell of

1864; the E window of the same date is an attractive work by the O'Connors (father and son).

NORTH TUDDENHAM, St Mary: Three C15 panels can be seen in the W window below the C19 figures, bought in by the Revd Barry in the C19: two have scenes from the life of St Margaret of Antioch, seen here as a shepherdess amid playful sheep and again refusing the advances of the prefect Olybrius who has rejected Christ; the third panel has a complex scene from the life of St George – and he can also be seen killing the dragon in a tracery light the westernmost S nave window; the traceries here have two figures, one with crossed legs. Around the rest of the church are eight sets of tracery lights with figures of saints and angels, shields, fragments and parts of scenes from all sorts of sources: amongst them Sts Edward, Leonard and (?)Hilda can be seen in one set of tracery lights, and Sts Matthew (with Creed scroll) and Laurence (with gridiron) in another. The porch has some fine fragments with fascinating details – including the figure of St Martin and some beautiful drawings of animals (*see illustration*).

NORWICH Cathedral: Hardly any of the Cathedral's original glass remains, but fragments from various sources can be seen in a number of places; in the S ambulatory, the St Luke's Chapel has a fine C15 Virgin and Child of the Norwich school, originally at Ringland and here set behind the famous C14 altarpiece; close by is the C16 St Brice's Window, originally from France, that found its way here via Langley Hall; St Saviour's Chapel has four East Anglian saints (Edmund, Fursey, Julian and Felix); reset fragments in a NW window here include St Matthew's angel, a centaur playing the bagpipes, some glass from Mehr (near Cologne), and heads of Christ and Moses. The N aisle has C16 and C17 coats-of-arms for (W to E) the Tudors, James I, Charles I, the Earl of Shrewsbury and Emperor Charles V. A collection of Flemish roundels in a S aisle window set around the modern figure of St Elisabeth of Hungary was installed by Dennis King in memory of his father, George King. In the N transept the St Andrew's Chapel has angels with shields of arms and other mainly heraldic C15 fragments, originally in the Deanery.

The huge W window of 1854 with biblical scenes is by George Hedgeland and has some of the first glass made following Winston's experiments to rediscover medieval methods of manu-

Two singing angels gritting their teeth, C15; North Tuddenham, Norfolk.

facture (see p.59). The E clerestory windows are earlier, by Warrington and dating from 1847. The W window medallions are by Clayton & Bell, and the glass in the St Luke's chapel by Hardman of 1868; that in the N transept with biblical warriors and St George is by Morris & Co. of 1902; by Hardman and Wailes in the S aisle; by Warrington of 1849 in the N aisle; and by Yarington in the presbytery triforium. In the Beauchamp Chapel is Moira Forsyth's own favourite window of 1964 – 'The Benedictines in England' – with scenes from St Benedict's life.

NORWICH Guildhall: The Council Room E window is divided into many sections and contains a number of C15 and C16 pieces: Sts Bartholomew, Thomas and Philip at the top, coats-of-arms for Elizabeth I, Anderson and one with sixteen quarterings involving the Dudley family; then the arms of Norwich, the Merchant Adventurers and France; then the First and

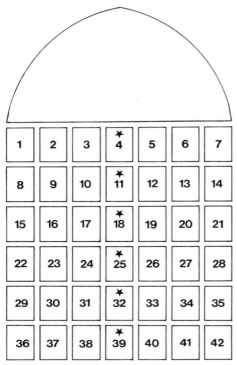

E window, St Peter Mancroft, Norwich.

Third Persons of the Trinity, a (?) Flemish panel with the Corrupt Judge (from Valerian II.6), and St John the Baptist in camel-skin and with Agnus Dei; in the tracery lights are the Apostles, the Assumption of St Barbara, Justice and Religion with Passion relics. Smaller N and S windows have St Barbara, St Luke, a double-headed eagle, part of the Holy Child and the Return of the Prodigal Son.

NORWICH, St Peter Hungate: Now a museum, this church has some indigenous C15 glass, e.g. the canopies in the N transept, angels on wheels in the N chancel and nine small figures in the E window (Sts Agatha, Bartholomew, James the Great, a king and patriarch, angels and John with chalice and devil). Glass from other parts of Norfolk is described in the museum's pamphlet and includes some fine C15 Norwich school work at the E end, St Peter with Christ in chancel N, and angels with Christ and the Virgin Mary in the W window.

NORWICH, St Peter Mancroft: A really fine display of C15 Norwich school glass in the

huge E window. It was assembled in 1741 and rearranged in 1947; seven of the forty-two panels that date from 1881 were made by Dixon (marked thus * in the diagram), the originals now being at Felbrigg (qv) and in the Burrell Collection, Glasgow (qv). Binoculars are essential in order to see the details – e.g. the Christ Child being portrayed in the rays of the Holy Spirit that descend to the Virgin Mary in No. 29. The panels show: (1) St Cecilia, (2) Arrest of St John, (3) St John on Patmos, (4) Trinity shield, (5) St Francis receives the Stigmata, (6) St John baptises a young man, (7) converts two others, (8) Sacrament shield, (9) St Stephen, (10) St Elisabeth of Hungary, (11) Ascension, (12) St Catherine (?), (13) St Faith, (14) Sts John and Peter at the Gate, (15) St Peter and Christ walk on the water, (16) St Peter fishing, (17) he preaches, (18) the Betrayal, (19) St Peter baptises Cornelius, (20) before Nero, (21) with Simon Magus, (22) the Circumcision, (23) Christ with St Thomas?, (24) Christ disrobed for the Crucifixion, (25) the Crucifixion, (26) the Entombment, (27) the Apostles gather for the Virgin's funeral, (28) Arrest of the Virgin's funeral, (29) the Annunciation, (30) the Visitation, (31 and 33) Adoration of the Magi, (32) the Resurrection, (34) Nativity with the Shepherds, (35) Massacre of the Holy Innocents, (36 and 41) the donors, Garnysh and Ramsey, (37) Thomas and Margaret of Ely, (38) the Trimphal Entry into Jerusalem, (39) the Last Supper, (40) Gethsemane, (42) donors. In the tracery lights are numerous saints and figures including the rare Canute, Owen and bishop Erconwald. On the S side of St Anne's Chapel are reset pieces of C16-C19 glass, mostly heraldic; over the S porch are the arms of Henry VI.

The S Chapel E window has glass by H. Hendrie of c. 1921, that in the Jesus Chapel is by J. Clement Bell and the tower window of c. 1968 is by Dennis King and Andrew Anderson.

PULHAM, St Mary: Early C14 glass can be seen in the head of a nave NE window with Christ and two angels from a Coronation scene; also in a N window are twelve small C15 figures of the Apostles with traditional attributes, and in a window by the porch numerous C14 and C15 fragments. In a N chancel window is a roundel with St Laurence and on the S side the figures of Sts Mary Magdalene, Barbara, Cecilia and Catherine also with attributes; in tracery lights to the right are fragmentary figures of Sts Peter, Andrew, James the Great and Christopher.

SALLE, St Peter and St Paul: Some remains of superb C15 glass but, alas, only in the tracery lights of a number of windows: eg in the S transept S and E windows are a fine collection of figures (some without heads) that include Sir Thomas Briggs and his two wives kneeling before their patron saint Thomas of Canterbury, Sts Jerome, Margaret, Catherine, Etheldred, a Helen and some beautiful angels. The E window has some superb angels and archangels from the Hierarchy placed amid the sun, moon, stars and remains that suggest the former presence of a Doom. On the N side of the chancel are eight figures of the Fathers of the Church and prophets with scrolls, and over the S side Sts Helen, Catherine and prophets (e.g. Daniel) below them but set in the clouds. In the N aisle E window is a restored Annunciation and next door to it in the N transept are parts of a Visitation scene and figures of the Virtues: Mercy, Truth, Justice and Peace. Some of the S aisle tracery lights have remains of figures that include prophets, patriarchs and cardinals.

SAXLINGHAM NETHERGATE, St Mary: A good collection of glass that can be described only briefly here; e.g. the four C13 panels (rare in Norfolk) in the S chancel with Sts John and James (both seated and labelled), St Edmund about to be shot with an arrow, then offering up his arrow, and a saint being beheaded. In the next window is some C13 *grisaille* with maple-leaf pattern and late C14 figures of Sts James and Philip. In a S window are panels of *c.* 1500 with St Anne, the Virgin and Child. The main E window tracery lights have an *in situ* part of the cycle of Christ and the Virgin, which begins with the Nativity and continues through to Pentecost and the Ascension, which flank a Coronation of the Virgin: the main lights have three large coats-of-arms of *c.* 1400. Fine C15 remains on the N side of the chancel include Jerome wearing a cardinal's hat, St Ambrose and Christ in Glory in the tracery lights. Two early C15 musician angels can be seen in the tower W window, and in the N aisle E window are canopy tops, the small bishop, an archbishop and St Edward the Confessor, all of *c.* 1400.

SCULTHORPE, St Mary and All Saints: Early Morris & Co. glass in the S aisle E window designed by Burne-Jones, with Faith, Hope and Charity; also Christ walking on the water and watching over the disciples by Ford Maddox Brown in the chancel S window; the charming window of Ruth Gleaning is by Heaton, Butler & Bayne. All the windows are of 1862.

STODY, St Mary: In a N nave tracery light are kings and prophets from a C15 Tree of Jesse, one of which surprisingly, is, St Edmund! Next door are the C15 remains of a Coronation of the Virgin Mary and Apostles including Sts Matthew, Philip and Bartholomew. Various fragmentary figures of female saints can be seen in the S transept.

WARHAM, St Mary Magdalene: Norwich school glass in the N nave includes C15 musical angels, some heads and early C14 figures of Adam and Eve. In the E window are six good imported Rhenish panels with scenes of the Transfiguration, the Entry into Jerusalem, the Deposition and other Passion incidents.

WEST RUDHAM, St Peter: David King reports glass of *c.* 1430 in a N nave window in two different styles: the westernmost window has Christ displaying the wounds; in the centre he is seated with the Crown of Thorns beneath a Coronation of the Virgin; on the right is Gabriel from an Annunciation, and St Mark with the lion in the easternmost tracery lights.

WIGGENHALL, St Mary Magdalene: The N aisle here has five windows with a host of C15 figures not often encountered in stained glass, e.g. Sts Calixtus, Hilary, Alshelm, Sixtus, Samson, German and Cuthbert at the W end, then a bishop, Sts Hippolytus, Leger, Botolph, Januarius, Prosdecimus, Giles and Romanus; then, standing behind battlements in the next window, are a bishop and a figure with a sword, below whom are Sts Medard, Gildard (in blue), Julian, Swithun and Albinus; in the fourth are Sts Victor, Silvester, (?), Desiderus with Paul, John, Thomas (in blue), Edmund, and one other below; and in the fifth St Felicianus above St Cornelius and two others. A few other fragments in chancel and aisle windows.

WIGHTON, All Saints: Some C15 saints in various tracery lights, but not readily identifiable even to the expert eye; David King suggests that these might include figures of Sts Catherine, Martha (or Julian with a devil on a chain), Agatha (with flesh hook), and in a SE window Sts Paul, Andrew, Bartholomew and Peter; angels on wheels in the W window and relics of the Passion in some others.

NORTHAMPTONSHIRE

There is a fair distribution of English and Continental glass throughout Northamptonshire. The C14 glass at Stanford-on-Avon and Lowick is splendid and there are lesser pieces at a number of other places. Outstanding are the C20 windows at Oundle School and All Hallows, Wellingborough, and there are good displays of C19 glass at Northampton and Middleton Cheney, the latter by Morris & Co.

MR	Place	12	13	14	15	16	17	18	19	20	Principal feature(s)
1	Abington									*	Annunciation (after Botticelli) by PR, 1982
2	Aldwincle		*								fine figs.: Sts Christopher and George, c.1290
3	Apethorpe					*	*				see below
4	Ashby St Ledgers								*		rare early C19 glass in the E w.
5	Aynho								*		TW glass, 1857; CEK ws., 1898 and 1899
6	Barby			*							Nativity in early C14 glass (N a. E w.)
7	Braybrooke									*	Virgin and Child, Evangelists by AV, 1969
8	Cranford St Andrew				*	F					C15 figs; Netherlandish Petrarch Triumphs
9	Croughton			H							early C14 royal and other heraldic panels
10	Deene								*	*	LBW E w., 1868; Bell, S a.w., 1919
11	Denford					O	O				roundels in the S a. E w.
12	Duston									*	abstract w. by G.Robinson, 1968
13	Fawsley				H	H	H				roundels and panels in a S a. w.
14	Gayton				O	O					roundels and panels in N chapel
15	Geddington								*		early CB glass in chancel, 1860; E w. by NC
16	Great Brington					H*					St John the Baptist; WM/Dearle ws., c.1910
17	Great Weldon			H	+	F					Flemish C16 Adoration Of The Magi (W w.)
18	Helmdon			H*							rare donor fig., William Campion, quarryman
19	Hinton-in-the-Hedges				*						Coronation of the Virgin (chancel S)
20	Holdenby		*								Coronation of the Virgin, c.1300 (chancel S)
21	Hollowell								*		early HH w. for JP, 1863
22	Irchester									*	St John the Baptist by E. Woore, 1924
23	Litchborough			*							Annunciation; Trinity shield (nave ws.)
24	Lowick			*	H						see below
25	Marston Trussell			*							early C14 St Peter (S clsty)
26	Mears Ashby						F*				see below
27	Middleton Cheney								*		see below
28	Northampton, Abington Mus.				*	+					2 Labours of the month, c.1500
29	– Church of Holy Sepulchre								*		see below
30	– Kingsthorpe			G							grisaille on N side of nave
31	– St Giles								*		C19 ws. by four leaders, JH, CEK, CB, HBB
32	Old				*						strange picture of a man carrying a devil
33	Oundle, School									*	see below
34	Raunds			+	*						St Elizabeth; Christ and angels canopy
35	Rushden				*						see below
36	Stanford-on-Avon			H*	*+	+			*		see below
37	Stoke Albany	G	H								arms for Roos plus C13 grisaille in chancel
38	Thenford				*						St Anne, Virgin, St Christopher, c.1480
39	Thorpe Malsor								*		E w.(1860); S Chancel w. (1889) by WN
40	Wellingborough	′								*	see below
41	Wilby							F			French C19 glass by A.Lusson
42	Woodford				*						early C15 prophets and apostles (Chancel N)

See page 280 for table of symbols

APETHORPE, St Leonards: The Last Supper in the E window is a painting on glass by John Rowell, 1732; he also did the coat-of-arms of Fane impaling Stringer, of the same date. Earlier glass can be seen in the E window of the Milway Chapel which depicts the Fall, Crucifixion, Resurrection and Last Judgement of 1621 in Flemish style, possibly by a van Linge.

160

LOWICK, St Peter: In four of the nave N windows are sixteen large figures in C14 glass, clearly from a Tree of Jesse that may have been in the former church; one of the figures is probably Sir Walter de Vere with Drayton arms; W to E, the other figures are Rehoboam, David, Solomon, Asa in the first window; then Jacob, Isaiah, Elijah and Habbakuk; Daniel, Ezekiel, Jeremiah and Isaac; and Joseph, Zachariah, Micah and Sir Walter in the easternmost. In each of the tracery lights are smaller figures set at an angle, which include Sts John the Baptist, Andrew, Michael, Mary and Margaret. In the chancel is some C14 heraldic glass set beneath the transoms of the C19 windows.

MEARS ASHBY, All Saints: C19 glass by the French glazier A. Lusson of 1859 in the S chancel; the E and W windows are by Clayton & Bell of a year later, and it is interesting to compare the two firms at this stage of the development in C19 glass. In the N aisle is a favourite window by Laurence Lee of 1970.

MIDDLETON CHENEY, All Saints: Fine early glass by Morris, Marshall, Faulkner & Co. in the 1865 E window, where the design was shared between Simeon Solomon (Twelve Tribes of Israel, David, Isaiah, Moses and Abraham), Morris (Eve, the Virgin Mary), Burne-Jones (the Fathers of the Church), angels and other details by Philip Webb. The Burning Fiery Furnace in the W window is by Burne-Jones, 1870, as is the chancel N window, 1893, and Samuel in the N aisle, accompanied by Rossetti's Elijah, 1880. In the rose of the E window is Morris's Annunciation – below it Sts Elizabeth and Anne are by Ford Maddox Brown and Mary by Burne-Jones of 1880.

NORTHAMPTON, Church of the Holy Sepulchre: An assorted collection of late C19 glass – e.g. the N aisle W window with a fighting Richard Coeur de Lion is by Mayer, 1883; he also did the 1899 window in the S aisle. Hardman's glass is in the tower W, Kempe's is in the N chapel E window, 1887, Burlison & Grylls' in the S chapel E window and A.J. Dix's of 1903 in the S aisle.

OUNDLE School Chapel: In the three E windows by John Piper and Patrick Reyntiens can be seen nine portrayals of Christ as the Eternal Qualities of the Son of Man: (left to right) they are The Way, The Truth, The Life; then The Vine, The Bread of Heaven, The Water of Baptism; and The Judge, The Teacher, The Good Shepherd. These almost expressionist windows that date from 1956 were a landmark in the evolution of British stained glass. Reyntiens has shown great originality of craftsmanship in order to translate Piper's ideas to glass, making wide use of flashing, etching and staining, and appliqué (*see illustration on* p.162). In the ambulatory Hugh Easton's Seven Ages of Man have some engaging little details in them.

RUSHDEN, St Mary: In the C15 E window tracery lights are some prophets and kings from a Jesse Tree. C19 E window of the North chapel has a C15 St James and one other figure. Four Apostles in some N aisle tracery lights.

STANFORD-ON-AVON, St Nicholas: Interesting panels that range from early C14 to C16, some recently restored but others in drastic need of attention. It would appear that there have been a number of periods of glazing but, with the exception of the E windows of the aisles and some of the chancel windows, these are mixed up within the various windows. In the S Chancel are fine early C14 panels with saints and good borders, some with a pattern of repeating covered cups (emblem of Eleanor of Castile) – those on the N side are almost illegible. Other pieces set into these windows against C14 *grisaille* are of a later date and include the Virgin Mary from a Coronation and various figures. The fine Decorated E windows of the nave aisle have mid C14 glass, well restored on the S side and in need of attention on the N: those in the S window have two female saints in the main lights – one is St Agnes – set in fine borders (note the heads and grotesques, reminiscent of the Lenton school that make up one border); above are fine canopies with birds and a grotesque on the pinnacle; the traceries have the Crucifixion with Sts Mary and John, angels and charming figures of birds; also in the S aisle are C14 angels and birds in the tracery lights, and donor panels, reset roundels and coats-of-arms of the C15 and C16 (*see illustration on* p.163). In the N aisle E window it is possible to discern St Anne teaching the Virgin Mary, a headless bishop in another border of heads, with canopies and tracery lights as on the S side, although here the near illegible subject is a Doom; other windows have C14 figures and decorations and later fragments. The main E window has glass from at least four different

Opposite: The Vine, The Bread and The Water by John Piper and Patrick Reyntiens, 1956; Oundle, Northamptonshire.

eras in its main lights and those formed by the intersecting tracery: in some of the latter panels can be seen small figures of Christ, two bishops, *grisaille* and coats-of-arms of C14-C16; the main lights have a charming little Virgin and Child at the head of the centre lancet and a large C19 version of an early C16 arrangement of Henry VII and Elizabeth of York astride the royal coat-of-arms with Tudor emblems – greyhound and lion supporters, portcullis and rose – all by T. Willement.

WELLINGBOROUGH, All Saints: An interesting collection of modern glass, notably Evie Hone's window (of 1955) in the S aisle: The Lamb, flames of the Holy Spirit, the Ark, the Loaves and Fishes and seven-branched candlestick. Of the three works by Piper and Reyntiens, the window with the Evangelists and emblems of the Prophets is the earliest (1961); their rose window dates from 1964, and the latest is the abstract work at the W end of the S chapel dating from 1969. The glass in the S chapel with the Virgin Mary, Sts Crispin and Crispinian is by Jean Barillet from 1962. The C19 E window is by Gibbs from 1871.

A charming C15 head; Stanford-on-Avon, Northamptonshire.

NORTHUMBERLAND

There is some excellent C14 glass at Morpeth which can be related stylistically to the glass on the W coast at Cartmel Priory in Cumberland, the link being the glaziers who almost certainly came from York. Otherwise both old and interesting recent glass in Northumberland is rather lacking.

MR	Place	Centuries								Principal feature(s)
		12	13	14	15	16	17	18	19	20	
1	Alnwick								*		see below
2	Bamburgh							*F		*	12 Dutch glass ws.; AKN Darling Mem.
3	Berwick-on-Tweed					O	O				many C16 and C17 Flemish roundels
4	Blanchland and Abbey			*							C15 abbot/donors; Qs with Passion emblems
5	Bothal			*	*						see below
6	Brinkburn Priory		G								similar pattern to that at York Minster
7	Bywell							*			good Wailes glass in N chapel E w.
8	Embleton							*			mature CEK E w. of 1884
9	Haltwhistle							*			WM 'Via Crucis', 1872; one by B-J
10	Hexham									*	HH's w. in S tspt; heraldics by S.Scott
11	Morpeth			*							see below
12	Ponteland			Q+H							arms of Aymer of Athol and de Valence
13	Rothbury,										
	Cragside Mansion							*			see below
14	Stannington			H							arms of St Oswin and St Etheldreda
15	Warkworth				*						part fig. of St Hilda as Abbess
16	Whitfield				*				*		good JP w. of 1862 designed by Mobberley

See page 280 for table of symbols

ALNWICK, St Michael: A good collection of C19 glass from the period 1865-75, notably by Clayton & Bell in the W window, Baptistry and S chancel windows; Lavers, Westlake & Barraud of 1871 in the N aisle; whilst the rest are by Powell, Bagulay (Baptistry S and at the W end of the N aisle), Burlison & Grylls, Atkinson and Ward & Hughes.

BOTHAL, St Andrew: There are eight windows here with remains in the heads of the lights and traceries, mostly of C14 on the S side and C15 on the N. The S aisle E window has remains of a Coronation scene and a few other fragments, whilst to the S of it are some quarries and border remains and a shield with Instruments of the Passion. On the N side, the C15 remains are probably from another church – they include a fine figure of the Virgin and part of Gabriel from an Annunciation in two tracery lights of the E window, and shields of arms above for England quartered with France, canopies and angels painted on blue glass; some good York roses and canopies in the others.

MORPETH, St Mary: The C14 Tree of Jesse in the E window is a splendid sight, despite much good restoration by Wailes in the C19. Spread across five lights, it is unusual in contain-ing only two kings and sixteen prophets (David with harp and Solomon with a scroll containing extracts from Psalm 72); Jesse is at the foot and the rest of the characters are set out thus:

Isaiah	Jeremiah	Virgin Child	Joel	Obadiah
Jonas	Nahum	Solomon	Habakkuk	Haggai
Zacharias	Daniel	David	Zephania	Ezekiel
Osyas	Micah	Jesse	Malachi	Amos

In the tracery lights can be seen other figures set against a beautiful foliage pattern. Over in the S aisle E window are C14 figures of Christ enthroned with the Orb and Blessing; to the left is St Blaise as a bishop also giving blessing, and on the right St Denis. In the westernmost window of the S chancel is Christ in Majesty with a red gown and green mantle and opposite in a tracery light a rather restored figure of St John (and St Dionysius?).

ROTHBURY, Cragside Mansion: In this mansion by Norman Shaw, much of the decorative work is by Morris & Co., notably the Library bay window with glass of 1873, appropriately portraying figures of literary giants such as Homer, Dante, Chaucer, Virgil, Horace and Aeschylus, all designed by Burne-Jones; Chaucer and Milton, by Ford Maddox Brown, and six scenes of St George by Rossetti.

NOTTINGHAMSHIRE

Much glass from the C14 in a number of places but outstanding at Newark and good at Fledborough, Halam, Southwell Minster and Woodborough; it is clearly related to glass of a similar age in Derbyshire, much of it being executed by the Lenton school of glaziers (*see* p.24). C15 pieces exist in a number of locations, best of all (again) at Newark and, to a lesser extent, at Papplewick. Both St Mary's and St Peter's at Nottingham have good representations of C19 windows – and there is some good post-war work around the county.

MR Place	Centuries									Principal feature(s)
	12	13	14	15	16	17	18	19	20	
1 Arnold									*	Biblical themes in d-d-v by RP, 1964-5
2 Aversham			+	*						see below
3 Babworth								*		see below
4 Balderton					+					early C16 Renaisance-style remains
5 Bleasby									*	early C20 ws. by Christopher Whall
6 Calrton in Lindrick				*						4 unusual late C15 roundels
7 Coddington								*		good WM glass in chancel and W w., 1965
8 Cossall				*						St Catherine (nave SE w.)
9 East Markham			H	*						C15 St Sitha (S a.E w.); late C14 arms, E w.
10 East Retford				*	F			*		Sts Laurence and Christopher, Magi, angels
11 Egmanton			*							Sts George and Michael, *c.*1360 (S tspt)
12 Farnsfield								*		W w. by CB, 1876; apse ws. by Wailes, 1862

MR	Place	Centuries								Principal feature(s)
		12	13	14	15	16	17	18	19	20	
13	Fledborough			*	+						see below
14	Greasley				*						Sts Agatha and Agnes
15	Halam			*					*		see below
16	Hucknall								*		25 ws. from CEK from the 1880s
17	– (RC)									*	19 ws. by RP
18	Keyworth									*	ws. by D. Fourmaintreaux for JP, 1967
19	Lambley			*	*						C14 Virgin; Virgin and Child; C15 Crucifixion
20	Laneham			*							late C14 Virgin plus angel from a Coronation
21	Mansfield Woodhouse					H					arms of D and Woodnoth (1617)
22	Marnham, Low				*						St James as pilgrim (in a. N w.)
23	Newark, St Mary Mag.			*	*				*		see below
24	– Wesleyan Chapel									*	'Holy Grail Quest' by WM, 1922
25	North Muskam				*						64 examples of the Barton rebus, c.1490
26	Nottingham, Boots Ltd									*	'Alchemical' ws. in Research Dept. by AH
27	– High Pavement Ch.									*	late WM ws. and one by HH, 1906
28	– St Barnabus (R.C.)							*			Pugin-designed ws. for Wailes, 1845
29	– St Mary								*		see below
30	Nuthall				H*						Crucifixion with Sts Mary and John (E w.)
31	Papplewick				*				*		see below
32	Pleasley									*	St Michael conquers Satan, F. Stephens, 1967
33	Plumtree								*		E w. and others by BG of mid 1870s
34	Saundby			*							Virgin; grotesques from the Lenton School
35	Southwell Minster			*		F			*	*	see below
36	Strelley Hall			F		F	F				see below
37	Thoroton								*		4 ws. by LB at their peak, 1868–9
38	Tuxford				*						St Laurence, c.1500 (S a.E w.)
39	West Bridgford									*	post-War glass by JP and A.Fisher
40	Woodborough			*					*		see below

See page 280 for table of symbols

AVERHAM, St Michael: The E window has C15 glass from Kelham Hall, whereas the C14 and C15 remains in a chancel N window are indigenous and include Christ and the Virgin Mary (in a quatrefoil), Christ giving blessing, a king and an angel; some grotesque-border suggests some work by the Lenton school.

BABWORTH, All Saints: The Resurrection window by Francis Eginton is a rare survivor of glass from the late Georgian period (most windows of this vintage were lost during the Gothic revival in the mid C19). The E window is by Wailes (1855) and W by Kempe (1879).

FLEDBOROUGH, St Gregory: In the N aisle E window is some restored C14 glass with figures of St John the Baptist and St Andrew (left), the Virgin and Child (with a bird) and knight (right); each figure is set within a rounded battlement arch. In the chancel N are two C14 saints, one possibly the Virgin Mary; also some C15 heraldic fragments.

HALAM, St Michael: Very fine C14 figures in the chancel tracery lights of St Christopher with the Christ Child (note the fish in the water

and, strangely, a garter on His right knee), of Eve spinning, Adam digging, and St Blaise with a (?) hog (which is strange, since this is usually associated with St Andrew and a carding comb with St Blaise); all four have canopies, and borders with white and gold eagles. Late Morris & Co. glass of 1919 in the N nave with the Visitation, Annunciation and St Michael; S aisle has the Transfiguration and Ascension; all are re-used cartoons of Burne-Jones, except for H. Dearle's Visitation.

NEWARK, St Mary Magdalene: Excellent medieval glass in the S chapel E window, reset by Joan Howson in 1957, where the two central lancets have panels of c. 1310 (and, incidentally, show very early use of yellow stain), and the other four are C15. A pamphlet in the church gives a key to the thirty main lights and fourteen tracery lights; it is briefly described as follows: (1) the first (left) lancet has (top to bottom) an incomplete Trinity panel, various figures, St Etheldreda with another saint, a pope and king; (2) a lute player, the Massacre of the Holy Innocents, a Visitation of the Virgin Mary and Elizabeth, the Annunciation; (3) the C14 scenes of the Creation, Expulsion of Adam and Eve, the

Magi at the Nativity, Christ in the Temple with Joseph and Mary, four shields of arms for Deyncourt; (4) C14 again, with figures from a Last Judgement, the Last Supper (Christ, chalice and one disciple only), then a double panel with Gethsemane (left) and Christ before his accusers (right), the three Marys at the tomb; (5) has C15 glass again with a lutenist, the suitors of the Virgin Mary attacking Joseph (a rare portrayal from an aprocryphal story), the Crucifixion (note the huge pincers for extracting the nails), the Ascension, and fragments that include the donors (Merings); (6) part of a Trinity, Instrumental angels, fragments that include parts of Christ and St Catherine, a Candlemas (or Corpus Christi?) procession, a shield of Henry VII. The tracery lights have the Seven Deadly Sins which are rarely seen in stained glass.

The huge, strongly coloured main E window of 1862 is by Hardman, who also did the N aisle E window. The S aisle has a window by Gérente of Paris in C13 style, with Wailes' windows to both sides of it and two by Kempe at the W end. The SE window in the chapel is a good work by Percy Bacon: other glass here by Comper.

NOTTINGHAM, St Mary: Masses of glass dating from the second half of the C19, the highlights of which are Hardman's E window of c. 1865, and the S transept S window by Heaton, Butler & Bayne, 1867. Also glass by Kempe (S aisle, 1895), by Clayton & Bell (1873-91) and Burlison & Grylls (mostly c. 1882).

PAPPLEWICK, St James: To the W of the S door are some C15 panels with the figures of St Peter (to the E) with chasuble and forked beard, six monks forming a kind of procession, St Stephen (to the W), and a kneeling knight holding a Book of Hours. The E window here is Francis Eginton's copy of J. Reynolds' Faith and Hope panels at New College, Oxford.

SOUTHWELL Minster: Most of the old glass is in the Chapter House, but above the altar of the Minster are four lancets with French Renaissance glass, c. 1555, bought in a pawnbroker's shop in Paris by the MPH. Gally in 1818: the panels come from the Paris Temple and include a Baptism of Christ, the Raising of Lazarus (note Francis I with red cup and beard), the Entry to Jerusalem (Louis XI with blue helmet), and a scene of Christ being mocked at the Passion which includes Luther raising his hand to strike Christ – real Counter-Reformation stuff! In the six windows of the Chapter House are numerous fragments, mostly C14, which include a Visitation scene with an Adoration of the Magi (in the first window to the left of the entrance), Christ and Apostles in glass of c.1300 (in third window), and Christ Resurrected (in fifth windows). Of the C19 glass O'Connor's characteristically bright work of the 1840s can be seen in the aisles; early Kempe in the E windows of the aisles, and later work of his in the N transept and N chapel of c.1907.

STRELLEY HALL, Chapel: Much Continental glass (brought here via Shirburn, Warwickshire?): in the nave can be see Sts Bartholomew and Ugbert in C14 glass with Lombardy lettering, and C16-C17 pieces which include a figure of St James the Great. C18 panels in the S chapel E window portray biblical scenes, coats-of-arms, saints and that favourite C18 subject, the Virtues such as Fortitude and Intelligence.

WOODBOROUGH, St Swithun: Fine C14 glass in the chancel: on the N side St Catherine trampling on the emperor, whilst next door St Margaret does likewise on a dragon; on the S is the Agony in the Garden with the disciples Peter and John sleeping and at the W end Christ with St Mary Magdalene at the Resurrection and Doubting Thomas touching Christ's side. In the E window is a fully blown Kempe window of c. 1897 that incorporates some C14 bits and eight-winged seraphim in the tracery lights. Elsewhere are various windows by Morris & Co., late works of c. 1910, either designed by H. Dearle (e.g. Virgin and Child) or re-used Burne-Jones cartoons, (e.g. St Dorothy).

OXFORDSHIRE

Oxfordshire is the only county that has had its pre-1540 glass thoroughly surveyed and published by the Corpus Vitrearium in a fine piece of research by Dr Peter Newton. Since this survey was carried out the northern part of Berkshire has been added to Oxfordshire, bringing the total number of places where old glass can be seen to over 150, of which twenty-nine are briefly described here and a further sixty-two referred to in the table below. As in Kent and Norfolk, the visitor to Oxford churches is likely to encounter old glass just about anywhere; most belong to the C14 and C15, although in the city of Oxford there are some good examples of later work. In fact Oxford has masses of glass of the highest quality and of all ages, notably at New College, All Souls, Christ Church, Merton, Wadham, Lincoln and some other colleges, as well as in a few churches.

MR	Place	12	13	14	15	16	17	18	19	20	Principal feature(s)
1	Asthall			H*							Crucifixion, canopies (N tspt and NE w.)
2	Banbury								*		HBB in medieval style, c.1870
3	Beckley			*	*						see below
4	Begbroke				*	O	HO		*		see below
5	Bicester								*		ws. by WM, B-J, PW; OC and Mayer ws.
6	Bix				F						early C16 French panels: Marriage at Cana
7	Bloxham			+							grotesque, castle and fleur-de-lis border
8	Brightwell Baldwin			*	*						see below
9	Broughton								*		LBW w., 1871; BG for G.G.Scott, 1870
10	Burford			+	H				*	*	see below
11	Buscot								*	*	Good Shepherd by B-J, 1892
12	Charlton-on-Otmoor		*	+							late C13 Virgin and Child
13	Childrey				*						Passion remains, Annunciation
14	Chilton								*		LBW ws. designed by J.F.Bentley, 1872–3
15	Chinnor			*					*		see below
16	Coleshill				F						early C16 Nativity panel from Angers
17	Combe				*						fine cherubim on wheels in E & N t.l.
18	Compton Beauchamp			*							Crucifixion (N tspt) and Annunciation (E w.)
19	Deddington									*	2 E ws. by AJD/Bromsgrove Guild, 1923
20	Dorchester		*	*					*		see below
21	Drayton								*		J.F. Bentley/LBW, 1872
22	East Challow				*	H					C15 Trinity. Arms of Russia Trading Co.
23	East Hagbourne			*							charming Virgin, Child and Nativity, c.1300
24	Enstone						*				Crucifixion and Nativity (S and E w.)
25	Eynsham				*						St Thomas (from Benedictine Abbey?) (S a.)
26	Great Milton			*							Lazarus begging, and with two angels
27	Hampton Poyle				*						in situ C15 Evanglist symbols, chancel N
28	Hardwick			*	*						The Baptist & Christ (E w.); C15 in W w.
29	Henley-on-Thames								*		JH E (1868) and NE ws.
30	Heythrop				*						saints, Evangelists plus symbols, donors
31	Holton		G	+	H						G in chancel; Brome/Baldington arms W w.
32	Horley			+	*						two donor figs. (canons) in N a.
33	Horspath			*	+	F	H				Sts Mary and John c.1300; Swiss glass
34	Kelmscot				*						St George and dragon (E w.)
35	Kidlington		*	*	*				*		see below
36	Lew								*		early HH for JP, 1865 – 'Charity'
37	Little Milton								*		many ws. by TW, 1853; one by HBB, 1869
38	Littlemore								*	*	ws. by TW, B-J, SH; also by L.Davis (1900)
39	Longworth									*	Crucifixion by Heywood Sumner, 1900
40	Lower Heyford			*							Christ in Judgement plus frags. (S a.)
41	Mapledurham			H*							c.1400 figs.; Sts Stephen, Sitha, Barbara
42	Marsh Baldon			*	H*	H					C14 St Anne, Virgin; C15 Virgin, donor
43	Milton, Manor			*	F						see below
44	Minster Lovell				*						see below
45	Nettlebed									*	PR Tree of Life and Resurrection
46	Newington				*						see below
47	North Moreton			*							see below
48	Over Worton								*		chancel ws. by Clutterbuck, 1845
49	Oxford All Souls Col.				*				*		see below
50	– Balliol Co.				*	*	*				see below
51	– Bodleian Lib.				*	O	O				numerous roundels: C15 panels of T.Becket

MR	Place	12	13	14	15	16	17	18	19	20	Principal feature(s)
52	– Braesenose Col.						*				– Christ and Evangelists by J.Pearson, 1776
53	Christ Church			*	*	*		*			see below
54	– Corpus Christi Col.									*	St Christopher by H.A.Payne, 1931
55	– Exeter Col.							*			see below
56	– Lincoln Col.						*				see below
57	– Magdalen Col.						*				8 Chiarascuro ws. by R.Greenbury, 1633
58	– Mansfield Col.									*	rich glass by JP, 1909
59	– Merton Col.		*	*	*						see below
60	– New Col.				*		*				see below
61	– Oriel Col.				*		*	*			C15 St Margaret; JD, 1885; Peckitt w.
62	– St Mary's Ch.								*		see below
63	– St Mary Magdalen								*		S chapel w. by OC; ws. by Wailes, 1844-64
64	– St Michael's Ch.		*		*				*	*	see below
65	– The Queen's Col.				*		*				8 A.Van Linge ws. (1635), restored by Price
66	– Wadham Col.						*				see below
67	– Worcester Col.								*		see below
68	Radley					H*			H		see below
69	Rousham				Q						Qs with lovers' knots (S a.)
70	Sandford-on-Thames			*						*	C14 Christ in Majesty; PR, 1974
71	Shellingford									*	'Childhood' by D.Strachan, 1935
72	Shiplake				F						see below
73	Shipton-under-Wychwood			H		O					8 shields of arms, c.1400
74	South Leigh				*						saints include St James; Adam digging (t.l.)
75	South Newington			*							Evangelist symbols, arms, grotesques
76	South Stoke		*								late C13 Virgin with Child (and apple)
77	Sparsholt			G*							mid C14 Christ, donor, archbishop
78	Stanton Harcourt		Q*		*						late C13 St James the Great; *grisaille*
79	Stanton St John		G	*							see below
80	Stonor Park					O		*			Salvator Mundi/Church Fathers by FE, 1800
81	Summer Field School								*	*	ws. by HH, 1895-1914
82	Sunningwell								*		Pre-Raph. ws. by J.P.Seddon/S. Belham, 1877
83	Tadmarton & Toot Baldon			*							both places have small t.l. head of Christ
84	Wantage			*	+				*		C14 figs., C15 frags. in chancel; TW ws.
85	Warborough			G	Q						*grisaille* Qs in N chancel
86	Waterperry		G		*	F					see below
87	Waterstock			*	*			*	*		C14 archbishop; C15 donors; TW, c.1850
88	Westwell					*					early C16 Crucifixion and 5 donors (nave S)
89	Wroxton, Abbey						*	*			see below
90	Wytham			*	*			*			see below
91	Yarnton				F*	F*	H				see below

See page 280 for table of symbols

BECKLEY, Assumption of the Virgin Mary: Some good early and late C14 glass, notably in the chancel tracery lights where two Assumption scenes can be seen in the E and S windows – in the former the subject is combined with a Coronation and St Thomas can be seen receiving the Virgin Mary's girdle as she ascends in accordance with an apocryphal account of her life; in the S window she is carried aloft in a mandorla borne by angels. On the N side there is a crowned and nimbed St Edmund carrying the arrows of his martyrdom. Two reset late C14 figures of Sts James and Christopher with the Christ Child can be seen in a N nave window (note in the latter how the fish in the river that the saints cross are painted on the outside of the glass in order to achieve the feeling of looking through water!). Next door is a C15 scene of St Anne teaching the Virgin.

BEGBROKE, St Michael: English and Continental glass given to the church in the C19 by Alderman Fletcher can be seen in the S chancel and nave: the S side of the chancel has various C15 remains including a rare portrayal of the head of God the Father with a petalled halo; next door are some C16 Flemish roundels (the Adoration of the Magi and St Bernard are C17); beyond are more of them, mostly of C17 age with biblical subjects. In a N nave window are yet more, mainly of the C16 with Old Testament subjects. The shields of arms in the nave are mostly by Willement (1827), plus the C17 arms of Charles II.

BRIGHTWELL BALDWIN, St Bartholomew: In the N Stone Chapel the left light has a much restored figure of St Peter, c. 1400, above a delightful scene of a cheeky devil trying to upset a pair of scales from a Judgement scene: next door is St Paul under a canopy and above him the Virgin Annunciate with dove beneath a canopy and shields of arms for Conyers and Norton above, as well as a stag and leopard. In the chancel S are the angel Gabriel and the Virgin at the Annunciation, and in a S tracery light a delightful little C14 saint. An early C15 Crucifixion is in the vestry E window.

BURFORD, St John the Baptist: The chancel E window has many reassembled C15 fragments with parts of saints (John the Baptist, Christopher, Barbara and Peter) and scenes (Annunciation). Seraphim can be seen in the W window of the nave along with St George (plus dragon), Mary Magdalene, Luke's Bull, a royal saint, Barbara (plus tower), Margaret (plus cross-staff and dragon). The N transept N window has a C16 shield of Edward the Confessor and a female head with a butterfly headdress (fashionable c. 1470-90); elsewhere are the radiant suns of Edward IV confirming a late C15 date. Interesting recent glass includes the large four-light W window, which is an early work by Kempe, and his window of more than thirty-five years later in the N aisle; the E window of 1886 by Hardman with healing miracles is in memory of Dr Cheadle and his wife; St John on Patmos, with his brother James and at the Crucifixion is an Arts & Crafts work by Christopher Whall from the early C20.

CHINNOR, St Andrew: Good C14 figures in the chancel of St Laurence with gridiron and St Alban with long rod both beneath canopies on the S side, with Clothing the Naked from the Corporeal Acts of Mercy above; opposite is Giving Drink to the Thirsty and a bishop and archbishop below. High up in the apex of the N aisle E window is Christ in Majesty between two angels, C14, and a shield for Zouche of Dene in a N window. Both E windows are by Clayton & Bell of 1865, competent work as always. The stained glass in the aisles is by William Aitken of the 1930s and 1940s.

DORCHESTER Abbey: Much of the old glass here dates from the C14, an exception being the roundel of c. 1250 in the N aisle E window, with St Birinius receiving his cross-staff from Pope Honarius. Most of it is in the main E window above the C19 glass in the bottom two layers; the main pieces in the lower layer have (left to right) an Annunciation, St Michael with the dragon (head of St Edmund above), the monk Radulpus de Tiwe in prayer, then (to right of the pillar) St Laurence, St Birinius converting the Saxons, and a bishop with crozier; in the second layer are fragments that include St Birinius' head, the Virgin and Child (one with an apple, the other a bird), Christ in Majesty and a Trinity shield. Above this are two heads from the same cartoon (one being a reversal of the other) and in the traceries a king and bishop from a Last Judgement; in the rose window is C19 glass by O'Connor mixed with C14 fragments, designed by Butterfield, c. 1847. The unique Tree of Jesse in the N chancel has the stone tracery forming the tree whilst what remains of the sixteen rather damaged stained glass kings and prophets is set in panels in the stone branches – figures (some of whom are not generally associated with a Tree of Jesse scheme) can be seen carved into the stonework, e.g. the Virgin Mary, three Magi and St Gabriel just above the recumbent Jesse. Opposite are various coats-of-arms and part of Jonah and the Whale, whilst the sedilia here have four panels of glass (c. 1300) in the pierced sexfoils — a Mass scene, an archbishop, a bishop (St Peter?), and fragments. Down in the nave are canopy remains and coats-of-arms for England, Cornwall, Lancaster, Marshall Hussey and others. Two of the C19 windows in the S Chapel are by Mayer of Munich, 1899, and the third by John Hardman.

KIDLINGTON, St Mary: The E window has some fine C13-C15 panels collected from other parts of the church; at the top is a dove, then the sun and moon, and below the transom a Crucifixion of c. 1300 with Sts Mary, John and two angels, one on a wheel; than a fine Trinity panel within a border of crowns and fleur-de-lis and between shields of arms (for Stapledon and Stafford) held by angels, a composite panel of the Virgin and Christ Child, parts of Jesse Tree kings, two small figures of prophets and St Anne teaching the Virgin to Read (with diaper background), all C15; in the bottom row are C14 figures, one composite, the other an archbishop and a C15 panel that Dr Newton identifies as the

Miracle of St Frideswide where one of Prince Akgar's messengers is healed before a crowd of royal figures. Also some C15 arms, quarries and a roundel in a S sanctuary window. The fifteen or so scenes in the W window are by O'Connor of 1857 and another C19 copy of Reynolds' Graces window at New College, Oxford.

MILTON Manor: The first-floor chapel in Gothic style has some interesting pieces of C14 English glass in the apse windows, said to have come from Steventon Church and set against fragments of *grisaille* with roundels and heraldic shields: the six panels have scenes of the Coronation with Christ top right and the Virgin Mary top left and four scenes below, the Nativity (left), Annunciation (left), Ascension (right) and Resurrection (right); the figure drawing is beautiful, but the glass has darkened somewhat in places. The large Flemish panels to the side have Christ with the Doubting Thomas in the centre, flanked by scenes from the Life of St Julian. Also here are some tiny enamel painted scenes of secular life and, in addition, a colourful parrot between two C17 coats-of-arms.

MINSTER LOVELL, St Kenelm: Various late C15 remains in tracery lights around the church. In the E window are Isaac and Daniel with scrolls, while the easternmost N window has a cherub, angel, a king and St (?) Helen; on the S side is a saint with a book – St Lucy? The N transept has two very corroded panels with figures, one of which might be St Agnes, whilst the N nave has St Peter the Martyr with sword in his head and another figure in dark blue; on the S side of the nave is the best figure of all, St Cosmas (or Damian) wearing academic robes and carrying a surgeon's knife and urine flask. In the W window are angels from the Hierarchy trampling devils underfoot.

NEWINGTON, St Giles: In a N chancel window is a good late C15 panel with the Assumption and Trinity represented as three crowned figures on a rainbow, the Son displaying the Crucifixion wounds; a nice head of the Virgin Mary with a dove from an Annunciation scene in a S window.

NORTH MORETON, All Saints: In the Stapleton Chantry five-light E windows are fifteen good figure panels of *c.* 1299 from which, alas, many of the original heads are missing. Restored (*c.* 1860), they portray incidents in the lives of Christ, the Virgin Mary, St Peter, St Paul and St Nicholas, but two of the panels are confusingly misplaced (shown in parenthesis below); thus in the central lancet are the Scourging, Crucifixion and Resurrection; second from the right has St Paul's Martyrdom, Preaching to Felix and (Nicholas' Entombment); second from the left has St Peter's Martyrdom, the Commission from Christ, and Draught of Fishes; the left light has St Nicholas giving alms, Raising Children from the tub, and (St Paul's Conversion); the right lancet has the Assumption, Burial and Death of the Virgin Mary. In a nave window is the figure of St Christopher with a staff and C14 flower-patterned *grisaille*.

OXFORD, All Souls College Chapel: Magnificent glass in the antechapel by John Glazier of 1440-47 with some restoration by Clayton & Bell in the late 1870s: in the E windows to N and S are the large figures of the twelve Apostles in the top row, each on a chequered floor, carrying traditional attributes, set within a canopy and with a label bearing their name beneath, six to the N and six to the S: beneath them are twelve female saints similarly disposed, the Holy Women and St Agatha to the N and Sts Elizabeth (with infant John the Baptist), Helen, Anastasia, Etheldreda, Katherine and Sidwell to the S. The rest of the glass here used to be in the Old Library and is now in two windows in the W wall and above the N door; these panels are smaller than those in the E windows but are similarly arranged beneath canopies, on a chequered floor and with labels: over the N door are Sts Dunstan, Edmund and Odo of Canterbury above and Archbishop Chichele, Henry IV and King Arthur below (C19 angels in traceries); those on the N side of the W wall feature bishops and Doctors of the Church, each with one of the symbols of the Evangelists (lion, ox, eagle and man/angel); on the S side is the Royal Window. The glass in the main chapel (1870s) by Clayton & Bell is deliberately 'antiquified', but still good – better at least than Hardman's Doom window of 1861.

OXFORD, Balliol College Chapel: There are a number of windows contemporary with the former chapel (1529), some of the C17, reset C15 glass, all restored in the C19, and some of the C20. In the E window amid New Testament scenes (mostly C16) are the arms, initials and rebuses of the donor Laurence Stubbs, (the Agony in the Garden and Ecce Homo panels use

Dürer's designs as a model). The six scenes from the life of St Catherine in the easternmost window on the S side are by Hugh Arnold, c. 1912; next door, an assemblage of C16 and C17 remains include Sts Edward the Confessor, Frideswide, Laurence, Hugh of Lincoln, Mary Magdalene and the Virgin Mary. A N window here has figures of Sts Margaret and Michael with their dragons, John and John the Baptist, Anthony Abbot and the Virgin and Child; next to it are coats-of-arms, the Virgin again and Thomas Chase (Master, 1421-8) and at the E end the Sickness and Recovery of Hezekiah, an incomplete work by A. van Linge, who also did the window in the antechapel with St Philip and the Eunuch, both of 1637.

OXFORD, Christ Church Cathedral: Much fascinating stained glass from the C14 to C19. Starting in the **N aisle** is the very scenic enamel painted window of 'Jonah Surveying Nineveh' by A. van Linge of c. 1631; Clayton & Bell did the next two biblical scenes and the huge St Michael window in the **N transept,** all 1875-80; also here are fragments of another van Linge window and one by William Price with angelic instrumentalists. In the **Latin Chapel** is the best glass, dating from c. 1360 and portraying under splendid canopies lovely large figures of: (left to right) St Catherine, the Virgin Mary and Child, and St Hilda (first window); a saint or archbishop flanked by Gabriel and the Virgin Annunciate (second); Sts Margaret, Frideswide and Catherine (third); three saints by Powell's, 1880 (fourth). The E window here is an early work by Burne-Jones for James Powell of 1859 with scenes depicting the death of St Frideswide. In the **Lady Chapel** next door is the Vyner Memorial Window, a later work by Burne-Jones (1871) to commemorate the death in Greece of four undergraduates, with Samuel, David, John the Evangelist, Timothy and related scenes underneath (note Burne-Jones's signature in the Timothy with Eunice panel – Topcliffe in Yorkshire has the only other signed window of his); Burne-Jones's work again in the Cecilia window close by. Clayton & Bell did the rose window and two E lights, c. 1875, and Burne-Jones yet again in the **Regimental Chapel** where his St Catherine window of 1877 commemorates Edith Liddell – the saint here is modelled on her; the Bishop Robert King window of c. 1630 is by B. van Linge. The E window of the **Lucy Chapel** has some fine glass of c.

1330, recently restored and cleaned: God is at the apex flanked by censing angels (below are some dogs eating the foliage!), then the coats-of-arms of England and France (old), the figures of St Augustine, the Martyrdom of St Thomas Becket, and St Martin dividing his cloak; below them are Sts Blaise and Cuthbert (carrying Oswald's head); in the three main lights are numerous fragments, including a donor figure and pieces out of the York Glaziers' 'bank' of medieval glass. The Tree of Jesse in the **S transept** is by Clayton & Bell (1891), as are the two biblical scenes in the 1875 window in the **S aisle:** others here by Burne-Jones yet again, the Crucifixion and Christ panels are Wailes (1858) and the Life of St Peter by Rogers for Powell's (1864). In the **Chapter House** are various panels and pieces that include (in S windows) a Virgin and Child, a roundel of the Assumption, Cardinal Wolsey's badge (crossed pole-axes) all early C16, and Flemish panels with Pilate Washing his Hands and St Jerome portrayed with a lion's paw! On the stairs is some unusual glass of c.1430, reassembled to give three fine roundels: M for Mary, the Assumption and Crucifixion inside the monogram IHS.

OXFORD, Exeter College Chapel: Most of the glass in this Sainte Chapelle-inspired building by Scott is by Clayton & Bell over the period 1859-80. The apse windows are the earliest in straight C13 style and utilising the then new glass from Chance Brothers of Birmingham. The window by the S door of 1914 is a good work by Powell's.

OXFORD, Lincoln College Chapel: On the S side is a complete set of Apostles in early C17 glass that face twelve prophets on the N, all by Bernard van Linge. The same type-antetype idea exists in the E window where his Old Testament scenes are set above their equivalents in the New: The Creation of Adam and Eve over the Nativity, Crossing the Red Sea above Christ's Baptism, the Passover above the Last Supper, the Brazen Serpent over the Crucifixion, Jonah and the whale over the Resurrection, and Elijah's Ascension over Christ's. Nearly all the colouring comes from enamel painting, but there are some stained pieces.

OXFORD, Merton College Chapel: In the fourteen windows of the N and S sides are figures prior to 1298 (restored in 1852 by Barraud, working for Powell's); each is set beneath

St Luke and Henricus of Mamesfeld, *c.*1295; Merton College, Oxford

a canopy and framed by *grisaille*, a style that thereafter became common in C14 English glass. In twelve of the windows the donor can be seen to appear twice – thus Henricus de Mamesfeld appears twenty-four times in all with each apostle (*see illustration above*). From W to E (N side are Sts Peter, Andrew, Simon, Philip, Bartholomew, James the Less, and John; then on the S side E end are an archbishop with Sts Paul and Nicholas, followed by Sts Laurence, (?), and Jude; the remaining five have the donor with Sts Thomas, Mark, James the Great, Luke and Matthew. In the E window are many panels of C14-C16 glass beneath *in situ* tracery glass, where the angel Gabriel and the Virgin Mary flank the rose window (and three coats-of-arms, for England, the Prince of Wales and Clare). In the main lights are more coats-of-arms (including those of the college) and nine superb panels from Thomas Glazier's workshop with seraphim, the Crucifixion, a Benedictine Abbess/saint, the Virgin and Child, another Benedictine (reversed cartoon of the former?), St John and the Virgin again; below are more shields of arms. In the Library are twelve panels of German glass and various other pieces.

OXFORD, New College Chapel: The original glass in the antechapel is by Thomas Glazier of *c.* 1380-86 with numerous large figures of biblical characters, each labelled and

set beneath a magnificent canopy (each of which is different); angels from the Hierarchy in the tracery lights. Starting at the N side of the W window are Jeremiah, Isaiah, (?), Hosea above Adam, Eve, Seth and Enoch with Thrones above; in NW windows Principalities look down on four prophets set above Methuselah, Noah, Abraham and Isaac; in the next window, four more prophets are over Jacob, Judah, Moses and Nahum with Dominations above; then in the E window (N side) six of the Apostles are above a female saint, part of the Crucifixion, St John and St Mary and with Angels above; over in the southern E window the other six are above another Crucifixion also with Mary and John and another saint – Angels and a Coronation above; the SE window has popes and bishops with Cherubim above and the SW a varied collection: Sts Mary of Egypt, Baruch, Jonah and Mary Magdalene above Martha, composite figures, St Withburga and six Seraphim overhead. More recent is the notorious W window with its painting on glass by Thomas Jervais after designs by Joshua Reynolds of 1785: above the clouds that envelope the Virtues set on their pedestals is a Nativity scene based on Correggio, in which Reynolds and Jervais appear as shepherds. However, Reynolds was not happy with the result – few people are, yet C19 copies of it abound in churches around Britain. In the chapel itself beneath some remains of medieval canopies are late C18 enamel-painted saints, patriarchs and bishops, mostly by William Price on the N side, and the Apostles with saints on the S side are by William Peckitt.

OXFORD, St Mary's University Church: In the N and S aisles are two windows by Pugin and Hardman of 1855 and 1843, both based on medieval style – the latter the better of the two. Two by Clayton & Bell in the S aisle, one of 1858 (a Tree of Jesse) the other in C15 style of the 1870s. A fine Tree of Jesse (W window) by Kempe, dating from 1891.

OXFORD, St Michael's Church: In a N aisle window can be seen a rare Lily Crucifixion: that is, the Crucifixion set on a lily, symbol of the Annunciation, an idea that would seem to symbolise the Word being made flesh, for the two events mark the beginning and end of the Incarnation of Christ on earth (*see illustration*). Other C15 Lily Crucifixions can be seen at Westwood (Wilts) and Long Melford (Suffolk), and one of later date at the Queens College, Oxford. In the E window are four reset panels of C13 glass with Sts Nicholas, Edmund of Abingdon, the Virgin and Child and Michael. Some rather overpainted early C20 windows also here.

OXFORD, Wadham College Chapel: The E window of Bernard van Linge is a huge colourful but rather awkward portrayal of the history of Christ, 1622 (there are also two C16 Flemish panels here). The N and S walls have earlier enamel painted figures with some staining of Christ, Prophets, Apostles and St Stephen, possibly by Robert Redland (whose work is also at Magdalen College): one is dated 1616.

OXFORD, Worcester College Chapel: All the windows here are early works by Henry Holiday dating from 1864-5 when he was twenty-four and working for Lavers & Barraud (he also painted the walls and ceiling). Paul San Casciani draws our attention to the magnificent Angel of the Annunciation, the Adoration of the Magi and other delights in this chapel, illuminated only, it would seem, by its rich glass.

RADLEY, St James: An interesting collection of royal coats-of-arms from Tudor times, though very restored by Willement in the mid C19. His elaborate resettings of the various

Lily Crucifixion, C15; St Michael's, Oxford.

coats include those for Henry VII between dragon and greyhound supporters, for Henry VIII between lion and dragon, for Richard III between the lion and the pig, and for Henry VI between a pair of amiable spaniels. Note Willement's attempts at setting jewels into the glass. Up in the tower W window is an early C16 largely original portrait of Henry VII as a young man. The E window has two panels of C16 French(?) glass with a donor, weeping women and indeterminate scenes.

SHIPLAKE, St Peter and St Paul: Five windows of French glass of *c.* 1500 from the church of St Berin at St Omer, given to the church in 1828. The particularly fine E window has charming busts, each surrounded by little angles: St John the Baptist is at the top, then St Andrew between two red-faced seraphim, and St Omer between God the Father and the Virgin Mary, forming a Coronation; below are Sts Barbara, Peter and Catherine (with symbols); then Sts Anthony Abbot, Peter of Luxembourg and John. In the chancel S some heads include those of a knight and priest; the S aisle E window has more of them and a large figure of St Peter beneath a huge papal tiara, donors and angels; next door there are two small English-looking royal saints under canopies and pieces that include a Christ Child and a monk. The W window is a bit messy, but the pieces include God the Father, the Virgin Mary (head missing) and the Christ Child, three very darkened Evangelists' symbols down the centre lancet and St John's fine eagle at the bottom, also exquisite angels and bizarre grotesques at the top.

STANTON ST JOHN, St John the Baptist: An unusual panel of *c.* 1300 in a S chancel window which portrays that part of the medieval legend of the Funeral of the Virgin Mary where a Jew tried to overturn the coffin, but his hands stuck to the wood until St Peter made the sign of the Cross and, with the Jew's instant conversion, he became unstuck and fell to the ground; he appears twice in the same panel, reaching up to the coffin and then on the ground after his release. Also here are two censing angels, a shield for Clare and a roundel of a man cutting branches from a tree. (*See illustration above of a C15 roundel.*) In the N chancel is a fine panel of C13 geometric *grisaille* (*see illustration on* p.23).

WATERPERRY, St Mary: Fine *grisaille* of *c.* 1250-70 in three chancel N windows, and in

C14 roundel – scaring away the birds; Stanton St John, Oxon.

the nave the mid C15 figures of the donor (Fitzellis) and family (Lady Fitzellis's headdress shows an interesting instance of back painting to give more of a three-dimensional effect). Next door in C14 glass are two more donors in a tracery light. On the S side a shield for Curzon, Curzon impaling Saunders, and Saunders alone, then the Curzons and a Virgin and Child. In a nave W window are C15 fragments of canopies, cherubim, seraphim, a sun *ensoleille* and a C16 Flemish panel of the Nativity.

WROXTON Abbey: The E window was put together in 1747 and contains much earlier work by B. van Linge, *c.* 1630. At the top are three little panels with four Apostles, whilst below are larger scenes of the Passion; then comes a row of well-painted little birds and, below them, three of the Evangelists: John, Mark and Matthew (with eagle, lion and angel). At the bottom are four of the ten Sibyls of Classical mythology: the Libyan, Cumaean, Delphic and Tiburtian.

WYTHAM, All Saints: A strange collection of glass of differing ages and from different sources; in nave N are four C14 roundels, possibly by Thomas Glazier, from the old church with a king, queen and sheep-shearing scene (from the months' labours?); by the pulpit is an Annunciation and St John's eagle, C15. The E window has a C18 Adoration of the Shepherds, and in the S chancel are some small Continental pieces from Alderman Fletcher's collection (see Yarnton), portraits of Edward IV and various coats-of-arms, Bertie and Willoughby alliances.

YARNTON, St Bartholomew: Much glass of Continental and English origin given by

Alderman Fletcher in 1813, although the only indigenous glass is in the four N traceries. Most delightful are the little birds in a small N chancel window of c. 1500 whose subject matter suggests that they once resided in an inn — each bird has a cup and scroll with inscribed comments such as 'who blayth this ale . . .', '. . . make God thy friend . . .' and 'ye: shall: praye: for: the: fox' (the latter from the popular Funeral of the Fox). In the chancel E are two six-winged cherubim on wheels, a composite yet beautiful C15 Virgin Mary, and St Thomas with spear. In the N nave windows, panels include a Virgin and rather chubby Child (Netherlandish, C15), Ablimech restoring Sarah to Abraham (mid C16), a C16 Flemish saint, the Prodigal Son being turned away from a brothel (Dutch?), and badges for Henry VII and Catherine of Aragon; in traceries are donor monks, Sts Nicholas, Thomas Becket, and a composite Jude and James the Great. Next door are Sts Christopher and Mary with the Christ Child, John and angel, all C15. In the W window (N side) are some rather composite figures of saints (Chad, John the Baptist and Thomas with T-square). A large collection of early C17 armorial glass can be seen in the Spencer Chapel, mostly with Spencer alliances.

SALOP

At Ludlow and St Mary, Shrewsbury, are two enormous collections of medieval stained glass, English at the former and mostly Continental at the latter. In the rest of the county, however, the mainly C14 and C15 remains tend to be fairly limited in quantity, although the quality of some of what amounts to only fragments is often high. Shrewsbury had an active firm of stained glass glaziers and painters in the early C19 – Betton & Evans – whose work can be seen not only in many parts of Salop but over the border in Wales, and in other parts of England, e.g. their name is particularly associated with Winchester College, though not always in the most complimentary terms! This is not because of the quality of their work (which is often of a high standard), but simply because on occasions they removed medieval glass, replacing it with their own copies, the original glass either disappearing or turning up in another church or even at Christie's, the auctioneers!

MR	Place	Centuries									Principal feature(s)
		12	13	14	15	16	17	18	19	20	
1	Alberbury			*					*		see below
2	Alveley				*						4 figs. in clsty ws.: Crucifixion (W w.)
3	Atcham			*							see below
4	Battlefield				F						early C16 French figs.
5	Calverhall								*		good WM ws. of 1875; also 1 by JP
6	Cheswardine								*		Queen Victoria w. by CB; CEK ws.1890s
7	Church Stretton					O	O				Flemish roundels in chancel ws.
8	Cleobury Mortimer								*		Piers Ploughman E w. by H.Burrow, 1875
9	Cound								*	*	see below
10	Cressage								*		see below
11	Donnington			*							Christ, Virgin from a Coronation in chancel
12	Ellesmere								*		ws. by Wailes, BG,OC,HBB, 1845-88
13	Eyton-on-the-Weald				H*						Sts Catherine and Christopher (N w.)
14	Hughley			+	+						figs. include the Virgin; canopy pieces
15	Kinlet								*		E w. is an early work by D.Evans, 1814
16	Ludlow			H*	*				*	*	see below
17	Meole Brace								*		see below
18	Morville			*							early C14 Crucifixion panel
19	Munslow				*						figs. of the Virgin and donor's family
20	Newport (RC)									*	ws. by R.F.Ashmead for Abbot & Co., 1975
21	Oswestry									*	the young Queen Victoria by SH, 1901
22	Prees								*		see below

MR Place	Centuries									Principal feature(s)
	12	**13**	**14**	**15**	**16**	**17**	**18**	**19**	**20**	
23 Shawbury				*						frag. Annunciation (chancel SW)
24 Shrewsbury,										
St Alkmund						*				Eginton's 'Faith and The Cross', 1795
25 – Clive House Mus.				*						6 Labours of the Month
26 – Holy Cross								*		early BE, 1806, in N a. E w.
27 – St Mary			F*	F	F			*		see below
28 Stanton Lacy								*		see below
29 Stokesay									*	2 very B-J inspired ws. by Harry Payne, 1904
30 Tong				*						figs. include St Peter, Virgin, c.1450
31 Uffington					O	F				German N.T. and apocryphal scenes
32 Worfield			*							3 early C14 panels: Crucifixion and groups

See page 280 for table of symbols

ALBERBURY, St Michael: Two small C14 figures of a king and queen can be seen in the S chapel SE tracery light, where there is also an outstanding Burne-Jones-inspired Art Nouveau work of 1897 by Mrs Southerby as a memorial to her father, Sir Baldwin Leighton. Most of the other windows here are by David Evans, c. 1840 (one has his signature).

ATCHAM, St Eata: Large C15 figures in the E window brought from Bacton (Herefordshire) in 1811: the unusual combination of the Virgin and Child, St John and God the Father, with the kneeling family of donors (Parry) below. Also from Bacton is a C15 angel in a N tracery light.

COUND, St Peter: In the S aisle E window C14 fragments include the figure of a saint within coloured border; also a head of Christ with a red and green nimbus. Windows by Kempe and his pupil Herbert Bryans (1891, 1909).

CRESSAGE, Christchurch: The E window by David Evans is an example of the early C19 predilection for copying masterpieces into enamel paintings on glass, in this case imitating some of the Flemish roundels at St Mary's, Shrewsbury, notably Raphael's 'Transfiguration' and Rubens's 'Deposition from the Cross'.

LUDLOW, St Laurence: An enormous collection of mostly late C15 glass, somewhat restored in 1828. (David Lloyd's guide, available as a pamphlet in the church, is highly recommended.) Starting in the **N aisle** (and moving clockwise round the church) one finds the oldest glass, three C14 shields of arms for Elizabeth Clare, Theobald de Verdun and Maud Mortimer. In the **N chapel** are three fine windows, the first being the 'Golden Window' which has Sts Catherine, John the Baptist and Christopher

beneath an Annunciation with Christ, all contained within a jewelled cloth-like canopy; above, in the traceries, are angels, God the Father and a small figure of Christ, and below are the donor (John Parys) and family. Next door is the **Apostles' Window,** where all twelve have traditional emblems (except Matthew and James who seem to have exchanged axe and spear). Unique here is the E window, or Palmers' Window, so called because it depicts in eight panels a local variant of the legend of Edward the Confessor and the visit of the Palmers of Ludlow to the Holy Land: (1) at the top left panel they board a ship; (2) the king meets St John disguised as a beggar in a wood and gives him a ring; (3) the Palmers meet St John in a wood and he asks them to return the ring to the king; (4) which they do; (5) a procession of Palmers (to celebrate their safe return?); (6) they receive their charter from the king?; (7) they return triumphantly to Ludlow; (8) celebration feast. The 'C15' glass in the chancel has been much restored over the years, to such an extent that at least fifty per cent of the work we now see is a copy of the original remains made by David Evans in the early and mid C19. The three **N windows** with nine lights each contain mostly saints with traditional attributes (note that St George appears twice), and some New Testament scenes such as the Resurrection and three Magi. The **E window** relates the story of St Laurence in twenty-seven panels: starting at the top left with his introduction to pope Sixtus II and moving to the right, we see how he gives away money, is taken prisoner, set before Decius, the idols dissolve in his presence, in prison he heals a blind man; in the middle row he converts the jailer, brings the lame to Decius who tortures them and St Laurence by numerous methods; in the bottom row he is finally roasted to death on the gridiron (second from left), is entombed, reappears, directs his followers and they build a church to his memory; in the traceries are the Trinity, angels from the Hierarchy, then a row of saints and coats-of-arms for Thomas (Bishop of Hereford) and Richard Neville. On the S side of the **chancel** is the unique portrayal in England of some of the Ten Commandments – only the last six are shown here: Moses announces them, whilst below each is a scene of their disregard; in the traceries are Sts John, Catherine, the Virgin and Christ. The other two S windows in the chancel portray numerous saints with their attributes. In the **Lady Chapel** is a much-restored Tree of Jesse with birds, a squirrel and monkey joining the six kings and six prophets in its branches plus, unusually, Joseph (with lily) and St (?) John the Baptist. The **S transept** has fragments made up into a cross, at the top of which is a mid C14 Virgin with a crown of fleur-de-lis.

Of the C19 is the W window with kings and prophets by Willement, and two N aisle windows by Hardman; and one here by Louis Davis of the 1920s (an Arts & Crafts colleague of Christopher Whall); in the S aisle are windows by Clayton & Bell (1884), Powell (Weyman Memorial, 1902) and Hughes (the Herbert Window, *c.* 1859).

MEOLE BRACE, Holy Trinity:

Good Morris & Co. glass of 1870-1921, many of the figures and scenes were designed by Burne-Jones; but a few are by Ford Maddox Brown (e.g. Noah, Simeon, Hope in the 1873 S aisle and all but two of the Old Testament scenes in the left-hand apse window of 1870), and by Dearle (Valour and Endurance, N aisle second from E window of 1921). A contrast is Kempe's S aisle E window of 1894.

PREES, St Chad:

Some interesting mid C19 glass, notably a reproduction of Holman Hunt's 'Behold I Stand and Knock', very much in the Nazarene tradition, by Chance Bros of Birmingham, *c.*1855. In the S nave is a rather conservative work by Betton & Evans of 1864, whilst Heaton, Butler & Bayne's window nearby of the same date is more in tune with the evolution of stained glass at that time.

SHREWSBURY, St Mary:

A treasure trove of medieval glass, mostly foreign, installed in the early C19. Beginning with the **chancel E** window is the huge Tree of Jesse of *c.* 1340 spread across eight lights; formerly in St Chad's Church, it was probably orginally given to a friary chapel by Sir John de Charlton who appears at the bottom together with his family,

three knights and their ladies, Edward II and the Virgin and Child; the Tree itself has the usual kings and prophets, finding its climax in the tracery lights with the Virgin, Crucifixion and Apostles. The **S chapel** E window is mainly C19 but the middle two windows of its S side have panels from St Jacques at Liège (*c.* 1525) with members of the Horne family with their patron saints (John, Joseph of Arimathaea, Anne and the Virgin). To the right in the lower part of the window are C14 panels with Sts Stephen, Catherine and Barbara. Moving into the **S aisle** the first window has glass from Treves Cathedral of 1497 with fine figures of Sts Barbara and Catherine flanking Helen with the Cross and a beautiful Virgin and Child: to the right are Charlemagne and St Goar between Peter and Paul (this Treves window is related to others in the N aisle, the former portraying St Agatha with pincers above the donor, Everard de Holnenfels, and the latter with Sts Sebastian, Lambert and Jerome). The middle window in the S aisle has four scenes from the life of St Bernard in the midst of other pieces which include a beautiful C14 Crucifixion – fourteen other related St Bernard panels can be seen in the triple-light N chancel window which these four continue – they will therefore be described later. In the next window is a rare portrayal of St Martin with geese, the Virgin and Child and an Adoration of the Magi, also from Treves; the westernmost window here has the figures of a donor and St Andrew. At the W end of the **N aisle** is the large figure of St John, *c.* 1450, probably from a Crucifixion scene that was part of the Herckenrode series (see Lichfield Cathedral, Staffs) – more parts of this glass may be among the fragments at the W end of the N aisle and include a Pieta, the Virgin Mary with seven swords pointed at her heart, Christ washing the disciples' feet, and Christ between St Mary and St Anne. In the **N and S porches** some Flemish roundels include strange portrayals of a grotesque elephant and the sign Cancer from the Zodiac (there are twenty-four more in the Vestry, including a fine St John on Patmos, and twelve in St Nicholas' chapel in the N transept that include scenes from the apocryphal Book of Tobit). In the E window of St Catherine's Chapel is a vivid Last Judgement, rather mutilated in order to fit in here, with an Assumption below, both C15 Flemish; the N wall here has an enamel painted Crucifixion beneath a fine scene of Christ's Betrayal, and flanked by donor canons apparelled in ermine: the Resurrected Christ is above with two Evangelist symbols. The fourteen painted panels of Cologne glass with the Life of St Bernard on the N side of the **sanctuary** begin on the top left-hand corner with his arrival at Citeaux, writing sermons, healing a man, building the monastery at Clairvaux; then in the centre light he persuades Henry II to accept the Pope's authority, sending his sister to a convent, teaching a peasant to pray, being punished for a misdemeanour, healing blind and deaf people, his vision of 'devotion'; in the third, he works in a field, cures a paralysed woman, bewails having not sung a penitential psalm, abducts a prisoner to Clairvaux. The previously mentioned four panels in the S aisle portray (left) the saint in bed (with a headache); (centre) excommunicating a vast number of flies that had been pestering the Abbey at Foigny, whereupon they drop dead on the spot and are shovelled out by a colleague! Below, an equally bizarre story concerning his scribe trying to write on parchment in the pouring rain – and miraculously succeeding – in order to persuade his brother to leave the luxurious Cluny and return to the more austere Clairvaux; on the right are St Bernard preaching the crusade, and deep in prayer at the altar. (These eighteen panels were bought by the Revd Rowland in 1845: there were sixty or so orginally at Altenburg, whence they were removed to avoid despoliation by Napoleon's troops; a few of the others can be seen at Marston Bigot in Somerset.) Most of the C19 glass is by Evans of various dates, e.g. the N transept N window of *c.* 1830, the chancel clerestory, 1820-29, and the copies of Murillo and Overbeck in the S chapel of *c.* 1846.

STANTON LACY, St Peter: A real oddity in stained glass is the early C19 copy of Faith, Hope and Charity at New College, Oxford, which here has the Honourable R.H. Clive, MP placed among their ranks. The glass in the S transept is by the local glazier, David Evans, who joined John Betton (later Sir John) in *c.* 1815 to found one of the earliest and most active of the C19 firms, Betton & Evans of Shrewsbury.

SOMERSET

Somerset is another of those counties (like Kent, Norfolk and Oxfordshire), where a few remains can be seen in a great number of places – but great remains at only a few. Wells is the supreme place for C14 glass; elsewhere in the county there is little of that age but much of the following century, although its quality overall is not as high as that generally seen in Yorkshire and Norfolk. In his book on Somerset glass Canon Woodford shows the stylistic, technical and iconographic points that C15 glass has in common at a number of locations in the county; he further suggests that there were a number of glaziers operating within a common style rather than an established school operating from a centre, as was the case at Norwich and York at the same time. The province of these glaziers would seem to reach beyond Somerset, as far as Gloucestershire, Dorset (e.g. Sherborne) and even Devon.

MR	Place	Centuries									Principal feature(s)
		12	13	14	15	16	17	18	19	20	
1	Alford			+		*					frag. of Mary Magdalene; Passion emblems
2	Badgworth								*		CEK ws. of the late 1870s and 1880s
3	Bicknoller·					*					St Sidwell, bishop and saint; Evangelists
4	Bishops Lydeard				*					*	Baptism scene; Virgin and Child; w. by NC
5	Brushford				F						French Virgin and Child; Flemish St George
6	Brympton d'Evercy			*	*						Sts Laurence, Stephen plus Qs (N chapel)
7	Butleigh								*		TW glass to Pugin designs, 1851
8	Charlinch				*						Sts Sitha, Catherine, Apollonia, Cecilia
9	Cheddar				*						saints, angels, arms, Evangelist symbols
10	Chewton Mendip		*		*						C13 & C15 Virgins; Sts Sidwell & Margaret
11	Compton Bishop			*							see below
12	Compton (nr Dundon)				*						Annunciation paint and stain on one pane

MR	Place	Centuries									Principal feature(s)
		12	13	14	15	16	17	18	19	20	
13	Compton Pauncefoot								*		5 characteristic ws. by Capronnier, 1860–70
14	Cothelstone				*						Sts Thomas of Canterbury & Hereford (N w.)
15	Curry Rivel		+		H*						C15 saints, angels and shields
16	East Brent				*				*		see below
17	East Coker				H	H					arms of Canterbury, Arundel, Carminow
18	Farleigh Hungerford			+	O	F	F				see below
19	Fivehead			Q		H					arms of England/France et al.
20	Frome								*		early OC 1848; CB, 1865; and JH
21	Glastonbury				*				*	*	see below
22	Halse				O						6 roundels with O.T. and N.T. scenes
23	Hatch Beauchamp				*						Virgin, St Paul, angel and frags. (N a.)
24	Huish Champflower				*						early C15 Tree of Jesse and 6 figures (N a.)
25	Kilmersdon								*	*	HH w. of 1878; Chapel E w., L.F.Day, 1912
26	Kingsbury Episcopi				H						arms for Mortimer, Stafford, Stourton et al.
27	Kingston					FH					small C17 German Nativity (S a. E w.)
28	Kingstone				*						St John the Baptist, angels, Qs (N ws.)
29	Langport				*				*		see below
30	Low Ham						*				H.Gyles Crucifixion, 1690
31	Lympsham								*		portraits of the vicar's children with Christ
32	Mark				*						see below
33	Marston Bigot					F			*		see below
34	Mells				*						see below
35	Middlezoy				Q	*					early C16 St Dorothy with roses (S a.)
36	Minehead									*	HH glass of c.1901
37	Montacute House				H	*H					see below
38	Moorlinch					*					Abraham and Isaac in late C16 Flemish glass
39	Muchelney				*O						N.T. scenes and saints
40	Nettlecombe˜					H*					see below
41	North Cadbury				*	H			*		see below
42	Norton Sub Hamdon				*				*		see below
43	Nynehead				*		H				C15 St Margaret and dragon
44	Oake				*						Sts Bartholomew, Thomas; 3 Church Doctors
45	Orchardleigh				*						see below
46	Othery				*						heads of three of the four Church Doctors
47	Over Stowey								*	*	ws. by WM, 1873 (N a.), 1906 and 1922
48	Pendomer				H*						pelican-in-her-piety; St James in E w.
49	Pilton				*						kneeling fig. of St Thomas Overay plus Qs.
50	Pitminster				*						St Catherine and Margaret in CEK 1894 w.
51	Seavington				*						figs. of Sts Margaret and Mary Magdalene
52	Taunton				*				*		'Infancy of Christ' ?remains; Gibbs ws.
53	Tintinhull									*	Fountain of Life by F.C.Eden, early C20
54	Trull				*						see below
55	Wedmore								*		William I, Victoria, Elisabeth by CB, 1887
56	Wells, Cathedral			*	+	F	*H		*		see below
57	West Bagborough									*	glass, rood, font cover, screen by NC
58	West Camel				*						Sts Andrew, Peter, Paul and others
59	West Monkton								*		rare glass from the 1820s by Grey & Son
60	Westonzoyland				Q	H					corn Qs; Seymour arms; RB for Richard Bere
61	West Pennard				*		F				see below
62	Winsford				*Q						small C14 Virgin and Child; star Qs
63	Yeovil, Crematorium									*	screen in waiting area by AF or JP

See page 280 for table of symbols

COMPTON BISHOP, St Andrew:

A beautiful tracery light arrangement of *c.* 1375 in the E window, where the Trinity is at the head, with God the Father holding the Cross of the Son (no dove of the Spirit), and God again from a Coronation (but no Virgin Mary), floral decoration and vine leaves; in lower lights can be seen (left to right) Sts Peter, Catherine (both with emblems but without heads, alas), Gabriel (from an Annunciation) and a fine figure of St Paul (bald, with sword).

EAST BRENT, St Mary:

At the E end of the N aisle are three large fine C15 figures set against quarries — Sts James the Great, John the Evangelist and John the Baptist, each with their

The Virgin and Child by Henry Holiday, 1878; Kilmersdon, Somerset.

attribute. The E window next to it is mostly of C19 origin but in C15 style, possibly Flemish; close examination reveals some charming ancient pieces, so much more subtle than the C19 imitation work. The E window is an exotic Ascension by O'Connor of 1858.

FARLEIGH HUNGERFORD, St Leonard:

In the E window is a rather fragmentary assemblage of C15 and early C16 glass where the Virgin and Child and St Leonard with his manacle can be made out in the centre: left and right lancets are said to contain Sts Christopher and Elizabeth with the infant St John the Baptist, but they are not all obvious. A north lancet has eight Flemish roundels that depict St Francis receiving the stigmata, St Giles with the hind, the Last Judgement, the Flight into Egypt, Tobit and the Fish, and the Woman Taken in Adultery. Some C14 fragments in a S window, and quarries with Hungerford scythes at the W end.

The CASTLE CHAPEL has many C15 and C16 panels and roundels, mostly Flemish, but some are said to be Spanish (a key to the layout is available at the turnstile).

GLASTONBURY, St John the Baptist:

In the N and S sanctuary windows (reassembled by Westlake in 1897) are C15 remains that on the N side include St Catherine, the Annunciation, St John on top, then the two panels of the Virgin Mary separated by an unknown and two angels, and with five donors kneeling below. On the S side is a veritable 'salad' of remains, amongst which are a number of coats-of-arms including those of Joseph of Arimathaea. The E window is by Westlake (plus a few C15 remains worked in), as are those in the S chancel. Clayton & Bell did most of the rest dating from 1857-85, except the E window of the N transept, which is by Danielli, 1924.

LANGPORT, All Saints:

A fine assembly of C15 Somerset glass reset in the E window by Clayton & Bell in 1867, comprising ten stately figures in two rows: top (left to right) are St Cecilia (palm and bell), Gabriel and the Virgin Mary (mostly modern), Elizabeth with rosary and Laurence (plus gridiron); then Anthony (mostly modern), Clement (anchor plus papal staff), Peter (keys and staff), (?) Gregory, Joseph of Arimathaea (two cruets); in the traceries are saints with attributes and arms of Paulet: James the Less (club), James the Great (staff and shell), Bartholomew (knife), John (chalice), Anthony (crutch, book, bell), Margaret (dragon) and Dorothy (flowers). Some C14 *grisaille* in the N transept and quarries in chancel N. The W window has figures by Hugh Kennedy, 1878.

MARK, St Mark: The N aisle W window has eight C15 figures reset in pairs, some of which have darkened or are rather fragmentary and not very easy to identify, but would seem to be (left to right) Sts Leonard and Stephen, Philip and Christ (from a Coronation?), Matthew and James the Less, Dorothy and John the Baptist.

MARSTON BIGOT, St Leonard: Splendid Flemish and German panels of *c.* 1500 in the E window, the centrepiece of which is the beautiful Annunciation; also a fine Crucifixion represented as a Pool of Life that flows into the mouths of the Evangelists; a good panel of The Spies with the Grapes (from Mariawald?), and another with scenes from incidents in the life of St Bernard where, after dinner with friends, his hostess (lurking in a doorway) tried to seduce him that night – but when she tried to 'invade his bed he shouted "thieves" each time and raised the household for trying to steal his irreplaceable treasure', as Woodforde puts it (*see illustration on* p.39). (See St Mary's, Shrewsbury.) Willement's nave windows of *c.* 1845 seem stark after this.

MELLS, St Andrew: Three sets of N aisle tracery lights have C15 remains, the best of which is the middle set, both from the point of view of drawing and its state of preservation; it is mostly the female saints that are represented: Sts Sitha (keys and loaves), Agatha (sword and saw), Mary Magdalene (casket and palm) and Apollonia (pincers, tooth and book); then Catherine, Helena, Margaret and (?) Hilda (palm and book); in the third are St John and St Laurence and other remains.

MONTACUTE House: In the Great Hall and Library are many coats-of-arms featuring the alliances of the Phelps family with friends at Court and in politics, as well as the arms of the Holy Roman Empire, England, Wales and Ireland (Phelps' arms are silver with a chevron between three roses gules). In the Hall are four C16 Flemish secular panels with (1) a ship in full sail; (2) a merchant's mark with a helm; (3) an angel with a shield; (4) an astronomer/navigator.

NETTLECOMBE, St Mary: Rare glass from the late C16 (reminiscent of Abbey Dore in Herefordshire) in two N windows: one with a nimbed bishop, St Catherine and (?) Clement; the other with Sts Laurence, the Virgin and John the Evangelist.

NORTH CADBURY, St Michael: In the tower W window are reset C15 panels hidden in the Court until after the Reformation. They portray good figures of saints, some with their traditional attributes: (left to right, top to bottom) Agatha and John the Baptist; then Barbara, Edmund (with book and arrow), Luke; then Giles (crook, rosary and hart), Edward the Confessor (staff and ermine coat), Etheldreda (crowned abbess). The E window with Christ in Judgement, St Michael, St Gabriel and related scenes is Clayton & Bell, 1877.

At **NORTH CADBURY COURT** are some coats-of-arms of the Hastings family, *c.* 1590.

NORTON SUB HAMDON, St Mary: All the tracery lights have C15 remains, some with recognisable figures: e.g. N aisle second from W has St Mary Magdalene in white and purple and another female saint with a sword; the third from W has remains of figures of the Evangelists. In the S aisle, the second from W has the Virgin Mary and Child, St Apollonia with tooth and pincers, and another Mary Magdalene above; the second from E has Sts Dorothy (flowers), an unidentifiable saint and Catherine (sword). Wailes's E window of *c.* 1861 and Heaton, Butler & Bayne's S chancel window of *c.* 1875.

ORCHARDLEIGH, St Mary: A fine collection of well-drawn C15 glass, rearranged and with some restoration. The E window has a figure traditionally labelled St Augustine, excellent musical angels (*see illustration on* p.3); also in the chancel are figures of the Apostles with emblems and Creed scrolls (not all correctly assigned!): St Bartholomew is on the N side with Jude (plus boat), Simon (plus fish), Matthias; on the S are Matthew (halbert), Andrew (Saltire cross), John (chalice and demon) and Philip (loaves); in the tracery light is a head of Deity. Particularly fine is the Trinity in a large trefoil over the vestry door, although it lacks the dove. In the S nave are the Evangelists' winged ox and lion set into the C19 window. The W window has two kings (one possibly St Edward the Confessor) and four musical angels; St Michael slays the dragon in a tracery light.

TRULL, All Saints: The E window has a large three-light, much restored C15 Crucifixion with Sts Mary and John, with Evangelist symbols above. In another C15 window are Sts Margaret, George and Michael.

WELLS Cathedral: Some excellent C14 remains in a number of places, yet little of the C15; much has been lost, from both neglect and ideological vandalism during the past. Starting in the **Lady Chapel,** glazed in 1300-05, are four large windows all with reset fragments – some are more complete than others (the fifth, the E window, is Willement's 1843 reconstruction version of what all the windows used to look like; the SE window has some figures under canopies, and in the tracery lights above some fine heads of popes and saints (also in the E window traceries); amongst the mosaic of bits in the N windows there can be seen an angelic trumpeter, two of the three Magi, St Mark's lion, Matthew's angel – otherwise we have very picturesque jumbles. In the SE chapel of the **retrochoir** are two figures of Christ in the tracery lights (in Majesty and from a Coronation) with bishops' heads below, fine canopies and a jumble in the main lights; over in the retrochoir SE transept is early C16 glass from Rouen by Arnout de Nimegue depicting incidents in the life of St John the Baptist and (on the right) his vision on Patmos, after Dürer: also two other French panels here of Joseph of Arimathaea asking Pilate for Christ's body. In the **S choir aisle,** four of the windows have C14 glass in their traceries with (E to W) St Michael, the Virgin and Child, heraldic glass, a Crucifixion; one window here has (in the main lights) some C17 coats-of-arms and Flemish panels, while over in the **N choir aisle** the traceries have St Michael, Crucifixion (possibly C12 from the earlier building), St John the Baptist (modern) with censing angels. The **choir** itself contains the superb Tree of Jesse of *c.* 1330 in the high E window in characteristic C14 green and yellow glass; some seventeen figures encircled by vine-type branches – David with his harp stands out –

focus to the Virgin and Child with the Crucifixion above; in the tracery lights above is a Doom. To the N and S of this window in the clerestories are large figures of saints and ecclesiatics, 'the most noble examples of English C14 painting', says Woodforde: (W to E) are Sts Richard of Chichester, Giles, Gregory, Blaise, George and Leo on the N side, and (E to W) Edward the Confessor and Ethelbert on the S. In the main body of the Cathedral there is little ancient glass – some C15 remains in the traceries of the westernmost **S aisle;** in the easternmost **N clerestory** are two small Coronations of the Virgin, and in the traceries of some S transept S windows (Sts John the Evangelist, Baptist and Dunstan, the latter tweaking a devil's nose!). The Death of St John the Baptist high up in the **N transept** is probably by Arnoult de Nijmegen again, whilst the great W window has much glass of 1660-70 (repaired by A. K. Nicholson) given by Robert Creyghton, Dean and Bishop, who appears above his coat-of-arms in the centre light. In the **Chapter House** there remain, alas, only a few C14 Resurrection scenes, coats-of-arms and foliage panels in white and ruby glass in the traceries.

Willement did the C19 glass in the **S clerestory** to the W of the C14 figures, and those to the N are by Joseph Bell of Bristol, 1851. The S aisle has four Kempe windows of *c.* 1900, and of 1903 are Powell's Virtues in the NE retrochoir, the Boer War memorials in the N transept and over the porches at the W end; finally there are Eginton's two figures of Sts Paul and Barnabas in the E windows of the S transept.

WEST PENNARD, St Nicholas: The tracery lights in the N aisle E window have four C15 figures, comprising a Coronation of the Virgin, St John and a saint with a sword (Paul?); the traceries in the second window from the E have four female figures of Sts Barbara (plus tower), Dorothy (plus flowers), Cecilia (plus bell) and one other. C19 includes four works by Mena of Paris, 1842-65, and one by Mayer in the chancel.

STAFFORDSHIRE

Some good C14 glass can be seen at a number of places in Staffordshire – as at Checkley, Church Leigh, Enville and Trysull. The glass at Lichfield Cathedral is a bit faded in places but still well worth seeing, as is other Continental glass at Biddulph. Hamstall Ridware has a varied collection that spans C13-C16.

MR	Place	Centuries									Principal feature(s)
		12	13	14	15	16	17	18	19	20	
1	Alrewas								*		good early glass by HH, 1860s
2	Amington								*		early B-J/WM ws. with N.T. scenes, 1864
3	Biddulph					FH					Abraham, Isaac, St Peter; Catherine, Christ
4	Blithfield, Church			GH							C14 arms and *grisaille;* C16 donors (W w.)
5	Hall			+	+	HO	O				various roundels; reset medieval frags.
6	Blore					HG					St Anne plus the Virgin, donor (S chancel)
7	Bradley			+	*						C15 angels, fig. with crozier, demon
8	Bramshall			HG		*					*grisaille* in E w. t. l.; part of donor fig.
9	Broughton			G*	*	H*	*		*		see below
10	Brown Edge								*		WM glass designed by B-J and FMB, 1874
11	Caverswall									*	S a. E w. by S. Image, 1907; HH in N a.
12	Chasetown									*	rose w. and 10 others by HH, 1961
13	Checkley			*		F					see below
14	Cheddleton								*		see below
15	Church Leigh			*							see below
16	Denstone								*		a fine early masterpiece by CB
17	Elford				F						3 Flemish panels from Life of the Virgin
18	Enville			*							see below
19	Hamstall Ridware		G	H	*						see below
20	Hanbury				*				*		C15 Trinity, John Baptist; C19 w. by WH
21	King's Bromley			G		+	F				part of Sts Giles, Elizabeth: Eginton reset
22	Leek									*	late WM ws. – rose w. by H.Dearle
23	Lichfield				F				*		see below
24	Longdon			G+	*	+			*		C15 donor/canon; early WH, 1858
25	Madeley								*		good C19 ws. by WM, CB, and CEK
26	Okeover			+	*						St Mary Mag., Peter, donors; Lenton border
27	Rolleston			H	*						see below
28	Seighford				*						St Christopher, Coronation (Coventry glass).
29	Stafford, St Mary								*		Gérente's C13-style w.; Pugin's N a. w. 1846
30	Statfold					F	F				St Augustine; Burning Fiery Furnace; *et al.*
31	Stoke-on-Trent, Mus.									*	4 recent panels by David le Versha
32	Stretton			+	*						frag. C15 Crucifixion (E w. t.l.)
33	Swynnerton								*		JP E w. of 1864 – B-J influenced
34	Tamworth								*	*	see below
35	Trysull			*							2 fine C14 figs., saint apostle (E w.)
36	Weston-under-Lizard			+		F					some Netherlandish pieces
37	Whittington				*						restored figs. of saints, donors, *c.* 1490
38	Wychnor			H							shield with arms of Zouch and Somerville

See page 280 for table of symbols

BROUGHTON, St Peter (this church is near Hookgate):

An odd collection of C14-C17 glass in this C17 church, some of which probably came from Wybunbury Church and Doddington Old Hall. The E window's four lights have reset and partially composite figures, e.g. a king, St George (with golden locks and a blue dragon), St Roche (pointing to a plague spot) – all C15 – and a C17 St Andrew set above some splendid heraldic achievements; the tracery lights have many figures and include some rather corroded C14 saints (one is a tiny St Laurence under a canopy), some C14 *grisaille*, a C17 Flemish Crucifixion scene, coats-of-arms and even a C16 choir in a rood loft. In the N chancel are nine shields of arms, some Gartered and some with complex alliances, set against C14 *grisaille* and other fragments. On the S side are some made-up figures, one of Christ or the Virgin holding an orb, an early C16 St Francis with the stigmata and donors kneeling below. In the S nave is a nice Kempe window of 1897 with the Three Marys at the Tomb.

CHECKLEY, St Mary and All Saints:

Some fine early C14 glass in the E window with two figures/scenes in each main light: (left to right) are a bishop set against *grisaille* with the Stoning of St Stephen below, then a S-shaped figure with Abraham and Isaac below, an archbishop above and Crucifixion with Sts Mary and John below and a border of fleur-de-lis and castles; a bearded figure above and St Margaret killing the dragon below; in the right light is a bishop and a scene of Becket's Martyrdom below. The three-light N chancel window has a Virgin and Child, St James and St Barbara, both on early C14 *grisaille* and castle/fleur-de-lis

183

border; to the S are the figures of St John and Moses, also on *grisaille*. Above the Foljambes' tomb are six C17 Labours of the Months, probably of Dutch origin: July (man with scythe), October (foraging pigs and fruit collecting), September (reaping), February (netting fish?), March (pruning) and April (tree planting).

CHEDDLETON, St Edward the Confessor: Much good Morris & Co. glass of the 1860s, a time when the firm acquired its mature style that was to see them through the rest of the century. Ford Maddox Brown designed the eight little figures of kings and queens in the chancel (1864), and the Old Testament scenes in the N aisle W window (1866); Burne-Jones's Baptism of Christ in the S aisle, his angels blowing trumpets and the N aisle window with St Cecilia (1892); in the N aisle NE window is Morris's design of Ruth and Boaz (1868).

CHURCH LEIGH, All Saints: Early C14 tall and dignified figures in the eastern chancel windows, set in vesicas: on the S side is the Coronation of the Virgin above Sts Laurence and Stephen, a Crucifixion with St John and the Virgin Mary (wearing a *barbette*), all set against maple-leaf *grisaille*; on the N side is a mostly modern Annunciation and a C14 roundel of a centaur-like creature at battle, set between an archbishop and St Giles (labelled Egidus in Lombardic script); above are shields of arms for Warenne and England. Other quartrefoils in chancel N have old glass with demi-figures of angels and one with another C14 armed centaur.

ENVILLE, St Mary: The E window of the S aisle has some good figures of *c.* 1330, St Michael with dragon, a somewhat restored but fine St James, Virgin with Child and St Thomas; the N aisle E window has some C14 *grisaille* in the heads of the lights and traceries. In the chancel are ten C14 coats-of-arms on the S side; the E window is a good work of Clayton & Bell of the 1870s.

HAMSTALL RIDWARE, St Michael and All Angels: In the N aisle are nine of the Apostles in C16 glass with the Creed scrolls: as is often the case with Creed scrolls, there appears to be some muddling over which apostle has which scroll, and this in turn causes the prophets to be occasionally mislabelled (here Matthias is mislabelled Thomas): in three windows it would seem that we have (left to right) Sts Peter,

Andrew, James; then John, Thomas, Simon; and Philip, Bartholomew, Matthias. In the N chapel is some C13 *grisaille*, and in the S chapel shields for Ridware (*c.* 1323) and Lord Leigh (also the figure of a crowned saint, possibly St Etheldreda, *c.* 1400, and above a Virgin Mary from a Crucifixion of *c.* 1500?).

LICHFIELD, Cathedral: Splendid – if somewhat faded – glass in the Lady Chapel where the central seven of the nine lancets contain numerous panels of *c.* 1540 from Herckenrode Abbey near Liège (demolished in 1802): the outer two contain later Flemish panels. It has been suggested that Lambert Lombard of the Italianised Flemish school did the designs. Numbering the lancets 1 to 9 (left to right) the main subject matter is the Passion and Resurrection (in 4-8), together with various founders and benefactors of the abbey and their patron saints (in 2 and 3) portrayed in the central three lancets, whilst 1 and 9 contain other Flemish glass of a slightly later date (Faith, Fortitude and Love on the N side, the Death of the Virgin and ? Thomas on the S side). More Herckenrode panels in the N and S choir aisles. Clayton & Bell's W window and Tree of Jesse in the N transept of 1893 and 1869, and works by Kempe and Burlison & Grylls in the N aisle.

ROLLESTON, St Mary: Unusual pieces in the S aisle E window: the heads of the lights have roundels of English C15 glass, possibly Coventry work, with the Offering of Samuel, a fragmentary figure of Christ and the Baptism in the Jordan with angels in attendance: at the foot are the months portrayed as zodiacal signs, Marcius for Aries, Aprilius as Taurus, and a damaged Leo. In the traceries C14 shields of arms for Edward I and II and Holland de Bohun.

TAMWORTH, St Editha: The W window is Alan Younger's 'Revelation of the Holy City' spread across five lights, dating from 1974. Also a Wailes E window of 1870 and glass by Henry Holiday for Powell's in the aisles. Morris & Co. windows in the chancel clerestory with the Legend of St Editha and the Occupation of Tamworth Castle by Marmion, designed by Ford Maddox Brown, 1873; Burne-Jones and Morris joined a year later in the design of the biblical E window of the S chapel. Also some later Morris & Co. of the early C20 that reuse Burne-Jones cartoons: e.g. in the chapel windows with saints and Old Testament figures.

SUFFOLK

Suffolk suffered more than the rest of East Anglia in the Puritan crusade against religious images in the 1640s: Dowsing, a particularly officious Parliamentary 'visitor', kept a diary of his destructive progress across the county, noting down his achievements day by day – and of others who had beaten him to it:

'Sudbury (Suffolk). Gregory Parish, January 9th. We break down 10 mighty great Angels in glass, in all 80.

'Eye, Aug. the 30th. Seven superstitious pictures in the Chancel, and Cross; one was Mary Magdalene; all in the glass; and six in the church windows; many more had been broken down afore.'

As a result of all this the remains in Suffolk are not nearly as extensive as those in neighbouring Norfolk (it, too, had its share of Puritan fanatics). Nevertheless, Long Melford, Hessett and Combs all have quite extensive remains where the quality of the C15 glass can be admired. The early C16 windows at Hengrave Hall are outstanding and miraculously remain virtually intact despite the C17 vandalism. As with Norfolk, Continental glass imported in the early C19 is well represented, e.g. at Nowton, Depden, Herringfleet and, to a lesser extent, at Saxmundham and Bury St Edmunds – and some good C19 windows at a number of places, well researched by Birkin Haward, a few of which are given below.

MR	Place	Centuries									Principal feature(s)
		12	13	14	15	16	17	18	19	20	
1	Aldeburgh									*	see below
2	Aspall								*		medallions and Qs by JP, c.1853
3	Assington								*		CB of 1861 — a good time for them
4	Bardwell				H*				*		Berdewell and Drury figs., c.1440; OC 1863
5	Barsham								*	*	large CEK E w., 1874; early ws. by F.C.Eden
6	Barton Mills								*	*	CB E w., 1868; N w. by HBB, 1907
7	Blythburgh				*						St Felix (t.l. by door); St Paul, Trinity shield
8	Boxford								*		E w. by Rosemary Rutherford, 1972
9	Bradfield Combust								*		good LBW E w. (1867) and C13-style S a. ws.
10	Brandeston				Q*						3 early C16 figs. of monks and Virgin
11	Brandon								*		Arts & Crafts style ws. by L. Walker, 1898
12	Brome								*		much good HBB glass of the early 1860s
13	Bury St Edmunds,										
	Cathedral					*			*		see below
14	– St Mary								*	*	see below
15	Chilton Street				*						small figs. of Sts Apollonia and Michael
16	Clare				H+						arms of St George, le Hunt, Haberdashers
17	Cockfield			+	*						good C14 border; St Anne and Virgin
18	Combs			+	*						see below
19	Dennington			+							early C14 canopies and border in chancel
20	Depden			*		F					see below
21	Drinkstone			*					*		see below
22	Easton			*							good C14 remains in t.l. include a king
23	Edwardstone								*		fine C19 w. by BG
24	Elveden									*	Iveagh Mem. by L. Lee, 1971
25	Fornham, St Martin								*	*	Wailes ws. 1846-73; w. by RFA, 1975
26	Gazeley				H*				*		C16 St Apollonia; LB 1858-64; BG 1886
27	Gipping				*						see below
28	Gislingham				*						Virgin, Coronation; fine columbine Qs.
29	Great Barton								*		peculiar assortment of queens (HBB, 1887)

MR	Place	Centuries									Principal feature(s)
		12	13	14	15	16	17	18	19	20	
30	Great Bricett			*							fine figs. of the Evangelists, c.1330, nave
31	Great Saxham				+	F	F				much Continental glass in E w.
32	Hawkedon				*						St Luke (writing) and Andrew (E w.)
33	Hawstead				*	F	H		*		see below
34	Hengrave, Hall					*					see below
35	Herringfleet			*	F	F	F	F	*		see below
36	Herringswell								*	*	exotic ws. by James Clark; CW's E w., 1900
37	Hessett				*				*		see below
38	Huntingfield				*						hare and hound border (after village's name)
39	Icklingham			*							canopy tops and two figs.
40	Ipswich, St Mary le Tower								*		N a. w. an early Wailes work of c.1852
41	Ixworth					O					Flemish roundels in E w.
42	Kentwell Hall					HF					Rouen glass; fine Last Judgement trumpeter
43	Leiston								*		see below
44	Long Melford				*						see below
45	Lowestoft								*	*	see below
46	Martlesham								*		exotic ws. by W. Pearce, 1930s, E w. by HBB
47	Norton				*						C15 Sts Margaret, (?)Etheldreda, Christopher
48	Nowton				*	O	O				see below
49	Oakley				*						St Christopher
50	Offton								*		much rich glass by JH and LBW, c.1860
51	Peasenhall								*		large Crucifixion w. by TW, 1861
52	Pettistree		G	H							C13 grisaille and arms of Ufford (S side)
53	Preston			H	H	H					50 heraldic pieces collected by R.Reyce
54	Risby			+	+						many frags. suggest fig. of St Edmund
55	Rougham				*						frag. Virgin and Child, King, Passion relics
56	Rushbrooke				*	HR	H				2 figs., arms of Edward Confessor; unicorns
57	Rushmere St Andrew								*		good ws. by LBW of the 1860s
58	Saxmundham					O			*		see below
59	Shimpling								*		good HH w., 1864; E w. by WW, 1841
60	Snape									*	Arts & Crafts E w. by M. Lowndes, c.1920
61	Sotterly				*						donor and children set into CEK E w.
62	South Elmham, All Saints				*						roundels with Sts Margaret and Ursula
63	Stratford St Mary				*						St Jude and fishing boat and 6 other apostles
64	Stuston								*		good HBB w. of 1861–3
65	Thorndon				+	F					Flemish glass in NW chancel
66	Thwaite								*		C13-style W w. by Clutterbuck, 1846
67	Ufford				*						small Annunciation (N w.). (E w. is C19 copy)
68	Westerfield								*		W w. by WM, 1867; B-J's N chancel w.
69	Weybread								*		glass by M & A O'Connor in E w.
70	Wilby				*						see below
71	Wrentham				*						St Nicholas panel in N a.
72	Yaxley			+	H*						Sts John, Catherine, Peter et al. (E w.)

See page 280 for table of symbols

ALDEBURGH, St Peter and St Paul: The 1979 Benjamin Britten memorial in the N aisle is a fine Piper/Reyntiens work with designs based on Britten's three Church Parable plays, The Prodigal Son (left), Curlew River where the dove-like curlew seemingly gives birth to the whole lancet with its natural forms as it touches the source of the river (centre), and the Burning Fiery Furnace (right).

BURY ST EDMUNDS Cathedral: Most of the glass here is C19, but in the six-light window at the W end of the S aisle is some C16 Flemish-style glass reassembled to give a Tree of Jesse in the upper outer two lights, with the figures Abia, Asa, Joram and one other; between them is St John beneath an exotic canopy, whilst the tracery lights have saints, other figures and fragments; the bottom three lights have rather fragmentary scenes connected with the story of Susanna and the Elders. Some splendid C19 windows here, notably Hardman's lively Last Judgement of 1869 in the huge W window, his Transfiguration in the E window, the Kempe-like, exotic Tree of Jesse by Clayton & Bell of 1898 (N aisle W), their many other windows,

St Margaret with the governor Olybrius' idol, C15; Combs, Suffolk.

notably the Creation (S aisle W window), and the early Kempe work of 1867 in the SE chancel.

BURY ST EDMUNDS, St Mary: Masses of C19 glass by various firms, notably Heaton, Butler & Bayne's Thanksgiving for the Harvest in the large W window, 1859 (they also did the S aisle windows twenty years later); Willement's unusual high-up rose window with the Martyrdom of St Edmund in its Star of David form, 1845; pictorial windows by Ward & Hughes of 1868-9 (with New Testament scenes, N aisle W end) and by Clutterbuck of 1854 (above S door); small scenes in medallions by Gérente of Paris, 1856, and H. Hughes's Ascension of 1873, both in the S chapel. Later is (?) Lavers & Westlake's E window: four archangels on white glass, 1914.

COMBS, St Mary: Much of the C15 glass here – given by Sir Christopher Willoughby, lord of the manor in the late C15 and a supporter of Richard III – was lost, not by Puritan fanaticism but due to an explosion in Stowmarket in 1871; mercifully, a quantity still remains, mostly in the S aisle which shows many figures from a Tree of Jesse in the tracery lights of a number of windows; the centrepiece, however, is the western-most S window with scenes from the popular medieval legend of the Life of St Margaret to whom, like St George, are attributed a farrago of bizarre events; St Margaret is shown keeping sheep and receiving the blessing from the Deity, then before the governor Olybrius whose demon idol on a pedestal she refuses to worship (*see illustration above*), then in prison, stepping into oil, being swallowed by the devil disguised as a dragon, whence she emerges and birches him! (In another version of the legend – e.g. at Mileham in Norfolk – she undergoes all this for refusing Olybrius' advances!); the last panel here has a baptism scene from another series involving a saint. Next door in the chapel are two scenes full of incident from a series of the Works of Mercy – Ministering to the Thirsty (a thirsty field-worker!), Feeding the Hungry and two Jesse Tree figures. The E window of this Chapel has numerous fascinating fragments – e.g. the little C14 trumpeter.

DEPDEN, St Mary: Some huge original C14 canopies beneath which are C16 scenes from the Abbey at Steinfield: Moses and the Burning Bush, Elijah Raising the Son of Zarephath, David Slaying Goliath, the Queen of Sheba before Solomon, Shadrach, Meshack and Abednigo before Nebuchadnezzar, and Job with his wife; also Christ Carrying the Cross and St Mary and the Virgin Lamenting.

DRINKSTONE, All Saints: Some S chancel tracery lights have several whole C14 figures in rich colours, of Christ in Majesty with

187

One of the many magnificent early C16 panels in the chapel at Hengrave Hall near Bury St Edmunds. Christ is portrayed as in St John's Revelation. Beneath him are the naked souls of the faithful between the two 'witnesses', and beneath them the General Resurrection and souls being tormented in hell.

four censing angels and three other figures; opposite is a restored Virgin and Child. The five-light E window is by Lavers & Barraud of 1865.

GIPPING, Chapel: The recently restored glass in the E window is probably work by late C15 glaziers from Westminster beginning to feel the winds of change of Renaissance realism: the more usual type of C15 tall silvery canopies have given way here to simpler golden structures, with more attention given to matters of perspective and executed with much subtle stipple shading; in the ten lights five figures can be made out, including an archbishop/saint, a mitred bishop with a red cape, a weeping young man (St John at the Crucifixion?), a knight, the Mater Dolorosa and (?) Lady Tyrrell.

HAWSTEAD, All Saints: In the N nave are four C15 roundels with Evangelist emblems and one referring to the finding of St Edmund's head in the custody of a wolf which cries 'heer, heer, heer', to indicate its whereabouts! Also here are the C17 arms of Drury impaling Hanningfield and Stafford. In the S chancel is a small Virgin and Child, C15. Interesting C19 glass includes an early window by Heaton, Butler & Bayne in the chancel window, *c*. 1860, in almost pictorial style, Burlison & Grylls' window, 1873, and two by Henry Holiday for Powell's.

HENGRAVE Hall: Magnificent glass in the chapel where the twenty-one C16 panels were possibly executed by either Galyon Hone or Robert Wright. The scenes here are much clearer, more concise and – like the chapel – more intimate than the vast panels at King's, Cambridge, that date from a few years before this display; the subjects range from Genesis to Revelation: God the Creator is a magnificent panel, with the universe being created by the Word issuing from his mouth as a cloud of breath and dissolving into concentric spheres with the signs of the Zodiac on the outer sphere (*see illustration on* p.51). After the Creation come four panels with Adam and Eve, then Noah and Lot on the same panel, leading straight to the New Testament with the Annunciation and Visitation, through the Childhood sequence to the Jordan Baptism and Entry into Jerusalem which begins the Passion series in five panels. After the Ascension comes Christ as described in St John's Relevation amidst the sun, moon and stars (*see illustration*). Coats-of-arms in other rooms and in the passage-ways include royal Tudor arms and alliances of the families of Hastings, Valence, Stafford, Bohun, Knevet *et al.*

HERRINGFLEET, St Margaret: The three-light E window has a fine collection of C15-C18 foreign glass, probably set by Yarington of Norwich in *c.* 1830; it includes three enamel painted scenes (one being Christ in Gethsemane), a Passion emblem shield, coats-of-arms that include those of Edward the Confessor, a rare Mass of St Gregory, a strange angel's face painted on to the moon (possibly the angel Gabriel with whom the moon was associated in C17 esoteric lore). In the S chancel are two fine C14 panels with Sts Catherine and Helen under canopies in an interesting C19 setting, probably by Robert Allen of Lowestoft who did the rosettes and geometrical tile patterns.

HESSETT, St Ethelbert: Numerous C15 remains and fragments in many N and S aisle windows, mostly reset by Warrington in *c.* 1850, of which the Passion scenes in the N aisle are full of incident and fascinating detail (eg. the Resurrection with the sleeping soldiers). Over in the S aisle, beneath rather orange-stained angels in the traceries, is St Nicholas blessing children, one of whom is playing with what seems to be a golf-club! Other fragments in S aisle windows include the figures a king with four people, the Ascension in typical C15 style inspired by the illustration in the *Biblium Pauperium* which a pair of feet disappear into the clouds leaving a pair of footprints behind; also St Paul with a sword and remains of Sts John and James. The three-light E window is by Warrington, *c.* 1850.

LEISTON, St Margaret: In the N transept are two Arts & Crafts styled windows by M.E.A. Rope (note her tortoise trademark), the earlier dating from 1927 with the Annunciation, Nativity and Childhood of Christ; her style is much the same in the window of 15-20 years later, with Nativity, Epiphany, Last Supper and Ruth. Her approach seems to have been popular in this part of Suffolk for she has similarly styled windows in Blaxhall, Little Glemham and Kesgrave.

LONG MELFORD, Holy Trinity: A fine collection of all the surviving original glass collected, restored and reset into the N aisle windows features some thirty-seven C15 figure panels and some tracery lights; each has a modern label, so we can see how the Clopton family and their friends take pride of place as

An alchemist examining his work beneath the zodiac signs Pisces, Aries and Gemini, C16; Saxmundham, Suffolk.

donors. Some good representations here of Sts Gabriel and Raphael (with trumpet and Cross chaplet respectively), Edmund, Andrew and a beautiful Pietà; at the W end are smaller figures of saints and Apostles. Not to be missed is the charming C15 Lily Crucifixion in the E window of the Clopton Chapel where the tiny Crucifixion is painted on to the six-leaf lily, and is set against a deep blue background.

LOWESTOFT, St Margaret: Some rare and interesting – but not exactly beautiful – early C19 glass by Robert Allen of *c.* 1819 in the S chancel window, with painted scenes of the Ascension, Crucifixion, two healing miracles and other scenes, all formerly in the E window. Allen began his working life as an enamel painter at the Lowestoft China Factory which closed in 1803, which is possibly why he turned his hand to staining and painting glass. The 1891 Te Deum (now the E window) is by Heaton, Butler & Bayne, whereas the W windows with Evangelists in the N aisle by Christopher Whall (*c.* 1903) were originally in St Peter's church.

NOWTON, St Peter: An enormous collection of Flemish roundels, dating from the C16 and C17, excellently set into the various windows in the early C19 by squire Orbell Rayoakes. Most are executed in yellow stain and dark paint, although a few are enamel coloured. Among the fifty or so in the E window are many familiar biblical scenes and panels of saints, including a strange portrayal of St Jerome beating himself with a stone (Pope Sixtus V is alleged to have remarked that Jerome – a prickly and sharp character as well as a brilliant scholar – had to stone himself in order to attain sainthood!); Adam is also pictured digging while his family hopefully watch him! In the S chancel are both biblical and non-biblical scenes, one of which has a young man riding a unicorn; there is, by contrast, a C15 English Virgin and Child and two Flemish Crucifixion panels.

SAXMUNDHAM, St John the Baptist: Among the nine reset (?) C16 roundels (reputedly from Innsbruck) is the unusual figure of an alchemist bending over a pot whilst Pisces, Aries and Gemini overlook his activities (*see*

illustration on p.189). In the tower is an indigenous angel holding a scroll, whilst in the S aisle is a striking C19 depiction of the Ascension by the illustrator the Dowager Marchioness of Waterford, a friend of Ruskin. The 1873 window in the S chapel was designed by Professor Wooldridge of the Slade Academy for Powell's.

WILBY, St Mary: Good C15 remains in the traceries and heads of the N lights include *grisaille*, an angel with a harp, a headless St Catherine, St Barbara (or Mary Magdalene?), Margaret (with dragon), Helen and a bishop; also some fine canopies with little figures of musical angels and St Sitha with a key inhabiting the niches in the turrets.

SURREY

Despite the presence of medieval glass furnaces at Chiddingfold, there seems to be surprisingly little glass left from that time. Much of the best glass is to be found amongst collections and bought-in panels at some churches, and a good part of that originates from the Continent, eg at Stoke d'Abernon, Gatton Chapel, Great Bookham and Ashtead. However, a few individual English pieces can be seen: Compton (C13), Buckland, Byfleet, Oxted and Worplesdon (all C14) and C15-C16 remains at a number of locations. There are some intriguing C19 and C20 pieces, notably the bizarre Fabian Society ensemble with George Bernard Shaw and H. G. Wells at Holmbury St Mary.

MR	Place	Centuries									Principal feature(s)
		12	13	14	15	16	17	18	19	20	
1	Abinger									*	The Cross/Tree of Life by L. Lee
2	Ashtead					F					see below
3	Banstead								*		DGR/WM W w., canopies by PW, 1863
4	Brookwood									*	Arts & Crafts w. by Edward Woore, *c.*1925
5	Buckland			*	*						C14 Sts Peter, Paul; C15 Virgin and Child
6	Byfleet			*							early C14 Coronation; saint, shield, canopy
7	Caterham								*		some nice Art Nouveau angels, 1885
8	Chiddingfold			+	F +						see below
9	Chipstead		*	*							see below
10	Cobham								*		early LB w. (designed by M.F. Halliday?)
11	Compton		*			*					C13 Virgin; C17 Flemish Jordan Baptism
12	Crowhurst				*						seraphim, Annunciation, canopies (E w.)
13	East Molesey								*		JP w. of 1876 and two by CEK, 1890s
14	Gatton					F			*		see below
15	Godalming								*		Light of the World by H. Kennedy, 1881
16	Great Bookham					F					see below
17	Guildford,										
	Abbots Hospital						*				3 Jacob scenes by B.Sutton, 1621 (Chapel)
18	– Cathedral										see below
19	Haslemere						*				6 C17 panels: Adam, Eve, Noah, saints *et al.*
20	Hindhead									*	early work by Karl Parsons, 1908
21	Holmbury St Mary								*	*	see below
22	Laleham									*	see below
23	Leatherhead				+					*	P.Woodroffe's 'Adoration of the Magi', 1936
24	Merstham				*						C15 Sts Peter, Catherine, Virgin (S chancel)

MR	Place	Centuries									Principal feature(s)
		12	13	14	15	16	17	18	19	20	
25	Mickleham				F						late C15 French (or Flemish?) Pentecost
26	Oakwoodhill		G								*grisaille, c.*1260 (S chancel)
27	Ockham			*			F				C14 musical angel; C18 scenes (German?)
28	Oxted, St Mary			*					*	*	Evangelist symbols; WM/B-J, c.1910; CEK
29	St John									*	rose w. by Jasper and Molly Kettlewell, 1962
30	Pyrford				*						mid-C15 Mercy-seat Trinity in apex of E w.
31	St Martha's									*	St Martha at the Ascension by MF, 1953
32	Shere			H*							C14 Evangelist symbols; Bray emblem
33	Stoke d'Abernon				F*	F	F				see below
34	Thorpe			+		O					L. Lee's Virgin and Child, 1973
35	Thursley				*						saint and donor fig. (N a.) from Costessy
36	Walton-on-the-Hill					F	F				on S side many Continental pieces
37	West Clandon						*	H			some elaborate royal coats-of-arms (W w.)
38	West Horsley		*	*							see below
39	Weybridge								*		St Francis by B-J for WM, 1887
40	Woldingham									*	D. Strachan's N.T. w.
41	Woodmansterne					*					C16 St Paul with sword (in vestry)
42	Worplesdon			*	*	H	H				C14 saints; arms of Henry VIII and Anne

See page 280 for table of symbols

ASHTEAD, St Giles: The C16 E window comes from Herckenrode Abbey (see also Lichfield Cathedral); it features the Crucifixion with Sts Mary and John, with St Michael spearing the dragon, St Anne teaching the Virgin to read and a nun praying in small panels below.

CHIDDINGFOLD, St Mary: In the thin W window of the S aisle are a number of pieces of clear and coloured glass, part of some 400 or so pieces excavated from three local sites of old glass furnaces: all but one date from the C14-C15, the earliest being before 1325 and the latest 1617; the blue, purple, green, yellow, red, grey and pink pieces show pot metal and flashing methods of colouring; the destination of the glass from this source remains a mystery, since all the records indicate that coloured glass came from abroad during the Middle Ages and that, although furnaces were used for firing painted glass, there is no record of glass actually being manufactured in this country – apart from the evidence here. The N chapel has four C15 Flemish roundels with scenes of Tobias and the Angel presented to the church in 1925.

CHIPSTEAD, St Margaret: In the S transept is a quatrefoil with C13-C14 fragments and, below, C13 figures of St Peter with a companion, (?), and St Paul, all in rich colours. The E window is a strange C19 assemblage that has a fair amount of C14 and C15 material including the four Evangelists with rather strange heads beneath C14-styled canopies: it is believed locally that some of this glass came with the Huguenot incumbents in the early C19.

GATTON, Chapel: Fitted out by Lord Marson in 1834, the chapel has mostly Flemish glass, such as the rather fragmentary Passover scene in the E window, three saints in the chancel (possibly women from the Crucifixion and a man reading). The S transept W window, also with fragmentary figures, has much enamel painting dating from the late C16; in the N transept are the Virgin and Child, St Mary Magdalene and a donor, possibly mid C16. C19 glass includes a coat-of-royal arms (Henry VII) by (?) Willement, c. 1830, and Kempe on the chapel S side of 1879. A small window of 1980 in the porch by Jane Grey with an agricultural theme.

GREAT BOOKHAM, St Nicholas: The E window has scenes from a type-antetype series in early C16 Flemish glass, originally in the Costessy Hall collection, e.g. the Mocking of Christ and its Old Testament equivalent of Joseph being sold to Midianites. Others from the same series can be seen in Exeter Cathedral.

GUILDFORD Cathedral: A number of windows by Moira Forsyth, notably the rose window of 1940, the Children's Window of 1952, the W.R.A.C. window, the Doctors' Window (with St Luke), and the Building Craft Livery Company Window, 1957-62. Engraved glass by John Hutton in the S transept and W doors, c.1950 and 1970, respectively. The 1955 Charterhouse Window is by R.E. Rutherford.

HOLMBURY ST MARY, Beatrix Webb House (Pasture Wood): Dr Pevsner reports in one of 'Flockhart's inglenooks' a bizarre window designed, it is said, by George Bernard Shaw and made by Caroline Townshend, depicting himself, Sidney Webb and E.R. Pease of the Fabian Society 'in medieval dress helping to build a new world . . . including H.G. Wells cocking a snook!'.

In the **Parish Church** the E window is a well-drawn, rather elaborate composition by Clayton & Bell of the mid 1870s.

LALEHAM, All Saints: Wilhelmina Geddes' St Christopher window of 1926 is a powerful portrayal that gives the saint an almost terrifying appearance – a distinct example of this Irish lady's characteristic style.

STOKE D'ABERNON, St Mary: A good collection of English and Continental glass, some from Costessy Hall, well explained in the church guide which points out how many of the panels are connected with the Virgin Mary, to whom the church is dedicated. The E window has magnificent C15 glass from the vicinity of Cologne with three Passion scenes, flanked by two from Trier with the Virgin and her mother, St Anne: some English heraldic and *grisaille* is

also here. In the chancel are Dutch roundels with scenes of the story of Susanna, and English C15 panels with Sts Apollonia, Bernard and Edmund, and the Crucifixion. Mary the Queen of Heaven is a beautiful piece in the S nave where it is accompanied by the Mater Dolorosa, a Rhenish Pieta, Netherlandish Crucifixion and English panel of God the Father, all *c.* 1500; the third window here has many reset English pieces, of which the Crucifixion originates from the York school. In the N transept is the Burial of the Virgin (1520) of the Flemish-inspired English school, and a French panel of 1540 with the Angel Appearing to the Shepherds. Amongst the Flemish, French and German C16 and C17 pieces in the Norbury Chantry are some rare subjects, e.g. the Desecration of the Temple by the Syrian Antiochus Epiphanes.

WEST HORSLEY, St Mary: In the E window are two panels of *c.* 1250, one with the Washing of Christ's Feet by Mary Magdalene and the other with St Catherine's soul ascending to heaven, having broken the wheel. In a N window is the fine late C14 kneeling figure of Sir James Berners.

SUSSEX, EAST AND WEST

Interesting C15 remains at Ticehurst and Westham and a few C14 at Hooe, Cowfold, North Stoke and Nuthurst. Otherwise medieval glass in both parts of the county is rather thinly spread. Of the C20, however, there are some interesting pieces at Northchapel and Chichester. Good Morris & Co. work in Brighton, Rotherfield and Haywards Heath.

MR	Place	Centuries									Principal feature(s)
		12	13	14	15	16	17	18	19	20	
	East Sussex										
1	Alfriston			*							C14 fig. of St Alphege (N tspt)
2	Battle				*						see below
3	Bexhill				F*						see below
4	Brighton, St Martin								*		E w. by Prof.Wooldridge/JP, 1874; HH, 1875
5	– St Michael								*		see below
6	– Synagogue									*	ws. by John Petts, late 1960s
7	Chalvington			*							part figure of St Thomas Becket, *c.*1300
8	Cooden									*	'Land and Sea' by J.&M.Kettlewell, 1980
9	Eastbourne				F						see below
10	Fletching								*		various ws. by CEK, 1883-98
11	Forest Row, Ashdown Park									*	see below
12	– Church								*		early Ward & Nixon w., 1850–98, NE nave
13	Frant			F*		F					Coronation of the Virgin (German glass?)
14	Glynde						O	H			32 Flemish panels (E ws.)
15	Heathfield									*	The Creation *et al* by P. Quail, 1968–80
16	Herstmonceux				*						2 t.l. figs. of Evangelists (plus 2 modern)

MR	Place	12	13	14	15	16	17	18	19	20	Principal feature(s)
17	Hooe			*							see below
18	Lewes, All Saints								*		ws. by HH
19	Michelham, Priory			+	+	+	+	+			20 panels of C14-C19 frags., some foreign
20	Newick			G*					*		2 Agnus Dei; Queen Victoria in Te Deum
21	Ovingdean								*		very early w. by CEK, 1867
22	Preston Manor				F						Swiss and English glass recently acquired
23	Rodmell			*							small Trinity panel, c.1400 (N w.)
24	Rotherfield								*		Salvator Mundi and saints by B-J/WM, 1878
25	St Leonards-on-Sea									*	11 ws. by RP, 1957
26	Seaford									*	The Creation and other ws. by Arthur Buss
29	Salehurst			*							fine C14 painted birds on green glass
28	Ticehurst				*		*				see below
29	Warbleton				*	+					2 C15 censing angels in N chapel
30	Westham				*				*		see below
31	Wilmington								*	*	'Butterfly' w.; Virgin by F. Stephens, 1960
	West Sussex										
1	Arundel, Castle								*		mid C19 w. with 15th Earl of Arundel by JH
2	Cathedral (R.C.)								*		the 15th Earl again!
3	Burpham								*	*	ws. by JP (1875), CEK, Wailes, L. Walker
4	Chichester, Cathedral								*	*	see below
5	– St Richard's									*	see below
6	Cowfold			*							small Crucifixion, c.1300
7	Cuckfield								*		ws. by CEK (1887), CB (1867/79)
8	East Grinstead									*	choice w. by AF in E w.
9	Haywards Heath								*		WM ws. by B-J and FMB, 1867
10	Henfield									*	glass by M. Lowndes and I. Gloag, c.1900
11	Hurstpierpoint				O	O	O				numerous C15-C17 roundels in S a.E w.
12	Lancing, College									*	see below
13	Linch			F	F						German (Flemish?) Deposition and Ascension
14	Lowfield Heath								*		lavish rose w. by ? in this building by Burges
15	Loxwood									*	Sermon on the Mount by P.Neave, 1982
16	Northchapel									*	see below
17	North Stoke			*							2 early C14 Coronation scenes (E w. and tspt)
18	Nuthurst			*							Christ in Majesty plus censing angels (E w.)
19	Paddockhurst									*	see below
20	Pagham				F						Magi Adoration & Presentation (ex Rouen)
21	Poling			*							yellow-stain fig. of St Paul (E w.)
22	Poynings			*							fine Annunciation and other remains, c.1400
23	Shermanbury			*							St Giles in W w.
24	Stopham				*	H					donor figs. (Stophams); arms of Barttelots
25	Tortington			*							C14 Evangelist symbols (E w.)
26	Walberton									*	Woolton Mem. w. by C. Edwards
27	West Grinstead			G*							canopies, *grisaille* and fig. of St George
28	Westhampnett							*			CB's E w. of 1867; W w. by JP, 1895

See page 280 for table of symbols

BATTLE, St Mary: In four N aisle windows are some rather faded but good Perpendicular (C15) remains, mostly in the tracery lights: starting at the W end they include two kneeling figures; then a part-figure in blue chasuble; in the third window Sts John the Baptist, Laurence, Dunston and one other with a sword; behind the organ are three crowned female saints, Margaret, Catherine and (?) Winefride, and another sword-bearing king in the tracery with God the Father above.

BEXHILL, St Peter: The N aisle W window has some fine C15 remains, removed from the church to Walpole's Strawberry Hill home before being returned in 1921: they include a Virgin Annunciate, Sts George, Peter, Andrew and a Coronation of the Virgin; in the tracery lights are the Apostles Peter, Andrew, Matthias and Laurence (with gridiron), a bishop, St Sitha (with book and flowers) and a six-winged cherub.

BRIGHTON, St Michael: Some fine glass by Morris, Marshall, Faulkner & Co. of 1862 (the firm's second year): the Three Marys at the Tomb is designed by Morris with Philip Webb's pelican above: Burne-Jones's Flight into Egypt in the E chapel S side, and his Baptism of Christ

193

One of the *dalle-de-verre* windows by Gabriel Loire, *c.*1970; St Richard's, Chichester, Sussex.

in the Baptistry (Agnus Dei by Webb). Of the three Annunciation and archangels in the W window Morris did all except the figures of Sts Michael and Uriel which are by Ford Maddox Brown, whilst the angels with bells in the rose window above are by Burne-Jones.

CHICHESTER Cathedral: Plenty of rather indifferent C19 glass – e.g. Wailes's W window of 1842 and Clayton & Bell's glass of the 1870s in the Lady Chapel, of which the earlier E window is the best. A monumentally formal window in the S transept by Marechal of Metz and more down-to-earth compositions by Kempe in the Retrochoir and SE chapel. Of 1949 are Christopher Webb's characteristic figures floating against plain glass in the N aisle, one of whom is Thomas Weelks, organist here, 1602-23; more exciting are Chagall's swirling colours that evoke Psalm 150, 'O Praise God in His Holiness' (*see illustration on* p.66).

CHICHESTER, St Richard's (R.C.): *Dalle-de-verre* windows by Gabriel Loire of recent date, with rich colours throughout; the composition by the font has an almost submarine quality about it, and the two large lights in the main body of the church are both effective, especially the Virgin Mary with the angels in the W window (*see illustration above*).

EASTBOURNE, St Mary: The S aisle E window of 1949 with the Empty Tomb and Sup-

per at Emmaus is reputed to be the last window by the prolific Scottish glazier Douglas Strachan.

FOREST ROW, Ashdown Park (Barclays Bank): The Adoration of the Magi and The Visitation by Harry Clarke, 1924-5 in his inimitable rich style and with unearthly yet expressive figures.

HOOE, St Oswald: Small figures of Christ and the Virgin Mary from a Coronation scene that dates from the Decorated-Perpendicular transition period in the second half of the C14: there are also two male heads, a canopy turret and the part-figures of Edward III and his wife, Queen Philippa.

LANCING College Chapel: The recently completed rose window here is one of the largest extant in Britain: designed by Stephen Dykes-Bower, the glass was made by Goddard & Gibbs, and features the coats-of-arms of the sixteen Woodard public schools and of the dioceses to which they belong in the inner ring: at the centre are those of the College. Other glass here by Comper.

NORTH CHAPEL, Parish Church: A Celtic-inspired window by Wilhelmina Geddes of 1930, less expressionistic and more in the Arts & Crafts tradition than her earlier works at Laleham and Wallsend; there is much action nevertheless in the elemental figures that surround the central figures of St Francis, i.e. in 'Sisters Moon and Water' and 'Brothers Weather and Wind'.

PADDOCKHURST, Worth Abbey: In the Assembly Hall (formerly Lady Cowdray's Music Room) is the History of British Music in glass from the prehistoric Gwydn Guabebob up to Sir Hubert Parry; it is by Ernest Heasemen, 1924.

TICEHURST, St Mary: On the N side of the sanctuary are four reset panels of fine C15 remains, with three large part-figures of St Christopher with the Christ Child blessing the saint, the Virgin and Child, and the rather faded group of Mary Salome with the infants John and James; in the fourth are some very picturesque fragments from a Doom scene with souls being carted off by devils (*see illustration*), roasting in the fire and rising from their tombs – and an angel descending from on high with a sword. In the N tracery lights is also a fine yellow-stained Coronation of the Virgin. The E window is a vast Te Deum by Margaret Holgate Foster of 1879, the central panel of which was exhibited at the 1878 Paris Exhibition.

WESTHAM, St Mary: Good remains of C15 glass in the tracery lights of the E window,

The Damned from a Doom window, C15; Ticehurst, Sussex.

somewhat restored, but displaying well thirteen figures, the twelve Apostles with St Paul, each conveniently labelled, carrying a traditional emblem and set on a chequered floor. Paul is given pride of place in the top row, flanked by Sts Peter and Bartholomew with Andrew and St James beyond; in the second row (left to right) are Sts John, Simon, Judas, Matthias, Matthew, Thomas, Philip and James the Less, between two angels at the extremities. Below are C15 canopy tops into which the heavy Te Deum by (?) Heaton, Butler & Bayne of 1897 has been set.

TYNE AND WEAR

Spectacular C20 glass by Wilhelmina Geddes can be seen at Wallsend, and good windows by Morris & Co. in Christchurch, Sunderland. A few small C15 pieces still remain at the Cathedral and St John's in Newcastle, and there is a good pair of heraldic panels at Earsdon that were at one time in Hampton Court Palace. The Jarrow Museum has some ancient pieces of glass which came from the Venerable Bede's C7 monastery.

MR	Place	Centuries								Principal feature(s)
		12	13	14	15	16	17	18	19	20	
1	Earsdon					H					see below
2	Gateshead					F			*		C13-style w. by Wailes; C16 from Tours
3	Jarrow, Museum										some coloured glass of Saxon date
4	Newcastle, Cathedral			*				*	*	see below
5	– Laing Gallery							*		WM & Co. ws. (ex St Cuthbert's), 1897
6	– Mus.		+							C13 frags. from Tynemouth excavations
7	– St Andrew							*		ws. by Wailes of Newcastle, c.1850
8	– St John			+	*	H				see below
9	– Cathedral (R.C.)							*		mid C19 ws. by Pugin/Wailes
10	North Shields								*	Martin Travers' Revelation w. of late 1920s
11	Roker								*	Arts & Crafts E w. by Harry Payne
12	Sunderland							*		see below
13	Wallsend								*	see below

See page 280 for table of symbols

EARSDON, St Alban: Two large, majestic, early C16 heraldic panels originally from Hampton Court Palace, given to the church in 1874. Made by Galyon Hone (see King's College Chapel, Cambridge) they portray the coats-of-arms of Henry VII and Henry VIII with Garter wreaths, crown, and supporters of dragon and greyhound for Henry VII underneath rather than at the side – lion and bear for Henry VIII.

NEWCASTLE Cathedral In the Chapel of St Margaret on the S side are C15 part-figures of a Virgin and Child of high quality, reminiscent of the York school of glazing. A number of C19 windows by A. Dunn, notably the E window of 1859 in pre-neo-Gothic style, whilst the S chancel window by Wailes of 1866 portrays an unusual subject: the chemist Joseph Garnett and his shop. On the N side is a contemporary abstract window by Stan Scott.

NEWCASTLE, St John: Only a few C14-C15 fragments of glass, but they include a C15 vesica-shaped medallion of the Virgin Mary and the arms of Hutton, Newcastle and Thornton. The N transept E window has some late C17 coats-of-arms for Percy quartering Lucy; in them the ruby colour was achieved by repeated yellow staining, flashed ruby glass being unavailable at the time, due to war in Europe.

SUNDERLAND, Christchurch: Ten fine scenes in the E window by Morris, Marshall, Faulkner & Co. of 1864, with the Sermon on the Mount designed by Rossetti, Christ with Children by Ford Maddox Brown, and the rest by Burne-Jones and William Morris, the latter designing the Miracle of the Loaves and Fishes, the Last Supper and the two men in white.

WALLSEND, St Luke: At the E end and spread across five lights is Wilhelmina Geddes' excellent and expressionist-inspired portrayal of the Deposition dating from 1922; it captures the spirit of its subject in a direct and uncompromising way that cannot help move the beholder.

WARWICKSHIRE

At the Beauchamp Chapel in St Mary's, Warwick, is some really superb late C15 glass that includes a remarkable set of angelic musicians. The Tree of Jesse in mid C14 glass at Merevale is also magnificent, and the figures of similar age at Caldecote and Wroxhall Abbey are good, despite some restoration at the latter place. Rugby School Chapel has an interesting collection of Renaissance and C19 glass, and foreign pieces can also be seen at Hatton and Chadshunt.

MR	Place	Centuries									Principal feature(s)
		12	13	14	15	16	17	18	19	20	
1	Arbury Hall, Chapel				H*	F					Christ, c. 1400; foreign glass in cloisters
2	Arley			*							the Virgin, saints, a priest
3	Bilton			+	*						Crucifixion; 'November' of Labours series
4	Bishop's Tachbrook								*		small early WM w. in N a. E w., 1864
5	Brinklow			*	*						birds in C14 canopies and C15 roundels
6	Caldecote			*							C14 St John, apostles
7	Chadshunt					F					12 medallions from (?)Italy: O.T. scenes
8	Charlecoat Park						H				early Victorian heraldic glass by TW
9	Cherington			+	+	HF					Apostles & Evangelists (German/Flemish)
10	Ettington									*	excellent E w. by Evie Hone
11	Fillongley			+	*						C15 donor with his 8 sons
12	Hampton Lucy								*		Life of St Peter in E w. by TW, 1837
13	Haseley				*	H					see below
14	Hatton					F					12 figs. from a German Tree of Jesse
15	Henley-in-Arden								*		E w. by Holland; also WM ws. 1865
16	Kinwarton			*					*		C14 Virgin, Child, donors; OC 1847, Gibbs w.
17	Ladbroke				*						Sts Cuthbert (with Oswald's head) and Giles
18	Lapworth								*		CB glass of the 1860s
19	Leamington								*		see below
20	Lighthorne						H				1640 arms of (?)Verney plus goat supporters
21	Mancetter			*							see below

MR	Place	Centuries									Principal feature(s)
		12	13	14	15	16	17	18	19	20	
22	Merevale			*	+				*		see below
23	Nether Whitacre			*							mid C14 censing angel (S chancel)
24	Packwood			*					*		Crucifixion, c.1300; Stubington w. 1913
25	Radway					F		*		*	Netherlandish panels: parables and Jacob
26	Rugby, St Oswald								*		rose w. by WM, 1863
27	– School Chapel				F				*	*	see below
28	Stretton-on-Dunsmore						*				Christ at Emmaus
29	Warwick, Market Mus.				H*	H					donor figs. (from Compton Verney)
30	– St Mary			*	*				*	*	see below
31	Whichford			*							early C14 Crucifixion plus two angels (E w.)
32	Whitnash								*		N chancel w. by A.Bell for Lavers, 1856
33	Willoughby									*	C. Townshend's cosmic Christ
34	Withybrook			+	*						small Crucifixion, figs., canopies plus angels
35	Wixford				H*						musician angels (S chapel)
36	Wootton Wawen								*		rare w. of 1814; Annunciation by S. Lowe
37	Wroxhall, Abbey			*	*						see below

See page 280 for table of symbols

HASELEY, St Mary: Some *in situ* C15 remains can be seen in the tower W window, where amid acanthus leaves can be seen an Annunciation with the Virgin Mary kneeling at a table and the archangel Gabriel; also the donor-priest and the inscription 'Orate iohis Aynolph'. In addition there are figures of St Catherine standing on a tiled floor, the abbess St Winefride with processional cross and, in the chancel, shields of Throckmorton quartering Neville and the date 1573.

LEAMINGTON, All Saints: Interesting glass of 1851 by Chance of Birmingham imitating C13 style in deep colours in the apse; of two years earlier is Holland of Warwick's colourful pictorial glass in the clerestory of the N transept. These transepts are interesting in that their rose windows – devoid of stained glass – are modelled on those in Rouen; the N rose here on the very geometric S rose at the Cathedral, and the S on the W rose at the church of St Ouen: what an opportunity they could present to an imaginative modern glazier.

MANCETTER, St Peter: The E window here, with its five tall lancets filled with numerous fragments of mostly C14 glass, has a small Tree of Jesse at its centre; the outer lancets (1) and (5) have angels, canopy parts and intertwined flowers; (2) has (from top to bottom) a Tudor rose, censing angel, St James with a staff and various bits; in (3) is a fine figure of St Margaret with dragon at the top, then David from a Tree of Jesse with harp (and squirrels in the branches), beneath whom are the prophets Iaconias, (?) Asa and a canopy; (4) has a censing

angel, a quatrefoil with a bearded saint (Paul?), then (?) Bartholomew and a canopy top; (5) is mostly fragments, apart from an angel at the top.

MEREVALE, St Mary: Although incomplete and much restored, the Tree of Jesse at the E end here is a superb window that represents Decorated glass at its best; there are eleven kings and four prophets but no Jesse or Virgin Mary, suggesting that the window has been truncated in order to fit in here; this would seem logical as the tracery is early Perpendicular and the glass at least fifty years earlier. Note the birds that inhabit the tree, and also how the same cartoon has been used for more than one figure (sometimes reversed). In the traceries are two C15 figures and some reset C14 heads. The S aisle E window has notable glass by Burlison & Grylls of 1885.

RUGBY School Chapel: Much C19 and Continental glass from a variety of sources and some mid C19 copies of the foreign style by Willement; at the E end is the fine Adoration of the Magi in majestic C16 Renaissance setting, a window that came here in 1834 from Aerschot near Louvain. Related to it is the Netherlandish Doubting Thomas in the N aisle E bay, probably from the same source. In the SE corner is the rather unexciting 1902 Boer War memorial by Morris & Co., followed by a fine Nunc Dimittis in C16 glass from Rouen. In the S and N transepts are the large well-drawn windows with clear figures and scenes by Gibbs of 1866 (*see illustration on* p.198), the Transfiguration of 1877 on the S side, and the Dr Arnold memorials with Old Testament characters on the N (1873

197

St Michael at the centre of a window by Gibbs, c.1866, Rugby School Chapel, Warwickshire.

Alban, St Elizabeth, Isaiah and the Virgin Mary, St Winifred, and St John of Bridlington in the upper lights, and composite figures below that include the donor Richard Beauchamp – but with his daughter's head rather than his own! Much coloured glass is used here, unusual for the late C15, in addition to high quality drawing; pearls and jewels can be seen in the border of some garments that have either been drawn on to the glass or inserted with their own little lead lines – sometimes even by drilling into a pane, a difficult process in the C15. Yet for all the expertise and high craftsmanship, something seems to be lacking in the actual characterisation of the figures who seem almost lost in the midst of all the splendour that surrounds them. A magnificent array of angel musicians and singers inhabits the tracery lights of the side and E windows, where all manner of instruments can be seen; although not always completely accurately represented, it is possible to make out many mid C15 instruments including monochord, tambourine, pipes, clavichord, double hornpipe (pibcorn), clavicymbal (a kind of psaltery), portable organ, positive organ, hautbois, bagpipes, triangle, pipe and tabor, rebec, psaltery, harp, crwths (old Welsh fiddle), mandoline, and glockenspiel with eight bells. In the vestry are a number of Flemish roundels of biblical scenes including Jacob's Ladder, and some C14 figures of saints and kings. Kempe & Co.'s luxurious Victorian glass in the chancel dating from c. 1900, and the huge Christ in Glory by Florence, Robert and Walter Camm of around 1952.

and 1878). (Earlier plans for these and other windows by the architect Butterfield led to a quarrel between him and his glazier John Hardman, such that in 1860 they broke company; Butterfield used Gibbs for this work – and for the next thirty-five or so years!) The huge seven-light Morris & Co. window with a Te Deum dates from 1902, ie after the deaths of Morris and Burne-Jones.

WARWICK, St Mary: Superb quality glass in the Beauchamp Chapel by John Prudde of Westminster in 1440-62. Much of it was destroyed by Cromwell's men in 1642; but some has survived, particularly the tracery lights round the chapel. In the E window some of the surviving figures – both complete and partial – have been assembled, so that above the singing cherubim stand on wheels and carry music scrolls with notes and words of the 'Ave Regina' (*see illustration opposite*), whilst below are the luxurious figures of St Thomas of Canterbury, St

WROXALL Abbey: Good C14 figures in a number of N windows that have been much restored: nevertheless there are some charming, mostly original donor figures looking adoringly at the saints with traditional attributes beneath canopies and set against *grisaille*: from W to E are Sts Peter, John the Baptist, Paul, with the angel Gabriel and the Virgin flanking a donor in the first window: then (?) Bartholomew, James, John and kneeling donors flanking a Virgin and Child below; then a single saint, two donors and a roundel; at the E end Sts Helen, Barbara, a charming Catherine and two donors. The E window has five much-restored C15 figures: Sts Leonard, Benedict, the Virgin Mary, a figure called 'Scholastica' and St Edmund with arrow, and a series of panels of the cycle of the Virgin below; some original angels with Passion shields in the tracery lights as well as Sts Michael and Thomas with a T-square.

Splendid musican angels with the 'Ave Regina', c.1450; St Mary, Warwick, Warwickshire.

WEST MIDLANDS

A few panels and pieces of medieval glass remain, of which the best are to be seen at St Mary's Hall in Coventry (C15) and Bushbury (C14). Some comparatively rare windows by Francis Eginton and William Peckitt survive from the Georgian era at Aston, Binley and St Paul's, Birmingham. The epoch-making glass at Coventry Cathedral seems to improve – or perhaps mature – with the passing years and will surely remain as a yardstick against which other British artistic creations in the world of stained glass will be measured for many years.

MR	Place	Centuries									Principal feature(s)
		12	13	14	15	16	17	18	19	20	
1	Aston							*			'Resurrection of Lady Dearden', 1793 by FE
2	Binley							*			Peckitt's Virgin and Child
3	Birmingham,										
	Art Gallery								*		The Seasons by B-J/WM, 1867
4	– Cathedral (R.C.)								*		see below
5	– Cathedral								*		see below
6	– St Mary, Oscott								*		early WW ws. to Pugin designs of Apostles
7	– St Paul						*				'Conversion of Paul', 1789 by FE
8	Bushbury			*							figs. of donor priest, Christ Child, Christ
9	Cheylesmore,										
	Christchurch									*	JH ws.; St Elisabeth by Fourmaintreaux
10	Coventry, Cathedral									*	see below
11	– St Mary's Hall				*						see below
12	– St Michael, Stoke		+								kneeling fig. with headscarf
13	Hampton-in-Arden			G	Q						bird Qs.
14	Walsgrave-on-Sowe				*						6 t.l. figs. of angels with shields, c.1530
15	Wolverhampton,					*					
	Art Gallery				F	F					some unusual secular glass
16	– Whitemore Reans									*	deep blue ws. by RP — 'Life in the Sea'

See page 280 for table of symbols

BIRMINGHAM, Cathedral of St Chad (R.C.): The earliest windows are those by Warrington in the apse of 1841, as are the later windows in the N chapel, but designed by Pugin; the rest is by Hardman, the best of which is perhaps that in the N transept of 1868, whilst a window in the S aisle shows the art of making stained glass windows.

BIRMINGHAM, Cathedral of St Philip: Late works of Burne-Jones for Morris & Co. in the chancel where the Ascension dates from 1885, and the Crucifixion and Nativity from 1885. The W window has his dramatic Last Judgement, a composition that caused him much 'physical fatigue' and 'mental weariness' – or so he claimed to Morris when submitting his bill for the designs and painting (for this and other Burne-Jones banter over such matters, see Charles Sewter's excellent book).

COVENTRY Cathedral: Glass of great quality in many parts of the cathedral, the most dramatic of which is perhaps the huge Baptistry window where Patrick Reyntiens has interpreted John Piper's design to evoke the idea of the Holy Spirit breaking through the complex pattern of life most admirably: 200 or so rectangular panels alternate with the concrete framework in such a way that the bright central section seems to burst through the exotically coloured walls of the Baptistry above the font. Such symbolical ideas are continued in the glass of the nave, where the five pairs of tall lights to north and south gradually unfold themselves as one progresses towards the altar: the N side represents Divine Order and the S the natural order with which man is associated. Thus the passage down the nave symbolically represents the individual's life from birth to death and to life after death, starting with the 'Green' pair of windows representing birth into the earth, followed by the 'Red' windows symbolising man's struggle in life, then the Multicoloured pair that evoke the idea of Salvation, whilst the 'Purple' tell of the redemption through the Resurrection, and finally the 'Golden' windows that shine on to the altar and symbolise the Kingdom of Heaven; these seventy-foot windows are mainly abstract in design, but a pair of binoculars reveals interesting little details of figured scenes. A team from the Royal College of Art worked on the windows over the period 1957-60, comprising Laurence Lee (the Red windows), Keith New (the Multicoloured), Geoffrey Clarke (the Purple), and all three collaborated on the other two pairs. Of a quite different character are the figures of saints in the window to the W of the altar by the Swedish artist Einar Forseth, and the abstract designs in the Chapel of Unity by Margaret Traherne. The engraved figures of saints on the W door are by John Hutton. In St Michael's Hall is some medieval glass; it includes some fine late C14/early C15 cherubim on wheels and carrying scrolls, and a C15 Resurrection scene reminiscent of that in St David's Church, Swansea.

COVENTRY, St Mary's Hall: Nine well-executed figures in 'jewelled' glass of *c.* 1500 in the N window – possibly by William Neve – portraying kings of England together with Arthur and Constantine: above are various coats-of-arms including those of the city of Coventry (with the Elephant and Castle). Fascinating fragments in the nearby oriel window include a roundel of a figure threshing the corn, probably September from a series on the months' labours.

WILTSHIRE

Wiltshire has a number of places where first-class medieval glass can be seen, Wilton Parish Church undoubtedly being the most fascinating with its twenty five or so panels from C12 and C13, some of which originate from the Sainte Chapelle and St Denis in Paris. Genuine indigenous displays are best seen at Edington Priory, Crudwell, Oaksey, Westwood, St Thomas', Salisbury, and to a lesser extent at the Cathedral. Lydiard Park and Church both demonstrate the kind of glass that was typical of the C17. Gabriel Loire's 'Prisoners of Conscience' window at Salisbury Cathedral is an interesting and bold but not totally successful attempt – amongst other things – to reintroduce something of the atmosphere generated by stained glass at Chartres, which may have existed at Salisbury.

MR	Place	Centuries									Principal feature(s)
		12	13	14	15	16	17	18	19	20	
1	Berwick St John								*		ws. of the 1860s by JH
2	Bishopstone			+							part figs. of St Peter and Virgin Annunciate
3	Blunsdon								*		LB w. for Butterfield, c.1865
4	Boyton		+		+				*		see below
5	Bradford-on-Avon				O	O	O				some scenes after J. Cornelius
6	Bromham				*						figs. of king, bishop, angels, a Pietà
7	Chippenham								*	*	various C19 ws.; C.Whall archangels, c.1918
8	Christian Malford			*							4 Church Doctors in red and blue glass
9	Clyffe Pypard				F	F					Swiss and Netherlandish glass
10	Crudwell				*						see below
11	Devizes									*	PR w., 1982
12	Edington, Priory			*							see below
13	Heytesbury								*		w. by Alexander Gibbs for Butterfield, c.1866
14	Lacock, Abbey				*						in Long Gallery Crucifixion and St Erasmus
15	Landford								*		E w. has Westlake design for LB, 1861
16	Littlecote House					F	F				foreign glass in the Great Hall
17	Lydiard, Park						*				see below
18	Tregoze			+	*		*				see below
19	Lyneham									*	recent unified scheme in cast glass by GR
20	Marden									*	two post-war ws. by J & MK
21	Marlborough									*	archangels by S.Image, 1913; ws. by WM/B-J
22	Mere			*					*		see below
23	Oaksey				*						see below
24	Purton				*						Sts Stephen, Laurence; 'Abraham's Bosom'
25	Rodbourne								*		early WM ws. by B-J, DGR, FMB, 1862
26	Rushall				*						Virgin and Child with angels (SE chancel)
27	Salisbury Cathedral		H*		F*	F	*		*	*	see below
28	– St Thomas				*						Sts Christopher, Thomas; E w. by A. Bell
29	Steeple Ashton				*						Coronation scene; apostles' emblems in t.l.
30	Stourhead, House							*			F.Eginton's lunette 'The School of Athens'
31	Swindon, Christchurch									*	glass by Martin Travers
32	– Holy Rood								*	*	C19 ws. by JH; C20 by Norris
33	Teffont Evias				*	O					bishop in N a.
34	Wardour Castle							*			Trinity lunette w. by F.Eginton
35	Westwood				*						see below
36	Wilsford				*						tiny C14 Crucifixion in chancel S w.
37	Wilton	F	F	F	F	F			*		see below
38	Woodborough								*		notable early w. by HBB, 1861
39	Woodford									*	three ws. by NC
40	Wootton Bassett								*		fine Tree of Jesse et al by JH, c.1871

See page 280 for table of symbols

BOYTON, St Mary: A rather mixed bag of remains and foreign panels, of which the two roundels with subjects from Petrarch's Triumphs is perhaps the most unusual; panels of German glass with the Annunciation and Assumption dated 1494 and an English C15 panel with Christ can be seen in the S chapel, with C13 remains possibly from Salisbury Cathedral. The huge C19 rose window in the S chapel has rather unexciting glass by Horwood of Mells.

CRUDWELL, All Saints: In a N window are five out of the Seven Sacraments in C15 glass surrounding the figure of Christ who stands against a blue background amid flowers and displaying the wounds of the Crucifixion (*see illustration on* p.203); the scenes are of Baptism, Last Rites, Confirmation, Marriage and Ordination. The painting of the faces is in some cases reminiscent of C15 work at nearby East Brent, Melbury Bubb and Sherborne Abbey, particularly of the face of Christ; note also the little angels in the canopies.

EDINGTON Priory: The E window of the N transept has an excellent C14 Crucifixion with Sts Mary and John set beneath large canopies, clearly of a standard befitting the importance of its donor, William Edington, Bishop of Winchester. In the tracery lights opposite are two angels, one with an organ and the other a lute. High in the nave clerestory are six figures, the sole remains of a frieze that originally filled all the lights with saints that thus paraded round the church: the westernmost is St William of York, then St Paul (or Stephen?), St Christopher, and the lesser known Sts Cuthbert, Aidon and Leodgar (i.e. a Celt and two Merovingians). At the W end of the S aisle are some fragments from Imber church, which is now derelict on Salisbury Plain.

LYDIARD Park: In an anteroom is a fascinating C17 window, probably by Abraham van Linge, comprising miscellaneous portrayals of animals, birds, plants and people, each painted on to a quarry; it is reminiscent of the encyclopedic window at Gorhambury (Herts, qv) also by van Linge.

LYDIARD TREGOZE: The three-light E window is a thoroughly C17 affair by Abraham van Linge of *c*.1630 (*see illustration on* p.52) with the two St Johns – Evangelist and Baptist – a pun on the name of the donor, St John St John Tregoze, who is also commemorated at Battersea Parish Church (qv); between the two saints is an olive tree with coats-of-arms that relate the descent of the manor from Ewyas to St John Tregoze; three further coats at the bottom. Earlier remains and fragments (mostly C15) can be seen in a number of windows, notably the C14 king with a sword, various shields of arms and *grisaille* in the S chancel, 'canopy' tops made of a trio of angels in the heads of some lights in the N windows, and a group of angels beneath one of these. There are some tracery light figures on the S side, of which St Blaise with his comb for carding wool is a prize specimen.

MERE, St Michael: Four good restored figures in quatrefoils in the S chapel with Sts Nicholas as a bishop, Martin on horseback, Christopher, a bishop (Thomas Becket?) and a coat-of-arms: all C14. There is much good C19 glass, eg the scenes under canopies by Henry Holiday for Powell's at the W end of the N aisle (1865) and the more Pre-Raphaelite-inspired trio in the W window on the S side; the S side of the Bettesthorne Chapel houses a rare early window by Thomas, Ward & Nixon, i.e. pre 1840; theirs also is the tower W window of a later date. The 'Suffer Little Children' window in the S aisle is by Kelley & Co. of London, *c*. 1909.

OAKSEY, All Saints: In a three-light N window are many late C15 remains that suggest the presence of a former Seven Sacrament series: e.g. in the right light is a priest kneeling at the

altar (Communion or Ordination?), and a rather orange yellow-stained St Catherine; to the left is St Anne with the Virgin, and a child in a font (Baptism), and in the centre a head of the Virgin Mary from a Coronation, a lady with a scroll and a kneeling penitent (Penance). Note also the pelican-in-her-piety, the tracery angels and Edward IV's badge of a radiant sun.

SALISBURY Cathedral: There has been much chopping and changing around of the glass here over the centuries, much destruction being wrought in 1788 when cartloads of medieval glass were said to have been dumped in the town ditch as part of James Wyatt's 'restoration and beautification' plans (some has been recovered and can be seen at the churches of Grateley, Boyton, Headley, East Tytherley). The only *in situ* remains to be seen are in the S transept (window No. **39** in the diagram, which is based on R.O.C. Spring's much-recommended pamphlet published by the Cathedral), whereas the *grisaille* at the W end of the aisles **(1)** probably came from the Chapter House: note the angel in

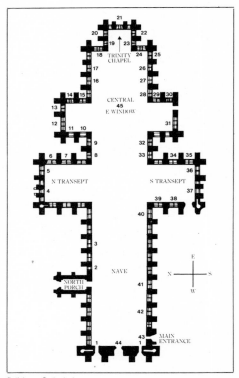

Salisbury Cathedral

202

each and the 1562 coats-of-arms of Bishop Jewel above (S) and those of 1558 of John Apice (N). *Grisaille* can also be seen in the SE transept **(31)** interspersed with rather darkened C13 glass, and again amongst the C19 *grisaille* in the S transept **(37)**. At the W end of the S nave aisle are the best old remains **(42)**, notably the Tree of Jesse (*c.* 1240) with two main figures in mandorla-shaped branches and a number of side figures and angels; next door are C13 panels of varying quality with the Angel Appearing to Zacharias in the Temple, a king and a bishop, two more bishops, six angels and a darkened Adoration of the Magi. Belonging to a different era – and vision – the high E window of the choir **(45)** in painted enamels is by Mortimer/Pearson of 1781 depicting the Brazen Serpent. The W window **(44)** is an assemblage of glass of different ages, partly from the Cathedral and part bought at auctions. It includes in the N light C13 *grisaille* and C15-C16 French panels with figures of St Anthony, the Betrayal, a female saint, bishop, and a C13 scene of a man with an angel (Zacharias?); in the centre are the arms of Henry VIII, Christ in Glory, a Crucifixion with Sts Mary and John, Mary Magdalene and Helen Finding the Cross; in the S light St Peter with a gigantic key and St Francis; along the bottom are six early examples of heraldic stained glass (*c.* 1280), originally in the Chapter House, with arms for (left to right) Gilbert de Clare, (composite), Eleanor of Provence (wife of Henry III), Louis IX, Henry III, Richard of Cornwall and Roger Bigod. Panels of French and Dutch glass formerly in the Trinity Chapel E window are now in the SE transept **(29)** and include scenes of Abraham's Visitation, Christ with Sts Mary and John, the Death of the Virgin and St Christopher.

Interesting amongst the post 1800 glass is the new (1980) 'Prisoners of Conscience' window by Gabriel Loire of Chartres, the deep blue five-light Trinity Chapel E window **(21)**, full of interesting details and effective but rather out of place in this otherwise brightly lit Cathedral, even in the marginally more intimate atmosphere of this Trinity Chapel; the other glass here is by Clayton & Bell, 1870s **(19, 20, 22, 23)**. To the E of the N porch are Harry Stammers' war Memorial with Elisha and Elijah **(2)**, and Christopher Webb's Sts Gabriel and George **(3)**. In the N transept are windows by A.O. Hemmings **(5, 6)**, imitation C13 glass and scenes with Moses in a more C19 style. Mostly Clayton & Bell's glass in **(7)**, as are **(8)**, **(9)** and

Christ displaying His Wounds from which were generated the Seven Sacraments, C15; Crudwell, Wiltshire.

(10) round the corner and into the N transept where the rest are by Powell of Whitefriars, except **(14)** with the Acts of Mercy which is by Burlison & Grylls, 1886. No. **17** with Ruth and Naomi is by Edward Woore and the George Herbert Memorial illustrating one of his poems is by C. Webb **(18)**. More engaging are Henry Holiday's windows of the Radnor Memorial in the choir aisle **(27, 28)**, his early work of 1871 in the S nave **(41)**, and Burne-Jones's angels **(32, 33)**.

WESTWOOD, St Mary: The E window has a much-restored yet fine C15 Lily Crucifixion, set between eight angels carrying instruments of

Two angels carrying shields with relics of the Passion – the whipping post and the crown of thorns; C15; Westwood, Wilts.

the Passion: in the traceries (left to right) are St John with book and Angus Dei, St Peter, St Paul and an angel whipping a devil. On the S side of the chancel are other Passion shields and to the W an Apostle with the mast of a ship and the portion of the Creed usually assigned to Simon Zelotes. In the N nave W end is the Horton rebus (*see illustrations on* p.31 *and above*).

WILTON, Sts Mary and Nicholas: Built in 1841-5, this church acquired at the time some C12-C17 Continental glass, some of which is truly remarkable. The finest is undoubtedly the collection of C12 and C13 panels set into the small N apse and into the seven large lights of the main apse, each of which has three medallions set against C19 blue glass; numbering the main apse lancets (1) to (7) and T, M, B for top, middle and bottom, they have tentatively been identified: the centre (4M) is a fine large late C12 head of a saint; three come from St Denis dating

from *c.* 1144: the Seated Virgin and Child (2M), the entry into Sotine (from apocryphal Gospel of Matthew) (3B) and the prophet Nathan from the Tree of Jesse (6T); there are also three panels from a series depicting the Parable of the Prodigal Son, *c.* 1270, in which He Receives His Heritage (4T), is Led Astray by Demons (7T) and The Return To His Father (1T). Four Normandy panels with scenes from Christ's Life date from *c.* 1230: Casting Out The Moneychangers (4B), with Apostles (5B), with three people (5T), and The Marriage At Cana (6M) (*see illustration on front cover*); other C13 panels include an angel (1B), cherubim (3T), St Catherine with the Emperor (1M), her decapitation (7M), scenes of the Mass (2B, 6B, 7B), scenes from the story of a king (2T, 5M), and a scene which is probably the raising of Tobias (3M). In a N lancet behind the organ console in the **N apse** are three more panels from St Denis with the prophet Hosea from the Tree of Jesse, and two groups of people, both probably from the Flight Into Egypt. To the left of it are some fine C14 censing angels set within C12 border, a C15 female saint, a panel of C16 Continental glass with two youths' heads and an archbishop; to the right are sainted bishops, archbishops and St (?) Denis carrying his head (German glass?). Over in the **S apse** are some English and Continental panels with C14 and C15 figures that include Sitha (with key), the decapitated St Regula, one with a rosary (St Dorothy?) and two feathered seraphim standing on wheels. At the E end of the **N aisle** are some darkened C14 German panels (which the interspersed C19 glass imitates) with scenes that include part of a Tree of Jesse and a Baptism with attending groups of people. At the W end of this aisle is the figure of St Nicholas, transformed from his original existence as God the Father, formerly the top part of a huge Tree of Jesse by Arnoult de Nijmegen, *c.* 1525, the bottom half of which can be seen at St George's, Hanover Square, London (qv); below is a German panel of the Pietà. In the **S aisle** are the arms of Mary Tudor and Philip II of Spain from the Earl of Pembroke's chapel and the kneeling figures are Pembrokes. The huge **wheel window** contains C16 Swiss and Austrian glass, notably a Trinity panel set sideways and heraldic pieces with the arms of the Abbey of St Gallen and of the Count of Feldkirch. Finally there are the C16 Flemish roundels in the **vestry** with subjects after Petrarch – The Triumphs of Chastity, and of Death and Life.

WORCESTERSHIRE

The county is fairly well endowed with C14 glass linked stylistically to that of neighbouring Herefordshire: small, well-drawn and richly coloured panels can be seen, particularly at Fladbury, Warndon, Kempsey, Mamble and Bredon, and lesser amounts at a number of other places (see below). A truly amazing collection from over a century later fills many of the windows at Great Malvern Priory and, again, lesser amounts can be found distributed around churches in the county (the remains at Birtsmorton, although few in number, are fascinating from the point of view of quality and iconography). Hanley Castle possesses a remarkable window of 1860 that is a landmark in Victorian stained glass design, and there is much from the C19 at Worcester Cathedral, but of lesser quality.

MR	Place	Centuries									Principal feature(s)
		12	13	14	15	16	17	18	19	20	
1	Abbots Morton				H	F*					David and Goliath, Burning Fiery Furnace
2	Alfrick					F	F				Netherlandish panels
3	Belbroughton				Q*						bird Qs.; 3 scenes of Labours of the Month
4	Birtsmorton				+						unique Baptism of St Christopher; donors
5	Bockleton			*							St Anne and/or Virgin and Child, c.1300
6	Bredon			*							see below
7	Bromsgrove								*		ws. by H. Hughes, LB, Capronnier
8	Childswickham			+*	+*						reset figs. of saints, angels et al.
9	Droitwich			*							Crucifixion, pelican-in-her-piety
10	Elmley Castle				H						royal arms and arms of Westminster Abbey
11	Evesham, All Saints			*					*		C14 Christ in N t.l.; HH ws. 1883
12	Fladbury			*					*		C14 Virgin, Child in lightbox; Preedy ws.
13	Great Malvern				*				*		see below
14	Great Witley						*				see below
15	Grimley				*						Annunciation with canopy of lilies; St John
16	Hagley							*	*		HH ws. in S a. (1876) and S a.E w. (1906)
17	Hanley Castle							*			see below
18	Himbleton		*	+	*						see below
19	Holt				*						Annunciation (S chapel)
20	Huddington				H*						Crucifixion, Cooksey rebus; Winter arms
21	Inkberrow				*						Sts Catherine, Margaret, angels, c.1500
22	Kempsey			*							see below
23	Little Malvern				*						Edward V, E. Woodville; Virgin Coronation
24	Madresfield Court									*	The Heavenly Kingdom, c.1900, by H.Payne
25	Mamble			*							see below
26	Oddingley			*							see below
27	Pebworth			*							Sts Catherine and Mary Magdalene (E w.)
28	Pershore								*		History of the Abbey w. by JH, 1870
29	Queenhill			H*							St Anne teaching the Virgin; royal arms
30	Ribbesford			H*							St George, angel, royal arms
31	Rochford								*		early B-J/WM w. of 1865 with the Nativity
32	Sedgeberrow			*							priest with keys and model of church
33	Warndon			*							see below
34	Wilden									*	late WM & Co. glass 1900–1914
35	Worcester, Cathedral				*				*		see below
36	Wyre Piddle				*						interesting frags. of St John's chalice et al.

See page 280 for table of symbols

BREDON, St Giles: Two fine early C14 figures set against *grisaille* in the N chancel, St Mary of Egypt to the left and St Mary Magdalene to the right; above them are the arms of Tattershall and the arms of Beauchamp are on the S side.

GREAT MALVERN Priory: One of the finest collections of medieval glass in the country dating from the mid C15; part of the work may have been executed by the glazier who did the St William window in York. The **E window**

205

Adam digging, C15; Great Malvern Priory, Worcestershire.

is a paean of praise to the New Testament, to the foundation of Christ's Church and its perpetuation under the guidance of the Virgin Mary; thus, apart from a few intruded pieces, we see the Coronation of the Virgin and Annunciation at the top of the tracery lights, with the Evangelists (and other saints) just below, and the twelve Apostles below in the main traceries; the eight main lights each have three scenes, such that the events from the Entry to Jerusalem (top left) to Pentecost (bottom right) are told in twenty-four panels, the bottom layer containing fragments, donors and benefactors. The Old Testament is featured in many panels on the S side of the **S chancel,** primarily Genesis and Exodus stories – note Noah's Ark with some bizarre animals on board! (*See illustration above.*) Over in the **N chancel aisle** is the so-called Museum Window, filled with a fragmentary assortment of pieces, the deciphering of which can reveal – amongst other things – parts of the Childhood of Christ and a number of panels concerned with the Church's teaching and traditions, such as the Four Doctors, the Seven Sacraments, the Apostles' Creed and even part of the Mass of St Giles; the tracery lights have a series of eight scenes depicting the life of the Virgin, from the meeting of her parents Anne and Joachim at the Golden Gate, their betrothal, her birth, presentation, refusal to wed, the selection of Joseph by the blossoming rod, to the Nativity, Annunciation and, above all, the Coronation. In the three

windows of the **S chancel clerestory** is glass from other parts of the Priory, with large figures of members of the Angelic Hierarchy (except Cherubim), the Doctors of the Church, some of the Apostles, other saints and coats-of-arms. Opposite in the N clerestory are scenes with the Legend and Martyrdom of St Werstan who first built a church on the present site of the Priory before the Conquest, then the Founder's Window that commemorates the Priory's foundation in 1085 (with William the Conqueror and Donation windows), followed by various saints (Blaise, Oswald, Wulstan), and part of the Legend of the Virgin that continues on into the third window. The great N window of the **N transept** is devoted to the Virgin Mary in the form of a Magnificat given to the Priory by Henry VII and Elizabeth who appear below; centrepiece is the Coronation panel where the Virgin is portrayed within a glowing vesica, flanked by Old Testament characters and angels; below are scenes of the Annunciation, Nativity, the Presentation, Christ with the Doctors, the Marriage at Cana and Raising of Lazarus, all scenes at which the Virgin was present; in the corners are the four Archangels; the W window here has panels of the Last Supper, Confirmation (from the Seven Sacraments), Sts Paul, John the Baptist and John the Evangelist. In the **N aisle** are remains of a Gospel History series and other New Testament panels that include three miracle scenes. Finally in the great W window are figures collected from various parts of the building that include archbishops and various saints such as Laurence, George, Christopher and some large angels.

Of the C19 is the extraordinary window in the N aisle by R.W. Winfield & Co. that portrays in a superficial C15-style Christ being revealed to the people of the world (or is it just to the British Empire?), with three scenes below of Queen Victoria to commemorate her Jubilee in 1887.

GREAT WITLEY, St Michael and All Angels: Designed by the Venetian Francisco Slater are the ten enamel-painted New Testament scenes that were painted by Joshua Price in 1719 for Lord Foley at Canons, the seat of the Duke of Chandos (*see illustration opposite*).

HANLEY CASTLE, St Mary: One of the best pieces of C19 stained glass work in this country can be seen in the W window where Clayton & Bell's Last Judgement is an immensely satisfying visual experience: some fifty-two figures are spread over three lights, yet without any feeling of overcrowding. The figure drawing is fine and economical, the colours clear and varied without the excessive shading that crept into so many of the firm's later works (*see illustration on* p.60). Some of these subtle shaded colours have never been seen before in C19 stained glass work, notably turquoise; note the fascinating details such as the coloured rims to the haloes. On the N side of this W end is the Ascension, executed by the same firm nearly ten years later, with more painting and deeper colours that impart a much heavier and more static feeling than its fresh and lively neighbour.

HIMBLETON, St Mary Magdalene: A few pieces of the C13-C15, the earliest being the rather darkened figure of St Mary Magdalene in the E window. Sts Mary and John of *c.* 1400 in the Shell Chapel E window and other slightly later figures in the N aisle and chancel (Sts Anne, Christopher, Catherine and the Virgin).

KEMPSEY, St Mary: Fine C14 figures of St Margaret and a bishop (Thomas Becket?) in the N chancel with St Catherine and another bishop of *c.* 1300 below. St Catherine appears again on the opposite side with St Cuthbert carrying Oswald's head, below, the slightly earlier figures (*c.* 1300) of St Edward and a bishop.

MAMBLE, St John the Baptist: A memorable C14 Crucifixion with Christ's drooping half-turned figure on the Cross, reminiscent of the Crucifixion windows at Eaton Bishop (Herefords, qv); note the strange outsized feet, borders of cups and castles and background of red and blue diaper set in crossing stripes.

ODDINGLEY, St James the Less: Large fine C15 figures in the E window of an archbishop, possibly St Thomas Becket rather than St Martin as labelled – the bishop below is either St Martin or Wulstan: also St Catherine with donor priest below, and another very fragmentary figure of St Helen (or Margaret?), three donors and the arms of Mortimer above (note the Pietà amongst the pieces). In the N chancel is a reset Coronation of the Virgin where both Christ and the Virgin (the latter with a head from elsewhere) are set against quarries and have fine yellow stain patterned orphreys.

WARNDON, St Nicholas: At the time of writing the glass here was being cleaned and

The Baptism in the River Jordan, one of the enamel painted windows by Joshua Price, 1719; Great Witley, Worcestershire.

restored, but it comprises fine mid C14 pieces of the Virgin and Child (reminiscent of the Virgin at Fladbury), and St Peter with keys, St Paul with sword, St Andrew and the Annunciation.

WORCESTER Cathedral: The only old glass in the Cathedral is the C15 panel in the S choir aisle with a king kneeling at a prayer desk set within an elaborate border. All the rest belongs to the C19, notably the great W window designed by Sir George G. Scott and executed by Hardman, and the E window of 1862, also by Hardman. Other examples include the rather Tree of Jesse-styled window in the S transept by Rodgers of Worcester (now mostly concealed by the organ), designed by the architect Preedy in 1853, a collaboration that came to an end after a dispute over this window; also some fine work of 1866 by Lavers & Barraud in the N transept and at the E end of the N aisle, 1862.

YORKSHIRE

Yorkshire is exceedingly rich in stained glass of all ages but particularly in work from the C14 and C15, much of which resides in York itself. Thanks to Lord Halifax's loyalty to the city's terms of surrender during the Civil War – i.e. not to desecrate the city's churches – Puritan excesses were very largely avoided. A proper examination of the glass in York alone would take at least a week – indeed a week is needed for the Minster itself if one is not to suffer indigestion from such a visual feast. Few people can afford such time in this busy twentieth century, so that repeated visits to York are a necessary alternative way of becoming gradually acquainted with its stained glass treasures. Work of the York glaziers can be seen in many of the city's churches, at many places in Yorkshire, and even further afield in the Lake District, Northumberland, even in Newark, Nottinghamshire – indeed ripples of their influence can be felt in the C15 glass in North Wales. The Freemen's Roll of the City mentions over 100 glaziers during the 200 or so years from the early C14 to the mid C16 – a number of them are buried at St Helen's Church, Stonegate, where the glaziers' coat-of-arms is displayed in one of the windows. A kind of universal style emerged whose characteristics can be seen over and over again: fine facial drawing and a fondness for wide-open eyes, bulbous noses and placing little figures in the tops and side shafts of canopy surrounds.

York glaziers and glass painters continued to make their mark around the country well beyond the Middle Ages. Henry Gyles was active, making mostly heraldic panels and sundials, during the latter part of the C17 before he died in 1709, whilst the contemporary brothers William and Joshua Price who lived until about 1722 concentrated more upon scene figure painting in enamels, a tradition that the prolific William Peckitt continued up to the end of C18. York seems to have been eclipsed by the London, Birmingham and Newcastle firms during the C19, but have come back fighting this century with a number of stained glass artists, notably H.W. Harvey and Harry Stammers.

Yorkshire is divided into North, South (p.216) and West (p.217).

NORTH YORKSHIRE

MR	Place	Centuries									Principal feature(s)
		12	13	14	15	16	17	18	19	20	
1	Acaster Malbis			*					*	*	see below
2	Aldborough								*	*	ws. by CEK, 1885–1907, some by Tower
3	Allerton Mauleverer						H*				pictorial panels by Wm.Peckitt, 1756
4	Birkin			*							fragmentary Trinity, Coronation, angels
5	Bishopthorpe, Palace					H	H				armorial ws. by H. Gyles & W. Peckitt
6	– St Andrew									*	several postwar windows by Harry Stammers
7	Bolton Percy			*					*		Raphael, St Anne, Virgin; WW, BG, CEK, WM
8	Castle Howard					F					Sts Catherine, John the Baptist (French)
9	Coxwold			*		H					see below
10	Cross Hills									*	ws. by PR, after 1966
11	Denton in Wharfedale						*				H.Gyles' King David; also St Cecilia
12	Easby	*		*							see below
13	Eryholme									*	E w. by D. Strachan 1935/45
14	Felixkirk		G	Q							heraldic border of the Ross (Roos) family
15	Gilling Castle				H						Dinnickhoff's panels of Fairfax alliances

MR	Place	12	13	14	15	16	17	18	19	20	Principal feature(s)
16	Goldsborough						H				H. Gyles w., 1696; Capronnier E w., 1859
17	Grinton				*						St George and donor (M.Bredlington?)
18	Hornby			*	*						C14 donor and Virgin; C15 Virgin
19	Howsham								*		see below
20	Kirkby Fleetham								*		good E and S a. ws. by JH, 1871
21	Kirkby Malham					O					St Anne, Virgin, Dürer's Nativity
22	Kirkby Wharfe			H	F*	F					see below
23	Knaresborough							*			see below
24	Middleham				*						Martyrdom of St Alkeda (N a.W w.)
25	Moor Monkton						H*				see below
26	Nether Poppleton			*							Virgin Coronation (School of Master Robert)
27	Nun Appleton Hall					*					Cupid sundial (Titian); H.Gyle's Seasons
28	Nun Monkton								*		C19 ws. by JP, Wailes, WM, SH
29	Patrick Brompton			*							York Minster-type frags.
30	Ripley, Castle							H			armorial history by Wm.Peckitt, 1785
31	Ryther			*H							see below
32	Scarborough, St Martin							*			see below
33	– St Mary							*	*		Gérente's C13-style ws.; H.Stammer's E w.
34	Selby			*	+						see below
35	Settrington				*						St Christopher (S a.E w.)
36	Sharow								*		notable w. by OC on S side, 1862
37	Skelton, Ch. of Consoler								*		good ws. by F.Weeks for Saunders & Co.
38	Skipton								*		Capronnier ws. spanning 30 years, 1869–99
39	Studley Royal								*		more good glass by Weeks (see Skelton)
40	Tadcaster			*	*			*	*		see below
41	Thirsk				*						see below
42	Topcliffe							*			see below
43	Wath			Q+	H						oakleaf Qs, Crucifixion, Fitzhugh arms
44	Well			H*							Neville family under canopies, c.1340
45	West Tanfield				*						see below
46	Whorlton							*	*		see below
47	Wiggington			*							small early C14 Crucifixion high in E w.
48	York, All Saints, N.St			*	*				*		see below
49	– All Saints, Pav'mnt			*							see below
50	– City Art Gal.							*			ws. by Wm Peckitt
51	– Gray's Court						H				coats-of-arms by Henry Gyles
52	– Guildhall									*	'History of York' by H.Harvey, c.1960
53	– Holy Trinity, G'gate			+	*						see below
54	– Minster	*	*	*	*	F*	F	*	*	*	see below
55	– St Denys		*	*	+						see below
56	– St Helen			+	*	O	H				see below
57	– St Martin-cum-Gregory			*	+	*					see below
58	– St Martin-le-Grand				*				*		see below
59	– St Mary, Castlegate			*							St John Baptist, St James (spider on hat!)
60	– St Michael, Sp'gate				*						see below
61	– St Michael-le-Bel'f			*	*						see below
62	– St Olave				*						Annunciation; Sts Dunstan and Olave

See page 280 for table of symbols

ACASTER MALBIS, Holy Trinity:

Fine mid C14 glass in the E window which David O'Connor suggests may be the work of Master Robert who did the splendid W window in York Minster; the figures of Christ and saints are set against beautiful *grisaille* quarries: St Bartholomew carrying his flayed skin over his arm (see also Grappenhall, Cheshire), St Andrew with Saltire Cross, St James with shells and other remains of various Apostles; also some shields of arms for Sutton and Holderness; C14 and C15 remains in other chancel windows. Christ, Mary and Martha in the N transept window of c. 1898, and St John in the chancel is by J.W. Knowles. A fine Burlison & Grylls window of 1902 with David, Moses and Isaiah.

COXWOLD, St Michael: There are some good C15 figures of saints amongst the rather fragmentary tracery lights on both sides of the church – St Christopher seems to be very popular here! On the S side, starting at the W end he appears with St James the Great, a deacon and lady donor in red, then Stephen, Catherine, (?), Barbara, Dorothy and Lucy, and angels from the Hierarchy in the third. On the N side (E to W) are St George's dragon, Margaret, Dorothy, two seraphim, Catherine and Mary Magdalene; followed by Sts George, Christopher, fragments and seraphim; then Sts John the Baptist, Christopher, part of John, a bishop; in the fourth window Christ and Christopher yet again above Mary Magdalene, Catherine, two angels and (?) Helen, whilst the fifth has St Dorothy, the Mater Dolorosa and part of a Resurrection scene. Aso some C17 heraldic glass by Peckitt.

EASBY, St Agatha: In the E window are two small figures, which David O'Connor suggests almost certainly belong to the late C12, of the Virgin (with a C15 head) and a patched-up St John, both with distinct C12 drapery (cf. the C12 figures in York Minster's nave clerestory); a charming C15 angel in the centre of the top light.

HOWSHAM, St John the Baptist: Fine early Clayton & Bell windows commissioned by Street in 1860, with the four Evangelists set against clear glass, showing fine features in great economy of drawing, each figure standing slightly forward of the border; there is no shading, just simple clear lines. There also is the Descent from the Cross window in the apse, and a fine rose window with Christ in Majesty, Evangelists and angels.

KIRKBY WHARFE, St John: An interesting collection of English and Continental glass in the S windows, eg six Austrian C16 panels with the Holy Family, Christ with the Doctors in the Temple, the Agony in the Garden of Gethsemane, the Adoration of the Magi, Flight into Egypt, and Virgin with Child; next to it are ten panels with the Deposition, Hope, the Sacrifice of Isaac, St Nicholas, St John the Baptist, the Flight into Egypt, which are all Swiss; then an English coat-of-arms for Hope family and an unusual representation of the Preaching of the Fox; the rest are Dutch and Flemish pieces. There is English glass also in the E window (Virgin Annunciate) and in the N aisle.

KNARESBOROUGH, St John the Baptist: Two good windows by Morris & Co. of 1873 in the S aisle where the figure design was shared between Ford Maddox Brown, Burne-Jones and William Morris; Burne-Jones was responsible for Samuel and the Virgin and Child; Morris for St John the Baptist and the Presentation scene, and Ford Maddox Brown for the rest. A Michael O'Connor window of c. is in the N aisle and the E window is by Edmundson of 1861.

MOOR MONKTON, Red House School Chapel: Some exotic late C16 heraldic glass by Dininckhoff recently restored by Dennis King of Norwich. In the centre are the arms of Slingsby with fourteen quarterings, and of Vavasour. Other Slingsby, royal, Percy arms, and vignettes with Justic, Charity, Faith, Prudence, Adam & Eve; the arms of Oxford, Cambridge, and See of Lichfield in traceries.

RYTHER, All Saints: In a S window glass of c. 1325 with a charming border of birds and squirrels, the arms of Rous and Ryther, and (?) the Virgin Mary under a canopy.

SCARBOROUGH, St Martin-on-the-Hill: A number of windows by Morris, Marshall, Faulkner & Co., the earliest of which dates from the firm's first year, 1861-2, notably the rose windows in the chancel with Morris's Crucifixion and Rossetti's Parable of the Vineyard and Virgin with Child. In the W window of 1862 are Adam, Eve and angels by Morris and Burne-Jones. The N aisle has P.P. Marshall's Joshua and (?) his St Michael: Gideon is by F.M. Brown, all of 1862, as is the E window. Various later windows by the firm date from 1863-73, mostly with figures designed by Burne-Jones, except the St Martin window in the S aisle which is by F.M. Brown.

SELBY Abbey: The much-restored Tree of Jesse of c. 1330 is in Master Robert's style (see York W window); it originally had sixty-eight figures, but after the 1906 fire most of the twenty-three that then remained were destroyed; what now remains is mostly a faithful copy by Ward & Hughes. It contains figures of two Herods, two Latin Fathers and Apostles – an interesting variation on the theme of a Jesse Tree. In the tracery lights are the much-restored remains of a Doom (cf. Carlisle and Wells where the same combination was used). C15 fragments

One of the soldiers at the Resurrection, C14; All Saints, North Street, York, Yorkshire.

in the Sacristy S windows and chancel include canopy tops and C14 coats-of-arms.

TADCASTER, St Mary: Morris & Co. in the E window of a later date than Scarborough, the late 1870s, with saints and angels mostly designed by Burne-Jones. The S aisle E window is by Powell of Leeds with Christ and Evangelists in 'sturdy Michelangelesque style' (David O'Connor); the London Powells did the Three Marys at the Tomb, 1925, and on the N side is a portrayal of the woman in Proverbs 31 in 'Walter Crane style' by the Scottish firm Adam & Small, 1879. The Acts of Mercy and Adoration of the Magi is by J.W. Knowles. There is also some medieval glass in the S aisle W window, notably a roundel of *c.* 1500 with St Catherine trampling on the Emperor (cf Clavering, Essex) and the C14 figures of St Peter, an archbishop and an early C15 figure of the Virgin Mary.

THIRSK, St Mary: In this spectacular church's S aisle E window are collected C15 fragments that include good figures of St Anne and Cleophas, St Leonard and two kneeling figures. In the tracery lights are St Giles and a bishop/abbot with a coat-of-arms for Ascouth. In the W window of the N aisle are

saint/archbishop, angels and another shield-of-arms for Ascouth.

TOPCLIFFE, St Columba: In the S aisle is a three-light Annunciation, Visitation and Nativity made by Lavers & Barraud in *c.* 1860 to the designs of M.F. Halliday, a pupil of Holman Hunt who died in 1869; it was exhibited at the 1862 Paris Exhibition.

WEST TANFIELD, St Nicholas: A few C15 remains with some figures in the N aisle E window includes a Crucifixion, the Virgin Mary holding a lily and with angels flanked by Sts James the Great with Gregory and John the Baptist with the Agnus Dei symbol; in the tracery lights are Sts William, Ambrose, Michael (with scales), an angel with a book, the sun and moon; also shields for Marmion, John of Gaunt and St Quentin.

WHORLTON, Holy Cross: A rather unusual collection of late C19/early C20 glass, notably two works by Kempe of 1879 in the chancel with Passion scenes, and a later one in the nave of 1902 with the two St Josephs. The W window is by Heaton, Butler & Bayne, dedicated to Ernest Augustus Charles and his friend Gordon of Khartoum: above it is a rose window with emblems of the four British countries and the Garter motto.

YORK, All Saints, North Street: A magnificent collection of C14 and C15 panels. The C14 E windows of the aisles have much restoration work in them, particularly that on the S side which is almost all by Wailes of 1844; there is a slightly higher percentage of old glass in the N aisle window of *c.* 1320-30 with New Testament themes and the Coronation of the Virgin. (*See illustration on* p.211.) Of the C15, however, there is much original work to admire. Starting at the E end of the **N aisle** are fifteen scenes that depict the Last Fifteen Days of the World, based on the Northumbrian poem 'The Pricke of Conscience' by Richard Rolle (b.1290), based on St Jerome's interpretations of the Book of Revelation – images that seem in places eerily relevant to our own age: it starts at the bottom left where (1) the sea rises, then (2) falls and (3) returns to its former level again (note the fish); (4) fish and sea-monsters rise from the deep; (5) the sea catches fire; (6) trees catch fire and the fruit falls; (7) earthquakes ensue; (8) rocks and stones are consumed into the earth; (9) people try to escape by hiding in holes; (10) only the earth and sky can be seen; (11) people emerge from their holes to pray; (12) the bones of the dead emerge from coffins; (13) the stars fall from heaven; (14) Death visits all; (15) the end of everything in an all-consuming fire; in quatrefoils above, St Peter receives the Blessed and a demon the Damned. Next door is the equally fine Acts of Mercy Window, beautiful work of the York school, probably executed by John Thornton: six of the Acts are represented under fine C15 canopies (the seventh – Burial of the Dead – is omitted for it is not in St Matthew's listing but in the Book of Tobit); the donor panel does not belong to this window, whereas the panel with sun surrounded by seven 'stars' symbolises the Acts revolving around Christ. Next door are three large figures, c. 1429, of Christ, Doubting Thomas and an archbishop – either Thomas Becket or the local St William. The main **E window** of 1412-27 has the figures of Sts John the Baptist, Anne teaching the Virgin and Christopher, and two groups of donors (the Blackburn family). In the **S aisle** are Sts Michael and John the Evangelist in one window, and the Nine Orders of Angels in another where each member of the Order leads off a different class of person: (left to right from the top) are Seraphim with archbishop and cardinal, Cherubim with doctors and clerics, Thrones taking care of the wealthy citizens; below, Dominations accompanying emperor, king and pope; Virtues lead off the affluent citizens; armed Powers take the clergy and a woman; then come the Principalities with sceptres who look after noblemen and bishops, Archangels with trumpets with the workers, and finally Angels with ordinary mortals — of whom one wears a pair of spectacles, certainly unique in C15 glass (*see illustration on* p.34). In the westernmost window are the Virgin and Child with St James (C19 head), and on the right either a Mass of St Gregory or the Miracle of St Bolsena.

YORK, All Saints, Pavement: The York school glass in the W window, c.1370, originally came from St Saviour's Church: it depicts eleven scenes from the Passion through to the Ascension. In the tracery lights are Christ and the Virgin Mary, with the Crucifixion and Scourging in the outer lights and an interesting shield with Instruments of the Passion.

YORK, Holy Trinity, Goodramgate: Very fine C15 York school work in a number of windows, notably the E window with large figures of Sts George, John the Baptist, the Trinity of Father with Crucified Son and Dove, then Sts John and Christopher; below them are smaller groupings of comparatively unusual subjects which are: (left to right) the Holy Family (St Mary Cleophas, Alphaeus and their children who were cousins of Christ, i.e. Sts Simon, Jude, James the Less and Joseph); then St Anne with the Virgin, Joachim (her husband) and the Christ Child; followed by another Trinity, this time represented as three Persons with crowns (and a strange picture of the Virgin Mary with a head from another window!); Zebedee, Mary Salome and their children (i.e. St John who here has an eagle, and a female child with a chalice; finally there is St Ursula protecting popes, kings and virgins alike. In the E window of the S aisle are a sainted archbishop and king (Paulinus and Olave?), and on the S side four shields in quatrefoil tracery lights. The N aisle E window also has some good pieces of the C14 and C15 of which the Virgin as the Queen of Heaven in a mandorla is a splendid panel.

YORK Minister: Magnificent glass mostly from the C14 and C15 with lesser amounts from the C12 and other periods. Entering by the W door and proceeding up the S aisle we pass **(3)** the fine but much-restored Tree of Jesse of c. 1310-20 and Peckitt's traceries, and six mid-C14 panels in **(5)** with the life of St John at Ephesus, including his stay on Patmos where he wrote the Revelation; here, too, is portrayed the legendary story of his drinking unharmed from the poisoned chalice, from which is derived his iconographic attribute as an apostle of the demon emerging from a chalice. In **(7)** is the late C12 panel of the conversion of the Jew by St Nicholas, e.g. where he heals cripples and revives the three boys. Below the early C16 rose window in the S transept, with its red and white roses symbolising the union of the Houses of York and Lancaster in 1486, are four windows of the same age with figures of Sts William of York, Peter, Paul and Wilfred, whilst below are Peckitt's C18 portrayals of Abraham, Solomon, Moses and Peter **(12-15)**; on the W wall here is the Te Deum of c. 1420, originally in the church of St Martin le Grand with God the Father as Creator, the Son and Holy Spirit as dove, all by John Thornton **(8, 9)**. Opposite on the E wall are fine C15 panels **(18-22)** with figures set against quarries: Sts William, Michael, Gabriel, John the Baptist and the Virgin and Child. This

Two delightful bird quarries in the Zouche Chapel, C15; York Minster, York, Yorkshire.

is a good place to look across at the great Five Sisters Window in the N transept **(62)** of *c.* 1250 where the *grisaille* is made from over 100,000 pieces of glass and at the centre of which is the inserted panel of Habakkuk visiting Daniel in the lion's den. In the S choir aisle window **(24)** is good C15 glass possibly by Thornton with the Holy Family and the events leading up to the birth of the Virgin and Annunciation; and **(25)** is the Tree of Jesse by Thomas of Oxford, *c.* 1385, formerly in New College, Oxford, and given to William Peckitt in part payment for windows he executed there in 1765 – a bad deal for the college if ever there was one! Next door is the huge St Cuthbert Window **(26)** of *c.* 1440 given by Thomas Langley who appears in a panel at the bottom: above him are numerous panels with no less than seventy-five incidents from the saint's life (ten of which are C19) – the masses of kneeling figures at the bottom are members of the House of Lancaster. This is perhaps the place to mention the Zouche Chapel where there are some charming C14-C15 quarries portraying birds (*see illustration opposite*), a monkey procession and other unusual subjects, as well as a splendid modern St Francis window by Ervin Bossanyi, a *tour de force* of stained glass work. Back in the choir aisle **(27)** is a C16 scene of the Crucifixion originally from Rouen and in Rickmansworth church before arriving here; **(30)** also includes some Rouen glass, a C17 Visitation after Raphael Sadeler and an unusual C16 Fall of Man where Adam and Eve leave the Garden of Eden accompanied by the Seven Deadly Sins. From this vantage point it is possible to see the clerestory of the N choir and presbytery with its C15 figures of popes, kings and ecclesiastics **(105-108)** and C14 Apostles **(103-104)**. This leads to the great E window **(32)**, which is undoubtedly one of the Seven Wonders of the stained glass world; commissioned from John Thornton of Coventry in 1405, completed three years later and given by Walter Skirlaw, Bishop of Durham, it protrays the Christian belief of the history of the world from beginning to end in 117 main light panels and 161 traceries, ie from Genesis and the Creation through the Old Testament to the Revelation, in which the twenty-two chapters of St John's book are depicted in all their details in eighty-one panels — not even the rose window in the St Chapelle at Paris surpasses this wonder! At the top of the window is God as Alpha and Omega, beneath whom are Old Testament figures, saints and the Angelic Hierarchy, followed by the Creation in seven of the panels in the first row of main lights and the Bible up to the death of Absalom in the next twenty, after which begins the Apocalypse of Revelation: in the bottom row are ecclesiastics and kings – and the donor Walter Skirlaw in the centre (who deserves to be a saint for making such a work of art possible!). In the N aisle of the choir and presbytery, **(35)** has fine figures of *c.* 1335, Sts Christopher with the Christ Child, Stephen, Laurence and a Coronation below; so too are those in **(36)** and in the S choir clerestory, which has some of the best C14 glass in the Minster and can be viewed well from here **(97-100)**. **(38)** In the NE transept is another long narrative C15 window where 100 or so panels relate the story of St William – into which have been

213

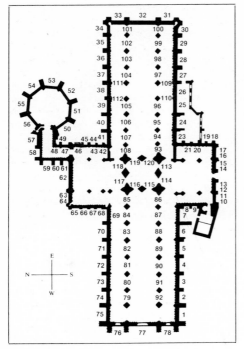

York Minster

de Dene window **(69)** in the N aisle of *c.* 1310 has panels depicting the life of St Catherine and heraldry of *c.* 1308 (interesting in that it is the oldest example in Britain of the use of yellow stain); next door has the Bell Founders' Window **(70)**, liberally and literally sprinked with bells of all sizes, given by Richard Tunnock who appears at the bottom in red and green presenting a window to St William. **(71)** has a Crucifixion and St Peter and in the border the charming wild life, hunting scenes and the famous 'Monkey's Funeral', possibly an echo of the funeral of the Virgin Mary at which strange things were believed to have happened (*see* Stanton St John, Oxon). **(72)** is the 'Penancers Window' with fine C14 faces and birch rods for correcting sins! Next door are the martyrdoms of Sts Peter and Paul in good C14 glass. The window labelled 'The Oldest Stained Glass in England' may well be true, contrary to prevailing views that would date this king from a Jesse Tree to *c.*1170 rather than *c.*1150 which is closer to the St Denis glass of *c.*1144 (in fact the St Denis glass at Wilton, Raby Castle and Twycross have the oldest glass), although this could well be the oldest English glass (*see illustration on* p.43). This is a good place to look at the magnificent glass of similar age high up in the S clerestory **(88-91)** where recently cleaned and restored panels from Archbishop Roger's choir of 1154-81 depict a variety of scenes, from Souls in Purgatory through to the life of St Benedict, the Supper at Emmaus, the Miraculous Draught of Fishes and Sts Peter and Paul; others can be seen opposite on the N side **(80-82)** and more are in the process of being restored: many of the new heads and details here have been drawn by Paul Jeffries of Dennis King's studios. Also up here in the clerestory are some of John Barnett's scenes of 1845. The glass in the great W window **(77)**, with the 'Heart of Yorkshire' in its magnificent tracery, was given by Archbishop Melton in 1338 and glazed by Master Robert: at the bottom are archbishops, then Apostles, and in the top row (left to right) the Annunciation, Nativity, Resurrection and Ascension, each taking up two lights, with the Coronation of the Virgin in the heads of the centre lights. Not to be missed is the **Chapter House** and its vestibule with many fine C14 windows; inside are seven magnificent windows with roundels of late C13/early C14 scenes — an exception is **(53)** which has C15-C16 glass that includes nine scenes from the life of St Thomas Becket; otherwise we have scenes from the lives of various saints –

metamorphosed details from other saints' lives and legends, probably to help fill up the space! It is followed by **(39)** and **(40)**, both of the C15, which include St Thomas Becket as Chancellor with Henry II and his martyrdom, and the three Sts Chad, Paulinus and Nicholas (note the hart below St Chad with a Crucifixion portrayed on its antlers). In **(41)** is one of the rare Crucifixion lilies, this time occurring in an Annunciation window where a tiny Crucifixion can be seen in the lily between Gabriel and the Virgin (cf. the large Crucifixion on a lily at Westwood, Wilts), and a Nativity with the Magi below, both C15. In the N transept the intricate pattern of the *grisaille* in the Five Sisters can be viewed from close to; **(66)** contains a superb Corpus Christi Trinity panel (God the Father holding the Son), a window that was formerly in St John's, Micklegate; then **(67, 68)** have C14 scenes of the life of John the Baptist, and from here the eight windows of the Crossing Tower with their forty-eight shields of arms of *c.* 1470 are well displayed **(113-120)**. On the E side of this transept are Kempe's restored figures of Sts Nicholas and Stephen, whilst Peter, Paul and Laurence are completely by him. The Peter

Catherine in (56), William of York (55), Peter (52), Paul (51), Margaret, Nicholas, John the Baptist, Edmund and Thomas Becket again, all in (50); The Life of the Virgin is in (54).

YORK, St Denys, Walmgate: Some very fine glass, particularly in the N aisle where the E window has a large but rather jumbled C14 Tree of Jesse – there are some fine heads in the tracery lights; in the other windows are mid C14 panels with donors whose costumes have some interesting details, whilst the main figures of saints are set against delightful quarries, some with roses and bees: (E to W) are St Thomas, Christ and St John, with castle-and-cup border and two saints in the traceries; then St Margaret with the Virgin and Child, and a Crucifixion with Sts Mary and John in the tracery lights; at the W end are scenes from the Life of St John the Baptist who wears a fine camel-skin complete with the animal's head; also two medallions of c. 1200, one with the Virgin Mary, the other St Michael with the devil. The C15 main E window has part scene of the Crucifixion flanked by Sts Mary, John, a sainted priest, an abbot with crozier and St Denys carrying his severed head. Over in the S aisle at the E end are C15 remains that include an angel with barrel-organ, the Virgin as the Queen of Heaven and a female saint.

YORK, St Helen: In the W window are four C15 made-up figures under C14 canopies, with Sts William of York, the Virgin as Queen of Heaven, Helen and Edward the Confessor with crown and holding his ring: below is a Coronation of the Virgin and groups of donors, some with their children with extraordinary faces! The S aisle W window has a figure made up from fragments, two (?) Flemish panels with the Nativity and St Francis receiving the stigmata, and the glass painters' arms by (?) Henry Gyles, late C17; Flemish roundels and quarries: one, a unicorn, another, a tiny mouse.

YORK, St Martin-cum-Gregory: Medieval glass in the E window of the S aisle where in C14 glass St Martin divides his cloak, flanked by two saints and with donors below; various C14-C15 fragments in three S aisle windows below. William Peckitt is the glazier/painter is buried here, his memorial being painted by his wife; Peckitt himself did the memorial of 1796 to his relations Anne and Charlotte with Sts John the Baptist and Catherine. Also C16 panels with the Kiss of Judas and David and Goliath.

YORK, St Martin-le-Grand: A magnificent wall of glass saved from destruction in the last war by the foresight of Dean Eric Milner White who removed it for safe keeping; glazed in 1437 and given by Robert Semer, it portrays incidents from the life of St Martin who seems to smile genially down from the central panel with his consecration below and the donor below that. Some of the scenes do not belong strictly to the cycle of St Martin's legend, an example of poetic licence on the part of the medieval mind to elaborate the story by borrowing from other legends, sometimes just to fill the space available! In the left-hand series (top to bottom) we see (1) Martin being received by a king; (2) he elevates the Host; (3) he heals a young girl; (4) stands with a crowd before a dove; (5) he receives another young girl (and also holds an instrument of correction?); (6) he appears in armour. On the right (7) he is ill in bed; (8) divides his cloak; (9) exorcises a devil; (10) has the vision of Christ; (11) his death — attended by the Devil; (12) his communion with animals where he protects the hares from the hounds; in the tracery lights are angels from the Hierarchy. Down the S aisle (W to E) are fragmentary panels that suggest figures of the Evangelists from St Crux's church, and four in the W wall from Wakefield Cathedral portraying female saints; to the E of the door is the figure of St Barbara (restored after bombing) flanked by two kneeling kings with God the Father and angels in the traceries, all C15. Next door is St George with the dragon and two martens in the tracery lights, and beyond is an unusual representation of the Trinity with Christ held almost Pietà-like by a ghost-like Father behind (head restored); in the other lights are a female donor and the trio of Joachim, St Anne and the Virgin, all beneath canopies with angels and other figures; in the tracery lights is a Trinity of God the Father with Crucified Son (no dove), two of the Evangelists and a Coronation of the Virgin; all C15. The E window is a dramatic portrayal of the old church amid flames, by Harry Stammers of York, c.1960.

YORK, St Michael, Spurriergate: Some fine C15 glass, notably in the E window with the 'Woman Clothed with the Sun' and moon from Revelation, set in a mandorla and the 'Man-child'; below is the Fall of Lucifer and St John the Baptist – note the jewelled border to both his and the Virgin's garment, the coloured glass 'jewels' being stuck on to the panes of glass as recommended by Theophilus – one or two have come off (cf. Beauchamp Chapel, Warwick: the jewels are leaded into holes in the panes).

YORK, St Michael-le-Belfrey: In the E window are collected C14 panels of Sts Peter and Paul, an Annunciation, Nativity, Resurrection and Coronation of the Virgin all under canopies, with donors below, one of whom presents the window; also here are a Crucifixion and St James below to the right: Jim Bracken is convinced that in the tracery lights is a scene depicting the Murder of St Thomas Becket: in the N aisle are some C16 legendary scenes concerning Becket's parentage, a series that is continued in the Minster Chapter House (53 in the diagram);

in other C16 glass here are St Michael, Christopher, the Virgin Mary, Ursula and the donor family; next door is St Christopher again with Sts Oswald, Catherine and Thomas with donors in the third window. In the S aisle (E to W) are four more windows with glass of *c.* 1530-35, rare for York. Each series has either donors or shields below, although in two cases there are charming groups of schoolchildren; the first is a C19 restoration, but it is followed by Sts John the Baptist, Peter, (?), Wilfred; then Hugh, Paul, Peter and William; George, Martin (both fine figures), a crowned bishop, St Christopher yet again; then a knight, James the Great, a bishop, James the Less and the 'Pierced Heart'.

SOUTH YORKSHIRE

MR	Place	Centuries									Principal feature(s)
		12	13	14	15	16	17	18	19	20	
1	Adwick-le-Street									*	J. Nuttgens' Life of St Francis, 1943
2	Arksey			H							Royal arms, arms of Marmion
3	Doncaster									*	see below
4	Ecclesfield				*					*	donors (Mounteneys); C19 ws. by JH, HBB
5	Harthill								*	*	HH/JP, 1874; CEK's E w.; M.Lowndes, 1908
6	High Melton			*							Christ Resurrected, Doom figs., prophet
7	Kirk Sandall					*					see below
8	Letwell								*		HH w. of the 1870s
9	Rotherham, Br.Chapel									*	historical w. by Alan Younger, 1972
10	Sheffield,Broomhall Ch.									*	glass by PR
11	– Cathedral								*	*	see below
12	– Fulwood Ch.									*	abstract glass by Alan Younger
13	– St Cuthbert									*	four early C20 ws. by A.J. Davies
14	– St Marie (R.C.)								*		Pugin/JH glass of early 1850s in W w.
15	– Woodthorpe Ch.									*	glass by PR
16	Sprotbrough			HG							arms of Deyncourt, Grey, Conyers, *et al*
17	Thrybergh				*						kneeling donor figs. (S a.E w.)
18	Todwick				*						St George with dragon (nave w.)

See page 280 for table of symbols

DONCASTER, St George: Glass by a variety of C19 firms, notably the W window modelled on the Tree of Jesse at Merevale (Warwicks, qv) by Ward & Hughes in 1873, the huge E window by Hardman, the E windows of the aisles by Capronnier, Clayton & Bell's S transept S window, Wailes in the chancel S, and by O'Connor in the N transept.

KIRK SANDALL, St Oswald: Interesting early C16 glass in the latest Tudor 'style', originally in three windows given by William Rukeby, now restored and assembled in the window of Rukeby Chapel. Two of the four figures can be identified as St Christopher with the Christ Child (and with the hermit from his story in the background), and St Margaret beautifully executed with much attention to characterisation through the subtle use

of stipple shading. Also angels with shields of the arms of Dublin and Rukeby (he was Archbishop of Dublin before becoming Chancellor of Ireland).

SHEFFIELD Cathedral: The often-cited 'C14 Spanish Tree of Jesse' is a C19 work – in fact it has recently been shown to be the original window by Gérente in All Saints, Margaret Street, London, supposedly 'drastically altered' by Gibbs in 1877 whose own work now fills the W window there; whatever its origins, it is a good piece of work. The main E and W windows are by Dixon of *c.* 1880, whilst the E windows of the N chancel chapel and Chapel of the Holy Spirit and the History of Sheffield window are by C. Webb. The splendid lantern filled with glass and wood is by Keith New, 1962.

216

WEST YORKSHIRE

MR	Place	Centuries									Principal feature(s)
		12	13	14	15	16	17	18	19	20	
1	Almondbury				*						see below
2	Baildon								*		good E w. by JP
3	Bradford, Bolling Hall			Q		H	H	H			bird Qs.; Tempest family arms
4	– Cathedral								*	*	see below
5	– City Art Gallery								*	*	see below
6	– St Brendon (R.C.)									*	'The Life of Christ' by James Crombie
7	St Paul, Man'ham								*		Christ in Majesty by DGR for WM, 1860s
8	Clifford								*		4 ws. by Pugin/JH; 2 by Lusson & J.Barnett
9	Dewsbury			*							see below
10	Drighlington								*	*	ws. by CEK spanning 40 years, 1875–1905
11	Elland				*						see below
12	Emley				*						Crucifixion plus Mary and John; St Michael
13	Ilkley									*	early C20 ws. by Martin Travers
14	Kildwick				H						arms of Henry VIII, Catherine of Aragon
15	Ledsham			*	*						C15 St Catherine, Margaret; C14 archbishop
16	Leeds, Good Shepherd									*	Arts & Crafts w. by R.Hallward, 1920s
17	– St Chad									*	E w. by Margaret A.Rope
18	– St Peter								*		see below
19	Methley				*				*	*	see below
20	Milnsbridge									*	St Luke, physician/painter, F.Cole, 1966
21	Normanton		G		H*	F	HF				see below
22	Ossett								*		ws. by F.Preedy, c.1865
23	Ripponden				*						figs. in S a. Sts Andrew, Peter, et al.
24	Thornhill				*						see below
25	Tong						H				sundial by Henry Gyles, 1702
26	Wakefield								*		a number of ws. by CEK of the 1870s
27	Woolley				*						Sts George, Catherine, The Virgin, Trinity
28	(Wragby)					F	F				(The 489 Swiss panels have been removed)

See page 280 for table of symbols

ALMONDBURY, All Hallows: Some nice C15 glass can be seen in the E window of the N chapel where the figures of Sts Elizabeth, John the Baptist and Helen have donors with shields below. On the N side are Sts Barbara, St Anne teaching the Virgin to Read, and Margaret; all of the York school – note how in places yellow stain is used on blue glass to give green.

BRADFORD Cathedral: Some Morris, Marshall, Faulkner & Co. windows of the early 1860s where designs have been made by Morris, Ford Maddox Brown, Rossetti, Philip Webb and Peter Paul Marshall, notably the S Chancel window with its saints, and the former E window where some twenty-eight or so figures have been distributed into three windows on each side of the triangular apse. Windows by Moira Forsyth, 1956-69, include the Hodgson Memorial.

BRADFORD, City Art Gallery (Cartwright Hall): The gallery has a number of interesting C19 windows, some of which are on loan and go on display from time to time: e.g. the Story of Tristram and Isoude told in thirteen panels, an early work by William Morris's firm of 1862 and formerly in Harden Grange, Bingley: Arthur Hughes designed (1) Tristram's Birth; Rossetti (2) the Fight with Sir Marhaus and (4) Drinking the Love Potion; Val Prinsep (3) where the couple leaves Ireland; Burne-Jones (5), (6), (7) and (11), i.e. Tristram's Marriage, his Madness, King Mark and La Belle Isoude, and the couple's tomb; William Morris (8), (9), (12) and (13), where Tristram is recognised by the dog he gave Isoude, where they land at Arthur's court, Queen Guinevere with Isoude, and Lancelot with Arthur; and (10) by Ford Maddox Brown, the Death of Tristram. There are also the Rossetti-designed panel of Abraham and Isaac, 1873, and Sts John and Matthew by Burne-Jones, 1874, Kempe's Annunciation, 1893, the four British saints by R.A. Bell, 1925.

DEWSBURY, All Saints: Some interesting pieces and small panels of glass that date from the mid C14, e.g. in the N transept N window where borderwork of chalices, lions and squirrels can be seen, quarries with birds and insects, and three fine roundels depicting the Labours of

217

the Months August, September and November (i.e. Harvesting, Threshing and Killing the Pig). Also some coats-of-arms for Warenne, de Spencer, Scarghill, Lathorne, St Martin and the remains of three figures under canopies, *c.* 1340, of the York school (Master Robert-style).

ELLAND, St Mary: An unusual collection of panels in the E window with twenty-one scenes from the life of the Virgin Mary according to the apocryphal gospel of St James, although only eleven of them are as they were in *c.* 1450, i.e. The Annunciation to St Anne, Joachim Meeting St Anne, the Nativity of Jesus, the Betrothal of the Virgin, the Assumption, Ascension, Resurrection, Adoration of the Magi, Descent of the Holy Ghost, the Annunciation and Visitation to St Elizabeth.

LEEDS, St Peter, Kirkgate: Much early C19 glass and late medieval Continental glass in the E window. St Peter in the S aisle is by Thomas Wright of Leeds and dates from 1811, which makes the glass somewhat rare since most glass of this era was removed during the enthusiastic refurbishment of churches later in the century; Wilmshurst's side windows in the chancel are typical of glass in the 1840s, i.e. just before the 'revolution' in design brought about by firms such as Hardman, Clayton & Bell, Heaton, Butler & Bayne and Morris & Co.

METHLEY, St Oswald: In the Waterton Chapel E window of three lights are eight late C15 figures standing rather stockily under canopies and with angels above: the four Doctors of the Church in traditional garb, Sts John the Evangelist, John the Baptist, Margaret and Christopher. The W window is by Willement, and the E by A.K. Nicholson of 1926.

NORMANTON, All Saints: An excellent collection of glass spanning 800 years, given to the church by Thomas Ward of the firm Ward & Hughes in the C19, recently cleaned and restored by the York Glaziers. Peter Gibson identified the following, which are now distributed (1) in the E window, a C16 German scene of the Pietá, three panels associated with the Death of the Virgin, and eight smaller pieces of C13-C20 glass; (2) a medley of C15 pieces with a coat-of-arms in one window, and next door some fine C13 *grisaille* set with roundels of C15 glass; (3) on the S side are C17 Swiss/German panels in the top row with events from the life of St Catherine and the Trinity with choir and musicians adoring: below is a panel with a large figure holding a chalice and to the left a C15 crowned head; in another window some good C17 coats-of-arms that include those of Sir Francis Chaplin, Lord Mayor of London in 1677, the royal arms, and those of John Morton of Canterbury *c.* 1500; (4) C15-C16 heraldic glass in the Memorial Chapel.

THORNHILL, St Michael and All Angels: The E window contains a fine Tree of Jesse dating from 1499, much restored but still with seven of the original figures; the donor was a Yorkshireman, Robert Frost, Chancellor to Prince Arthur at the Tudor Court. The work is very much of its era, when Continental influences were making themselves felt and certain stained glass artists strove to improve characterisation in their portrayals of figures which during the C15 had gradually become more stilted and mannered, but here shows the subtle use of brushwork in the figuration of some of the saints and Apostles in the Tree. Unfortunately this delicate work probably required more gentle firing in the kiln, and this in turn may have contributed to the loss of paint over the centuries, as can be seen particularly in the Saville Chapel E window next door. This interesting work of 1493 portrays Last Judgement – or *La Vie de l'Homme* – where figures rise from their graves at the sound of the trumpet; in the midst of the scene are the Trinity, the Assumption, the Resurrecting Christ and the Virgin with Child to whom the donors (Savilles) pray, and in the tracery lights are many figures of saints. On the N side of the chancel are a number of windows, the easternmost of which has scenes from a cycle of the Virgin Mary at the Coronation, Annunciation, Death, Assumption, Nativity and Resurrection, together with three sainted bishops on thrones. Then comes a comparatively rare portrayal of the Holy Family, i.e. of the families of the Three Marys: in (1) is St Mary Cleophas with Alpheus, and the children James the Less, Jude and Simon; (2) Joachim and St Anne with the Virgin Mary; (3) Mary Salome with Zebedee and their children James and John the Evangelist; above them is a Trinity and Agnus Dei (restored), and below the donor Sir Thomas Saville; in the third window there is a much-restored Crucifixion with Sts Mary and John (the latter with enormous toes!). In the N window of the Saville Chapel is a C14 Crucifixion, set against a trellis of quarries.

WALES

North Wales has some fine medieval glass that has been the subject of a thorough survey by Dr Mostyn Lewis who has shown that not only is the work related to that in neighbouring Cheshire and Salop but influence of the C15 York school can also be perceived; at Tremeirchion, for example, the large open eyes with curve line at the outer corner, the rather bulbous noses and haloes with a little inward-projecting trefoil are all reminiscent of their style. The county richest in medieval glass is without doubt Clwydd where fine C15/C16 displays can be seen at Llanrhaeadr, Dyserth, Llandyrnog and particularly Gresford; earlier pieces from the C14 still exist at Treuddyn and Worthenbury.

South Wales on the other hand has hardly any old glass: a few pieces have turned up in St David's, Swansea (R.C.), Newport, a nice St Catherine at Old Radnor, and fragments at Cardigan and Mathern. It is comparatively rich, however, in C20 glass, both from the Arts & Crafts followers of *c.* 1910 onwards and from the Celtic Studios and, particularly, glaziers connected with the Swansea College of Art. At the College, developments in stained glass design on the Continent have been felt under the guidance of Tim Lewis: Bridgend Crematorium and St Mary's, Swansea, boast examples of this progressive work.

CLWYDD

MR	Place	12	13	14	15	16	17	18	19	20	Principal feature(s)
1	Abergele, Gwrych Castle							H*			early C19 Acts of Mercy w.
2	Buckley									*	3-light w. in nave by the Celtic Studios, 1967
3	Cilcain					*					early C16 Crucifixion plus Sts Mary and John
4	Colwyn Bay									*	Infancy of Christ series by H.Clarke, 1930s
5	Dyserth					*					see below
6	Gresford				*				*		see below
7	Gwyddelwern					*					part of a bearded man, c.1500; female saint
8	Hawarden								*	*	WM glass from the period 1898–1913
9	Hope				+						see below
10	Llanasa					*					see below
11	Llandegla								*		rare early C19 enamel w. by F. Eginton
12	Llandyrnog					*			*		see below
13	Llanelidan				Q	*					Passion relics and Wounds on a shield
14	Llanferres								*		Clutterbuck's St Paul at Athens, c.1844
15	Llangernyw								*		Clutterbuck again, Last Judgement, c.1830
16	Llangollen				+F	F			*		see below
17	Llanrhaeadr				+	*					see below
18	Llantysilio				*						2 York-type figs., one St James
19	Mold						H+				some arms and York-type frags. c.1460
20	Nercwys					*					Crucifixion in E w. includes some old glass
21	Northop								*		5-light w. by OC, 1850
22	Penrhyn Colwyn Bay Col.									*	Conquest of Everest and S.Pole; R.Ashmead
23	St Asaph, Cathedral						H		*		arms by FE, c.1795; Clutterbuck's E w.
24	Tremeirchion				*	*					see below
25	Treuddyn			*							see below
26	Worthenbury			+					*		see below
27	Wrexham								*		Evans' 'Flemish' ws. 1841; WM ws.
28	Ysceifiog								*		rather faded 3-light E w. by JH, c.1845

See page 280 for table of symbols

DYSERTH, St Bridget: The E window has a fine Tree of Jesse of *c.* 1533 and a complete set of Apostles carrying Creed scrolls in the tracery lights above of *c.* 1500; unfortunately the lower layer of panels has been damaged so that Jesse is missing. The Tree, which is not indigenous to the church, is unusual in not having any prophets, whilst the kings and Christ's ancestors, all labelled in Latin, are well drawn and grouped in threes amid the abundant and intricate foliage – Ioras appears three times, Asa and Josaphat twice each! The use of yellow staining throughout is both subtle and effective.

GRESFORD, All Saints: The finest ancient glass in North Wales, mostly dating from the C15. In the **Trevor Chapel** on the S side the four main panels depict scenes of the Beheading of John the Baptist, Herod's Feast, St Anthony Entering Religious Life, and his death – all scenes with some fascinating details in the drawing, with lively and sometimes bizarre faces, reminiscent of Dutch paintings at the time; below them are Evangelist symbols, four saints (Apollonia, Christopher, Michael and Sitha with keys) and, above this, numerous fragments which include angels, kings, St John with cup and dragon and musical angels; and in the traceries some little angels painted on pale pink glass; at the very bottom of the window (behind the memorial) in double lights it is possible to make out parts of St George in armour, St John the Baptist, part of the Virgin Mary, angels with shields, donors and possibly a scene of the Flagellation. In the **Lady Chapel** (on the N side) is glass with scenes connected with the life and death of the Virgin Mary; on the N side in the heads of lights are four recently restored panels (by Dennis King) with the Entombment, Funeral of the Virgin (note the Jew with his hands stuck to the coffin; see Stanton St John, Oxon), the Assumption and Coronation of the Virgin with angels, fragments of enamel-painted portraits above; in the much-restored E window here are scenes of Joachim in the Wilderness, St Anne in the Garden, Meeting Joachim, the two Being Blessed; then below the Birth of the Virgin, Anne Taking Mary to the Temple, the Annunciation and Visitation with St Elizabeth (the Nativity, Flight into Egypt and parts of some of the other panels are of 1872); the donor and his family below, with St Apollonia, the four Evangelists delightfully portrayed with their beast-symbols and another saint in the tracery lights. The main E window of the chancel is 'about a fifth medieval (Mostyn Lewis), ie of *c.*1500, whereas the fine Tree of Jesse in its tracery lights is comprised mostly of old glass: thus, of the figures in golden mandorlas at the top of the seven main lights, the Virgin with lily, Christ with the Virgin, God the Father (with new head), and The Spirit all mostly have old glass, whereas St John with chalice and dragon, Gabriel and Mary are mainly modern — the rest of the thirty-five panels form a Te Deum with 105 figures, an impressive sight, but mostly modern work which becomes obvious when seen close to. There are some old pieces also in the porch windows, notably in the traceries of the N side, whilst those on the S side have C18 Italian painted pieces with some charming cherubs! The C19 glass is generally rather disappointing — a vivid battle of St Michael's angelic forces in action by Clayton & Bell, windows by Ward & Hughes and a damaged work by Lobin of Tours in the N aisle at the W end.

HOPE, St Cynfarch: Late C15 glass, some of which resembles that at Gresford, but mainly of reassembled fragmentary scenes; some panels suggest the former presence of a sequence depicting the life of the Virgin, eg Joachim in the Wilderness, St Anne Praying in the Garden and (?) The Purification, all in the northernmost E window. Other lights have fragments and small pieces that include inscriptions of words and phrases from the Te Deum, canopies, heraldic unicorns, hind and antelopes, and parts of figures; in the traceries the Virgin's Coronation.

LLANASA, St Asaph: Good glass of the early C16 mixed with good restoration of 1877. In the E window of the S side is a fairly complete Crucifixion with the Virgin and St John set between the sun and moon, with Instruments of the Passion above and a background of star quarries. On the N side the E window has figures on acorn/maple-leaf quarries: a bishop, Sts Catherine, James the Great and Laurence.

LLANDYRNOG, St Tyrnog: An interesting E window with much-reset glass of *c.* 1500, reminiscent of Gresford. Centrepiece is the Crucifixion with beautiful ministering angels from which streams the Blood of Christ to five of the Seven Sacraments, some of which are rather fragmentary: Penance (below), Mass and Extreme Unction (left), Holy Orders and Matrimony on the right are the best; in the extreme left and right lights are panels with Apostles and Creed Scrolls, St James the Great and John on the right; on the left is a little panel with fragments that have some splendid faces and a fine St Mark with a lion perched on his Gospel; the tracery lights have a Coronation and a superb Annunciation in the centre (note the huge and elaborate lily plant) and below four female saints all labelled: Marcella, Winifred, Frideswide and Catherine: above are a nimbed bishop and archbishop. (Close by is a C19 Annunciation reminiscent of early Kempe, by Cox & Buckley.)

LLANGOLLEN, Plas Newydd: Various pieces collected in the late C18/early C19, mainly of the C17-C18 but also some of the late C15-early C16, now set in the Oak Room, Anteroom and by the Front Door; they include Crucifixion and Circumcision scenes in monochrome and enamel colours, and various heads; in the Library is a rose *ensoleille, c.* 1470, and enamel painted pieces of fruit flowers, animals and birds. At the church of **St Collen** is a typically colourful window (by Holland of Warwick, 1849), at the E end of the N aisle, with scenes from Christ's Life. Slightly earlier is the Nunc Dimittis window in the tower by David Evans of Shrewsbury, 1833.

LLANRHAEADR, St Dyfnog: The fine Tree of Jesse of 1533 is described by Dr Mostyn Lewis as being 'the most beautiful window in North Wales' (*see illustrations on this page and* p.16). Fortunately it was hidden during the Civil War so most of the window remains intact to view today. Spread across its five main lights are eighteen figures, each labelled, Jesse taking up three panels, and a further six prophets in the tracery lights (note the eye in the exploding sun here!). The figure of David is particularly interesting in that his red tunic has yellow buttons, achieved by abrading the flashed red and yellow-staining the clear areas; David's lips are painted with enamel paint, which makes this one of the earliest examples of enamels in Britain. On the W wall are some reset fragments of *c.* 1400, 'found in a heap in a cottage' says the local guidebook! They include a beautiful Annunciation.

TREMEIRCHION, Corpus Christi: In a S window of the vestry is St Anne Teaching the Virgin to Read, reminiscent of the York school of glass painting. There are also some later fragments of *c.* 1500 that include parts from a Crucifixion, a Doom Window and St Catherine's wheel, and unusual portraits on glass of Charles I, a cleric and James I, dating from *c.* 1625.

Zadok the Priest from the Tree of Jesse 1533; Llanrhaeadr, Clwydd.

TREUDDYN, St Mary: The oldest glass in Wales, dating from the early and late C14 in the E window of the chancel; the figure of a monk beneath a canopy probably dates from *c.* 1305 – i.e. contemporary or soon after similar-styled glass at Merton College, Oxford; in the tracery lights is a roundel of *c.* 1330 with the head and shoulders of a female, and over on the S side canopy work and part of the Virgin Annunciate, beautifully drawn and of the late C14.

WORTHENBURY, St Deiniol: Interesting fragments of late C14 glass in the E window, some of which may have come from Winchester College Chapel when Betton & Evans removed and copied the late C14 Tree of Jesse – note the vine leaves, grapes and stems: there are one or two later medieval fragments with painted heads here, and some C19 copies: the main figures of King Edward, Sir Roger Pulston and wife, and St Leonard are of the C19; Betton & Evans also did the copies of prints by William Fowler (1806) of a saint and Sir William Berdewell of Suffolk.

221

DYFED

MR	Place	Centuries									Principal feature(s)
		12	13	14	15	16	17	18	19	20	
1	Aberporth								*		notable early w. by LBW, 1857
2	Aberystwyth									*	Sts Cecilia and Francis by L. Lee
3	Bosherston								*		E w. by CB, c.1872
4	Burry Port									*	Last Judgement by Celtic Studios, 1978
5	Caldy Island									*	'Arthurian' St Illtud, 1920
6	Cardigan			+							some indigenous frags., some from Hafod
7	– Our Lady									*	Sacraments and Works of Mercy by AH, 1980
8	Carew (and Lawrenny)								*		Light of the World at both by A.L.Moore
9	Castlemartin									*	The Ascension by HBB, 1922
10	Cilgerran & Crunwear									*	ws. by Celtic Studios, 1970 and 1952
11	Fishguard									*	see below
12	Haverford West									*	see below
13	Lampeter									*	see below
14	Little Newcastle									*	Christ's Charge to Peter, E w., Roy Lewis
15	Llandefaelog								*		B-J/WM ws., 1895; also HD, 1928
16	Llandovery (R.C.)									*	ws. by M.E.A. Rope, 1938, and Nuttgens
17	Newport			*	F	F			*		see below
18	Pembroke Dock								*		see below
19	St Brides								*	*	W w. by Cox & Sons; E w., H.Davies
20	St David's, Cathedral			+	+					*	see below
21	St Florence								*		Annunciation in N tspt by WM, 1873
22	St Ishmael's									*	ws. by CEK, WT and R.J.Newberry, c.1921
23	St Twynnells									*	see below
24	Spittal								*	*	see below
25	Stackpole Elidyr								*		OC's w. of 1862 with King Solomon
26	Templeton									*	St John the Baptist w. by W.P.Wilkins
27	Tenby								*	*	see below
28	Wiston								*	*	Christ and St Peter by SH; CK/WT, 1920

See page 280 for table of symbols

FISHGUARD, Parish Church: A number of C20 windows of which the E window of 1906 with the Good Shepherd and Suffer Little Children is by Burlison & Grylls; also theirs is the War Memorial in the N chancel. More recent is the two-light Annunciation by Celtic Studios, 1970.

HAVERFORD WEST, St Martin and St Mary: Both churches have glass of the first half of the C20: at **St Martin** is the three-light 1909 window in the Lady Chapel by Heaton, Butler & Bayne, and the Annunciation by C. Powell of Highgate, part of which was designed by Lawrence Davies, the curate-in-charge. Powell of Whitefriars did the Annunciation with rose and town crest in the S chancel of **St Mary** where there are also windows by Kempe (of 1893), by Kempe and Tower on the S side, 1910-29 (i.e. after Kempe's death), and there is a N light by the Celtic Studios.

LAMPETER, Parish Church: A powerful window of 1934 with rich colours by Wilhelmina Geddes with her own brand of expressionist figures: here St Peter and St Andrew have Christ between them and angels attending above

and below. The E window and four to five in the nave are by Clayton & Bell of c. 1860.

NEWPORT, St Mary: In the S chancel is a beautiful C14 medallion with a Nativity scene, probably of Continental origin. Two Flemish roundels in a N window: one depicts St John with a chalice and a rather harmless-looking little bird emerging from it, rather than the demon usually associated with the saint; he is also standing barefoot amid hills, possibly portraying the saint in later life in exile on the Isle of Patmos – i.e. we have three portrayals of the saint in one: as Evangelist with (baby) eagle, as Apostle, and as the writer of Revelation! (*See illustration opposite.*) The other has musical angels with a Dutch text and the date 1631. These foreign panels were all installed in c. 1880. Also C19 and C20 glass by Heaton, Butler & Bayne.

PEMBROKE DOCK, St John: Most of the windows are by C.E. Kempe and Kempe & Tower, dating from 1896-1918, work of a high standard but tending to the monotonous and standard formula; some after 1900 bear his wheatsheaf signature and those after his death in

St John on Patmos, C17?; Newport, Dyfed.

Becket Chapel the window with the saint, Henry II and arms is by Carl Edwards, 1958.

SAINT TWYNNELS, St Twynnell: The E window with the Crucifixion is by Heaton, Butler & Bayne of 1919; it makes an interesting contrast to Celtic Studio's St Francis Window, 1963, with its exotic birds attending the saint.

SPITTAL, St Mary: The two-light E window (the Colonel Higgin Memorial), with an Australian soldier crossing the stream of death to Christ, is a work of 1917 by Mary Lowndes who founded the firm of Lowndes & Drury: (their premises in London were used by many stained glass designers of the Arts & Crafts movement early this century). Also some windows by A.L. Moore: the Women at the Tomb, *c.* 1898, and St Michael, *c.* 1918.

1907 have the tower superimposed on it. The E window is a well-drawn and deeply coloured work by Herbert Davis of 1898.

SAINT DAVID'S Cathedral: Some old medieval fragments can be seen, made into a border in a N aisle window, and Frederick Cole's glass in the two rose windows. The angelic musicians with the Virgin and Child and Evangelists in the Lady Chapel Window is Kempe & Tower work of 1923-4, as are the W windows and two in St Thomas's Chapel of 1909. In the St Thomas à

TENBY, St Mary: A good five-light W window by Clayton & Bell of 1865 in characteristic style: the E is by Wailes, *c.* 1856. Very good is the Henderson Memorial on the N side and very much in Arts & Crafts style of the turn of the century, but with Karl Parsons' own characteristically exuberant style utilising deep colours and a kind of gritty-jewel effect (there is a better window of his at Porthcawl, qv). Slightly later is the splendid S aisle W window with the Crucifixion and Virtues by Kempe & Tower; they also did the Virgin & Child in a N window.

GLAMORGAN (MID, SOUTH AND WEST)

MR	Place	Centuries									Principal feature(s)
		12	13	14	15	16	17	18	19	20	
1	Abercynon									*	ws. by A. Wilkinson and M. Lowndes
2	Baglan								*		E w. of 1880 by B-J for WM & Co.
3	Bridgend									*	see below
4	Cardiff, Rumney									*	'Fire, Light, Water, Tree of Life' by GR
5	– St John, Canton									*	see below
6	– St John the Baptist								*		WM ws. in N a., some by FMB
7	– St Stephen									*	w. by Martin Travers, *c.* 1922
8	– University									*	Lecture Hall d-d-v by PF, 1968
9	Coity								*		see below
10	Laleston									*	Christ and Mary Magdalene by GR, 1980
11	Llandaff, Cathedral								*	*	see below
12	Llansamlet									*	S a. w. by David LeVersha
13	Mountain Ash									*	early C20 w. by M.Lowndes
14	Mumbles, All Saints									*	Lifeboat w. by T. Lewis; W w. by M. Walters
15	Peterston & Sully									*	notable ws. by A. Wilkinson
16	Porthcawl									*	see below
17	Port Talbot, St Theodoric									*	three large ws. over altar by Tim Lewis
18	Pyle									*	a small light by Karl Parsons in a S a. w.
19	Swansea, Col. of Art									*	contemporary stair w. by Joannes Schreiter
20	– St David (R.C.)				*					*	see below

MR Place	Centuries									Principal feature(s):
	12	13	14	15	16	17	18	19	20	
21 – St Gabriel									*	good w. by Celtic Studios/H. Martin
22 – St Mary									*	see below
23 – Sts Michael, Jude,Peter									*	see below
24 Ystalyfera									*	ingenious recent w. by Yvonne Daters

See page 280 for table of symbols

The oldest glass in Wales, the Resurrection, C15; St David's, Swansea, Glamorgan.

BRIDGEND, Crematorium (on the Coity Road): A remarkable array of modern stained glass by the contemporary German glaziers, students, ex-students and teachers at the Swansea College of Art. The Chapel of Ease has probably the most accessible set of windows – the Four Seasons in long colourful lancets by Roger Hayman of the late 1970s (*see illustration opposite*). Along the passage into the main chapel the right-hand side has some very mannered glass, some of which is inspired by the thinking of Klee: glass of all shapes and sizes is used, from very thick circular lenses to thin opalescent sheets of colour; they are by Johannes Schreiter, Joachim Poensgen, Joachim Klos, Ludwig Schaffrath and Wilhem Buschulte; the colourful sequence on the right are memorial windows by members of the College of Art. At the end of the passage is a rather kaleidoscopic small panel and other windows by Tim Lewis, while inside the Chapel itself is an interesting large pastel-coloured creation by Yanous Boujioucos.

224

CARDIFF, St John, Canton: In the S aisle is an interesting work by Geoffrey Robinson of 1981 evoking Life in the church's liturgical colours – red, green, yellow, blue, purple and white.

COITY, St Mary: The E window of 1863 with the three Healing Miracles is one of the few designs solely by Peter Paul Marshall, a founder member of Morris, Marshall, Faulkner & Co.

LLANDAFF Cathedral: A number of early windows by Morris & Co. of the late 1860s, the earliest being the S choir aisle E window designed jointly by Morris and Ford Maddox Brown. In the N aisle the scenes are by Burne-Jones and musical angels by Morris; all three combined in the windows with Christ and the Evangelists in the choir S; the Old Testament figures in the S nave are Burne-Jones again of 1869, whilst those of the New Testament are by Ford Maddox Brown (except Burne-Jones's St Peter) of 1874. The Tree of Jesse in the Lady Chapel is by Geoffrey Webb of 1951 and The Supper at Emmaus is the subject in the high E window of three lights and a rose above the altar by Patrick Reyntiens to designs of John Piper, 1961-2. But who is responsible, one might wonder, for the extraordinary and powerful design of the window in the N aisle with the Crucifixion set on Eve and the serpent?

PORTHCAWL, Parish Church: An excellent five-light E window of 1928 by Karl Parsons in his own brand of the Arts & Crafts style, rich and glowing (almost like C13 glass at, say, Canterbury or Chartres).

SWANSEA, St David (R.C.): A fine and unusual C15 Resurrection panel recently given to the church: note the figure behind the tomb and the subtle but rather odd use of yellow stain that has gone – or been made to go – orange in places (*see illustration*). Also here is a whirling Annunciation window by Catrin Jones, *c.* 1982.

Detail from one of the Seasons by Roger Hayman, late 1970s; Bridgend Crematorium, Bridgend, Glamorgan.

SWANSEA, St Mary: In St Mary's is some interesting modern glass: two windows in the W wall of 1982 by Catrin Jones to commemorate the marriage of the Prince and Princess of Wales with nice colours, clasped hands and flowers. The N aisle has a pair of recently made windows by Kuni Kajiwara that form a kind of butterfly astride the font behind which they are placed; the images in them are inspired by Swansea's history and industry. The Lady Chapel has two windows by John Piper and Patrick Reyntiens of 1965-6 in their abstract/symbolical style. Most of the chancel windows have rich glass by J. Powell of Whitefriars, 1960s – two on the S side with Sts Barnabas and James are recent and by Alf Fisher. A window by Rodney Bender is to be installed by 1985.

SWANSEA, The Churches of St Michael, St Jude, St Peter: All of these places have windows by the Celtic Studios, whose work can be seen throughout South Wales.

GWENT

MR	Place	12	13	14	15	16	17	18	19	20	Principal feature(s)
1	Caldicot									*	Annunciation in N a. by GR, 1981
2	Ebbw Vale & Risca									*	both have ws. by The Celtic Studios, 1968/70
3	Liswerry									*	Christ in Majesty and work by J.Crombie
4	Llanarth & Llanelly									*	both have ws. by The Celtic Studios, 1968/70
5	Llangattock Lingoed				+						in E and S ws. white rose and sun *ensoleille*
6	Llantrisant & Nash									*	both have recent ws. by G.Robinson
7	Mathern				+						large panel of frags. in a W w.
8	Newport, St Woolo									*	see below
9	Pontnewydd									*	The Holy City as 12 jewels, by G.Robinson
10	Rogiet									*	Annunciation by GR, 1981
11	Tredegar									*	see below

See page 280 for table of symbols

NEWPORT, St Woolo's Cathedral: The rose window at the E end (of 1964) with an abstract design by John Piper was made by Patrick Reyntiens – with some subtle and complex staining work.

(NEW) TREDEGA, Parish Church: Geoffrey Robinson reports a fine delicate window at the E end of the church with the Ascension, dating probably from the turn of the century and by an unidentified artist.

GWYNEDD

MR	Place	12	13	14	15	16	17	18	19	20	Principal feature(s)
1	Aberdovy (Aberdyfi)								*		see below
2	Aberffraw								*		Faith, Hope, and Charity by Gibbs, 1849
3	Bangor								*		D. Evans O.T. figs. & Apostles, 1839
4	Beaumaris (Anglesey)					H*	H				fig. of the Virgin from a Crucifixion
5	Bodedern								*		fine Crucifixion w. by ? of 1849
6	Dolwyddelan					*					fig. of St Christopher in yellow stain
7	Glynllifon Llandwrog							H			largest heraldic w. in Wales by (?)D.Evans
8	Harlech & Llanddona									*	Celtic Studios ws. *c.*1965
9	Holyhead								*	*	see below
10	Llanbedrog & Llandegfan								*		both have D. Evans ws., 1850 & 1832
11	Llandudno & Llanfairynghornwy								*		both have ws. by David Evans of *c.*1840
12	Llanenddwyn & Llanllechid								*		both have Clutterbuck ws., 1850/44
13	Llanfechell (Anglesey)				*	H					York-type Trinity; Christ on Tau Cross
14	Llanuwchllyn				*	*					see below
15	Llanwenllwyfo (Anglesey)					F					Flemish and other foreign glass
16	Penrhyn, Castle								*		see below

See page 280 for table of symbols

ABERDOVY, Parish Church: Dr Mostyn Lewis reports that on the S side is a 'beautifully decorative' window by David Evans of Shrewsbury, dating from *c.* 1837, with geometric, leaf and petal design partly in pot metals and part yellow stain.

HOLYHEAD, Parish Church: More decorative windows by David Evans of the 1840s. In the S aisle are the figures of the three female saints Dorothy, Theresa and Agnes, designed by Burne-Jones for Morris & Co. in 1897; they also did the E window in the same year, whereas the firm's S window with St Michael and two angels of 1921 is mostly designed by Henry Dearle; the 1927 E window of the N transept is also theirs.

LLANUWCHLLLYN, Church: Some nice remains and fragments of the C15 and C16 in a number of windows: the small Crucifixion in the E window of the N side is reminiscent of the simple example in the chapel of Bramall Hall. However, the Trinity of *c.* 1460 with the Father, the Crucified Son and dove of the Holy Spirit in the E window of the S aisle suggests the influence of the York school.

PENRHYN Castle: Some fine work by Thomas Willement in the Great Hall, especially in the pairs of roundels with the months and signs of the Zodiac of *c.* 1835 which imitate C13 style. There are two more windows by him on the stairs (of 1832) and some fine heraldic glass in the tympana of three windows in the Drawing Room. In the Chapel the Adoration of the Magi and Nunc Dimittis Window is by David Evans of *c.* 1833; so, too, are the figures of the Evangelists and the copy of Rubens' 'Descent from The Cross' on the triptych at Antwerp.

POWYS

MR	Place	Centuries									Principal feature(s)
		12	13	14	15	16	17	18	19	20	
1	Abbeycwmhir								*		fine w. by HBB, 1866
2	Bettws Cedewain				F	*					Nativity, Crucifixion; Merchant marks
3	Beulah								*		two notable works by BG, 1878
4	Brecon, Cathedral									*	Bishop Bevan Mem. by Horace Wilkinson
5	Bwlch & Dolanog									*	Celtic Studios ws. 1951/68
6	Castle Caereinion								*		decorative w. by David Evans, *c.*1840
7	Leighton								*		see below
8	Llandysilio								*		the E w. is a good work by CB of 1868
9	Llanllugan					*					St John, Crucifixion, other figs. *c.*1500
10	Llanwnog					*					early C16 frags.; canopy and a bishop
11	Llanwrin				*						see below
12	Llyswen									*	four small ws. by Carl Edwards, *c.*1946–73
13	Manafon					*					angels (not very well drawn)
14	Meifod								H		fine heraldic glass by D.Evans, 1838
15	Old Radnor				*						see below
16	Welshpool								*		see below
17	Ystradgynlais									*	rose & W ws. by Celtic Studios

See page 280 for table of symbols

LEIGHTON, Holy Trinity: There are two windows here by the Liverpool firm of Forrest & Bromley of *c.* 1873, of whose work elsewhere little seems to remain. One window has the figure of St James and the other the Return of the Dove to the Ark, both framed within exotic canopies and surrounds.

LLANWRIN, St Gwrin: Late C15 glass in the E window, notably the Crucifixion in the main light with Christ on a 'Tau Cross', with cherubim in attendance and set against roses in the sun *ensoleille.* Also note a part of a Virgin and Child window.

OLD RADNOR, Church: In the vestry E window is the charming late C15 figure of St Catherine with a huge wheel, set against the 'rather wild emotion' (Dr Mostyn Lewis) of roses in the sun *ensoleille.* (As a bonus for coming to see the Welsh St Catherine here, the visitor is also confronted by a C7 Celtic font and an organ that dates from 1500.)

WELSHPOOL, Christchurch: There are some brilliantly coloured pictorial windows by David Evans of Shrewsbury in the chancel. The windows date from *c.*1844. Note that one light is a copy of Raphael's 'Transfiguration'.

SCOTLAND

With the exception of the magnificent collection of stained glass in the Burrell Museum, some C13 panels in the chapel of St Bride at Douglas, of the foreign panels at Provands Lordship (Glasgow) and fragments set into a window at Holyrood Palace, there is virtually no pre-Reformation glass in Scotland – and even these exceptions originate from outside Scotland. This sad situation has been brought about partly by the zeal with which certain aspects of the Reformation's philosophy were put into action and partly through Scottish wars of independence, not to mention the all-too-familiar problem of neglect and removal through changing fashions. And yet documentary evidence points to there having been widespread amounts of stained glass in Scotland during medieval times; this is supported by the bits and pieces that have ended up in various museums and private collections. Much research has still to be done on this matter and on the whole of stained glass in Scotland. Michael Donnelly's preliminary study (*see* Bibliography) is an invaluable document, even though it concentrates on glass that originated in and around Glasgow. Therefore, apart from the four more or less *in situ* panels of heraldic glass of 1542 in the Magdalene Chapel at Edinburgh, our examination of Scottish glass has to begin in Scotland of the 1840s.

In the first half of the C19 Scotland had a number of firms and individual glaziers producing painted windows, although here again little of their work remains. (Donnelly points out that over 300 churches in Glasgow alone have been demolished since 1900!) The firm of Ballantine & Allen was founded in 1837, and by 1845 James Ballantine was criticising other glaziers for copying Gothic medallions – even though the English were doing the same thing – that is, if they were not churning out outdated panels in Georgian poses or copying classical paintings on to glass. It must be said that Ballantine's own work was on the stodgy side – if his quartet of windows still in the Scott Memorial is anything to go by. It was possibly the disastrous decision by the authorites in the mid 1860s to install sixty Munich-designed windows at Glasgow Cathedral (*see* the entry for Glasgow Cathedral) that stimulated action towards what might be described as Scottish self-sufficiency in stained glass. Daniel Cottier was an important figure at this time, fresh from an apprenticeship with Morris & Co. in London; in fact he subseqently set up an office in London and, through his interest in art dealing, kept abreast of development in aesthetic matters not only in London but across the Atlantic as well. There is a fine set of his windows at the Ruthven Hotel at Auchterarder that dates from 1882 and which in most respects is as good as anything in England at the time. The firm of Adam & Small was founded in 1870 and produced windows to Stephen Adams's designs that were consistently of the highest standard (see for example Pollockshields Parish Church and the Clark Memorial Church in Largs of the early 1890s). Another key personality at this time was the artist James Guthrie who, with like-minded souls, formed a group that became known as the Glasgow Boys, out of which emerged the Glasgow School of painting and, amongst other things, many freelance designers of

Dancing by Daniel Cottier, *c.*1882; Ruthven Hotel, Auchterarder, Tayside.

stained glass windows – notably David Gauld and Harrington Mann. Guthrie's firm, Guthrie & Wells, often made the windows designed by these people. Christopher Whall was also commissioned by Guthrie to design windows for the firm (eg at the Largs Church) and so the Arts & Crafts tradition was well and truly established in the world of Scottish stained glass; many famous names subsequently emerged, including Robert Anning Bell and Louis Davis. It was from this tradition that sought to combine the potentialities of the exotic new glass and techniques that were being discovered with the personal vision of the artist that came the kind of mild expressionism which can be felt in so much Scottish glass from the first half of this century. These stained glass artists initially included Douglas Strachan and Alfred Webster and subsequently Gordon Webster and William (Willie) Wilson. Each has a fundamentally different style, yet they all share a desire to establish a harmony of their glass with the surroundings in which they have to live; moreover they also manage to maintain a kind of Celtic streak of starkness and clarity in figure and facial drawing and intricacy in surrounding designs.

BORDERS

MR Place	Centuries									Principal feature(s)
	12	13	14	15	16	17	18	19	20	
1 Jedburgh									*	Nativity by designer Alex Walker, 1902
2 Melrose, Holy Trinity									*	two ws. by W.Wilson, 1963
3 Morebattle									*	Simeon and Infant Christ by DS, c.1910
4 Roxburgh									*	a single-light w. by W.Wilson, 1947

See page 280 for table of symbols

CENTRAL

MR Place	Centuries									Principal feature(s)
	12	13	14	15	16	17	18	19	20	
1 Dunblane, Cathedral									*	see below
2 Grangemouth									*	a work by J.E. Nuttgens dating from 1936
3 Stenhousemuir									*	4 ws. by DS, one unfinished (1950)
4 Stirling, Holy Rood								*	*	ws. by J & W Keir, Adam and Small, DS

See page 280 for table of symbols

DUNBLANE Cathedral: A number of windows by Douglas Strachan of the mid 1920s, e.g. in the Lady Chapel and on the S side of the nave. Of a few years earlier are the works by Louis Davis whose splendid six Benedicite windows in the choir show him at his best: from left to right they represent Allegory, Chaos, Earth and Humanity, with archangels in the two outer windows; the E window here is by Kempe and those in the little N chapel off the choir are small scenes by Gordon Webster and D. Strachan. A charming Magnificat and Nunc Dimittis windows on the S side of the nave by Louis Davis again, and G. Webster's window with little scenes on the N side of the nave and the tiny little St Clement figure in the equally tiny chapel by the font. Clayton & Bell did the W window with its rich glass.

DUMFRIES AND GALLOWAY

MR Place	Centuries									Principal feature(s)
	12	13	14	15	16	17	18	19	20	
1 Dumfries, St Michael								*		see below
2 – St Ninian									*	appliqué ws. by Jeffries/JP
3 Tinwald									*	some ws. by G. Webster, 1938-55

See page 280 for table of symbols

DUMFRIES, St Michael: Twelve extraordinary windows by the Viennese firm Rihurer and Koeningenen 1885-90: the style is Pre-Raphaelite inspired and the windows executed mostly in enamels. Also windows here by Ballantine, A. Webster and W. Wilson.

FIFE

MR Place	Centuries									Principal feature(s)
	12	13	14	15	16	17	18	19	20	
1　Culross, Abbey									*	see below
2　Dunfermline			?+						*	see below
3　Kircaldy								*	*	see below
4　Leuchars									*	one w. by W.Wilson, 1958
5　Methil, Community Centre									*	7 foot appliqué ws. executed by local children
6　St Andrews,										
– Holy Trinity									*	see below
7　– Martyr's Church									*	1950s ws. by W. Wilson; and DS, 1929
8　Upper Largo								*	*	see below

See page 280 for table of symbols

CULROSS Abbey: A fine small modern panel by Douglas Hogg that utilises glass in a kind of three-dimensional manner, here using glass on edge to generate a cross. Also a window in the porch by Sadie McLellan of 1963 that seems to suggest St Catherine's wheel; in a N transept window a series of scenes by Stephen Adam, 1906.

DUNFERMLINE Abbey: Some pre-Reformation glass said to be in the Durie window in the N aisle, but this is not obvious to the eye. Otherwise most of the glass belongs to the first half of the C20 with the exception of the Bruce Memorial with its long thin figures in the N transept by Gordon Webster of 1974; these include the single-light S transept window by Alexander Strachan of 1932 with Christ in the Temple, his Livingstone Window of 1937 in the S chapel and the small, almost jewel-like window of 1916 by Strachan's brother, Douglas, in the S aisle of the Abbey.

KIRCALDY, St Brycedale: Two windows by Morris & Co. of 1889 and 1892 depicting Moses and the Burning Bush and The Burial of Moses. The five-light War Memorial in the W window is by Douglas Strachan of 1923.

ST ANDREWS, Holy Trinity: A large number of interesting windows, notably eleven by D. Strachan! The huge, richly coloured W window is possibly the best of them and the E window is also good. On the S side is a large Arts & Crafts six-light window by Reginald Hallward, and in the N transept a rather Pre-Raphaelite Benedicite by Powell of Whitefriars. Not to be missed is Wilson's Shepherd Boy of 1950. The clerestory windows are by Douglas Strachan's brother, Alexander.

UPPER LARGO, Parish Church: The Praise Window of 1896 at the E end is a fine work by David Gauld filled with happy figures; Gauld was generally more at ease with secular windows, being much inspired by Rossetti and the Pre-Raphaelites; this is one of the windows he did for J. & W. Guthrie of Glasgow. Also by Guthrie is the window of *c.* 1881 based on the hymn 'The Church is one Foundation. Strachan's window of 1934 has the theme 'Behold I make all Things New'.

GRAMPIAN

MR Place	Centuries									Principal feature(s)
	12	13	14	15	16	17	18	19	20	
1　Aberdeen, various churches								*	*	see below
2　– University									*	see below
3　Crathie								*		see below
4　Elgin									*	St Michael w. by DS, 1910

MR	Place	Centuries									Principal feature(s)
		12	13	14	15	16	17	18	19	20	
5	Fochabers								*		a w. by WM & Co., 1877 (in Gordon Chapel)
6	Forres									*	14 ws. by Strachan, mostly c.1939
7	Fyvie									*	see below
8	Lossiemouth									*	Miraculous Draught by C. Florence, 1971
9	Pluscarden Priory									*	Woman Clothed with the Sun, S. McLellan

See page 280 for table of symbols

ABERDEEN, various churches: There is glass by Douglas Strachan at numerous places throughout the region, representing examples from just about every stage of this prolific artist's career which spanned over fifty years, before his death in 1950. The earliest examples are probably those in St Nicholas, Union Street, or at the South Parish church, both in Aberdeen, dating from before 1900, whilst at Rubislaw Church in the same city there is one that dates from 1947. In fact examples from each decade can be seen in churches or chapels in the city at:

1899: South Parish Kirk
1900–10: Gilcomston, King's College, St James, St Ninian, St Machar's Cathedral
1911–20: St Machar's Cathedral, Queen's Cross (rose window), King's College
1921–30: Holborn West Kirk, St Marchar's Cathedral
1931–40: King's College (chapel and library)
1941–50: Rubislaw

ABERDEEN, King's College Chapel: Apart from the glass by Douglas Strachan mentioned above, there are two windows by William Morris & Co. of 1897 in the chapel and on the N side of the chancel.

CRATHIE, Royal Church: A five-light window in Arts & Crafts style of c. 1895 by Robert Anning Bell, with figures of Christ, St Margaret, St Andrew, St Columba and Bridget.

FYVIE, Parish Church: A fine window by Tiffany of New York, c.1901, with St Michael.

HIGHLANDS

MR	Place	Centuries									Principal feature(s)
		12	13	14	15	16	17	18	19	20	
1	Beauly									*	see below
2	Inverness, St Columba									*	rose w. by Gordon Webster, 1957

See page 280 for table of symbols

BEAULY, Parish Church: Two windows by W. Wilson of the 1960s, one before he went blind and one after, designed and executed by John Blythe to Wilson's instructions.

LOTHIAN

MR	Place	Centuries									Principal feature(s)
		12	13	14	15	16	17	18	19	20	
1	Dalkeith, St John									*	see below
2	– Buccleuch Ch.									*	a late w. by W.Wilson, 1962
3	Edinburgh, Café Royal								*		see below
4	– Caledonian Ins. Co.									*	see below
5	– Castle, Chapel									*	see below
6	– Cathedral								*	*	see below
7	– Crematorium									*	contemporary glass by Sax Shaw
8	– Holyrood Palace		*	*							frags. in the Wardrobe Room
9	– Magdalene Chapel					H					see below
10	– New College Hall									*	in Lib. many ws. by Strachan, 1911–34
11	– Old Greyfriars								*		eight early ws. by Ballantine, c.1857
12	– Royal High School									*	3 large ws. with famous Scots by W.Wilson
13	– St Cuthbert									*	see below
14	– Scott Memorial								*		4 early heraldic ws. by Ballantine, c.1845
15	Gladsmuir									*	David Muir Mem. by Rona Moody, 1982

MR	Place	Centuries									Principal feature(s)
		12	13	14	15	16	17	18	19	20	
16	Linlithgow								*	*	see below
17	Musselburgh, Loretto									*	20 interesting ws. by Nina Davidson, c.1951
18	Newbattle									*	rose and other ws. by W. Wilson, 1945-60
19	Roslin, Chapel								*	*	see below

See page 280 for table of symbols

DALKEITH, St John and Park Church: On the N side is a fine double-light window by W. Wilson in rich medieval style with the artist's characteristic facial drawing; opposite are two more good windows of his.

EDINBURGH, Café Royal, Oyster Bar: Overlooking the bar and keeping an eye on the customers are eight fine sportspersons set with quarries and elaborate surrounds by Ballantine of the 1890s, designed by Tom Wilson (uncle of Willie) (*see illustration*).

EDINBURGH, Caledonian Insurance Co.: Five massive windows of 1937 by Wilson evoking Scottish industry – one includes a self-portrait. 'Lots of whimsy, strong portraits and a fascinating social document,' says Rona Moody.

EDINBURGH Castle Chapel: Windows by Douglas Strachan of 1922-9, thought at the time to be outstanding; they certainly seem to have affected the Scottish stained glass fraternity, for his style of rather angular faces (a kind of overall mosaic-like texture of small pieces of glass, the use of thick clear quarries lightly painted, coupled with the Arts & Crafts jewel-like look) crept into other glaziers' work soon after this.

EDINBURGH, Cathedral, St Giles: Much glass by Ballantine of the 1870s, but a Ballantine trying to conform to the prevailing taste and standard set by Mayer of Munich at Glasgow Cathedral, thought at the time to be the last word in stained glass – he was helped in this venture by Robert Herdman. There are two works by Daniel Cottier, the W window and one at the E end of the N nave, although the former has aged badly and is due for replacement (at the time of writing, a window on the theme of Robert Burns by the Icelandic glazier Leifur Breidfjord is planned). The Argyl Window in the SE corner is by the prolific Oscar Patterson of Glasgow. The ubiquitous Morris and Kempe have glass here, the latter pulling out all the stops in his window in the side chapel by the SW door – with plenty of fine drawing and even leaded-in 'jewels' Beauchamp Chapel-style, whereas the Burne-Jones designed window in the NW corner has some fading in the paintwork. More recent are the windows by W. Wilson in the clerestory (1954); the 'Blue Window' with Christ Amid the Storm in the N transept by Strachan, who also

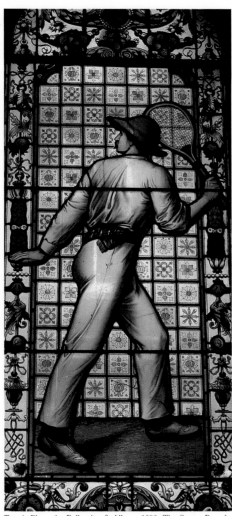

Tennis Player by Ballantine & Allen, c.1890; The Oyster Bar of the Cafe Royal, Edinburgh, Tayside.

233

David, by Louis Comfort Tiffany, c.1900; St Cuthbert, Edinburgh, Tayside.

did the elaborate armorial glass in the Thistle Chapel; the three-light window in the N aisle by Francis Spear of 1957 is very much of its time.

EDINBURGH, Magdalene Chapel, Cowgate: Four panels dating from 1542 – the oldest *in situ* glass in Scotland; these include the coats-of-arms of Mary de Guise (Lorrainne), consort of James V, the royal arms of Scotland, of Michael Maquhen, and Maquhen impaling those of the chapel's founder, J. Rynd.

EDINBURGH, St Cuthbert's, Lothian Road: Sixteen windows by Ballantine of various dates, but the real gem here is one by Tiffany of New York, *c.* 1900, a Boer War memorial for W.V.S. Clair McLaren in the gallery, of the young David as a shepherd boy with a sling – note how it uses moulded glass with a thick rippling surface, the fascinating sky and the large water-bottle made out of the eye of a piece of crown yellow glass (*see illustration*). Note the War Memorial of 1922 by D. Strachan.

LINLITHGOW, St Michael: A notable if not entirely beautiful collection of glass from the period 1885-*c.*1950 by English and Scottish glaziers. Clayton & Bell did the long lights of the E window with Psalm 104 and its 'rotating' wheel atop, as well as the large six-light with rose S transept window housing large figures. On the S side of the nave are the Evangelists to Burne-Jones's designs, and H. Hendrie's fine window at the W end; the main W window with the Transfiguration is by Ballantine of *c.* 1890. On the Choir S side is Cottier's very Victorian three-light window. Alfred Webster did the rich and colourful four-light War Memorial – and William Meikle & Co. the small 'Boy Samuel'.

ROSLIN Chapel: In this charming chapel, most of the glass is poor, rather faded C19 work, but the porch by the W door has two good modern windows: a work of 1957 by W. Wilson, 'The Airman', and St Francis by Carrick Whalen, 1970. In the crypt is 'The Ascension' by Pat Pollen of The Tower of Glass in Dublin.

STRATHCLYDE

MR Place	Centuries									Principal feature(s)
	12	13	14	15	16	17	18	19	20	
1 Ardrossan								*		see below
2 Bearsden, Kilpatrick									*	see below
3 – St Andrew's Col.								*	*	see below

MR	Place	Centuries									Principal feature(s)
		12	13	14	15	16	17	18	19	20	
4	Bellahouston									*	an early C20 w. by David Gauld
5	Dalry								*	*	see below
6	Douglas		*								see below
7	Glasgow, Burrell Mus.	*	*	*	HF*	HF*	HF*	H*	*		see below
8	– Cathedral				O	*			*	*	see below
9	– Hughendon House								*		see below
10	– People's Palace								*	*	see below
11	– Pollokshields Ch.								*	*	see below
12	– Provands Lordship				O	O					Flemish roundels and other panels
13	– Royal Infirmary									*	see below
14	– Royston								*		see below
15	– St Andrew								*		several ws. by Stephen Adam, 1875
16	– St James, Bishopsbriggs									*	see below
17	– St James, Pollok								*		good Ascension w. by A.Walker, c.1896
18	– School of Art									*	see below
19	– University Chapel									*	see below
20	Greenock								*		see below
21	Helensburgh								*		see below
22	Iona, Abbey									*	lancet by W.Wilson 1965, and 1 by Strachan
23	Irvine								*		see below
24	Largs, Clark Mem.Ch.								*		see below
25	– St Columba									*	Pilgrim's Progress et al by DS, 1914/36
26	Larkhall									*	sermon on the Mount by J.T. Stewart, 1901
27	Paisley, Abbey								*	*	see below
28	Skelmorlie								*		good Ascension w. by D.Gauld, 1895

See page 280 for table of symbols

ARDROSSAN, St Andrew: A fine Ascension window of 1896 by Harrington Mann who for a while shared a studio with David Gauld, both products of the rich vein of stained glass design that was generated in the 1890s around the Glasgow School of Art.

BEARSDEN, New Kilpatrick Church: A good four-light W window with scenes from the Life of Christ by the prolific designer Stephen Adam, a late work (c. 1909) with almost Pre-Raphaelite – Burne-Jones inspired – figures. Daniel Cottier's also influenced Stephen Adam.

BEARSDEN, St Andrew's College: A number of windows were transferred here from Dowanhill Convent including some fine portrait pieces by Daniel Cottier; mounted in a light box is a window by Harry Clarke.

DALRY, St Margaret: A good collection of glass, notably those from the late 1950s by Guthrie & Wells, two of which were designed by Nina Davidson, the cartoonist, one – 'Suffer Little Children' – by R.A. Bell, and the 'Peace, Be Still' window by Charles Payne, which is particularly good work. Also an earlier work (1925) by Charles Davidson and three of the C19 by the Royal Factory, Munich.

DOUGLAS, St Bride's Chapel: Two C13 panels said to be from Canterbury Cathedral, one with the Virgin and Child, the other with saints and scrolls bearing Lombardic inscriptions.

GLASGOW, Burrell Museum: Part of Sir William Burrell's magnificent collection of stained glass, given to the City of Glasgow in 1944, has at last gone on permanent display at the new museum in Pollok Park. Burrell collected over 600 pieces during the period 1911-37, over a third of which were leaded into the windows of his home, Hutton Castle. All the glass on display is well set and labelled. Some of the best specimens came from the sales of the collections of Randolph Hearst and Sir William Jerningham at Costessy in Norfolk; the collection is particularly strong on glass of the C15 and early C16, especially by Flemish and French artists, although there is much from Germany and England, and lesser amounts from Holland and Switzerland. Particularly well displayed are the panels from the Church of St John at Rouen with scenes from the lives of Sts John the Evangelist and the Baptist, the former portrayed on Patmos, boiling in oil, raising Susanna to life (there are related panels at Wells and Ely cathedrals); the latter have the birth and death of the saint; there are also figures from a Tree of Jesse of the early

235

St Mary of Egypt, C14 French glass; Burrell Museum, Glasgow, Strathclyde.

light box; from an earlier age and also in light boxes are the superb late C13 panel with Beatrix van Valkenburg and the prophet Jeremiah from St Denis of *c*.1144 (companion panels at Raby Castle, Wilton and Twycross qv). Elsewhere are some splendid pieces that include a fine English C13 king from a Jesse Tree, a Marriage at Cana in three medallions of French C13 glass, numerous C14 panels from England, France and Germany (*see illustrations on this page and opposite*) with figures under neat canopies; there is some nice work from the C15 Norwich school and other English C14 panels. For heraldic glass the collection is without equal — it represents over half the 600 or so panels. A few of these date from the C14 and C15, but the greater part come from the C16, notably the forty or so coats-of-arms displayed around the museum's dining room. Originally they were installed in the Banqueting Hall at Fawsley Hall in Northampton. These arms record the alliances with various families connected with the place, notably De Vere, St John, Dillon-Lee, Knightly and The Crown. Also of the C16 are the forty or so panels with Gartered arms and other heraldic pieces originally at Vale Royal.

GLASGOW Cathedral: The saga of the Munich windows chosen for the Cathedral in the last century has just about faded away; little eviden⌐⌐ remains of the era and the whole episode has become a classic example of how high ideals founder from over-planning and what the *Glasgow Herald* later described as making the 'snobbish mistake of trusting in great names'.

It was decided that the cathedral should have a set of windows befitting so great a monument. So 123 biblical subjects were selected according to a 'harmonious plan' that, admirably, followed the medieval practice of setting Old and New Testament scenes alongside each other in a sequence that began with the Fall of Man in the NW corner. Partly at the recommendation of Charles Winston and partly because of fashion, the Royal Bavarian Glass Painting Studio at Munich was chosen. Under the direction of Max Ainmuller, ten artists worked as one to produce a highly coloured but monotonous set between the years 1859 and 1864. The problem was that these artists, nurtured under the inspiration of the Italian Cinquecento, produced windows that were woefully out of place in Glasgow – and in more sense than one, for Glasgow's polluted air caused the figures to fade prematurely.

Over the years just about all the Munich win-

C16, formerly at Rouen, by Arnoult de Nijmegen, whose work can also be seen at Wilton and St Georges, Hanover Square in London. A little earlier is the charming portrait of Princess Cecily from the 'Royal' Window at Canterbury (she was a daughter of Edward IV) and set in a

dows have been removed – a nice little rose re-mains over the S door, as well as some figures high in the E walls of the transepts – but it has to be admitted that not all the replacements are an unqualified improvement. The present assorted collection includes two large works by Francis Spear of the 1950s at the E and W ends, the lat-ter depicting Adam and Eve, Dark and Light, the Alpha and Omega with a predominantly yellow/gold tone. More gentle are the windows in the transepts by Willie Wilson (on the N side) and Gordon Webster of 1951 on the S with its severe four figures in the lower lights and more overhead. In the N choir aisle are works by H. Hendrie (notably 'Christ and the World's Work' in a kind of mannered medieval style) and a more colourful work by Ceri Richards. Harry Stam-mers' memorial windows at the W end of the nave (both sides) are less interesting than his more characteristic set of windows in the small downstairs chapel from the 1960s. The crypt E window has two Swiss panels dated 1620 with a 'comic strip' style of painted scenes round a cen-tral subject, which in both cases is the Passion; also two oval C17 painted roundels of the Last Supper and Resurrection set in elaborate sur-rounds. In the Lower Church are a number of C15 and C16 Flemish roundels with subjects that include the Annunciation, St John's Revelation, St Martin dividing his cloak, Christ in Geth-semane as The Gardener, and others; also here is a recent colourful little two-light window of 1979 by Gordon Webster. Other windows in the Cathedral by Marion Grant, D. Strachan (in N ai-sle), Ballantine and Bertollini of Milan.

A donor with a fashionable wig before the Virgin and Child, North German, c.1400; Burrell Museum, Glasgow, Strathclyde.

GLASGOW, Hughendon House, Langside Drive: A fine window portraying the Harvest on the south stair by Harrington Mann (of 1898) using opalescent glass, one of a number of windows that Hugh McCulloch commissioned for this, his own house.

GLASGOW, The People's Palace: Panels of stained glass by Glasgow glaziers recovered from various churches are now, alas, back in store after an excellent exhibition in 1982. All that remains on display is the figure of St Mungo — patron saint of Glasgow — in the entrance hall by Charles Baillie (and Guthrie & Wells) and up-stairs in light boxes panels by Stephen Adam of 1877 with scenes of the traditional industries of Maryhill. (In store are an early panel by Daniel Cottier of c. 1864, formerly in Trinity, Irvine; an old man praying, by Stephen Adams Jr in rich colours, c. 1900: a panel with Elijah, by Charles Stewart, formerly a display piece in the studio that Stewart and his father founded after 1907; some fine windows by Norman Macdougall, formerly in Springbourne Parish Church, and his harp-playing angel of 1887, originally in Trinity Church, Claremont St. Also numerous cartoons of windows spanning the past 100-odd years.

GLASGOW, Pollokshields, Parish Chur-ch: Fine windows by Stephen Adam spanning much of his career. The good but slightly senti-mental Eadie Memorial in the clerestory with 'Suffer Little Children' is by R.A. Bell; note some of the other richly coloured windows up here – e.g. 'Cast Thy Bread Upon The Waters' at the W end.

GLASGOW, Royal Infirmary, Ante Chapel: The Healing of the Sick is a splendid window by Adam & Small. Stephen Adam who

237

died in 1910 has been described as the pioneer of modern stained glass in Scotland; this window has certainly evaded the trap of sentimentality into which the artist could so easily have fallen.

GLASGOW, Royston Hill, Parish Church: A three-light window by Morris & Co. of 1866 with Moses and St Paul in one light and with related scenes of the Golden Calf and Preaching at Athens below, all in one light, and David (with Goliath) and John the Baptist (with Christ's Baptism) in the second.

GLASGOW, Episcopal Church of St James, Bishopsbriggs: New Testament window, formerly in Trinity Church, Claremont Street, include scenes of the Temptation, the Calling of Sts Andrew and Peter, the Sermon on the Mount and Christ Blessing Children, by Stephen Adam Jr (c. 1900?).

GLASGOW, School of Art: Near the main entrance is Tristan & Isolde, fine work by Dorothy Smyth of the School, 1901.

GLASGOW University Chapel: Windows by Strachan and his pupil, Gordon Webster – and by Laurence Lee and his pupil, Keith New.

GREENOCK, (Old) West Kirk: Faith and Charity were designed by Burne-Jones for Morris, Marshall, Faulkner & Co., c. 1867, to which Hope by Daniel Cottier was added some time later. Although much influenced by Burne-

Jones, Cottier's style is markedly different and individual – and, one may say, less affected.

HELENSBURGH, Caindhu Hotel: Built in 1872-3 by William Leiper for John Ure, Provost of Glasgow, this splendid place has a number of fine figures of the Virtues – Beauty, Love, Truth, Audacity etc. – by Daniel Cottier, portrayed in rectangular panels and set against nicely drawn quarries.

IRVINE, Trinity Church: A rose window and one with three lights of 1861 by the Edinburgh firm Field & Allen.

LARGS, Clark Memorial Church: Some fine windows by Stephen Adam from the early 1890s, the 'last and greatest period of his artistic career', says Donnelly; the E window of 1894 is by old Glasgow firm of William Meikle & Co., and the Thanksgiving of Noah is a splendid early work by Christopher Whall, as are the Vision of Samuel, the Sacrifice of Abraham and the Good Samaritan, all c. 1890.

PAISLEY Abbey: Some fine windows by various Scottish and English glaziers, notably Daniel Cottier, Douglas Strachan (the E window, 1931, and S choir, 1932), Herbert Hendrie (on S side), Gordon Webster (1951 in the choir), Louis Davis in the N transept, C. Webb and F. Stephens (in St Mirins aisle, 1955); Morris & Co. in the E window of the S aisle, 1874, in the N aisle and N transept, 1876.

TAYSIDE

MR Place	Centuries									Principal feature(s)
	12	13	14	15	16	17	18	19	20	
1 Alyth, St Andrew									*	a w. by John Blythe of the early 1950s
2 Auchterarder								*		see below
3 Brechin, Cathedral									*	see below
4 Dundee, St Andrew									*	ws. by W.Wilson from the period 1957–71
5 Kenmore									*	four-light w. by W.Wilson, 1969
6 Murthly								*		see below
7 Perth, St John									* *	see below

See page 280 for table of symbols

AUCHTERARDER, Colearne House (Ruthven Hotel): In this former mansion built in 1882 for the industrialist Alexander Mackintosh by William Leiper are three fine little portrait panels set against quarries in the stair window, designed by Daniel Cottier fresh from London and inspired by a spell with Morris & Co.; his also are the figures of Music, Dancing

and Art in the Front Hall, and the Four Seasons personified in the Dining Rooms. The three beautiful Japanese-inspired natural themes are a fine piece of design and execution by William Stewart for J. & W. Guthrie, c. 1888. Also the nursery rhymes painted like Flemish roundels in the bay window of the old nursery. (*See illustrations on p.229 and opposite.*)

Japanese influenced Art Nouveau panel by William Stewart, c.1888; Ruthven Hotel, Auchterarder, Tayside.

BRECHIN Cathedral: A three-light window by Morris & Co. of 1907; various windows by Willie Wilson 1952-8, one of Douglas Strachan's last windows – a War Memorial of 1949, a three-light work by Hugh Easton, 1953 and one by G. Webster.

MURTHLY, Chapel of the Eremite: An interesting early window by Ballantine of 1846 which makes it one of the earliest stained glass windows in Scotland.

PERTH, St John: A fine collection of Scottish glass in twenty-two windows dating from the period 1894-1975, some good and others repre-

sentative work by eleven different artists. They are well described in a superbly written booklet available in the church. Hendrie has seven windows here, there are two each by Wilson, Strachan, Ballantine and Miss Kemp, and one each by Isabel Goudie, Guthrie & Wells, Miss Chilton, Louis Davis, Harvey Salin and Meredith Williams. It is difficult to highlight some rather than others, but Salvin's modern work of c.1975 is particularly pleasing, as is 'Music' by Davis and Wilson's two-light window with St Christopher and St Nicholas. Also satisfying are the small scenes with a rather medieval look about them in Miss Kemp's windows of 1932 at the W end of the S aisle.

239

GLOSSARY

Note Heraldic terms are listed separately on page 28.

Abrade *see* p.18.

Acanthus a type of leaf that is thick and scalloped; its appearance, particularly in tracery lights, suggests a Perpendicular date.

Aciding *see* p.19.

Agnus Dei The Lamb of God symbol carried by John the Baptist: lamb carrying the flag.

Aisle *see* Diagram.

Alb full-length tunic with narrow sleeves.

Ambulatory *see* Diagram.

Amice neck-cloth with an apparel on one edge.

Angelic Hierarchy the nine Orders of Angels.

Antetype an Old Testament scene that foreshadows one from the New.

Antiphon a verse of a psalm intoned or sung.

Apparel the decorated portion of a dalmatic.

Appliqué *see* p.19.

Apse semicircular end to chancel.

Armature *see* p.44.

Babuineries grotesques derived from female baboons, one of the characteristic devices of the Lenton school.

Back Painting *see* p.17.

Bay Window a window, usually curved, that projects outwards from a wall.

Biblia Pauperum Poor Man's Bible (*see* p.29).

Black Letter the Gothic script that replaced Lombardic script in *c.*1380.

Bull's Eye *see* p.17.

Cartoon the full-sized drawing of the intended window with lead lines (*see* p.17.)

Censer a container for burning and waving incense.

Chancel *see* Diagram.

Chasuble principal garment worn by a priest officiating; oval-shaped with a hole for the head.

Chiaroscuro painting in monochrome by working on the qualities of light and shade.

Choir *see* Diagram.

Cinquefoil an opening in stone formed by five cusps surrounding a central circle.

Clerestory the upper level of the church beneath the vaults, often pierced by windows.

Corrosion generally a pitting or flaking-off of the surface of the glass, brought about by bad firing, the presence of potash in the glass or other impurities, accelerated by modern pollution.

Crocket pinnacles, gables and other projections on the sides of spires or canopies.

Crossing *see* Diagram.

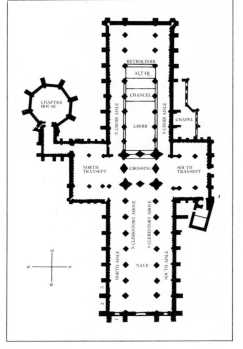

Diagram showing areas in a church.

Cross Paty an equal-arm cross with each arm thicker at its extremity.

Crown Glass *see* p.15.

Dalle-de-verre *see* p.17.

Dalmatic a sleeved open-sided tunic worn by deacons and bishops.

Decalogue the Ten Commandments.

Decorated the style of architecture prevalent from *c.*1290-*c.*1380.

Diaper a geometric pattern of small squares and lozenges.

Drolleries amusing grotesques or bizarre creatures sometimes found in decorative parts of the window.

Enamelling painting with a compound made up of ground powdered coloured glass mixed with a fusible medium: after painting on to the glass it was fired in a fairly hot kiln, such that the mixture fused to the surface.

Finial the top piece of a canopy.

Flashing *see* p.17.

Foil opening formed by cusping circle or arch.

Fused Glass *see* p.19.

Golden Legend a book of *c.*1275 by Jacobus de Voraigne on the lives of saints.

Grisaille (from the French *grisailler,* to make grey) clear glass painted with a foliage pattern, usually geometric and sometimes interspersed with small coloured pieces of glass (*see* p.22).

Grozing Iron *see* p.17.

Halation the phenomenon whereby light coming through a bright or lightly coloured piece of glass spills over into darker areas, imparting a blurred edge around the boundaries.

Impaled the heraldic division of a shield into two vertically.

Lancet a long slender window terminating in a pointed arch.

Light architecturally it refers to an opening between stone mullions.

Lombardy Script the earlier form of lettering used in windows before *c.*1375.

Mandorla an oval shape generated by two intersecting curves within which holy figures – usually Christ or the Virgin Mary – are placed; often decorated by emanating rays or waves.

Medallion a window made up of panels, all linked by a narrative sequence, within one light.

Merchant's Mark as the name implies, a symbol made from items connected with the merchant's business.

Mouchette a curved dagger-shaped opening in tracery, characteristic of the Decorated period.

Muff *see* p.15.

Mullion the stone shaft that divides a window into lights.

Murrey a pinky-brown colour, introduced in the late fourteenth century.

Nave *see* Diagram.

Nimbus a bright disc, aureole or halo surrounding the head of saints.

Norman Slab *see* p.18.

Ogee an arch formed by two intersecting concave and then convex curves, characteristic of the Decorated period.

Orphrey richly ornamented (often embroidered) stripes and borders of an ecclesiastical garment.

Pallium a vestment worn by archbishops over the shoulders and falling down the back and front.

Passion Shield a shield with emblems of the Passion, nails, hammer etc.

Perpendicular the period of architecture from *c.*1380–1530.

Pick Out *see* p.17.

Pot-Metal *see* p.15.

Quarry a small, usually diamond-shaped piece of glass individually painted, fired and leaded up with other quarries to form a field, often as a background to figures. They probably evolved from geometric *grisaille* as an easier and more convenient way of 'mass-producing' background material. Some are nevertheless exquisitely painted, decorated with birds, flowers, leaves, initials, symbols and rebuses.

Quatrefoil an opening generated by four symmetrically meeting cusps.

Reamy *see* p.19.

Rebus the translation of a name into an image; a play on a name.

Rood the Crucifixion, usually attended by St Mary and St John.

Rose Window circular window sometimes large, divided radially by the tracery; occasionally called a wheel window.

Roundel a circular piece of glass or pieces of glass, usually of a single colour; but, from the Perpendicular period onwards, they are common in clear glass with scenes painted in dark pigment and yellow stain — later with coloured enamels (*see* p.41).

Ruby red glass — *see* p.17.

Saddle Bar *see* p.18.

Saltire Cross a diagonal cross, the emblem of St Andrew; *see also* heraldic glossary, p.28.

Scratch Out *see* p.17.

Sedilia seats for the clergy along the sides of the chancel.

Silver Stain also called yellow stain — *see* p.18.

Smear Shading *see* p.17.

Strapwork decoration consisting of an interlacing network of bands.

Streaky Glass *see* p.19.

Sun Ensoleille *see* sun-in-splendour.

Sun-in-Splendour radiant suns, popular as cusp fillings, border and other decoration, a badge of Edward VI, common 1461-85.

Transepts *see* Diagram.

Transom major horizontal division of the tracery part way up.

Trefoil an opening generated by three symmetrically meeting cusps.

Tribune the gallery at triforium level of a church/cathedral, usually over aisle; became obsolete by introduction of flying buttresses.

Triforium the level below the clerestory, sometimes glazed.

Tunicle similar to a dalmatic but longer and rarely with apparels.

Type-Antetype/Typology *see* p.29.

Undercroft a chapel below the main floor level, sometimes underground.

Vesica similar to mandorla (qv) but with a sharp intersection of the curves.

241

THEMATIC GUIDE

CROSS REFERENCE BY
SUBJECT MATTER AND AGE

Note 1: The number after examples at York Minster refers to the number of the window in the diagram (*see* p.214)

Note 2: FR in the list means the example exists in a Flemish or other painted roundel form.

Note 3: The location at each place is the cathedral or church unless otherwise stated.

THE PASSION CYCLE

The Entry to Jerusalem: **C15** St Kew; **C16** Cambridge – King's Col., Eccles, Hengrave Hall, Lichfield, Southwell, Warham, Wimborne St Giles; **C17** Wroxton Abbey.

The Washing of Christ's Feet: **C13** Canterbury; **C15** St Kew; **C16** Hengrave Hall; **C20** Broomfield.

The Last Supper: **C13** Canterbury, Madley, Lincoln; **C15** Great Malvern, St Kew; **C16** Cambridge – King's Col., Hengrave Hall, Lichfield; **C17** Oxford – Lincoln and The Queen's Col.; FR Blithfield, Warwick; **C18** Apethorpe, Audley End, South Perrott; **C19** Cheltenham; **C20** Cambridge – Robinson Col.

The Agony in The Garden: **C16** Woodborough, York – All Saints North Street; **C15** Glasgow – Burrell, Herringfleet, St Kew; **C16** Cambridge, King's Col., Hengrave Hall, Hevingham, Kirkby Wharfe, Noak Hill; FR South Ormsby; **C17** Oxford – Balliol Col., Wroxton; **C18** City of London – St Botolph; **C19** Pott Shrigley.

The Betrayal By Judas: **C14** Clavering; **C15** East Harling, Salisbury, St Kew; **C16** Bristol, Cambridge – King's Col., Exeter, Hengrave Hall, Lichfield, Shrewsbury – St Mary; FR South Ormsby, Nowton; **C17** Little Easton.

The Trial Before Pilate (or Herod) – and/or Pilate Washing His Hands: **C15** Glasgow – Burrell, St Kew; **C16** Cambridge – King's Col. (before Herod), Ely, Fairford, Lichfield; FR Llanwarne; **C17** Little Easton; **C18** Wroxton Abbey.

The Scourging of Jesus: **C15** Hessett, Martham, St Kew, York – All Saints Pavement; **C16** Cambridge – King's Col., Hengrave Hall, Lichfield, Noak Hill; FR Muchelney, Nowton.

The Mocking of Christ and The Crown of Thorns – 'Ecce Homo': **C15** Hessett, Littleham, Thorney; **C16** Biddulph, Cambridge – King's Col., Great Bookham, Lichfield, Sherborne St John, Southwell; **C17** Oxford – Balliol Col.

Christ Carrying the Cross – 'Via Crucis': **C13** Hereford; **C15** St Kew; **C16** Cambridge – King's Col., Depden, Great Bookham, Hengrave Hall, Lichfield; FR Begbroke, South Ormsby; **C19** Haltwhistle; **C20** Cricklewood.

The Nailing to The Cross: **C16** Chelwood; FR Mapperton.

The Crucifixion: **C13** Cowfold, Hereford, Horspath, Kidlington, Leigh Church, Packwood; **C14** Asthall, Bredon, Compton Beauchamp, Checkley, Cosby, Eaton Bishop, Edington, Egginton, Glasgow – Burrell, Great Bardfield, Kelston, Mamble, Shrewsbury, Stanford-on-Avon, Thornbury, Thruxton, Tickenham, Warfield, Wells, Whichford, Whitwell (Leics.), Wigginton, Wilsford, York – All Saints Pavement, York – St Denis, York – St Michael-le-Belfrey; **C15** Alveley, Ayston, Brightwell-Baldwin, Childrey, East Harling, Glasgow – Burrell, Great Malvern, Hardwick, Horspath, Lacock, Lambley, Lea, Llanuwchllyn, Martham, Morville, Nettlestead, Newark, North Cerney, Nuthall, Oxford – Merton Col., Rushall, St Catherine's Court, St Winnow, Salisbury, Sproxton, Stoke D'Abernon, Taverham, Trull, Winscombe; **C16** Aldbury, Ashtead, Barton, Bettws Cedewain, Bramall Hall, Cambridge – King's Col., Cilcain, Cotehele, East Retford, Glasgow – Burrell, Hingham, Llanasa, Llanwrin, Greenwich, Madingley, Shrewsbury, Stradsett, The Vyne, Westminster – St Margaret's, Withcote Hall; **C17** Apethorpe, Cambridge – Peterhouse Col.,

242

Enstone, Little Easton, Low Ham, Prittlewell, Wroxton Abbey; **C18** South Perrott; **C19** Buxton, Doddington, Dorchester (Dorset), East Buckland, Hanley Castle, Landford, Whaddon; **C20** Llandaff.

The Taking Down From The Cross: **C13** Canterbury, Twycross; **C15** East Harling, St Kew; **C16** Ashcombe, Cambridge – King's Col., G. Bookham, Hingham, Kirkby Wharfe, Lichfield, Warham; **C19** Penrhyn Castle.

The Pieta and Mater Dolorosa: **C15** Bromham, Coxwold, Gipping, Long Melford, Much Hadham, Stoke D'Abernon, Thorney; **C16** Aldbury, Depden, Normanton, Wilton; FR Begbroke, Nowton; **C20** Bristol – St Mary Redcliffe, London – St Clement Dane's.

The Harrowing of Hell: **C14** Warfield; C15 Messingham, St Kew, Thorney, York – All Saints Pavement; **C16** Cambridge – King's Col., Hengrave Hall, Hingham.

The Resurrection: **C13** Twycross; **C14** Milton Manor, Newark, North Moreton, Stamford-on-Avon, York – St Michael-le-Belfrey; **C15** Broughton, East Harling, Elland, Glasgow – Burrell, Martham, Stamford – St Martin, Swansea, Thornhill, Wistow, Wrangle, York – All Saints Pavement; **C16** Cambridge – King's Col., Glasgow – Burrell, Hengrave Hall, Hessett, Hingham, Lichfield, Seal, The Vyne; **C17** Apethorpe, Little Easton, Oxford – Lincoln and The Queen's Cols.; **C18** Great Witley, Shrewsbury – St Alkmond; **C19** Babworth, Bovingdon, Hopton; **C20** Broomfield, Mill Hill.

Mary Magdalene and Christ After The Resurrection – 'Noli Tangere': **C12** York Minster (91); **C13** York Minster (47, 53); **C14** Newark,

Okeover, Woodborough, York Minster (6, 35, 98); **C15** Disley, Glasgow – Burrell, York Minster (37); Cambridge – King's Col., Fairford, Llanwenllwyfo; **C19** Waterford.

The Three Marys in The Garden: **C12** York Minster (91); **C13** Hereford, Madley; **C15** Newark, Stamford – St Martin, Thorney; **C16** Cambridge – King's Col., Erpingham, Fairford, Hingham, Lichfield; **C19** Ladock, Lowestoft, Watton-at-Stone.

The Supper at Emmaus: **C12** York Minster (91); **C13** Lincoln, York Minster (53); **C15** Thorney; **C16** Cambridge – King's Col., Fairford, Lichfield; **C17** Stretton; **C18** Great Witley; **C20** Waterford.

St Thomas's Doubt: **C14** Woodborough; **C15** York – All Saints North Street; **C16** Erpingham, Exeter, Fairford, Hingham, Milton House; **C17** Lambourne, Noak Hill.

The Ascension: **C13** Canterbury, London – Victoria & Albert Museum, Westminster Abbey, York Minster (53); **C14** Milton Manor, Weston Underwood, York Minster (77); **C15** East Harling, Elland, Hessett, Martham, Newark, York – All Saints P'ment; **C16** Bampton, Cambridge – King's Col., Fairford, Greenwich, Hingham, Rendcombe, York Minster (75); **C17** Abbey Dore, Oxford – Lincoln and The Queen's Cols.; **C19** Funtley, Lowestoft, Staveley, Tunbridge Wells; **C20** Islington, Portsmouth, Skelton.

Pentecost: **C13** Westminster Abbey, Canterbury; **C14** Harbledown, York Minster (98); **C15** East Harling, Elland, Saxlingham Nethergate; **C16** Cambridge – King's Col., Fairford, York Minster (75); **C17** Oxford – The Queen's Col.; *C20* Bristol – St Mary Redcliffe.

PORTRAYALS OF CHRIST

Christ in Glory: **C12** Rivenhall; **C13** Canterbury, Hereford; **C14** Acaster Malbis, Brinsop, Bushbury, Chartham, Chinnor, Drinkstone, Eaton Bishop, Evesham, Hardwick, Morpeth, Nuthurst, Sandford (Oxon), Southwell, Tickenham, Wycliffe, York Minster (72, 76); **C15** Abbots Bickington, Ludlow, Norwich – St Peter Hungate, Oxford – St Peter-in-the-East, Salisbury, South Creake, Westminster (All Saints), Whittington;**C16** Leadenham,

Reymerston; **C17** Shrewsbury – St Mary's; **C19** Bradford, Crewe, Howsham, Kingsbury, Slough, Waltham Abbey, Willoughby; **C20** Hillingdon, Ockbrook.

Christ Showing His Wounds: **C13** Lincoln; **C14** Lower Heyford, Sparsholt; **C15** Cadbury, Chewton Mendip, Crudwell, Greystoke, Hardwick, Melbury Bubb, Newington, Sherborne, St Weonards, Sidmouth, West Rudham.

THE CYCLE OF THE VIRGIN MARY

Incidents From The Lives of Anne and Joachim, Parents Of The Virgin: **C14** York Minster (1); **C15** Elland, Erpingham, Great Malvern, Gresford, Sherborne St John, York – Holy Trinity Goodramgate, York Minster (24), York – St Martin; **C16** Cambridge – King's Col., Fairford, Glasgow – Burrell; FR Stonor Park.

The Betrothal of Joseph and Mary: **C13** Lincoln; **C15** Elland, Great Malvern, Newark; **C16** Bristol – St Mark, Cambridge – King's Col.

The Birth and Childhood of The Virgin Mary: **C15** Great Malvern, Gresford, York Minster (24); **C16** Cambridge – King's Col., Fairford, Glasgow – Burrell, Lichfield.

Teaching The Virgin Mary To Read: **C14** Bere Ferrers, Fawkham, Marsh Baldon, Queenhill, Upper Hardres; **C15** Astbury, Almondbury, Beckley, Blithfield, Bolton Percy, Cockfield, Dyrham, Haddon Hall, Kempsford, Kemsing, Kidlington, Kirkby Wharfe, Lullingstone, Mulbarton, Norbury, Oaksey, Oxford – All Souls Col., Ross on Wye, Saxlingham Nethergate, Stamford – St George, Stanford-on-Avon, Stoke D'Abernon, Taunton, Tremeirchion, York – All Saints North Street, York – Holy Trinity Goodramgate, York Minster (24), York – St Martin, Winchester; **C16** Hingham, Kirkby Malham, Rendcombe, Shrewsbury – St Mary; **C17** Oxford – The Queen's Col.

The Annunciation: **C12** Rivenhall; **C13** Aldermaston, Canterbury, Lincoln, York Minster (53); **C14** Compton Beauchamp, Ely Museum, Litchborough, Milton Manor, Oxford – Christ Church, Saundby, Shotwick, Thornton, Treuddyn, Warndon, York Minster (6, 33, 35, 74, 77), York – St Michael-le-Belfrey; **C15** Attleborough, Bale, Bexhill, Bondleigh, Bothal, Brightwell Baldwin, Burford, Canterbury, Childrey, Cirencester, Compton Dundon, Dymock, East Harling, Elland, Glastonbury, Glasgow – Burrell, Great Malvern, Gresford, Grimley, Haddon Hall, Haseley, Hessett, Holt, Langport, Ludlow, Melbury Bubb, Newark, Norwich – St Peter Mancroft, Poynings, Ringland, St Neot, Salisbury – St Thomas, Salle, Shawbury, Shelton, Stamford – Brown's Hospital, Stamford – St Martin, Stratton Strawless, Thaxted, Tong, Tortworth, Ufford,

Wistow, Witherley, Wytham, York – St Olave; **C16** Cambridge – King's Col., Cotehele, East Shefford, Fairford, Glasgow – Burrell, Hengrave Hall, Lichfield, Ludlow, Rugby; **C17** Lambourne, Oxford – The Queen's Col., Temple Ewell; **C18** Great Witley; **C19** Frinton, Landford, Middleton Cheney, Oxted, Pixley, Sherborne, Surbiton, Waterford, Wickhambreaux; **C20** Abington, Bristol – St Mary Redcliffe, Canterbury, Corfe Castle, Easton, Market Harborough, Mill Hill, Upper Hardres.

The Visitation: **C14** Southwell, Stanford-on-Avon, Upper Hardres; **C15** East Barsham, East Harling, Elland, Gresford, Newark, Norwich – St Peter Mancroft; **C17** Oxford – The Queen's Col., York Minster (30); **C18** Great Witley; **C20** Forest Hill.

The Nativity: **C13** Canterbury, East Hagbourne, York Minster (33, 35); **C14** Barby, Milton Manor, Newport (Dyfed), Rochford, York – All Saints North Street, York Minster (6, 74, 77), York – St Michael-le-Belfrey; **C15** Childrey, East Harling, Elland, Great Malvern, Nantwich, Norwich – St Peter Mancroft, Saxlingham Nethergate; FR Leicester Museum, South Ormsby, York – St Helen; **C16** Cambridge – King's Col., Coleshill, Fairford, Glasgow – Burrell, Hatfield Peverel, Hengrave Hall, Langley, Pagham, Waterperry, York Minster (75); **C17** Enstone, Kingston (London), Oxford – Lincoln and Wadham Cols.; **C18** Oxford – New Col., Wytham, York Minster (34); **C19** Audlem, Fawley, Funtley, Ottery St Mary, Shropham, Whissendine, Windsor; **C20** Bristol – St Mary Redcliffe, Camden, Dorchester, Farnworth, High Easter, Martindale, Mill Hill, Northill, Waterford.

The Adoration of the Magi: **C13** Ashbourne, Canterbury, Dorchester (Oxon.), Lanchester, Lincoln, Madley, Salisbury; **C14** Southwell, Thornton, York – All Saints North Street, York Minster (74, 99); **C15** East Harling, Glasgow – Burrell, Norwich – St Peter Mancroft, Taunton, York Minster (41); **C16** Almer, Cambridge – King's Col., East Retford, Fairford, Great Weldon, Hengrave Hall, Hevingham, Kirkby Wharfe, Langley, Rugby, Stradsett; FR Begbroke, Blithfield, Muchelney; **C17** Lambourne; **C19** Bolton, Bury St Edmunds, East

Hempstead, Knutsford, London – Surbiton, Oxford – Worcester Col., Stamford – St John Baptist, Sunningwell, Watton; **C20** Cambridge – Robinson Col., Forest Hill, Hatch End, Leatherhead, Woldingham, Woodbridge.

The Adoration of the Shepherds: **C13** Ashbourne, Lincoln, Lanchester; **C14** London – Victoria & Albert Museum; **C15** East Harling, Norwich – St Peter Mancroft, Stoke D'Abernon; **C16** Erpingham, Kirkby Malham, Patrixbourne, York Minster (75); FR Llanwarne, Nowton; **C17** Lambourne, Little Easton, Oxford – The Queen's Col., Temple Ewell; **C18** The Vyne; **C19** Lanercost Priory, Sunningwell; **C20** Hatch End.

The Massacre of The Holy Innocents: **C13** Ashbourne, Westminster Abbey; **C14** York Minster (28, 31, 99); **C15** Erpingham, Newark, Wormbridge; **C16** Cambridge – King's Col., Elham, Hengrave Hall; **C17** Bishopsbourne.

The Flight into Egypt: **C12** Raby Castle, Wilton; **C13** Doddington, Lanchester; **C14** Thornton, York Minster (99); **C15** Durham; **C16** Cambridge – King's Col., Erpingham, Hengrave Hall, Kirkby Wharfe; **C17** Temple Ewell; **C18** Oxford – The Queen's Col.

The Circumcision: **C16** Cambridge – King's Col., Chadshunt; FR Nowton; **C17** Broughton.

The Presentation in The Temple: **C12** Twycross; **C13** Ashbourne, Canterbury, Madley, London – Victoria & Albert; **C14** York Minster (99); **C15** East Harling, Erpingham, Glasgow – Burrell, Hessett, Martham, York Minster (24); **C16** Cambridge – King's Col., Elford, Fairford, Great Bookham, Hengrave Hall, Pagham, York Minster (1); **C18** Oxford – Oriel Col.; **C19** Eastling, Northill; **C20** Bristol – St Mary Radcliffe.

In The Temple: **C13** Canterbury, Lincoln; **C14** Newark, York Minster (28); **C15** East Harling,

Kirkby Wharfe; **C16** Cambridge – King's Col., Disley, Fairford, Hengrave Hall.

The Death of The Virgin Mary: **C12** (?)Rivenhall; **C13** Lincoln Col., Woodchurch; **C14** York Minster (98, 99); **C15** Gresford, Norfolk – St Peter Mancroft, Salisbury; **C16** Cambridge – Corpus Christi Col., Normanton.

The Funeral of The Virgin Mary: **C14** North Moreton, Stanton St John, York Minster (98); **C15** Gresford, Norwich – St Peter Mancroft; **C16** Cambridge – King's Col.

The Assumption of The Virgin Mary: **C14** Beckley, North Moreton, Stanford-on-Avon; **C15** Boyton, Childrey, East Harling, Elland, Great Malvern, Gresford, Newington, Oxford – Christ Church, Thornford, Wrangle; **C16** Bristol – St Mark's, Fairford; FR Nowton; **C19** Wavendon; **C20** Westminster (Farm Street).

The Coronation of The Virgin: **C13** Aldermaston, York Minster (55, 58); **C14** Beckley, Birkin, Bothal, Boughton Aluph, Chartham, Crundale, Donnington, Frant, Gloucester, Holdenby, Milton Manor, Nether Poppleton, North Stoke, Stanford-on-Avon, Tewkesbury, Wormshill, York Minster (73, 74, 77, 88), York – St Michael-le-Belfrey; **C15** Bexhill, Bledington, Bradford Peverell, Clevedon, East Malling, Gislingham, Glasgow – Burrell, Great Malvern, Gresford, Himbleton, Hinton-in-the-Hedges, Ketteringham, Long Ashton, Molash, Mottisfont, Norwich – St Peter Mancroft, Oddingley, Saxlingham Nethergate, Steeple Ashton, Stody, Thaxted, West Pennard, West Rudham, York Minster (35, 53, 68, 95, 107), York – Holy Trinity Goodramgate, York – St Helen's; **C16** Awliscombe, Cambridge – King's Col., Llandyrnog, Stratton Strawless; FR Begbroke, Nowton; **C17** Temple Ewell.

The Virgin as Queen of Heaven: **C15** York – St Helen's, York – Holy Trinity Goodramgate; **C16** York Minster (30); **C19** Stoke Poges.

OTHER BIBLICAL THEMES

The Creation: **C14** Newark; **C15** Great Malvern, Ludlow, York Minster (32); **C16** Hengrave, St Neot, Walton-on-the-Hill; **C17** The Tower of London; **C19** Bury St Edmunds, Camden, Cirencester, Selsley, Southwark,

Waltham Abbey; **C20** Heathfield, Middleton, Ruislip, Seaford.

Adam and Eve: **C13** Canterbury, Lincoln; **C14** Halam, Newark, Oxford – New Col., Warham;

C15 Malvern, Martham, Mulbarton, Thaxted, York Minster (32); C16 Apethorpe, Cambridge – King's Col., Disley, Glasgow – Burrell, Hengrave Hall, Moor Monkton, York Minster (30); C17 Haslemere, London – Tower of London, Oxford – Lincoln and University Cols.; C19 Bradfield Col., Brampton, Bury St Edmunds, Camberwell, Daylesford, Ealing, Hackney, Middleton Cheney, New Bradwell; C20 Cambridge – Robinson Col., London – St Michael Paternoster Royal, Pimlico.

Noah and The Ark: C13 Canterbury, York Minster (55); C15 Malvern, York – St Michael Spurriergate; C16 Hengrave, St Neot; C17 Haslemere; C19 Bolton Percy, Cambridge – All Saints, Camden, Rochdale, Waterford; Wellingborough.

The Tree of Jesse – and figure remains: C12 Glasgow – Burrell, York Minster (74), Wilton; C13 Canterbury, Clevedon, Kidlington, London – Victoria & Albert Museum, Nackington, Salisbury, Westwell; C14 Barkway, Bristol, Cartmel Priory, Dorchester, Gloucester, Lowick, Ludlow, Madley, Mancetter, Merevale, Morpeth, Selby, Shrewsbury – St Mary's, Tewkesbury, Wells, Wilton, York – St Denys, York Minster (25); C15 Combs, Gedney,

Gresford, Huish Champflower, Leverington, Margaretting, St Kew, Stody, Thornhill, Winchester Col., Wrangle, York – St Michael; C16 Dyserth, Glasgow – Burrell, Hatton Hall, Llanrhaeadr, London – St George's Hanover Square, Prittlewell, Wimborne Minster; C17 Greenham; C19 Ascott, Ashbourne, Beverley Minster, Burford, Cattistock, Conningham, Doncaster, Hunstanton, Knightsbridge, Preston (Herts.), Prittlewell, Tideswell, Waltham Abbey, Westminster – All Saints, Wootton Bassett; C20 Hayling, London Colney.

Last Judgement: C12 York Minster (89); C13 Lincoln; C14 Carlisle, Goodnerstone, Newark, Selby, Shrewsbury – St Mary's, Tewkesbury, Wells, York Minster (25); C15 Purton, Thornhill; C16 Almer, Fairford, Hengrave; FR Farleigh Hungerford, Nowton; C17 Oxford – The Queen's Col.; C19 Bury St Edmunds, Cambridge – King's Col., Chipping Camden, Hanley Castle, South Dalton, Taunton, Windsor.

The Apocalypse and Scenes From St John's Revelation: C13 Lincoln; C15 Norwich – St Peter Mancroft, York – St Michael Spurriergate; C16 Glasgow – Burrell, Harefield, Hengrave; FR Muchelney; Shrewsbury; C17 Lambourne; C20 Burford, Hillingdon, Tamworth.

GROUPS OF FIGURES

The Trinity: C13 Hever Castle; C14 Birkin, Cheriton, Compton Bishop, Lockington, Norbury, Purford, Trottiscliffe, Wycliffe, York Minster (68); C15 Bilsington, Burnham Deepdale, Doddiscombsleigh, East Challow, Gresford, Kidlington, Llanfechell, Llanuwchllyn, Mottisfont, Newington, Orchardleigh, Ringland, Rodmell, South Creake, Stamford – Brown's Hospital, Thornhill, Thurton, Winchester, Woolley, York – Holy Trinity Goodramgate, York Minster (2, 29, 68); C16 Bampton; C17 Normanton; C18 Wardour Castle; C20 Chelsea, Liverpool (R.C.).

The Holy Family: C13 York Minster (59); C15 Burrington, Lanteglos, Oxford – All Souls Col., Thirsk, Thornhill, Tong, York – Holy Trinity, York Minster (24); C16 Rendcombe; FR Muchelney, Nowton.

The Angelic Hierachy: C14 Aldwincle, Hitcham, Sheering, Oxford – New Col., Wood-

borough; C15 Combe Martin, Coxwold, Great Malvern, Great Snoring, Harpley, Hessett, Martham, Minster Lovell, Mulbarton, Orchardleigh, Salle, Sandon, Westwell, Yarnton, York – All Saints North Street, York – St Martin's, York – St Michael Spurriergate; C16 St Neot; C19 Cambridge – Jesus Col., Torquay.

The Four Evangelists: C13 Hereford; C14 Chartham, Great Bricet, Hitcham, Oxted, Potsgrave, Sevington, Shere, Snodland, South Newington, Tortington, Whichford; C15 Bledington, Cheddar, Chelvey, Doddiscombsleigh, Great Malvern, Gresford, Hampton Poyle, Hawstead, Herstmonceux, Melbury Bubb, Ockbrook, Odell, Orchardleigh, Sherborne – Almshouses, Shiplake, Stratton Strawless, Theddingworth; C16 Chessington, Glyne, Heythrop, Langley, Lincoln, Oxford – Trinity Col., Tottenham; C17 Abbey Dore, Oxford – St Peter-in-the-East, Wroxton Abbey;

C18 Oxford – Brasenose Col.; C19 Barnsley, Howsham, Thornbury; C20 Plymouth.

The Four Fathers – or Doctors – of the Church: C15 Ashill, Cirencester, Dunsford (?), Great Malvern, Launde Priory, Long Ashton, Christian Malford, Methley, Oake, Oxford – All Souls Col., Saxlingham Nethergate; C16 Fairford, Windsor; C18 Stonor Park.

The Twelve Apostles – (complete or near-complete sets): C13 Oxford – Merton Col.; C14 Oxford – New Col., Southwell, Wramplingham, York Minster (77); C15 Bledington, Boston, Canterbury, Cockington, Drayton Beauchamp, Dyserth, Great Malvern, Great Massingham, Field Dalling, Horwood, Metheringham, Norbury, Orchardleigh, Oxford – All Souls Col., Pulham, Westham, Woodford; C16 Cherington, Hamstall Ridware, Ludlow, Withcote Hall; C17 Abbey Dore, Oxford – Lincoln, Trinity and Wadham Cols.; C19 Birmingham – Oscott, Hanley Castle, London – Holy Trinity Sloane St, Wroxton; C20 Liverpool.

THE SAINTS

Agatha: C15 Cley, Greasley, Mells, Norwich – St Peter Hungate, Oxford – All Souls Col., Shrewsbury, South Creake, Wighton.

Agnes: C15 Field Dalling, Greasley, Lichfield, Lullingstone, Martham, Winchester, Wrangle.

Alphege: C13 Canterbury; C14 Alfriston; C15 Deerhurst; C20 Weston-super-Mare.

Andrew: C13 Canterbury, Oxford – Merton Col.; C14 Acaster Malbis, Exeter, Fledborough, Landwade, Ripon, Warndon, York Minster (4, 70, 71, 99 104); C15 Beverley, Bexhill, Broughton, Doddiscombleigh, Frolesworth, Greystroke, Hawkedon, Lanteglos, Long Melford, Mottisfont, Much Hadham, Orchardleigh, Oxford – All Souls Col., Shiplake, South Creake, West Camel, Wighton; C16 Fairford, Hamstall Ridware, Shrewsbury – St Mary, Wimborne St Giles; FR Llanwarne, Stonor Park; C17 South Weald; C18 Ely, Wroxton Abbey; C19 Alderley Edge, Brown Edge, Ottery St Mary, Redcar; C20 Abbotsbury, Bearsted.

Anthony: C14 Kelston; C15 Abbots Bickington, Cartmel Fell, Crosthwaite, Golant, Gresford, Langport, Long Ashton, Salisbury, Sandhurst, Shiplake, Winscombe, FR Nowton.

Apollonia: C14 Long Sutton, Payhembury; C15 Charlinch, Chilton Street, Clavering, Cley, Gresford, Long Melford, Mells, North Cadbury, Norton-sub-Hamdon, Winchester Col.; C16 Gazeley, Rendcombe; FR Stoke D'Abernon.

Barbara: C14 Checkley, Exeter, Kelston, North Luffenham, Shrewsbury, York Minster (68); C15 Almondbury, Awliscombe, Bawburgh, Burford, Cheddar, Cley, Coxwold, Cucklington, Gresford, Ketteringham, Keyston, Loders, Mapledurham, Mileham, Much Hadham, North Cadbury, Norwich – Guildhall, Pulham, Shiplake, West Pennard, Wilby, Winchester Col, Wrangle, York – St Martin; C16 Bristol – St Mark's, Glasgow – Burrell, Lichfield.

Bartholomew: C13 Canterbury, Oxford – Merton Col.; C14 Acaster Malbis, Landwade, Strelley, York Minster (99); C15 Butleigh, Grappenhall, Haddon Hall, Langport, Mersham, Nettlestead, Norwich – St Peter H'gate, Oake, Orchardleigh, Stody, Wighton; C16 Hamstall Ridware, Rendcombe, FR Mapperton.

Blaise: C14 Halam, Morpeth, Oxford – Christ Church, Payhembury, Wells; C15 Doddiscombsleigh, Great Malvern, Harpley, Lydiard Tregoze, Stamford – St John.

Catherine: C15 West Horsley, Wilton, York Minster (56); C14 Compton Bishop, Cubley, Deerhurst, Ely Stained Glass Museum, Exeter, Glastonbury, Herringfleet, Kempsey, Mileham, Oxford – Christ Church, Newport, Pebworth, Risby, Shrewsbury; Woodborough, Woodton, York Minster (5, 69); C15 Battle, Biddulph, Blythburgh, Bowness, Charlinch, Chelwood, Chilham, Cirencester, Clavering, Cossall, Coxwold, Cranbrook, Dean (Beds), Edenham, Field Dalling, Framingham Earl, Glasgow – Burrell, Glastonbury, Gloucester, Griston, Guestwick, Haseley, Ketteringham, Kingerby, Launde Priory, Ledsham, Mells, Merstham, Merton, Methley, Mottisfont, Much Hadham, Newark, Normanton, North Cerney, Norton-sub-Hamdon, Norwich – St Peter Mancroft,

Oaksey, Oddingley, Old Radnor, Pitminster, Pulham, Salle, Shiplake, Shrewsbury, Stamford – St George, St Kew, Stamford – St John Baptist, Stody, Sustead, Tadcaster, Thirsk, Thaxted, Whittington, Wighton, Winchester Col., Winscombe, Woolley, Wormbridge, Yaxley, York Minster (29); **C16** Awliscombe, Birtles, Bristol – St Mark's, Castle Howard, Cotehele, Eyton, Greystoke, Kimberley, Leicester Museum, Llandyrnog, Ludlow, Oxford – Balliol Col., St Neot, St Weonards, Stratton Strawless, Tixover, West Wickham, Windsor; FR Nowton, St Catherine's Court; **C18** York – Sts Martin & Gregory; **C19** Cambridge – All Saints, Oxted; **C20** Abbotsbury, Coggeshall, Plymouth.

Cecilia: **C14** Dronfield; **C15** Cley, Charlinch, Field Dalling, Glasgow – Burrell, Langport, Norwich – St Peter Mancroft, Pulham, West Pennard, Wrangle, Yaxley; FR Nowton; **C18** Denton; **C19** Oxted, Shobrooke; **C20** London – St Paul's Onslow Square, Martindale.

Christopher: **C14** Aldwincle, Broughton Aluph, Burford, Dunston, Halam, Halvergate, Mere, Pembridge, York Minster (35, 68), York – St Michael-le-Belfrey; **C15** Abbots Bickington, Beckley, Birtsmorton, Bledington, Burford, Cirencester, Coxwold, Doddiscombsleigh, Durham, Edington, Eyton-on-the-Wold, Glasgow – Burrell, Great Malvern, Gresford, Littlehempton, Mersham, Merton, Methley, St Winnow, Salisbury, Seighford, Settrington, Stamford – St John Baptist, Stockerston, Thenford, York – All Saints North Street, York – Holy Trinity Goodramgate; **C16** Dolwyddelan, East Retford, Glasgow – Burrell, Heythrop, Lichfield, Rendcombe, West Wickham, York – St Michael-le-Belfrey; FR Farleigh Hungerford, Leicester Museum, Nowton; **C17** Lambourne, Oxford – The Queen's Col., Oxford – St Peter-in-the-East; **C19** Wigan; **C20** Laleham.

Clement: **C14** Glasgow – Burrell, Gloucester, Wells; **C15** Chilham, Langport, Stockerston; **C16** Glasgow – Burrell, Rendcombe, **C17** Oxford – The Queen's Col.; **C19** Ilford.

Cuthbert: **C13** York Minster (60); **C14** Cockayne Hatley, Kempsey, Oxford – Christ Church, York – St Michael-le-Belfrey; **C15** Edington, Emneth, Gloucester, Great Malvern, Ladbroke, Methley, Stamford – St John Baptist, Wiggenhall, York Minster (26, 106); **C16** Greystoke; **C19** Durham – St Oswald.

Denis: **C14** Morpeth, York Minster (72); **C15** Methley, York – St Denis.

Dorothy: **C14** Hereford; **C15** Gloucester, Coxwold, Langport, Loders, Mark, Middlezoy, North Cerney, Norton-sub-Hamdon, West Pennard, Wilton; **C16** West Wickham; **C17** Oxford – St Peter-in-the-East.

Dunstan: **C14** Cockayne Hatley; **C15** Battle, Canterbury, York – St Olave.

Edmund: **C13** Edworth, Saxlingham Nethergate, York Minster (50); **C14** Beckley, Exeter, Heydour, Risby, Upper Hardres, York Minster (72); **C15** Denton, Harpley, Hawstead, Ketteringham, Long Melford, Martham, Methley, North Cadbury, Norwich, Stody, Thaxted, Torbryan, Wiggenhall, Wormbridge, Wrangle, York Minster (77b); FR Stoke D'Abernon.

Edward the Confessor: **C13** Kempsey, York Minster (60); **C14** Cockayne Hatley, Exeter, Heydour, North Luffenham, Stapleford Abbotts, Wells, York Minster (2, 28, 31); **C15** Canterbury, Doddiscombsleigh, Glasgow – Burrell, Harpley, Kelly, Ludlow, North Cadbury, Orchardleigh, Oxford – Merton Col., Ross-on-Wye, Sandringham, Tong, York – St Helen, York Minster (23); **C14** Oxford – Balliol Col.; **C17** Oxford – The Queen's Col.

Elizabeth: **C13** York Minster (59); **C14** Hereford; **C15** Almondbury, King's Bromley, Langport, Lullingstone, Morley, Norwich – St Peter Mancroft, Oxford – All Souls, Raunds, Stamford – St John Baptist, Warwick; **C16** Noak Hill, Patrixbourne; **C17** Oxford – St Peter-in-the-East.

Elizabeth of Hungary: **C15** Disley; **C20** Sturminster Newton.

Etheldreda: **C14** Hamstall Ridware; **C15** Cartmel Priory, Ely, Newark, North Cadbury, Salle.

Francis: **C15** Norwich – St Peter Mancroft, Salisbury; **C16** Broughton, York – St Helen; FR Farleigh Hungerford; **C19** Hertford, Nettleham, Weybridge; **C20** Castlemartin, Twickenham, Woburn.

Frideswide: **C14** Oxford – Christ Church; **C15** Begbroke, Kidlington; **C16** Llandyrnog, Oxford – Balliol and Trinity Cols.; **C19** Oxford – Christ Church Col.

Gabriel: **C14** Compton Bishop, Exeter, Kingsland; **C15** Banningham, Bawburgh, Launde Priory, Long Melford, West Rudham, Westwell, York Minster (18); **C16** Rendcombe; **C17** Herringfleet.

George: **C14** Aldwincle, Barton-on-Humber, Brinsop, Egmanton, Hereford, Heydour, Long Sutton, Stanford-on-Avon, Wells, West Grinstead, Wimbledon; **C15** Bexhill, Binfield, Bledington, Bowness, Broughton, Burford, Castle Acre, Cranbrook, Doddiscombsleigh, Glasgow – Burrell, Gloucester, Great Chart, Great Malvern, Gresford, Grinton, Haddon Hall, Ketteringham, Lullingstone, Mersham, Nettlecombe, North Tuddenham, Ribbesford, Sandhurst, St Neot, St Winnow, Stamford – St John Baptist, Trull, Woolley, Wrangle, York – Holy Trinity Goodramgate, York – St Martin, York – St Michael-le-Belfrey; **C16** St George's Hanover Square; FR Leicester Museum; **C18** Preston (Warwicks); **C19** Hessett, Rothbury; **C20** Manchester.

Giles: **C14** Church Leigh, Wells; **C15** Hawkesbury, Kings Bromley, Ladbroke, North Cadbury, Shermanbury, Stamford – St John Baptist, Thirsk; FR Farleigh Hungerford, Llanwarne.

Helen: **C13** Havering(?); **C14** Exeter, Herringfleet, York Minster (98); **C15** Almondbury, Ashton-under-Lyne, Coxwold, Haddon Hall, Kelling, Mells, Morley, Oxford – All Souls, St Weonards, Salisbury, Salle, Shrewsbury, South Creake, Stamford St Martin, Stody, Wilby, York – St Helen.

Hugh of Lincoln: **C13** Lincoln; **C16** Oxford – Balliol Col., York – St Michael-le-Belfrey; **C19** Oxford – Museum.

James the Great: **C13** Canterbury, Oxford – Merton Col., Saxlingham Nethergate, Stanton Harcourt; **C14** Acaster Malbis, Barton-on-Humber, Bere Ferrers, Checkley, Enville, London – Victoria & Albert Museum, Mancetter, Saxlingham Nethergate, Woodborough, York Minster (28, 31, 33, 104); **C15** Beckley, Butleigh, Combe, Coxwold, Cranbrook, Diddington, Doddiscombsleigh, East Brent, Edlesborough, Edworth, Grappenhall, Haddon Hall, Harpley, Langport, Lanteglos, Llantisilio,

Marnham, Mark, Norwich — St Peter Hungate, Oxford – All Souls, South Leigh, Stamford – Brown's Hospital, Stowting, Tattershall, Tong, Weston Longville, West Tanfield, Wilden, Winscombe, Yarnton, York – St Mary Castlegate; **C16** Fairford, Hamstall Ridware, Harefield, Islington, Ketteringham, Llandyrnog, Long Melford, Rendcombe, Strelley, York Minster (34), York – St Michael-le-Belfrey; **C17** London – Lincoln's Inn; **C18** Wroxton Abbey.

James the Less: **C13** Canterbury; **C14** York Minster (103); **C15** Astbury, Beverley Minster, Haddon Hall, Langport, Mark, South Creake, Thornhill, West Hallam; **C16** York – St Michael-le-Belfrey.

John the Baptist: **C13** Chetwode, Westminster Abbey, York Minster (50, 58); **C14** Glasgow – Burrell, Fledborough, Hardwick, Ipplepen, Lowick, Meldreth, Mileham, Rolleston, Selling, Weston Underwood, Wickhambreaux, Willesborough, York Minster (4, 6, 28, 36, 67); **C15** Almondbury, Battle, Bristol – St Mary Redcliffe, Brympton, Cartmel Priory, Coxwold, Durham, Dyrham, East Brent, Gloucester, Great Malvern, Gresford, Haddon Hall, Harbury, Ketteringham, Kingstone, Launde Priory, Long Ashton, Long Stretton, Ludlow, Lullingstone, Luton, Malvern, Methley, Mottisfont, Norwich – Guildhall, Norwich – St Peter Mancroft, Oxford Balliol Col., Oxford – Trinity Col., Pott Shrigley, Ringland, Sherborne Abbey, Shiplake, South Ormsby, Stowting, Tong, West Tanfield, Yarnton, York – Holy Trinity Goodramgate, York Minster (18, 23, 78), York – St Mary Castlegate, York – St Michael Spurriergate, York St Michael-le-Belfrey; **C16** Almer, Cambridge – King's College, Castle Howard, Chelwood, Compton, Great Brington, Kirkby Wharfe, Lichfield, Ludlow, Noak Hill, Norwood Green, Patrixbourne, Southwell, Thorpe, York – St Helen, York – St Michael-le-Belfrey; **C17** Lydiard Tregoze, Oxford – Lincoln Col.; **C18** Great Witley, York – St Martin and Gregory; **C19** Congleton, Kentish Town, Kingston, Landford, Waterford; **C20** Cossington (Leics), Dronfield, Radstock, Woldingham.

John the Evangelist: **C12** Easby; **C13** Canterbury, Hever Castle, Lincoln, Madley, Saxlingham Nethergate, Twycross; **C14** Caldecote, Glasgow – Burrell, Great Malvern, Kelston,

Kimberley, London – Victoria & Albert, Selling, Stanford, Upper Hardres, Weston Underwood, York – St Denys, York Minster (5, 28, 31, 99, 104); **C15** Atcham, Brympton, Binfield, Cheddar, Clifton, Denton, Doddiscombsleigh, Dyrham, East Brent, Glasgow — Burrell, Gresford, Harpley, Langport, Llanllugan, Long Melford, Ludlow, Mells, Methley, Mileham, Nantwich, North Cadbury, Norwich – St Peter Mancroft, Orchardleigh, Oxford – Merton Col.; Oxford – Balliol Col., Sherborne Abbey, Shiplake, Shrewsbury, Stamford – St John Baptist, Stanton St John, Tattershall, Tong, Weston Longville, West Pennard, Westwood, Wrangle, Yarnton, Yaxley, York – All Saints North Street, York – Holy Trinity Goodramgate, York – St Michael Spurriergate; **C16** Birtles, Bury St Edmunds, Clyffe Pyppard, Ely, Lichfield, Llandyrnog, Rendcombe, Reymerston, St Neot, Shrewsbury, Wells; FR Blithfield, Newport (Dyfed), South Ormsby; **C17** Lydiard Tregoze, Patrixbourne, South Weald; **C20** Cerne Abbas.

Jude: **C13** Lincoln; **C14** Elsing, York Minster (98); **C15** Mark, Orchardleigh, Oxford – All Souls, Stratford St Mary, Thornhill, Wrangle.

Laurence: **C13** Dorchester, York Minster (49); **C14** Beverley, Chinnor, Ely – Museum, Glasgow – Burrell, Great Bardfield, Leigh Church, Pembridge, York Minster (1, 33, 35, 72); **C15** Addlesthorpe, Battle, Bexhill, Bowness, Bristol – St Mary Redcliffe, Broughton, Brympton, Cambridge – Magdalene Col., Castle Bromwich, Denton, Doddiscombsleigh, Great Malvern, Harpley, Headcorn, Langport, Ludlow, Mark, Mells, Nettlecombe, Nettlestead, Purton, St Kew, St Neots, Thaxted, Tuxford, Wilden, Wrangle; FR Sherborne St John; **C16** East Retford, Outwell; **C17** Oxford – The Queen's Col.

Leonard: **C14** Chilham, Drayton; **C15** Beverley Minster, Cartmel Fell, Haddon Hall, Old Buckenham, St Neot, Stamford – St John Baptist; FR Farleigh Hungerford.

Lucy: **C15** Addlethorpe, Coxwold, Guestwick, Minster Lovell.

Luke: **C13** Oxford – Merton Col.; **C14** Landwade; **C15** Hawkedon, St Neot, Stamford – St John Baptist, Stratton Strawless; **C18** Lullingstone; **C19** Cambridge – Jesus Col., Laner-

cost Priory; **C20** Abbotsbury, Milnsbridge.

Margaret of Antioch: **C13** York Minster (50); **C14** Checkley, Exeter, Kempsey, Kimberley, Landwade, Mancetter, Mileham, Old Warden, Oxford – Christ Church, Payhembury, Selling, Willesborough, Woodborough, Woodton, York – St Denys, York Minster (5, 50); **C15** Almondbury, Battle, Burford, Combs, Coxwold, Diddington, Framingham Earl, Gloucester, Ketteringham, Langport, Martham, Mells, Methley, Mileham, Much Hadham, North Tuddenham, Nynehead, Oxford – Balliol Col., Pitminster, Salle, Seavington, South Elmham, Stody, Torbryan, Trull, Weasenham, Wilby, Winslade, Wrangle, York – St Michael Spurriergate; **C16** Lichfield, Oxford – Oriel Col., Stratton Strawless; FR Leicester Museum, Oxford – Trinity Col., South Ormsby; **C17** Oxford – The Queen's Col.; **C19** Romsey, Staveley.

Mary the Virgin (with and without the Christ Child): **C12** Easby, Rivenhall, Wilton; **C13** Charlton, Compton, Hever Castle, Kemsing, Oxford – St Michael's, Stoke (Oxfords), York – St Denys, York Minster (58, 59); **C14** Bristol, Brougham, Checkley, Chilham, Clevedon, Dorchester, Drinkstone, Eaton Bishop, Enville, Fledborough, Harlow, Hereford, Kinwarton, Lambley, Leigh, Milton, Monks Risborough, Notgrove, Oxford – Christ Church, Radclive, Selling, Sevington, Stanford-on-Avon, Stowting, Warndon, Wells, Winsford, Wycliffe, York – St Denys, York Minster (33, 72, 74), York – St Michael-le-Belfrey; **C15** Atcham, Banham, Bilsington, Bishops Lydeard, Buckland (Surrey), Cartmel Priory, Clifton, Diss, Glastonbury, Gresford, Hughley, Kidlington, Lindsell, Llanwrin, Long Melford, Ludlow, Luton, Madingley, Merstham, Morley, North Cerney, Norton-sub-Hamdon, Norwich, Oxford – Balliol Col., Oxford – St Peter-in-the-East, Oxford – Trinity, Ringland, Rushall, Seighford, Stockton, Stoke D'Abernon, St Catherine, St Neot, St Winnow, Sherborne, Shrewsbury, Thornhill, Tong, Tyneham, Warwick, Waterperry, West Tanfield, Willesborough, Woolley, Wormbridge, Wyre Piddle, Yarnton, York Minster (41); **C16** Almer, Begbroke, Brushford, Cambridge – King's Col., Greystoke, Exeter, Kirkby Malham, Lichfield, Rendcombe, Stratton Strawless; **C18** Binley; **C19** Kendal, Scarborough, Waterford; **C20** Bristol — St Mary Redcliffe, Leigh, Sturminster Newton, Whitehaven, Wilmington.

Mary Magdalene: **C13** Canterbury, Selling, West Horsley; **C14** Bredon, Cockayne Hatley, Glasgow – Burrell, Payhembury, Hereford, North Luffenham, Okeover, Oxford – New Col., Petworth; **C15** Bledington, Burford, Coxwold, Diss, East Harling, Field Dalling, Grappenhall, Launde Priory, Madingley, Mells, Morley, Much Hadham, North Ockendon, Norton-sub-Hamdon, Oxford – All Souls, Pulham, Salisbury, Seavington, Stamford – St John Baptist, Stody, Wells, Winchester Col., York Minster (78); **C16** Alford, Awliscombe, Oxford – Balliol Col.; **C19** Mere, Easthampstead, Pulham Market, Rochdale Troutbeck; **C20** Dorchester.

Matthew: **C13** Lincoln, Oxford – Merton Col.; **C14** Elsing, Landwade, York Minster (98); **C15** Mark, Nettlestead, Orchardleigh, Stody; **C16** Falmouth.

Matthias: **C13** Canterbury – Merton Col.; **C14** York Minster (99); **C15** Bexhill, Bristol – St Mary Redcliffe, Orchardleigh; **C16** Hamstall Ridware.

Michael: **C12** Dalbury; **C13** York – St Denys, Oxford – St Michael; **C14** Boughton Aluph, Dorchester, Eaton Bishop, Egmanton, Enville, Exeter, Goodnestone, Kingsland, Lowick, Newport, Meysey Hampton, Ruckinge, Wells, York Minster, York – St Michael-le-Belfrey, York – St Michael Bishopsgate; **C15** Bristol – St Mary Redcliffe, Chilham, Doddiscombsleigh, Emley, Great Chart, Gresford, Haddon Hall, Ketteringham, Kingsnorth, Littleham, Long Sutton, Martham, Mersham, Oxford – Balliol Col., Sandhurst, Sellindge, Stamford – Brown's Hospital, Thaxted, Trull, York – All Saints North Street, York Minster (18), York – St Mary Bishopshill; **C16** Glasgow – Burrell; **C19** Cattistock, Hanley Castle, Waterford; **C20** East Hempstead, Grantham, Mill Hill.

Nicholas: **C13** Canterbury, Lincoln, Westminster Abbey, Oxford — Merton Col., Oxford – St Michael, York Minster (50); **C14** Mere, North Moreton, York Minster (7); **C15** Abbots Bickington, Banwell, Eaton Socon, Hessett, York Minster (39, 62); **C16** Glasgow – Burrell, Hillesden, Kirkby Wharfe, Wilton, Yarnton; FR South Ormsby, Muchelney, Nowton, Yarnton; **C20** Abbotsbury, Martindale, North Cerney.

Paul: **C12** York Minster (88); **C13** Chipstead, Lincoln, Oxford – Merton Col., York Minster (59); **C14** Buckland, Cockington, Exeter, North Moreton, Ripon, Trumpington, Warndon, Westham, Weston Underwood, York Minster (70, 72, 73, 99), York – St Michael-le-Belfrey; **C15** Beverley, Binfield, Blythburgh, Brightwell Baldwin, Butleigh, Canterbury, Doddiscombsleigh, Edington, Great Malvern, Haddon Hall, Hatch Beauchamp, Hessett, Poling, Shrewsbury, Stamford – Brown's Hospital, Tattershall, West Camel, Westwood, Wiggenhall, Wighton, York Minster (41); **C16** Cambridge — King's Col., Diddington, Heythrop, Rendcombe, St Neot, Woodmansterne, York — St Michael-le-Belfrey; **C17** Bedingham, Chedgrave, Erpingham; **C18** Birmingham – St Paul's, London – St Andrew's-by-the-Wardrobe; **C19** Beverley Minster, Halewood, Ottery St Mary, Ponsonby, Sheepy; **C20** Thorpe (Lincs).

Peter: **C12** Lincoln, York Minster (88); **C13** Chipstead, Oxford – Merton Col., York Minster (52, 58); **C14** Buckland (Surrey), Compton Bishop, Exeter, Landwade, Marston Trussell, North Moreton, Ripon, Tadcaster, Trumpington, Warndon, Weston Underwood, Woodborough, York Minster (70, 72, 76, 104), York – St Michael-le-Belfrey; **C15** Beverley Minster, Bexhill, Binfield, Brightwell Baldwin, Burford, Canterbury, Frolesworth, Grappenhall, Gresford, Hessett, Lanteglos, Long Melford, Marsh Baldon, Merstham, Molash, Morley, Mottisfont, Nettlecombe, Norwich – St Peter Hungate, Norwich – St Peter Mancroft, Oxford – All Souls, Oxford – St Peter-in-the-East, Okeover, Papplewick, Salisbury, Shiplake, Shrewsbury, Tattershall, Thorney, Tong, West Camel, Westwood, Wighton, Wormbridge, Wrangle, Yaxley, York Minster (37, 41); **C16** Fairford, Glasgow – Burrell, Hamstall Ridware, Rendcombe, Reymerston, St Weonards, Thorpe, York Minster (15, 75), York – St Michael-le-Belfrey; FR Claverton, Long Stretton, Muchelney; **C17** Chedgrave, Hatherleigh, Oxford – The Queen's Col.; **C18** Great Witley, Wroxton Abbey; **C19** Alderley Edge, Cambridge – All Saints, Doddington, Hampton Lucy, New Ferry, Sheepy, Waterford.

Philip: **C13** Oxford – Merton Col.; **C14** Elsing, Exeter, Saxlingham Nethergate, York Minster (103); **C15** Astbury, Bedingham, Grappenhall, Mark, Norwich – Guildhall, Orchardleigh,

Stody, Weston Longville; **C16** Falmouth, Hamstall Ridware; **C17** Oxford – Balliol Col., South Weald; **C18** Ely – Prior Cauden Chapel.

Roche: **C15** Barkway, Broughton, Launde Priory, Littleham; **C16** Glasgow – Burrell, Llanwerne.

Sidwell: **C14** Exeter; **C15** Chewton Mendip, Oxford — All Souls Col.

Simon: **C13** Oxford — Merton Col.; **C14** Gloucester, Landwade; **C15** Orchardleigh, Thornhill; **C16** Hamstall Ridware, Islington.

Stephen: **C13** Grateley, Church Leigh, Westminster Abbey, York Minster (49, 52); **C14** Checkley, Great Bardfield, Heydour, Mapledurham, Payhembury, Shrewsbury; **C15** Addlethorpe, Bowness, Brympton D'Evercy, Coxwold, Doddiscombsleigh, Harpley, Headcorn Littlehempston, Nettlestead, Norwich – St Peter Mancroft, Papplewick, Purton, St Neots, Thornford, Wormbridge, Wrangle, York Minster (62); **C16** Chelwood, St Neot; **C17** Bedingham, Oxford – Wadham Col.

Thomas the Apostle: **C13** York Minster (47, 53); **C14** Beckley, Enville, Ipplepen, Woodborough, York Minster (98, 104), York – St Denys, York – St Michael-le-Belfrey; **C15** Abbotsbury, Butleigh, Eynsham, Glasgow – Burrell, Gloucester, Grappenhall, Lytchett Matravers,

Mersham, Nettlestead, Oake, Wiggenhall, Yarnton, York – All Saints North Street; **C16** Cambridge – King's Col., Erpingham, Exeter, Fairford, Hamstall Ridware, Hingham, Lichfield, Milton Manor, Norwich – Guildhall, Rugby; **C17** Lambourne, Noak Hill, South Weald.

Thomas à Becket: **C13** Canterbury, Lincoln, York Minster (50); **C14** Chalvington, Checkley, Credenhill, Fordham, Mere, Oxford – Christ Church, York – St Michael-le-Belfrey; **C15** Cothelstone, Elham, Gloucester, Nettlestead, Oddingley, Oxford – Bodleian Library, Salle, Warwick, Yarnton, York Minster (23, 40); **C16** Greystoke, Oxford – Trinity Col.; **C20** Peterborough.

William of York: **C14** York — All Saints North Street, York Minster (14); **C15** York Minster (15, 18, 38, 40, 109), York – St Helen.

Ursula: **C14** Long Sutton, York – St Michael-le-Belfrey; **C15** London Victoria & Albert, South Elmham, Morley, Thaxted, Winchester Col., York – Holy Trinity Goodramgate; **C19** Skelton.

Zita (or Sitha): **C15** Addlethorpe, Barkway, Bexhill, Charlinch, Cirencester, Clavering, East Markham, Emneth, Gresford, Mells, Norbury, Wilby, Wilton, Winchester Col., Wrangle.

OTHER SCENES

Labours of the Months (one or more months represented): **C15** Biddenden, Bilton, Brandiston Hall (Norfolk), Checkley, Chelmsford Museum, Denton (Norfolk), Dewsbury, Foulsham, Norbury Hall, Northampton – Museum, Rolleston, Shrewsbury – Clive Museum.

Magnificat: **C15** Great Malvern; **C20** Brasted, Luton, Wellington.

The Seven Sacraments: **C14** York Minster (73); **C15** Bishop's Lydeard, Buckland (Glos), Burrington, Cartmel Fell, Crudwell, Doddiscombsleigh, Durham, Great Malvern, Leicester Museum, Llandyrnog, Melbury Bubb,

Oxford – Bodleian Library, Tattershall, York — St Michael Spurriergate; **C16** Litchfeld.

The Seven Works of Mercy: **C14** Chinnor; **C15** Combs, Leicester Museum, Tattershall, York – All Saints North St; **C19** Abergele, Denton (Gt. Man), Highgate, Llangernyw, London – Holy Trinity Sloane St.

Te Deum: **C15** Beverley Minster, Gresford, Morley, York Minster (8, 9); **C19** Bournemouth – St Peter, Kingston, Ladbroke, Landford, Lowestoft, Plymstock, Sherborne Abbey, Ticehurst; **C20** Eryholme, Liverpool, Rugby, Westminster – St James, Worplesdon.

GREATER LONDON

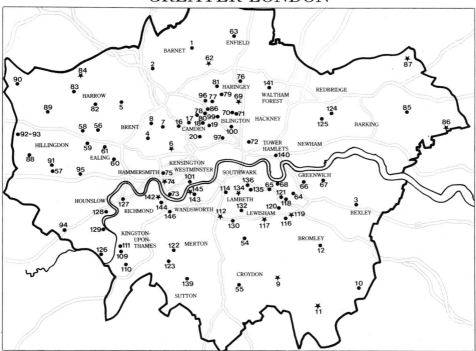

CENTRAL LONDON

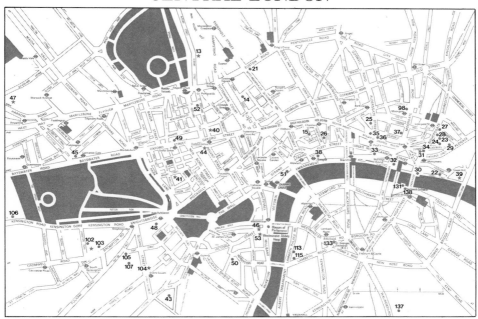

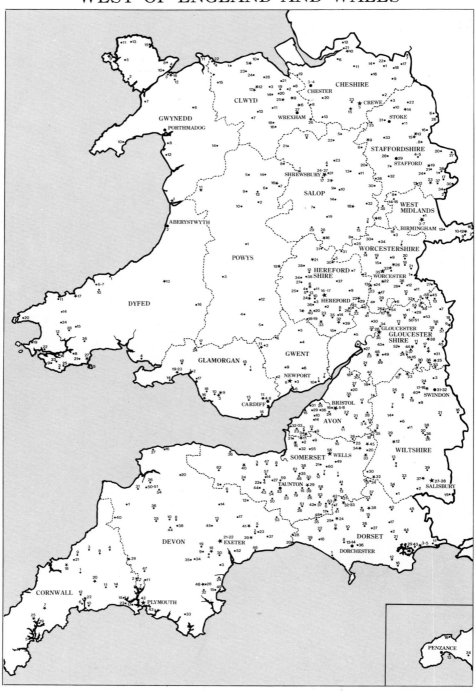

EAST OF ENGLAND

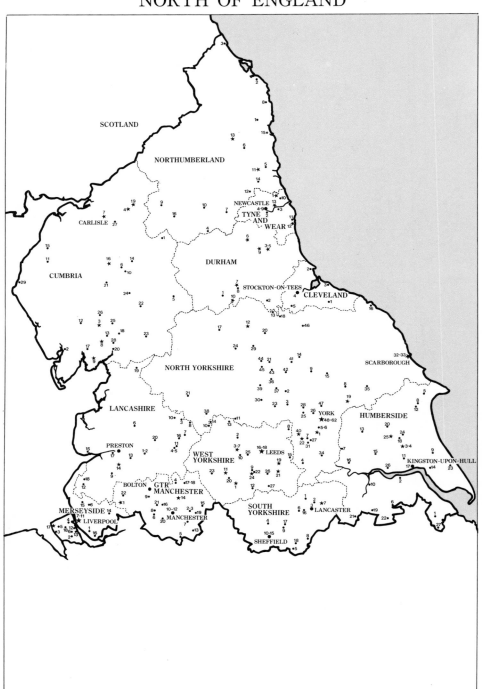

SCOTLAND

NORTHUMBERLAND

CARLISLE

CUMBRIA

NEWCASTLE
TYNE
AND
WEAR

DURHAM

STOCKTON-ON-TEES

CLEVELAND

SCARBOROUGH

NORTH YORKSHIRE

LANCASHIRE

PRESTON

YORK

HUMBERSIDE

WEST
YORKSHIRE

LEEDS

KINGSTON-UPON-HULL

BOLTON
GTR.
MANCHESTER

MERSEYSIDE
LIVERPOOL

MANCHESTER

SOUTH
YORKSHIRE

LANCASTER

SHEFFIELD

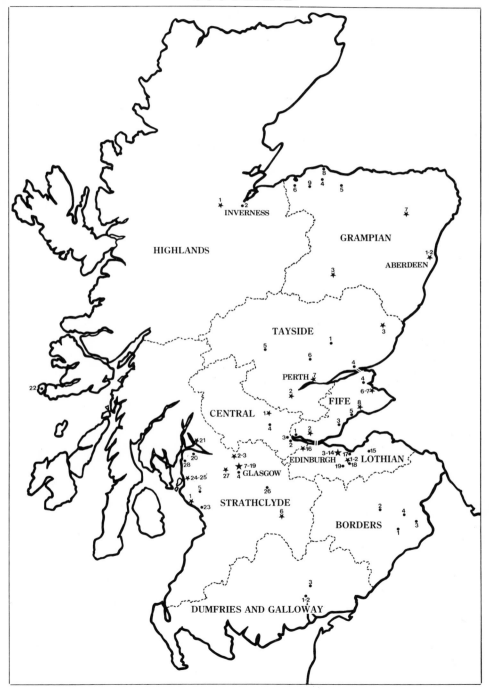

BIBLIOGRAPHY

Anderson, M.D., *History and Imagery in British Churches*, 1971

Angus, M., *Modern Stained Glass in British Churches*, 1984

Arnold, H., *Stained Glass of the Middle Ages in England and France*, 1913

Attwater, A., *Penguin Dictionary of Saints*, 1965

Baker, J., *English Stained Glass*, 1962

Binnal, P., *The 19th Century Stained Glass in Lincoln Minster*

British Society of Master Glass Painters, *Journal*, Var. dates

– – *Directory of Master Glass Painters, var. dates*

Caviness, M.N., *Early Stained Glass of Canterbury Cathedral*, 1977

Clarke, B.(ed)., *Architectural Stained Glass*, 1979

Coe, B., *Stained Glass in England & Wales*, 1980

Colchester, L.S., *Stained Glass in Wells Cathedral*, 1977

Connick, C.J., *Adventures in Light & Colour*, 1937

Day, L.F., *Windows*, 1909

Donnely, M., *Glasgow Stained Glass: a Preliminary Study*, 1981

Drake, M.A., *A History of English Glass-Painting*, 1912

Farmer, O.G., *Fairford Church and its Stained Glass Windows*, 1962

Gibson, P., *The Stained and Painted Glass of York Minster*, 1979

Glasgow Art Gallery and Museum, *Stained and Painted Glass in the Burrell Collection*, 1965

Hamand, L.A., *The Ancient Windows of Great Malvern Priory Church*, 1978

Harrison, K.P., *The Windows of King's College Chapel, Cambridge*, 1952

Harrison, M., *Victorian Stained Glass*, 1980

Haward, B., *Nineteenth Century Norfolk Stained Glass*, 1984

Hill, Revd. D.I., *The Stained Glass of Canterbury Cathedral*

Holiday, H., *Stained Glass as an Art*, 1896

Hunt, J.E., *The Glass in St Mary's Shrewsbury*, 1951/80

Jeavons, S.A., *Medieval Painted Glass in Staffordshire Churches*, 1952

Kendrick, Sir T., *Nineteenth Century Stained Glass, c.*1950 (in ms. form only)

King, D., *Stained Glass Tours of Norfolk*, 1980

King's College, *An Illustrated Guide to the Windows*, 1965

Knowles, J.A., *Essays in the History of the York School of Glass Painting*, 1936

– – *The Stained Glass of York Minster*, 1936

Larkworthy, P., *Clayton and Bell, Stained Glass Artists and Decorators*, 1984

Le Couteur, J.D., *English Medieval Painted Glass*, 1926

Lee, L., *The Appreciation of Stained Glass*, 1977

Lee, Seddon, Stephens, *Stained Glass*, 1976

Lewis, Dr M., *Stained Glass in North Wales up to 1850*, 1970

Male, E., *The Gothic Image*, 1961

Morgan, F.C., *Hereford Cathedral Glass*, 1967

Nelson, P., *Ancient Painted Glass in England 1170-1500*, 1913

Newton, P., *The County of Oxford*, 1979

Osborne, J., *Stained Glass in England*, 1981

Panovsky, E., *Meaning in the Visual Arts*, 1955

Peatling, A.V., *Ancient Stained and Painted Glass in the Churches of Surrey*, 1930

Pevsner et al. *The Buildings of England.*

Piper, J., *Stained Glass: Art or Anti-Art*, 1968

Rackham, B., *Victoria & Albert Museum: A Guide to the Collections of Stained Glass*, 1936

Read, Sir H., *English Stained Glass*, 1926

Read, H. and Baker J., *English Stained Glass*, 1960

Reyntiens, P., *The Technique of Stained Glass*, 1977

Rushforth, G., *Medieval Christian Imagery as Illustrated by the Painted Windows of Great Malvern Priory Church*, 1936

San Casciani, P. and P., *The Stained Glass of Oxford*, 1982

Schiller, G., *Iconography of Christian Art*, 1969

Sewter, A.C., *The Stained Glass of William Morris & His Circle*, 2 vols, 1974-5

Skeat, F.W., *The Stained Glass Windows of St Albans Cathedral*, 1977

Sowers, R., *Stained Glass: An Architectural Art*, 1965

Spring, R.O.C., *The Stained Glass of Salisbury Cathedral*, 1979

Theophilus (trans. R. Hendrie), *De Diversis Artibus (A Treatise Upon Various Arts)*, 1847

Whall, C., *Stained Glass Work*, 1905

Westlake, N.H.J., *A History of Design in Painted Glass*, 1881-94

Winston, C., *Hints on Glass Painting*, 2 vols, 1847

Woodforde, C., *English Stained and Painted Glass*, 1954

Stained Glass in Somerset, 1250-1830
The Medieval Glass of St Peter Mancroft, Norwich, 1934
The Norwich School of Glass Painting in the Fifteenth Century, 1950

INDEXES
ARTISTS, FIRMS AND THEIR WORK

The page numbers after each name refer to examples of their work or reference in the text. Those numbers in **bold** indicate illustrations.

PLACE NAMES

Page numbers appearing in **bold** indicate where an illustration appears.

GENERAL INDEX

See other indices for places and names not listed here:

TABLE OF SYMBOLS AND ABBREVIATIONS

*	figures, scenes or panels	F	glass of Continental origin	O	Flemish roundels
+	fragments	fig.(s)	figure(s)	O.T.	Old Testament
a.	aisle	frag.(s)	fragment(s)	Perp.	Perpendicular
A & C	Arts & Crafts	G	*grisaille*	Q(s)	quarries
C	century	H	heraldic coats-of-arms	qtfl	quatrefoil
Ch.	Church			R.C.	Roman Catholic
clsty	clerestory	Lib.	Library	S	South
Col.	College	Mem.	Memorial	t.l.(s)	tracery lights
d-d-v	dalle-de-verre	Mus.	Museum	tspt	transept
Dec.	Decorated	N	north	v.	very
E	East	N.T.	New Testament	W	West
				w.(ws.)	window(s)

Also abbreviated are the following artists and stained glass firms and authorities:

AF	Alfred Fisher	FE	Francis Eginton	LL	Laurence Lee
AH	Antony Hollaway	FMB	Ford Maddox Brown	ML	Mostyn Lewis
AHT	Amber Hiscott			MMF	Morris, Marshall, Faulkner & Co.
AJD	A. J. Davies of the Bromsgrove Guild	FRA	F. R. Ashmead		
		FS	Francis Skeat	MR	Moira Forsyth
AKN	A. K. Nicholson	F St	Frances Stephens	NC	Sir Ninian Comper
AM	Albert Moore	FXE	F. X. Eggert	OC	Michael O'Connor
AW	Alfred Wilkinson	GG	Goddard & Gibbs	PF	Pierre Fourmaintreau
AY	Alan Younger	GM	Gerald Moira		
BB	Barbara Batt	GR	Geoffrey Robinson	PQ	Paul Quail
BE	Betton and Evans of Shrewsbury	GW	Geoffrey Webb	PR	John Piper and Patrick Reyntiens
		HBB	Heaton Butler & Bayne		
BG	Burlison and Grylls			PW	Philip Webb
B-J	Sir Edward Burne-Jones	HD	H. Dearle	RB	Ray Bradley
		HH	Sir Henry Holiday	RC	Roy Coomber
CB	Clayton and Bell	HS	Harry Stammers	RP	Patrick Reyntiens
CEK	C. E. Kempe (or Kempe & Co.)	J & MK	Jasper & Molly Kettlewell	RR	Rosemary Rutherford
CW	Christopher Whall	JC	James Crombie	SH	Shrigley & Hunt
DBB	Dom B. Bailey	JH	John Hardman & Co.	TW	Thomas Willement
DGR	Dante Gabriel Rossetti	JHY	John Hayward	WH	Ward & Hughes
		JP	James Powell & 'Sons	WM	William Morris and his Company
DK	David King	JR	James Rowell		
DOC	David O'Connor	LB	Lavers & Barraud	WN	Ward & Nixon
DS	Douglas Strachan	LBW	Lavers, Barraud & Westlake	WW	William Warrington
FB	Michael Farrar Bell				
		LCE	L. C. Evetts	WT	Water Tower